The Impact of Self-Concept on Language Learning

MIX
Paper from
responsible sources
FSC
www.fsc.org   FSC® C014540

SECOND LANGUAGE ACQUISITION

Series Editor: **Professor David Singleton**, *University of Pannonia, Hungary* and Fellow Emeritus, *Trinity College, Dublin, Ireland*

This series brings together titles dealing with a variety of aspects of language acquisition and processing in situations where a language or languages other than the native language is involved. Second language is thus interpreted in its broadest possible sense. The volumes included in the series all offer in their different ways, on the one hand, exposition and discussion of empirical findings and, on the other, some degree of theoretical reflection. In this latter connection, no particular theoretical stance is privileged in the series; nor is any relevant perspective— sociolinguistic, psycholinguistic, neurolinguistic, etc.— deemed out of place. The intended readership of the series includes final-year undergraduates working on second language acquisition projects, postgraduate students involved in second language acquisition research, and researchers and teachers in general whose interests include a second language acquisition component.

Full details of all the books in this series and of all our other publications can be found on http://www.multilingual-matters.com, or by writing to Multilingual Matters, St Nicholas House, 31-34 High Street, Bristol BS1 2AW, UK.

SECOND LANGUAGE ACQUISITION: 79

The Impact of Self-Concept on Language Learning

Edited by
Kata Csizér and Michael Magid

MULTILINGUAL MATTERS
Bristol • Buffalo • Toronto

Library of Congress Cataloging in Publication Data
A catalog record for this book is available from the Library of Congress.
The Impact of Self-Concept on Language Learning/Edited by Kata Csizér and Michael Magid.
Second Language Acquisition: 79
Includes bibliographical references.
1. Language and languages–Study and teaching. 2. Language and languages–Self-instruction. 3. Independent study. I. Csizér, Kata, 1971-editor. II. Magid, Michael, 1974-editor.
P53.445.I67 2014
418.0071–dc23 2014014811

British Library Cataloguing in Publication Data
A catalogue entry for this book is available from the British Library.

ISBN-13: 978-1-78309-237-6 (hbk)
ISBN-13: 978-1-78309-236-9 (pbk)

Multilingual Matters
UK: St Nicholas House, 31-34 High Street, Bristol BS1 2AW, UK.
USA: UTP, 2250 Military Road, Tonawanda, NY 14150, USA.
Canada: UTP, 5201 Dufferin Street, North York, Ontario M3H 5T8, Canada.

Website: www.multilingual-matters.com
Twitter: Multi_Ling_Mat
Facebook:https://www.facebook.com/multilingualmatters
Blog: www.channelviewpublications.wordpress.com

The policy of Multilingual Matters/Channel View Publications is to use papers that are natural, renewable and recyclable products, made from wood grown in sustainable forests. In the manufacturing process of our books, and to further support our policy, preference is given to printers that have FSC and PEFC Chain of Custody certification. The FSC and/or PEFC logos will appear on those books where full certification has been granted to the printer concerned.

Typeset by Exeter Premedia Services, Chennai, India
Printed and bound in Great Britain by Short Run Press Ltd.

Contents

Contributors

Nicolette Bramley is currently enrolled in a Master of Teaching at the University of New England, majoring in Language Teaching and ESL. At the time of writing, she was a lecturer in Japanese at the University of Canberra. Her research interests include the ESL migrant experience, Japanese language education, and language and gender studies. She has published work on Japanese language education, and language and gender in the political media interview.

Damon Brewster is the director of the English Language Programme at J.F. Oberlin University. His research interests include motivation in learning, particularly concepts of self in L2 learners and self-efficacy, as well as practical applications of web-based tools to encourage learner autonomy in ELT.

Letty Chan is an assistant professor at the Department of English Language and Literature, Hong Kong Shue Yan University. She has recently obtained a PhD in Applied Linguistics at the University of Nottingham (UK) and was supervised by Professor Zoltán Dörnyei. Her current research interests include the L2 Motivational Self System, vision and mental imagery, and the Dynamic Systems Theory.

Kathryn Everhart Chaffee is a graduate student studying at the University of Alberta under Dr Kim Noels' supervision. She completed her BA in psychology in 2007 at the University of Delaware. Her research interests include cross-cultural differences in control strategies and learning motivation.

Kata Csizér holds a PhD in Language Pedagogy and works as a lecturer in the Department of English Applied Linguistics, Eötvös University, Budapest, where she teaches various L2 motivation courses. Her main field of research interest focuses on the socio-psychological aspects of L2 learning and teaching as well as second and foreign language motivation. She has published over 50 academic papers on various aspects of L2 motivation and has co-authored three books, including *Motivational*

Dynamics, Language Attitudes and Language Globalisation: A Hungarian perspective (2006, Multilingual Matters, with Zoltán Dörnyei and Nóra Németh).

Zoltán Dörnyei is a professor of Psycholinguistics at the School of English, University of Nottingham. He has published widely on various aspects of second language acquisition and language learning motivation, and he is the author of several books, including *The Psychology of Second Language Acquisition* (2009, Oxford University Press), *Teaching and Researching Motivation* (2nd edn, 2011, Longman, with Ema Ushioda), *Motivating Learning* (2013, Pearson, with Jill Hadfield) and *Motivating Learners, Motivating Teachers: Building Vision in the Language Classroom* (2014, Cambridge University Press, with Magdalena Kubanyiova).

Kay Irie is a professor at Gakushuin University, Tokyo where she is developing a CLIL-based English programme. She also teaches in the Graduate College of Education at Temple University Japan. Her current research interests include learner autonomy and motivation in language education. She is a co-editor of *Realizing Autonomy: Practice and Reflection in Language Education Contexts* (2012, Palgrave Macmillan).

Janina Iwaniec is a PhD student in the Department of Linguistics and English Language at Lancaster University. Her research interests lie in the area of individual learner differences as well as the impact of gender and the rural/urban divide on the motivation to learn English. She has a diverse experience of teaching academic English and has been involved in teaching undergraduate and postgraduate courses at Lancaster University.

Jeremy F. Jones is a senior lecturer in TESOL and Foreign Language Teaching at the University of Canberra. He has taught EFL/ESL and language teacher education in the Middle East, Japan, Cambodia, China and Vietnam as well as in Australia. He has researched and published in the areas of language teaching methodology, assessment, discourse analysis and intercultural communication.

Jim King is a lecturer in Education at the University of Leicester, UK. He holds a PhD in Applied Linguistics from the University of Nottingham and is a post-doctoral fellow of the Japan Society for the Promotion of Science (JSPS). His book *Silence in the Second Language Classroom* has been published by Palgrave Macmillan (2013).

Tae-Young Kim (PhD OISE/University of Toronto) is an associate professor in the Department of English Education at Chung-Ang University, where he teaches both undergraduate and graduate courses in applied linguistics, and coordinates the Graduate School of Education (English major). His research interests include ESL/EFL learning/teaching motivation, demotivation, sociocultural theory and qualitative methodology. He has published over 50 papers on various topics in L2 motivation. His recent studies have been published in *The Canadian Modern Language Review, System, The Asia-Pacific Education Researcher* and *Asia Pacific Education Review.*

Yoon-Kyoung Kim is a PhD candidate at Chung-Ang University, South Korea. She completed her master's thesis on Korean EFL secondary school students' English learning motivation focusing on the perspective of the L2 Motivational Self System. Her current research interests involve changes in L2 learning motivation, L2 learning demotivation, teacher motivation and demotivation, sociocultural theory and activity theory.

Yuzo Kimura is a professor of English in the Department of English, Faculty of Medicine, University of Toyama, Japan. He teaches English to medical, nursing and pharmaceutical students and has been conducting research on L2 teaching and learning motivation in three countries in the Far East; Japan, China and South Korea. His research interests lie in L2 teaching/learning motivation, teacher development and classroom research. His recent longitudinal research concerns a dual comparative study of L2 teaching/learning motivation; first, among these three countries, and second, from the perspectives of the Sociocultural Theory and the Complex Dynamic Systems Theory.

Judit Kormos is a reader in Second Language Acquisition at Lancaster University in the United Kingdom. Her research interests include the role of motivation and cognitive variables in language learning, the psycholinguistic aspects of speech production and special needs in foreign language education. She is the author of several books and over forty research articles in the field of second language acquisition.

David Lyons is an assistant lecturer in the Department of English Language and Literature at Keimyung University, South Korea, where he teaches undergraduate and graduate classes and is involved in secondary teacher training. He is also a PhD candidate in the School of English, Drama and Canadian & American Studies at the University of Birmingham. His main research interests lie in the areas of L2 motivation, learner beliefs and task-based learning.

Jessica Mackay is a teacher and teacher trainer at the School of Modern Languages of the University of Barcelona, where she is also a PhD candidate under the supervision of Dr Elsa Tragant. Her research interests include L2 motivation in EFL contexts, classroom dynamics and materials development.

Michael Magid is an English language pedagogy specialist at the English Language Institute of Singapore. As an English language pedagogy specialist, Michael draws on his experience of teaching English at all levels in Canada, England, China and Japan as well as his background in applied linguistics. He graduated from the University of Nottingham and holds a PhD in Applied Linguistics which was written under the supervision of Zoltán Dörnyei. As a part of his PhD, Michael designed a programme to motivate learners of English and build their self-confidence. His publications are in the areas of L2 motivation, sociolinguistics and materials development.

Maya Sugita McEown is a post-doctoral fellow at the University of Alberta. She completed her PhD at the Graduate School of Foreign Language Education and Research, Kansai University. She has established expertise in teachers' motivational strategies through her doctoral studies, in which she carried out observational and self-report studies, some of which included a longitudinal design. Through her training in the disciplines of applied linguistics, she is currently working on a comparative study of teachers' motivational instruction in the language classrooms between Japanese and Canadian contexts based on the Self-Determination Theory.

Sarah Mercer teaches at the University of Graz, Austria, where she has been working since 1996. She completed her PhD at the University of Lancaster and her habilitation at the University of Graz. Her research interests include all aspects of the psychology surrounding the foreign language learning experience, focusing in particular on the self. She is the author of *Towards an Understanding of Language Learner Self-concept* published by Springer and is a co-editor of *Psychology for Language Learning* published by Palgrave and *Multiple Perspectives on the Self* published by Multilingual Matters.

Gabriella Mezei is a teacher at the National University of Public Service, Faculty of Public Administration, Centre for Foreign Languages. She holds a PhD in Language Pedagogy obtained at Eötvös Loránd University, Budapest, and an MA in Applied Linguistics. Her research interests include language teaching and learning, motivational strategies, autonomy and self-regulation. She is a member of the MTA TK Lendület Research Centre for Educational and Network Studies (RECENS). The research team focuses on mechanisms of negative relationships and networks in different social contexts, including the achievement, integration and negative relationships of elementary and secondary school students.

Megan Michalyk completed her BA (Honors) degree in Psychology at the University of Alberta in 2007. As an undergraduate student, she explored research interests in the area of cross-cultural differences in second language learning motivation. She went on to complete her Master of Science degree in Clinical Psychology from the University of Western Ontario in 2009 before leaving psychology to enter the health care field where she is now a registered nurse practising in critical care.

Masuko Miyahara is a lecturer at International Christian University, Tokyo. She holds an MA in TESOL and a PhD in Second Language Learning from the Institute of Education, University of London. Her research interests focus on identity studies and autonomy in language education. She is also interested in research methodology and methods in language learning research, particularly in the area of narratives.

Kimberly A. Noels is a professor in the Social and Cultural Psychology area of the Department of Psychology and an adjunct associate professor in the Department of Educational Psychology at the University of Alberta. Her research focuses on the role of the socio-ecological context in language learning and the implications of language learning for ethnic identity, psychological well-being and intergroup relations. This research has been recognised through awards from the Modern Language Association, the International Association of Language and Social Psychology and the Society for the Psychological Study of Social Issues.

Nihat Polat (PhD, The University of Texas at Austin) is an associate professor of Applied Linguistics and L2 teacher education and the director of the Master's and Teacher Certification Programme in ESL at Duquesne University. His research interests include identity, socialisation, motivation, beliefs, self-concept, cyber ecologies and gender in L2 acquisition as well as the nature of change in teachers' pedagogical beliefs and practices. He has published in numerous journals, including *The Modern Language Journal, Language Learning & Technology, Linguistics and Education*. He is also a consulting editor for the *Journal of Educational Research*.

Elke Stracke is an associate professor and Associate Dean International in the Faculty of Arts and Design at the University of Canberra, Australia. Prior to joining the University of Canberra, she held university teaching and research positions in New Zealand (University of Otago), Australia (Australian National University) and Germany (University of

Münster). As an educator and researcher she is interested in language learning and teaching, and feedback practices and peer learning in postgraduate supervision practice.

Zhen Yue is a PhD student in the School of Education, University of Birmingham, where she obtained her MA in TEFL. Her main research output has been her master's thesis entitled *Exploring English Language Learning Motivation of Chinese Overseas University Students in the UK* (University of Birmingham, United Kingdom, 2010). Her research interests include second language learning motivation and willingness to communicate, particularly the dynamic and complex interactions in terms of the language learner's agency and learning practice.

1 The Self-Concept and Language Learning: An Introduction

Kata Csizér and Michael Magid

Introduction

A learner's sense of self plays a key role in academic achievement (Pajares & Schunk, 2005) and plays a more significant role in language learning since 'language, after all, belongs to a person's whole social being; it is a part of one's identity, and is used to convey this identity to other people' (Williams & Burden, 1997: 115). Recently in second language (L2) acquisition, scholars have focused on the importance of self-concept as a result of Zoltán Dörnyei's L2 Motivational Self System (e.g. Dörnyei, 2005; Dörnyei & Ushioda, 2011), which is based on Higgins's (1987) self-discrepancy theory, in which an L2 learner compares their current self-concept to their self-guides, which are their ideal self and their ought self. Self-concept may be 'conceptualised in global terms or in respect to specific domains and includes both cognitive and affective dimensions' (Mercer, 2011: 65).

The paradigmatic shift of L2 motivation research brought about by not only the interest of and research into self-related concepts in second language learning but as well as the apparent need of reconceptualising L2 motivation concepts and processes in light of the emergence of Global English resulted in a wealth of publications in recent years. One of the most comprehensive summaries of the developments of the new century was presented in Dörnyei and Ushioda's 2009 volume, also published by Multilingual Matters. Dörnyei and Ushioda (2009) called for papers discussing various aspects of L2 motivation as related to students' selves and identities, and as a result of their edited volume they concluded that 'motivation conceived as part of the learner's identity/self is a workable concept from several perspectives' (Dörnyei & Ushioda, 2009: 350). Research into identity and self-related issues in very recent years not only proved the above quote to be true but also created a research niche for a new wave of studies that aimed at finding out how self-related issues actually impact L2 learning in general and L2 motivation processes in particular. Our present volume contributes to this line of research by including theoretical works about the L2 Motivational Self System and self-guides and empirical investigations targeting both learners and teachers of English. A particularly important line in empirical research is that of the intervention studies, as these investigations measure the effects of strategy training on students' L2 motivation. Strategy training concerning students' selves can take many shapes: various motivational programmes, imagery training and self intervention programmes can prove to be successful in motivating L2 learning both in the short and long run in various learning contexts around the world.

A Brief Overview of this Book

This edited volume highlights the effects of self-concept on L2 learning and teaching by considering a wide range of theories related to self-concept as well as their practical applications. As far as the structure of the book is concerned, four main parts are presented: (1) chapters featuring various theories related to the self-concept; (2) empirical studies related to the selves of the learners; (3) teachers' perspectives on students' self-concept and (4) L2 motivational intervention studies associated with the development of the self-concept of language learners.

Part 1 begins with Zoltán Dörnyei's chapter highlighting the importance of and relationship between future self-guides and vision. He argues that vision and mental imagery should be considered as an essential part of motivation and language learning. The second chapter in this part written by Maya Sugita McEown, Kimberly A. Noels and Kathryn Everhart Chaffee details conceptual differences and similarities among the Socio-educational Model, Self-Determination Theory and the L2 Motivational Self System. The authors not only discuss theoretical considerations but empirical data are also presented to underline their arguments. Part 1 is concluded by Sarah Mercer's chapter, which investigates how self and one's network of relationships are linked. She has designed a conceptual model of the self, which contains personal and social aspects as well as takes time and context into consideration.

Part 2 of the book includes studies that set out to research how self-related concepts might contribute to the process of language learning. In terms of thematic categorisation, several chapters have dealt with how selves, L2 motivation, self-regulation and autonomy are related. Kata Csizér and Judit Kormos (Chapter 5) investigate possible relationships between motivational selves, self-regulation and autonomy. Tae-Young Kim and Yoon-Kyoung Kim (Chapter 6) research differences between elementary and junior high school students concerning their L2 Motivational Self System and self-regulatory processes. Kimberly A. Noels, Kathryn Everhart Chaffee, Megan Michalyk and Maya Sugita McEown (Chapter 8) add culture to the picture and consider how contextual aspects might factor into autonomy. The role of self-regulation is the topic of Janina Iwaniec's work (Chapter 11), which deals with a number of self-constructs and their relevance in regulating the learning process. Another interesting trend in this part of the book relates to students' identities. David Lyons (Chapter 7) puts forward a longitudinal study to map how self-concepts influence motivation. Elke Stracke, Jeremy Jones and Nicolette Bramley (Chapter 9) map bicultural identities in an Australian context. Kay Irie and Damon Brewster (Chapter 10) introduce the notion of experiential capital and its role in language learning. Masuko Miyahara (Chapter 12) writes about emerging self-identities and emotions as well as identity construction. Jim King (Chapter 13) discusses social anxiety and silent behaviour in a Japanese context. Zhen Yue's investigation (Chapter 14) provides complex and dynamic information on Chinese university students' willingness to communicate. Last but not least, Nihat Polat (Chapter 15) investigates how the L2 Motivational Self System relates to socialisation, identification and L2 accent attainment.

Part 3 contains studies from the teachers' perspectives. Gabriella Mezei (Chapter 16) presents a study on how teachers' motivational strategies impact students' selves and motivation. Yuzo Kimura's (Chapter 17) longitudinal case study puts teachers at the centre of interest and looks at how dynamically changing their motivation is.

Part 4 consists of three intervention studies that examine how self-related training enhances students' motivation. Michael Magid (Chapter 18) describes his motivational programme and presents his results concerning the effects of the programme through which students' Ideal L2 selves are strengthened. Letty Chan (Chapter 19) reveals results of her imagery training programme on students' possible L2 selves. Jessica Mackay (Chapter 20) discusses the practical implications of her Ideal L2 self intervention programme in a Spanish context. Part 5 presents future research directions on the impact of self-concept on language learning. These directions originate from the authors of the chapters outlined above and are both theoretical and practical in nature.

Based on the above brief summary, we are proud to present a book on L2 motivation, which not only includes studies from all over the world (Central Europe, Canada, Asia and Australia) but also contains many different research methods. In fact, we feel that one of the main strengths of the book lies in the high quality of varied research methods employed in the studies with both qualitative and quantitative data as well as longitudinal and cross-sectional investigations.

Acknowledgements

First and foremost, we would like to thank Zoltán Dörnyei for encouraging us to embark on this rewarding enterprise. Secondly, we feel deeply indebted to our contributors. Needless to say, we could not have done this without them! We would also like to thank those researchers whose work we could not include in the volume for answering our call for chapters and putting forth such excellent proposals. Finally, we would like to express our gratitude to Multilingual Matters for agreeing to publish this volume. We thank the staff and editors for their highly professional work and support. We would also like to thank the reviewers for their valuable feedback.

References

Dörnyei, Z. (2005) *The Psychology of the Language Learner: Individual Differences in Second Language Acquisition*. Mahwah, NJ: Lawrence Erlbaum.

Dörnyei, Z. and Ushioda, E. (2011) *Teaching and Researching Motivation* (2nd edn). Harlow: Longman.

Dörnyei, Z. and Ushioda, E. (eds) (2009) *Motivation, Language Identity and the L2 Self*. Bristol: Multilingual Matters.

Higgins, E.T. (1987) Self-discrepancy: A theory relating self and affect. *Psychological Review* 94 (3), 319–340.

Mercer, S. (2011) The self as a complex dynamic system. *Studies in Second Language Learning and Teaching* 1 (1), 57–82.

Pajares, F. and Schunk, D.H. (2005) Self-efficacy and self-concept beliefs. In H.W. Marsh, R.G. Craven and D.M. McInerney (eds) *International Advances in Self Research* (vol. 2) (pp. 95–121). Greenwich, CT: Information Age Publishing.

Williams, M. and Burden, R.L. (1997) *Psychology for Language Teachers*. Cambridge: Cambridge University Press.

Part 1

Theories Related to Self-Concept

2 Future Self-Guides and Vision

Zoltán Dörnyei

Introduction

Recent theorising on second language (L2) motivation has introduced two new terms, 'future self-guides' and 'vision'. They refer to interrelated concepts that have partly emerged from a continuous line of research on L2 motivation that goes back to Robert Gardner and Wallace Lambert's pioneering study in 1959, but which also added new twists to the traditional conceptualisations: future self-guides drew attention to the importance of one's self-concept in understanding motivational dispositions, while vision highlighted the potential significance of mental imagery – and especially future self-images – in energising goal-specific behaviour. This chapter describes the two concepts and discusses how they are related to each other.

Future Self-Guides

A person's self-concept has traditionally been seen as the summary of the individual's self-knowledge related to how the person views him/herself (Dörnyei, 2009). One specific aspect of this complex notion has been identified as particularly relevant to motivation researchers: the future dimension of the self-concept, that is, not so much how people view themselves in the present as how they imagine themselves in the future. In a seminal paper, Markus and Nurius (1986) labelled the mental representations associated with this future dimension as 'possible selves' and distinguished three main types depending on the overall quality of the imagined future selves: they can represent individuals' ideas of what they *might* become, what they *would like* to become and what they are *afraid of* becoming.

Projected future self-states have a strong motivational impact (cf. Markus & Nurius, 1987), and this motivational function was made explicit by Higgins's (1987, 1998) self-discrepancy theory. Higgins focused only on two types of possible selves, the *ideal self*, referring to the characteristics that someone would ideally like to possess, subsuming hopes, aspirations and wishes, and the *ought self*, referring to the attributes that one believes one ought to possess, subsuming someone's sense of personal or social duties, obligations or responsibilities. Higgins then argued that people have a feeling of unease when there is a discrepancy between their actual real-life self and their aspired future self. This psychological tension, in turn, spurs the desire for action towards reducing the gap, and it thus becomes a potent source of motivation. In this sense, possible selves act as 'future self-guides', reflecting a dynamic, forward-pointing conception that can explain how someone is moved from the present towards the future.

The L2 Motivational Self System

I have described elsewhere how L2 motivation research reached a stage when past traditions could be meaningfully fused with lessons learnt about future self-guides in social psychology (e.g. Dörnyei, 2009, 2010; see also Csizér & Dörnyei, 2005), resulting in a tripartite construct, the L2 Motivational Self System. This is partly an application of possible selves theory to second language acquisition contexts, proposing the L2 equivalents of the ideal and ought selves:

- *Ideal L2 self*: if the person we would like to become speaks an L2 (e.g. the person we would like to become is associated with travelling or doing business internationally), the ideal L2 self is a powerful motivator to learn the L2 because we would like to reduce the gap between our actual and ideal selves.

- *Ought-to L2 self*, which concerns L2-related attributes that one believes one *ought to* possess to avoid possible negative outcomes and which therefore may bear little resemblance to the person's own desires or wishes.

However, besides these two sources of L2 motivation – that is, the learner's internal desire to become an effective L2 user and social pressures coming from the learner's environment to master the L2 – the L2 Motivational Self System also includes a third main component to reflect the main findings of motivation research in the 1990s, which highlighted the motivational significance of the immediate learning situation in which the mastery of the L2 occurred:

- *L2 learning experience*, which concerns situation-specific motives related to the immediate learning environment and experience (e.g. the positive impact of success, the rapport between teachers and students or the enjoyable quality of a language course).

Thus, the new approach concerned two future self-guides associated with imagined experience and a third constituent rooted in actual experience. Over the past five years, several studies have validated this broad tripartite construct (cf. e.g. the papers in Dörnyei & Ushioda, 2009, as well as Busse, 2013; Csizér & Lukács, 2010; Henry, 2009, 2010, 2011; Hiver, 2013; Islam *et al.*, 2013; Kormos *et al.,* 2011; Lamb, 2012; Magid, 2009; Papi, 2010; Papi & Teimouri, 2012), confirming the overall explanatory power of the model, with the ideal L2 self, in particular, playing a substantive role as a future self-guide in determining motivated behaviour.

Conditions for the Motivating Capacity of Future Self-Guides

A key aspect of the L2 Motivational Self System is the recognition that although future self-guides have the capacity to motivate action, this does not always happen automatically: in many cases, the desire to learn the L2 that has been generated by constructive future self-images fails to be realised in actual action. Therefore, Dörnyei (2005) has proposed a number of key conditions that need to be in place for future self-guides to be able to exert their motivational impact. Dörnyei and Ushioda (2011) offer the following list of the main prerequisites:

- The learner *has* a desired future self-image. People differ in how easily they can generate a successful possible self, and therefore, not everyone is expected to possess a developed ideal or ought-to self-guide.
- The future self is sufficiently *different* from the current self. If there is no observable gap between current and future selves, no increased effort is felt necessary and no motivation emerges.
- The future self-image is *elaborate* and *vivid*. People vary in the vividness of their mental imagery, and a possible self with insufficient specificity and detail may not be able to evoke the necessary motivational response.
- The future self-image is perceived as *plausible*. Possible selves are effective only insofar as the individual does indeed perceive them as *possible*, that is, realistic within the person's individual circumstances. Thus, a sense of controllability (i.e. the belief that one's action is conceivable and can make a difference) is an essential prerequisite.
- The future self-image is *not* perceived as *comfortably certain* to reach, that is, within one's grasp. The learner must not believe that the

possible self will happen automatically, without a marked increase in expended effort.

- The future self-image is in harmony – or at least does not clash – with other parts of the individual's self-concept (e.g. a conflict between the ideal and the ought-to selves), particularly with expectations of the learner's family, peers or other elements of the social environment.
- The future self-image is accompanied by relevant and effective *procedural strategies* that act as a *roadmap* towards the goal. Once our vision generates energy, we need productive tasks into which to channel this energy or it will ebb away.
- The future self-image is *regularly activated* in the learner's working self-concept. Possible selves can be squeezed out of someone's working self-concept by other contenders for attention and will therefore become relevant for behaviour only if they are primed by frequent and varied reminders.
- The desired future self-image is offset by a counteracting *feared possible self* in the same domain. Maximal motivational effectiveness is achieved if the learner also has a vivid image about the *negative consequences* of failing to achieve the desired end state.

It has become clear over the past few years that these conditions are not just additional corollaries of the new conceptualisation of L2 motivation but also form an integral part of it because without them the three primary motivational dimensions lose their motivational capacity (for a discussion, see Dörnyei, 2009). Furthermore, it has also been realised that the summary of the necessary conditions carries considerable practical significance: the conditions outline in effect a principled novel approach for teachers to motivate their students by ensuring that the conditions are met, a point I will come back to in the concluding section of this chapter.

Vision

A key aspect of future self-guides – one that has also been emphasised with regard to the L2 Motivational Self System – is that they involve images and senses; as Markus and Nurius (1986) stated, possible selves are represented in the same imaginary and semantic way as the here-and-now self, that is, they are a reality for the individual: people can 'see' and 'hear' their possible future self (see also Ruvolo & Markus, 1992). This means that, in many ways, possible selves are similar to dreams and visions about oneself. Indeed, Markus and Nurius (1987: 59) confirm,

'Possible selves encompass within their scope visions of desired and unde-sired end states' – thus, possible selves can be seen as the 'vision of what might be'. The use of the term 'vision' has not been restricted to possible selves theory in the social sciences but has been applied widely to refer to a variety of diverse contexts and areas, including the popular media, so much so that van der Helm (2009: 96) actually talks about 'the vision phenomenon' to cover 'the ensemble of claims and products which are called "visions" or could be called as such'. In his insightful analysis, he distinguishes between seven different types of vision: religious, political, humanistic, business/organisational, community, public policy and per-sonal visions. Within these contexts, he argues, the actual meaning of vision is fairly homogeneous, capturing three defining aspects: (1) the *future*, (2) the *ideal* and (3) the *desire for deliberate change*.

In agreement with the significance attached to vision in the social sci-ences, in our book-length overview of the theory and practice of language vision, we have expressed their belief that 'vision is one of the single most important factors within the domain of language learning: where there is a vision, there is a way' (Dörnyei & Kubanyiova, 2014). This, however, begs the question: if vision is such an important motivator of human behaviour, how does it relate to the notion of motivation in gen-eral? In fact, we could ask, should a vision-based approach replace pre-vious motivational frameworks? The answer is no. We must realise that the plurality of motivational constructs in the psychological literature has to do with the multi-faceted nature of human behaviour and with the various levels of abstraction that we can approach human behaviour from. Motivation by definition subsumes every factor that impacts on human behaviour, and the range of potential motives that can initiate or modify our actions is vast: people might decide to do something for rea-sons as diverse as physical needs, financial benefits, moral or faith convic-tions, cognitive curiosity or because they like someone who already does it – the list is virtually endless. Various motivation theories in the past have highlighted different clusters of the vast array of potential motives in order to explain certain specific behavioural domains under focus, such as voting, mating, learning or working behaviours. In my summary of motivational techniques – *Motivational Strategies in the Language Classroom* (Dörnyei, 2001) – I surveyed a wide selection of diverse motives that are relevant to sustained learning behaviours in foreign language classes, and a focus on vision does not replace or invalidate the principles and proce-dures presented there.

The attraction of using 'vision' in our thinking of motivation is that it represents one of the highest-order motivational forces, one that is par-ticularly fitting to explain the long-term, and often lifelong, process of mastering a second language. While the day-to-day realities of one's L2 learning experience are the function of multiple factors related to diverse aspects of the learning environment or the learner's personal life, the concept of vision offers a useful, broad lens to focus on the bigger picture, the overall persistence that is necessary to lead one to ultimate language attainment. In other words, while individuals pursue languages for a variety of purposes and an equally wide array of reasons keep their motivation alive, the vision of who they would like to become as second language users seems to be one of the most reliable predictors of their long-term intended effort.

Vision and Goals

A key question we need to address in order to understand the exact nature of vision is in what way it is dissimilar to a 'goal' – after all, goals also represent directional intentions to reach future states. Dörnyei and Kubanyiova (2014) argue that there is a qualitative difference between the two concepts: unlike an abstract, cognitive goal, a vision includes a strong *sensory element* – it involves tangible images related to achieving the goal. Thus, for example, the vision of becoming a doctor exceeds the abstract goal of earning a medical degree in that the vision involves the individual actually seeing him/herself receiving the degree certificate or practising as a qualified doctor. That is, the vision to become a doctor also involves the sensory experience of *being* a doctor. More generally, the main feature of a vision is that it subsumes both a desired goal and a representation of how the individual approaches or realises that goal. In this sense, a vision can be understood as a *personalised goal* (Markus & Ruvolo, 1989) that the learner has made his/her own by adding to it the imagined reality of the actual goal experience. Talking about the vision of an organisation, Levin (2000: 95) articulates this sensory element when she says that effective visions 'should outline a rich and textual picture of what success looks like and feels like'. She goes on to say that a vision 'should be so vivid as to enable the listener or reader to transport himself or herself to the future, so to speak, to witness it and experience it'.

Vision and Imagery

According to the *Oxford English Dictionary*, a vision is 'a vivid mental image, especially a fanciful one of the future'. *Mental imagery*, which is the technical term for the phenomenon used in psychology, is a relatively unknown concept in L2 studies, even though it has been highlighted in various areas of L2 learning in the past few decades, for example in grammar teaching (Gerngross et al., 2006), vocabulary learning (Cohen, 1987; Ellis & Beaton, 1993; Shen, 2010; Stevick, 1986), reading (Arnold, 1999;

Green & Donahue, 2009; Krasny & Sadoski, 2008), writing (Wright & Hill, 2008) and listening comprehension (Center *et al.*, 1999). The concept refers to generating mental representations of perceptual or emotional experiences and situations in the mind in multiple sensory modalities (visual, auditory, tactile, olfactory and gustatory) – in other words, it involves generating an imagined reality that we can see, hear, feel and taste. This quasi-perceptual experience is often described in everyday parlance as 'visualising' or 'seeing in the mind's eye' (a term originally coined by Shakespeare in *Hamlet*) or 'hearing in the head' or 'imagining the feel of'.

From a neurobiological perspective, all imagery falls under the broad category of 'mental simulation', because the mental processes involved in it emulate the neural processes that would actually operate if the person were in the simulated scenario (Moulton & Kosslyn, 2009). Interestingly, neurobiological research has confirmed that mental imagery relies to a large extent on the same neural mechanisms and pathways as actual perception, and studies of brain damage have also shown that such injuries often produce parallel deficits in imagery and in perception (Reisberg & Heuer, 2005). That is, to put it broadly, the brain cannot tell the difference between an actual physical event and the vivid imagery of the same event (Cox, 2012). For this reason, the principled manipulation of mental imagery lends itself to versatile applications in a range of diverse areas and can be used for the purpose of preparation, repetition, elaboration, intensification or modification of behaviours. For example, virtually all world-class athletes use *guided imagery* as an integral part of their training programme, because it is a well-documented fact in sports psychology that imagery can be used for mentally practising specific performance skills, improving confidence, controlling anxiety, preparing for competitive situations and enhancing actual performance (cf. Morris *et al.*, 2005). Similarly, imagery is a basic tool in psychoanalysis and other forms of psychotherapy (e.g. Katz, 2000; Singer, 2006), and successful applications of imagery techniques have also been reported in various educational contexts (e.g. Berkovits, 2005; Clark & Paivio, 1991; Murdock, 1987).

The stimulatory nature of mental imagery is at the heart of its potency. Learners with a vivid and detailed ideal self-image that has a substantial L2 component are more likely to be motivated to take action in pursuing language studies than their peers who have not articulated a desired future goal state for themselves. Until recently, there has been rather limited research in this area within the L2 literature. Some validation of the imagery-motivation link has been offered by recent intervention studies in which various possible selves enhancement activities were employed to facilitate future identity formation and to strengthen students' future self-images (Fukada *et al.*, 2011; Jones, 2012; Magid & Chan, 2012; Sampson, 2012; see also Chapters 18, 19 and 20 of this volume). These have consistently reported that most participants have found visualisation tasks focusing on their future self-guides motivating, and they tended to invest more effort in language learning as a result of the programme, thereby attesting to the impact of the treatment.

Imagery Capacity and Sensory Preferences

Besides the intervention studies mentioned above, the connection between imagery skills and future self-guides has been examined by another line of inquiry over the past five years that investigated the motivational relevance of imagination and sensory preferences (e.g. visual style). First, a pilot study by Al-Shehri (2009) examined the relationship of L2 learners' visual learning style preferences and self-reported imaginative capacities with their motivation to test the hypothesis that learners who exhibit a visual learning style preference are more likely to possess a stronger capacity for visual imagery and imagination, and are therefore more likely to develop a stronger ideal L2 self than their visually less capable peers. In accordance with this hypothesis, the obtained results revealed strong positive associations between students' visual styles, imagination, ideal L2 selves and motivated L2 behaviour.

In subsequent large-scale studies in Korea, Kim (2009) and Kim and Kim (2011) confirmed the positive association between motivation, imagery capacity and sensory styles – both visual and auditory – suggesting that these are key components in the formation of a vivid ideal L2 self. Most recently, in a study of Hong Kong secondary school pupils studying two target languages, English and Mandarin, Dörnyei and Chan (2013: 454) have also found future self-guides to be associated with salient imagery/visualisation components, which, in their view, 'justifies the use of the term "vision" when referring to them'. They showed that vision is multisensory in nature, involving all the senses and not just visualisation. An important characteristic of the imagery skills involved was their language-independent nature, pointing to the conclusion that L2-related mental imagery is part of the more generic mechanisms underlying human vision rather than a function of specific target languages.

An additional result of the Dörnyei and Chan (2013) study was the finding that the two different target languages they studied were associated with distinct ideal language selves, thus forming distinct L2-specific visions. This added to the growing consensus in the field of L2 motivation research that coexisting ideal L2 self-images constitute fairly distinct L2-specific visions, which can then interfere with each other both in a positive way (e.g. transferable linguistic confidence from one language experience to the other) or in a negative, demotivating manner (e.g. competition for space in the working self-concept).

Practical Implications and Future Directions

Perceiving L2 motivation in terms of future self-guides and vision has considerable practical implications, because mental imagery is an important internal resource that can be intentionally harnessed (Sheikh et al., 2002; Taylor et al., 1998). We saw earlier that the motivational capacity of future self-guides is dependent on a number of key conditions, and therefore, the essence of any motivational practice in this vein is to create or enhance these conditions. Dörnyei and Kubanyiova (2014) provide ample evidence that it is possible to devise varied classroom activities to train imagery skills, thereby helping students to generate personal visions supported by vivid and lively images and then to sustain this vision during the often challenging everyday reality of the language-learning process. As mentioned above, there have already been promising attempts to develop visionary training programmes (e.g. Fukada et al., 2011; Magid & Chan, 2012; Sampson, 2012) and teachers can also consult two available practical resource books for vision-enhancing classroom activities (Arnold et al., 2007; Hadfield & Dörnyei, 2013).

Regarding the future of self-guides and vision within the understanding of language learning motivation, I believe that there is considerable mileage in pursuing these lines of inquiry. Given that vision is one of the highest-order motivational constructs and that it transfers from one domain to another relatively freely (i.e. the vision to become a successful language learner is not that different in its underlying mechanisms from the vision to become, for example, an applied linguist), it seems a useful concept for addressing some of the ultimate Wh- questions of human behaviour. One particularly fruitful research direction is to investigate what kind of behavioural pathways are needed to be able to channel the energy generated by vision into human action. We know from sports psychology that successful athletes manage to match their highly developed imagery skills with corresponding training plans to good effect, and therefore, there is a strong likelihood that certain fitting combinations of visionary goals (i.e. future self-guides powered by mental imagery) and well-designed action sequences (i.e. learning plans) can generate powerful motivational currents that can be utilised to combat apathy and demotivation in diverse educational settings.

References

Al-Shehri, A.S. (2009) Motivation and vision: The relation between the ideal L2 self, imagination and visual style. In Z. Dörnyei and E. Ushioda (eds) *Motivation, Language Identity and the L2 Self* (pp. 164–171). Bristol: Multilingual Matters.

Arnold, J. (1999) Visualisation: Language learning with the mind's eye. In J. Arnold (ed.) *Affect in Language Learning* (pp. 260–278). Cambridge: Cambridge University Press.

Arnold, J., Puchta, H. and Rinvolucri, M. (2007) *Imagine that! Mental Imagery in the EFL Classroom*. Cambridge: Cambridge University Press & Helbling.

Berkovits, S. (2005) *Guided Imagery: Successful Techniques to Improve School Performance and Self-esteem*. Duluth, MN: Whole Person Associates.

Busse, V. (2013) An exploration of motivation and self-beliefs of first year students of German. *System* 41, 379–398.

Center, Y., Freeman, L., Robertson, G. and Outhred, L. (1999) The effect of visual imagery training on the reading and listening comprehension of low listening comprehenders in year 2. *Journal of Research in Reading* 22, 241–256.

Clark, J.M. and Paivio, A. (1991) Dual coding theory and education. *Educational Psychology Review* 3 (3), 149–210.

Cohen, A. (1987) The use of verbal and imagery mnemonics in second-language vocabulary learning. *Studies in Second Language Acquisition* 9, 43–61.

Cox, R.H. (2012) *Sport Psychology: Concepts and Applications* (7th edn). New York: McGraw-Hill.

Csizér, K. and Dörnyei, Z. (2005) The internal structure of language learning motivation: Results of structural equation modelling. *The Modern Language Journal* 89 (1), 19–36.

Csizér, K. and Lukács, G. (2010) The comparative analysis of motivation, attitudes and selves: The case of English and German in Hungary. *System* 38, 1–13.

Dörnyei, Z. (2001) *Motivational Strategies in the Language Classroom*. Cambridge: Cambridge University Press.

Dörnyei, Z. (2005) *The Psychology of the Language Learner: Individual Differences in Second Language Acquisition*. Mahwah, NJ: Lawrence Erlbaum.

Dörnyei, Z. (2009) The L2 Motivational Self System. In Z. Dörnyei and E. Ushioda (eds) *Motivation, Language Identity and the L2 Self* (pp. 9–42). Bristol: Multilingual Matters.

Dörnyei, Z. (2010) Researching motivation: From integrativeness to the ideal L2 self. In S. Hunston and D. Oakey (eds) *Introducing Applied Linguistics: Concepts and Skills* (pp. 74–83). London: Routledge.

Dörnyei, Z. and Chan, L. (2013) Motivation and vision: An analysis of future L2 self images, sensory styles, and imagery capacity across two target languages. *Language Learning* 63 (3), 437–462

Dörnyei, Z. and Kubanyiova, M. (2014) *Motivating Learners, Motivating Teachers: Building Vision in the Language Classroom*. Cambridge: Cambridge University Press.

Dörnyei, Z. and Ushioda, E. (eds) (2009) *Motivation, Language Identity and the L2 self*. Bristol: Multilingual Matters.

Dörnyei, Z. and Ushioda, E. (2011) *Teaching and Researching Motivation* (2nd edn). Harlow: Longman.

Ellis, N.C. and Beaton, A.A. (1993) Factors affecting the learning of foreign vocabulary: Imagery keyword mediators and phonological short-term memory. *Quarterly Journal of Experimental Psychology 46A*, 533–558.

Fukada, Y., Fukuda, T., Falout, J. and Murphey, T. (2011) Increasing motivation with possible selves. In A. Stewart (ed.) *JALT 2010 Conference Proceedings* (pp. 337–349). Tokyo: JALT.

Gardner, R.C. and Lambert, W.E. (1959) Motivational variables in second language acquisition. *Canadian Journal of Psychology* 13, 266–272.

Gerngross, G., Puchta, H. and Thornbury, S. (2006) *Teaching Grammar Creatively*. Crawley: Helbling Languages.

Green, M.C. and Donahue, J.K. (2009) Simulated world: Transportation into narratives. In K.D. Markman, W.M.P. Klein and J.A. Suhr (eds) *Handbook of Imagination and Mental Simulation* (pp. 241–256). New York, NY: Psychology Press.

Hadfield, J. and Dörnyei, Z. (2013) *Motivating Learners*. Harlow, England: Pearson.

Henry, A. (2009) Gender differences in compulsory school pupils' L2 self-concepts: A longitudinal study. *System* 37, 177–193.

Henry, A. (2010) Contexts of possibility in simultaneous language learning: Using the L2 Motivational Self System to assess the impact of global English. *Journal of Multilingual and Multicultural Development* 31 (2), 149–162.

Henry, A. (2011) Examining the impact of L2 English on L3 selves: A case study. *International Journal of Multilingualism* 8 (3), 235–255.

Higgins, E.T. (1987) Self-discrepancy: A theory relating self and affect. *Psychological Review* 94, 319–340.

Higgins, E.T. (1998) Promotion and prevention: Regulatory focus as a motivational principle. *Advances in Experimental Social Psychology* 30, 1–46.

Hiver, P. (2013) The interplay of possible language teacher selves in professional development choices. *Language Teaching Research* 17 (2), 210–227.

Islam, M., Lamb, M. and Chambers, G.N. (2013) The L2 motivational self system and national interest: A Pakistani perspective. *System* 41, 231–244.

Jones, K. (2012) *Visualising Success: An Imagery Intervention Programme to Increase Two Students' Confidence and Motivation in a Foreign Language*. Nottingham, UK: University of Nottingham.

Katz, A.N. (2000) Mental imagery. In A.E. Kazdin (ed.) *Encyclopedia of Psychology* (Vol. 5, pp. 187–191). Oxford: American Psychological Association and Oxford University Press.

Kim, T.-Y. (2009) Korean elementary school students' perceptual learning style, ideal L2 self, and motivated behaviour. *Korean Journal of English Language and Linguistics* 9, 261–286.

Kim, Y.-K. and Kim, T.-Y. (2011) The effect of Korean secondary school students' perceptual learning styles and ideal L2 self on motivated L2 behavior and English proficiency. *Korean Journal of English Language and Linguistics* 11, 21–42.

Kormos, J., Kiddle, T. and Csizér, K. (2011) Systems of goals, attitudes, and self-related beliefs in second-language-learning motivation. *Applied Linguistics* 32, 495–516.

Krasny, K. and Sadoski, M. (2008) Mental imagery and affect in English/French bilingual readers: A cross-linguistic perspective. *Canadian Modern Language Review* 64, 399–428.

Lamb, M. (2012) A self system perspective on young adolescents' motivation to learn English in urban and rural settings. *Language Learning* 62, 997–1023.

Levin, I.M. (2000) Vision revisited: Telling the story of the future. *Journal of Applied Behavioral Science* 36 (1), 91–107.

Magid, M. (2009) The L2 Motivational Self System from a Chinese perspective: A mixed methods study. *Journal of Applied Linguistics* 6 (1), 69–90.

Magid, M. and Chan, L.H. (2012) Motivating English learners by helping them visualise their Ideal L2 Self: Lessons from two motivational programmes. *Innovation in Language Learning and Teaching* 6 (2), 113–125.

Markus, H. and Nurius, P. (1986) Possible selves. *American Psychologist* 41, 954–969.

Markus, H. and Nurius, P. (1987) Possible selves: The interface between motivation and the self-concept. In K. Yardley and T. Honess (eds) *Self and Identity: Psychosocial Perspectives* (pp. 157–172). Chichester: John Wiley & Sons.

Markus, H. and Ruvolo, A. (1989) Possible selves: Personalized representations of goals. In L.A. Pervin (ed.) *Goal Concepts in Personality and Social Psychology* (pp. 211–241). Hillsdale, NJ: Lawrence Erlbaum.

Morris, T., Spittle, M. and Watt, A.P. (2005) *Imagery in Sport*. Champaign, IL: Human Kinetics.

Moulton, S.T. and Kosslyn, S.M. (2009) Imagining predictions: Mental imagery as mental emulation. *Philosophical Transactions of the Royal Society B* 364, 1273–1280.

Murdock, M. (1987) *Spinning Inward: Using Guided Imagery with Children for Learning, Creativity and Relaxation*. Boston, MA: Shambhala.

Papi, M. (2010) The L2 motivational self system, L2 anxiety, and motivated behaviour: A structural equation modeling approach. *System* 38, 467–479.

Papi, M. and Teimouri, Y. (2012) Dynamics of selves and motivation: A cross-sectional study in the EFL context of Iran. *International Journal of Applied Linguistics* 22 (3), 287–309.

Reisberg, D. and Heuer, F. (2005) Visuospatial images. In P. Shah and A. Miyake (eds) *The Cambridge Handbook of Visuospatial Thinking* (pp. 35–80). Cambridge: Cambridge University Press.

Ruvolo, A.P. and Markus, H.R. (1992) Possible selves and performance: The power of self-relevant imagery. *Social Cognition* 10 (1), 95–124.

Sampson, R. (2012) The language-learning self, self-enhancement activities, and self perceptual change. *Language Teaching Research* 16 (3), 317–335.

Sheikh, A.A., Skeikh, K.A. and Moleski, L.M. (2002) Techniques to enhance imaging ability. In A.A. Sheikh (ed.) *Handbook of Therapeutic Imagery Techniques* (pp. 383–399). Amityville, NY: Baywood.

Shen, H.H. (2010) Imagery and verbal coding approaches in Chinese vocabulary instruction. *Language Teaching Research* 14, 485–500.

Singer, J.L. (2006) *Imagery in Psychotherapy*. Washington, DC: American Psychological Association.

Stevick, E.W. (1986) *Images and Options in the Language Classroom*. Cambridge: Cambridge University Press.

Taylor, S.E., Pham, L.B., Rivkin, I.D. and Armor, D.A. (1998) Harnessing the imagination: Mental simulation, self-regulation, and coping. *American Psychologist* 53 (4), 429–439.

van der Helm, R. (2009) The vision phenomenon: Towards a theoretical underpinning of visions of the future and the process of envisioning. *Futures* 41, 96–104.

Wright, A. and Hill, D.A. (2008) *Writing Stories: Developing Language Skills through Story Making*. Crawley, UK: Helbling Languages.

3 At the Interface of the Socio-Educational Model, Self-Determination Theory and the L2 Motivational Self System Models

Maya Sugita McEown, Kimberly A. Noels and Kathryn Everhart Chaffee

For what you see and hear depends a good deal on where you are standing.
C.S. Lewis, 1955, *The Magician's Nephew*

Introduction

Although it is a key predictor of learners' eventual proficiency in their target language (TL), motivation has been a tricky construct to define. As many language learning motivation (LLM) researchers have argued, motivation is best understood as an umbrella term for a broad concept that covers a variety of cognitive, affective and behavioural processes explaining: (1) why people decide to do something; (2) how long they will sustain the activity and (3) how much effort they will expend to pursue it (Boekaerts, 1995; Dörnyei, 2001). Indeed, a recent volume has a dozen or more chapters on different psychological constructs that arguably have motivational implications (see Mercer *et al.*, 2012). Because of the diverse aspects of motivation, teachers and researchers might face a quandary deciding which constructs are most useful for understanding learners' motivation in their particular social and educational context.

There are many ways to deal with theoretical diversity. Some choose one framework and eschew all others. Others seek to integrate the diverse approaches in a single grand theory. Still others would rather have nothing to do with theory, arguing that it can constrain thinking and result in dogmatic adherence to one way of thinking. We choose to adopt the perspective-taking approach advocated by MacIntyre *et al.* (2010), which maintains that different theories reflect different perspectives, such that any point of view will simultaneously reveal some aspects of the phenomena of interest and conceal others. MacIntyre *et al.* (2010: 1) liken this theoretical perspective-taking to viewing a garden:

> A famous garden at the Ryoanji Temple in Japan has 15 stones. The positioning of the stones is fascinating; from any vantage point an observer will see 14 stones, never all 15. Contemplating the meaning of the garden at Ryoanji raised for us 'what does it mean to take "A" perspective?'

MacIntyre and his colleagues stress the value of being acquainted with diverse points of view, arguing that by considering the theories together, we can see complementary, and perhaps richer, ways of understanding motivation and language learning (LL).

With this idea in mind, we will consider the concepts of self and identity as they are framed in three widely used motivational frameworks, including the Socio-Educational Model (SEM) (Gardner, 1985, 2010), Self-Determination Theory (SDT) (Deci & Ryan, 1985; Ryan & Deci, 2000) and the Second Language (L2) Motivational Self System (L2MSS) (Dörnyei, 2009). In so doing, we hope to identify areas of convergence and divergence, which will provide a more nuanced understanding of the role of the self in L2 motivation. We also hope to point out directions for future research, primarily by directing attention to the methodological and contextual trends in current research and suggesting how these trends can not only offer affordances but also place constraints on our thinking about motivation. To accomplish these goals, we first present an overview of the self- and identity-relevant aspects of the SEM, SDT and L2MSS and consider their similarities and differences conceptually and empirically. As part of this discussion, we report the results of an empirical study that examines the overlap of the three theories. Lastly, we highlight some methodological and contextual issues with our study and with studies in this area more generally that we feel need to be addressed in future theorising and empirical research.

Three Theoretical Frameworks

The Socio-Educational Model (SEM)

Gardner's (1985, 2010) SEM was formulated at a time when ethnolinguistic group relations in Canada and elsewhere were particularly politically charged (see Noels & Giles, 2009, for a review). In light of this, it is not surprising that an important aspect of this model concerns learners' attitudes towards the TL community. Gardner (2010) argued that language learning involves more than just learning new words and grammatical structures; there is an acculturative aspect such that when one learns another language, one is encouraged to learn and internalise something from another cultural group, much as a child imitates its caregiver and is reinforced with the caregiver's feedback. This aspect, termed 'integrativeness', reflects 'a general openness to adopting characteristics of other cultural communities' (Gardner, 2010: 85), and includes an interest in foreign languages, positive attitudes towards the TL community and an integrative orientation.

An orientation represents 'the underlying force directing the choice of a particular reason' (Gardner, 2010: 16). The integrative orientation is characterised by an interest in and desire to communicate with the TL community, and in some definitions includes the possibility of identifying with the TL group (e.g. Masgoret & Gardner, 2003). To have an impact on volitional behaviour, any orientation must also be linked with a drive to learn and effort extended towards the goal of language learning. An integrative motivation thus includes not only an integrative orientation towards language learning but also motivational intensity, the desire to learn the TL and affective aspects, which include positive attitudes towards the specific language learning situation, language learning in general, the specific TL group and ethnic out-groups in general. Individuals with an integrative orientation want to approach and integrate with the TL group, although Gardner specifies that this does not necessarily mean that they want to assimilate into that group (albeit that may happen in extreme cases), rather, they want to engage with the TL community (Gardner, 2010: 88).

Several orientations other than the integrative orientation can direct motivation; one alternative (but not necessarily oppositional) orientation is the instrumental orientation. This orientation involves a desire to learn the TL for practical, utilitarian reasons such as 'because it will make me more educated' and 'it will be useful in getting a good job' (Gardner et al., 1997: 361). Although Gardner and his colleagues did not extensively examine the instrumental orientation, it is useful to contrast it with the notion of integrativeness in order to highlight the latter's emphasis on intergroup relations and social identity concerns.

Self-Determination Theory (SDT)

Drawing from principles in humanistic psychology, SDT (Deci & Ryan, 1985) maintains that people have an innate tendency to explore and master novel aspects of their environment and assimilate these new experiences into their existing self-structures. This process is not random; rather persons are assumed to regulate their behaviour in line with their sense of self. That is, with each new experience, a person considers other possible actions in light of her/his current interests, and then acts in a way that reflects the best correspondence with these interests. A person's actions are considered authentic when they are endorsed by the person and are congruent with other value commitments that a person holds.

Extending these principles to the study of motivation, it is assumed that if people feel that an activity is consistent with their sense of self, they will be more motivated to engage in that activity. With regard to language learning, the more people feel that learning and using a language are congruent with the other values that they have, the more motivated they will be to engage in learning and using the language. This experience is termed integrated regulation.

Of course, we are not all motivated to learn languages because doing so is integral to our sense of self. We may see the value of learning and using a language even if we don't see the language as self-defining. For instance, the language may help us to achieve goals that we feel are important to us (e.g. an English as a foreign language (EFL) teacher learns the native language of her students to better communicate with them; a fiancé learns his sweetheart's language to better understand her and her familial background). Such an orientation, where the person has personally identified the value of the activity, is termed identified regulation.

Alternatively, we might be motivated less because of our own sense of what is important and valuable, but more because we have a generalised sense of what ought to be important. Perhaps this sentiment arises because of the values of those around us. For example, parents might emphasise that knowing another language is an important educational goal, and students might internalise this belief to some degree. Even if they can't see the value or relevance of learning the language for themselves, personally, they might feel that learning a language is something that every good child and/or good student should do. This feeling that one should or ought to learn a language is termed introjected regulation.

In still other cases, we may engage in an activity not because we feel it is self-relevant or have some sense that it might be good to do, but rather because there is some obvious reward or punishment for doing so. For instance, learning a language might be a means to getting a required course credit, or failure to do so might result in the denial of a job promotion. Such reasons have very little to do with a learner's sense of self, but rather are driven by people or circumstances external to the learner. Hence, such an experience of motivation is termed external regulation.

These experiences of motivation, then, vary in the extent to which the regulation of action is self-determined. SDT proposes another form of motivation which relates back to the idea that we have 'an inherent tendency to seek out novelty and challenges, to extend and exercise our capacities, to explore, and to learn' (Ryan & Deci, 2000: 70) about our physical and social worlds. Engaging in such an activity brings about a feeling of enjoyment, absorption and fulfilment, termed flow by Csik-szentmihalyi (1990). Thus, the process of learning a language could be experienced as being a pleasurable process in and of itself; a person might not necessarily feel that the activity is tied to their sense of self, but simply enjoy engaging in the activity for its own sake. This experience of intrinsic motivation then is distinct from the other forms of regulation that are subsumed under the term extrinsic motivation.

It should be noted that these are not categories into which people neatly fall. Rather, drawing on the discourse of dynamic systems theory, intrinsic and extrinsic motivation might be described as two motivational systems (Noels, 2005), one reflecting the extent to which the activity is regulated by internal or external sources and the second reflecting an innate proclivity to explore novelty and seek out new challenges. Because of diverse interactions in their social world, people could hold multiple orientations, and the prominence of one or another might shift from situation to situation and from time to time. Moreover, there is really no objective way to say that one motivational orientation is superior to another. If students value and identify with the language and feel intrinsically motivated, they are more likely to engage creatively with the language. Language instructors might find that such an orientation facilitates the teaching and learning process. However, there might be circumstances where such an orientation is fraught, as might be the case when learning the language of a colonial oppressor, which might result in linguistic and cultural assimilation or marginalisation.

L2 Motivational Self System (L2MSS) model

Dörnyei's (2009) L2MSS framework draws from work by social psychologists, who study the self as an aspect of social cognition and the thinking of applied linguists interested in dynamic systems theory. The L2MSS has been strongly influenced by the possible selves theory of Markus and Nurius (1986) and Higgins's (1987) self-discrepancy theory. The possible selves theory concerns how people conceptualise their potential and think about their future (Markus & Nurius, 1986). Possible selves act as future self-guides, representing a dynamic, forward-focusing conception that can explain how people are moved from the present to the future. Likewise, self-discrepancy theory postulates that people are motivated to reach a condition where their self-concept matches their personally relevant self-guides (Higgins, 1987).

Synthesising the self-images introduced in the theory of possible selves (Markus & Nurius, 1986) and the self-discrepancy theory (Higgins, 1987), Dörnyei developed three components for the L2MSS. The central concept is the ideal L2 self, which refers to the attributes that one would ideally like to possess in connection with L2 learning. A complementary concept is the ought-to L2 self, signifying the attributes that one believes one ought to possess in connection with L2 learning. The L2 learning experience consists of 'situated "executive" motives related to the immediate learning environment and experience (e.g. the impact of the teacher, the curriculum, the peer group, the experience of success)' (Dörnyei, 2009: 29).

Dörnyei (e.g. 2009) maintains that key self-related constructions of the ideal L2 self and ought-to L2 self extend the scope of Gardner's (1985) notion of integrativeness, making it applicable in diverse language learning environments in our globalised world (Dörnyei, 2010). He claims (2005: 105) that 'our idealised L2-speaking self can be seen as a member of an imagined L2 community whose mental construction is partly based on our real-life experiences of members of the community/communities speaking the particular L2 in question and partly on our imagination'.

Empirical Comparisons of the Three Theories

Convergence and divergence

There are several points of convergence and divergence between the self and identity constructs in these models, some of which have been substantiated through empirical examinations. We thus turn to review empirical studies, which compared self- and identity-related constructs between the three theories (see Appendix for a summary). The purpose is to consider empirical evidence concerning the relations between the models.

SEM and SDT

Although some have equated the intrinsic–extrinsic and integrative–instrumental distinction, these two pairings are not synonymous. Gardner (2010) suggested that the integrative orientation is better classified as a type of extrinsic motivation because it does not pertain to engaging in the activity for enjoyment per se. We would agree to some extent with this position, but argue that the relationship between these two sets of constructs is more complex. Empirical research indicates that the integrative orientation is strongly associated with intrinsic motivation, but it is also highly associated with more self-determined forms of extrinsic motivation (Noels, 2001; Sugita McEown et al., under review). In their study of Japanese EFL high school students, Kimura et al. (2001) found that the largest factor of LLM observed was complex, consisting of intrinsic, integrative and instrumental subscales.

However, the integrative orientation is not synonymous with either type of motivation in that it is not perfectly correlated with either, and it tends to predict different kinds of outcome variables. For instance, Pae's (2008) study demonstrated that integrative orientation was distinct from both intrinsic and extrinsic motivation (identified, introjected and external regulations), although the integrative orientation was relatively closer to intrinsic than to extrinsic motivation. Noels (2001, 2005; see also Sugita McEown et al., under review) found that whereas the SDT orientations tended to be stronger predictors of learning and classroom engagement, the integrative orientation was a better predictor of community and cultural engagement. Because of these findings, Noels argues that the integrative orientation references issues related to social identity and intergroup relations that might be distinct from the processes taking place in the immediate learning situation. In contrast, Landry (2012) suggests that an SDT approach could also be useful for understanding intergroup relations in language learning.

SEM and L2MSS

The conceptual differences between SEM and L2MSS have been much discussed since Dörnyei (2005, 2009) proposed the L2MSS as an alternative framework to the SEM. According to Dörnyei (2010), the central theme of L2MSS was the elaboration of the motivational dimension that has traditionally been interpreted as integrativeness/integrative motivation with the ideal L2 self. Lamb (2012) claims that the key differences between the two theories are in whether they are more affectively (SEM) or cognitively (L2MSS) based, and whether the motivationally important identifications are with others (SEM) or with future versions of the self (L2MSS). There are several empirical examinations of the relations between the self-related variables in these two frameworks. The study of Kim and Kim (2012) of Korean EFL secondary school students found that the ideal L2 self was a better predictor for explaining participants' motivated behaviour than integrativeness, and argued that the ideal L2 self could replace integrative orientation. On the other hand, in their study of Hungarian EFL secondary school students, Kormos and Csizér (2008) found that the ideal L2 self and integrativeness are not interchangeable concepts and the ought-to L2 self could not be identified in their participants. They concluded that integrativeness was more closely related to cultural interest, while the ideal L2 self was more closely related to international posture (Yashima et al., 2002). Although both of the studies investigated a large number of EFL secondary level students using a cross-sectional questionnaire survey, their results were inconsistent.

SDT and L2MSS

As Dörnyei (2009) pointed out, SDT and the L2MSS frameworks have several conceptual similarities, but there are important divergences as well. The ought-to L2 self and introjected regulation would seem to be definitionally congruent. The ideal L2 self would seem to be most similar to the notion of identified and integrated regulation, in that both reflect personally held values and goals. Indeed, in his study of Japanese EFL university students, Nishida (2012) found that the ideal L2 self was most strongly correlated with integrated regulation. These constructs differ, however, in their temporal orientation. The integrated self-regulation refers to well internalised values and goals that comprise one's current, authentic sense of self. In contrast, the ideal L2 self refers to a vision of a future self, as one would like to be. It may be that this ideal self is integrated into a person's self-concept, but it might not be.

These studies generally indicate that although there is considerable overlap between these sets of self-related constructs, they are not isomorphic. To the best of our knowledge, however, no study to date has simultaneously investigated the connections between all three theories, nor how these self-related variables are linked with other motivational variables. To this end, we conducted a study with two purposes: (1) to examine the relations among key concepts in the three theoretical frameworks (i.e. integrative orientation, intrinsic motivation, integrated regulation, identified regulation, introjected regulation, external regulation, amotivation, ideal L2 self and ought-to L2 self) and (2) to explore differences in the predictions among three theories for various affective and behavioural implications of these self-relevant constructs (i.e. engagement in LL, LL anxiety, intention to learn the TL and self-evaluation of TL competence).

An Empirical Study

Participants

A total of 167 university-level language learners were surveyed (gender: 67.7% female; age: $M = 18.88$, SD $= 1.71$), including 51.2% who reported that they had been studying the TL for two years or less, 15.8% who studied the TL for between two and five years, and 21.9% who studied the language for 6–19 years. Most indicated that their native language was English (85.6%) or English and another language (14.4%). About 20% reported that one or both of their parents spoke the TL and hence these students could be considered heritage language learners (HLLs). The language courses in which the students enrolled included French (29.3%),

Spanish (24.0%), Italian (9.0%), German (6.6%), Chinese (6.0%) and Ukrainian (3.6%), along with other languages (e.g. Arabic, Cree, Punjabi, etc.).

Instruments

The questionnaire consisted of 55 items to assess the self-relevant constructs proposed by the three frameworks (SEM, SDT and L2MSS). Items were rated on a five-point scale. Twenty-eight items from Noels *et al.* (2000) assessed SDT orientations: intrinsic motivation (four items: e.g. 'For the pleasure I experience as I get to know [TL] better'; α = .91); integrated regulation (four items: e.g. 'Because it is a part of my identity'; α = .91); identified regulation (five items: e.g. 'Because it helps me to achieve goals that are important to me'; α = .87); introjected regulation (seven items: e.g. 'Because I would feel guilty if I didn't know a second language'; α = .87); external regulation (four items: e.g. 'In order to have a better salary later on'; α = .70) and amotivation (four items: e.g. 'Honestly, I don't know; I truly have the impression of wasting my time in studying [TL]'; α = .86). A total of 23 items from Dörnyei (2010) represented: the ideal L2 self (12 items: e.g. 'I often imagine myself in the future speaking [TL] very well'; α = .95) and the ought-to L2 self (11 items: 'If I fail to learn a foreign language like [TL] I'll be letting other people down'; α = .87). A total of four items from Gardner (1985) assessed integrative motivation (e.g. 'Because it will allow me to meet and converse with more and varied people'; α = .85).

Additional instruments assessed engagement, affect and proficiency indices that are hypothesised to be predicted by the self-relevant variables. Nine items assessed schoolwork engagement (e.g. 'I am enthusiastic about my [TL] studies'; α = .95; Salmela-Aro & Upadaya, 2012) and 10 items assessed anxiety (e.g. 'I get nervous when I am speaking in my [the TL] class'; α = .86; Clément & Baker, 2001). Five items assessed the students' intention to continue learning the language (Noels *et al.*, 1999; e.g. 'I want to keep on learning [the TL] as long as possible'; α = .94) and four items from Clément and Baker (2001) assessed the students' self-evaluation of their reading, writing, speaking and understanding of the TL on a scale ranging from 1 to 7, where a high mean score indicated a high self-evaluation of TL competence (α = .83).

Data collection and analysis

Students who were enrolled in diverse language courses at a Canadian university completed an online questionnaire that was part of a larger study on LLM (Chaffee *et al.*, in preparation). The questionnaire wording was adapted to each student's TL and completed at individual computer terminals during group testing sessions. Prior to completing the survey, participants completed an informed consent procedure as outlined by the Tri-Council Policy of the Government of Canada and the Canadian Psychological Association to ensure their voluntary, informed participation and assure them of the confidentiality of their responses.

In order to examine the overlap between the key variables from the three theoretical frameworks, a principal axis factor analysis with oblimin rotation examined the relation between the self-related variables. The results (Table 3.1) yielded a two-factor solution (based on the Kaiser criterion) accounting for 72% of the variance in the correlation matrix. These factors exhibited a low, positive correlation of .29. The first factor was defined by positive loadings (>.35) by intrinsic, integrative orientation and the ideal L2 self, as well as by identified and integrated regulation; this factor was also defined by negative loadings associated with amotivation. This factor suggested an orientation characterised by a high degree of internalised reasons for learning the language, combined with enjoyment in learning, which were in contrast to having no purpose or meaning for learning the language. The second factor was defined by the ought-to L2 self, introjected regulation and external regulation. This factor seemed to reflect an orientation in which motivation was controlled by pressures that are either internal or external to the self. In sum, these

Table 3.1 Results of the principal axis factor analysis of motivational variables

	Factors	
Variables	1	2
Intrinsic motivation	.84	
Integrative orientation	.83	
Ideal L2 self	.80	
Identified regulation	.79	
Integrated regulation	.64	
Amotivation	-.57	
Ought-to L2 self		.88
Introjected regulation		.76
External regulation		.66
Eigenvalue	4.74	1.75
Percentage of variance	52.61	19.38

results suggest that there are at least two distinct (but not oppositional) subsystems, the first reflecting motivation defined by personal values and goals (including the integrative orientation) and the second reflecting motivation defined by external pressures and/or introjects.

With regard to the prediction of the affective and behavioural variables, a series of stepwise regression analyses were conducted with the self-related indices as the predictor variables and the affective and behavioural indices as the criterion variables (Table 3.2). The best model to predict engagement contained four predictor variables, such that intrinsic motivation and the ideal L2 self positively predicted engagement, but external regulation and amotivation negatively predicted engagement ($R^2 = .63$, $F(4,155) = 65.96$, $p < .01$). With regard to the prediction of classroom anxiety, the best model was one in which the ideal L2 self negatively predicted and introjected regulation positively predicted anxiety ($R^2 = .14$, $F(2,157) = 12.54$, $p < .01$). Concerning the prediction of the intention to persist in learning the language, the best model contained four predictor variables ($R^2 = .73$, $F(4,155)$

Table 3.2 Summary of the results of the stepwise regression analyses with integrative orientation, SDT orientations, ideal L2 self and ought-to L2 self as the predictor variables and engagement, anxiety, continue to learn the language and self-evaluation as the criterion variables

	Criterion variables			
Predictor variables	Engagement	Anxiety	Continue to learn the language	Self-evaluation
	β	β	β	β
Integrative orientation				
Intrinsic motivation	.47**	.17**		
Integrated regulation				.59**
Identified regulation				
Introjected regulation		.20**	-.12*	
External regulation	-.15**			
Amotivation	-.17**		-.29**	
Ideal L2 self	.30**	-.41**	.60**	
Ought-to L2 self				

Notes: *$p < .05$; **$p < .01$.

$= 105.62, p < .01$); the ideal L2 self and intrinsic motivation positively predicted students' intentions, while amotivation and introjected regulation negatively predicted the students' intentions. Finally, the best model to predict students' self-evaluation of their TL competence was one that included only integrated regulation ($R^2 = .34, F(1,156) = 81.83, p < .01$).

Discussion

The results show that key concepts from two of the theoretical frameworks (SDT and L2MSS) significantly predicted engagement, anxiety and the intention to continue learning the language. However, a striking point is that these outcome variables were best explained by a combination of the key concepts from the different theories. This might again indicate that these theories overlap with each other to some extent. However, considering that self-evaluation was significantly predicted by only one predictor variable from SDT, the key concepts from the different theoretical frameworks might predict different learning outcomes. The integrative orientation did not significantly predict any of these outcomes. One possible reason was that the criterion variables used in this study were learning-related outcomes that did not include any cultural or TL community aspects. As indicated in Noels (2001; see also Sugita McEown et al., under review), the integrative orientation tends to better predict language community engagement. Moreover, these regression analyses do not consider the possibility that there might be mediated relations between variables; Kim (2012) found that Gardner's L2 motivational constructs may have an indirect impact on English proficiency that is mediated by the ideal L2 self and the ought-to L2 self. Based on these analyses, we could say that although some conceptual overlaps were confirmed between the three theoretical frameworks, the frameworks might differentially predict learning outcomes.

Methodological and Contextual Issues

The empirical work just described examined the relations among key concepts in the three theoretical frameworks and differences in their predictive power. Although the findings provide some support for the interplay between these three sets of self-related constructs, this topic needs to be further investigated using different methods and in different learning contexts. In the next section, we will elaborate on such directions for future research, but first we broaden the discussion by considering methodological and contextual trends in research using these three theories over the last two decades. We do so because, in addition to theoretical stances, the methodological tools we use and contexts within which we carry out our research have the potential to affect our understanding of motivation and the self; our tools limit the kinds of questions we answer and the contexts we work in make certain issues more or less salient. This point is illustrated by calls for more studies using research methods and analytical strategies that can capture the dynamic aspect of LLM (Dörnyei, 2009), and by claims that the integrative orientation may be less relevant in contexts where an opportunity to interact with the TL community is not available and/or a TL community is not clearly associated with the language (e.g. Dörnyei, 1990; Lamb, 2004). Given that methodological practices and research contexts can impact understanding, we reviewed over 70 empirical studies conducted since 1990 that have used one or more of these three theories in order to identify important trends (see Appendix for a summary).

We focused on two methodological dimensions: (1) the design and (2) the type of data collected, following Nakata's (2006) categorisation of common LL research designs into four categories: (a) cross-sectional quantitative studies; (b) longitudinal quantitative studies; (c) cross-sectional qualitative studies and (d) longitudinal qualitative studies. Cross-sectional studies typically sample the participants' thoughts, behaviours or emotional stances at one point in time, while longitudinal studies observe the same participants for an extended period in order to detect patterns of development over time. To this scheme we added another category, repeated cross-sectional design, in which data collection occurs across time, but the samples at each timepoint comprise different participants (also termed trend analysis; see Taris, 2000). Moreover, some longitudinal studies include an intervention in their design (e.g. to examine the effects of a new teaching practice on motivational intensity compared to the current practice; see Taris, 2000). In such pre-test–post-test designs, measurements of the variable of interest (i.e. the dependent variable, e.g. motivational intensity) are taken before and after the intervention (i.e. the independent variable; e.g. type of teaching practice). More rigorous designs might include a control group that does not receive this kind of treatment (termed pre-test–post-test control group design). These types of studies can take place in the field or in a laboratory (termed quasi-experimental or experimental designs, respectively).

The most common examples of quantitative data in LLM research are responses to closed-ended questions that are usually answered on a numerical scale, or qualitative responses that are coded into numerical categories or scales. Usually this information is collected with questionnaire surveys. The most common examples of qualitative data in the field are verbal or written responses to open-ended questions, whether elicited through open-ended items in a questionnaire, verbal responses in personal or focus group interviews or researchers' field notes from observational studies. These two forms of data are not exclusive, and many researchers mix both types of data to address the issues in which they are interested.

As can be seen in the Appendix, 76.9% of the reviewed studies used a cross-sectional design, and 80% of these used questionnaires to collect quantitative data. Four cross-sectional studies collected only qualitative data, but six studies collected mixed data. Among the longitudinal studies (21.8%), almost half of the studies used mixed data (41.2%), and 41.2% reported only quantitative data. Qualitative data from interviews and/or open-ended questionnaires were elicited less often. Thus, there is a pre-ponderance of cross-sectional research designs using questionnaire surveys to elicit quantitative information. If, as a field, we wish to better under-stand the dynamics of motivation and assess our causal claims, we should conduct more studies with longitudinal and experimental designs (cf. Reinhart et al., 2013). We would likely also develop a richer understanding by collecting mixed data in our studies.

We examined three contextual aspects: (1) the level of education in which a student enrolled (and, relatedly, the age of the language learner); (2) the nature of the language contact situation and (3) the country in which the data collection took place. The educational level of learners has been argued to be important for understanding self-related aspects of moti-vation because it corresponds with the age of the learner. Age is an impor-tant aspect because research shows that there are developmental differences in the structure and dynamics of the self-concept across the lifespan (Har-ter, 2012), and dynamics of motivational processes could have different impacts during different periods in learners' development (Dörnyei, 2001). We thus coded the studies across three age-related categories: (a) elementary level learners (E); (b) secondary level learners (S; age 13–17 years) and (c) post-secondary level learners (PS; over 18 years). As shown in the Appendix, post-secondary students have been the focus of 61.5% of the reviewed stud-ies, particularly in studies using SEM and SDT. In contrast, studies employ-ing the L2MSS framework have recruited more young learners than post-secondary language learners. This would suggest that we need additional research across age groups. Moreover, comparisons between theoretical frameworks may be problematic because different age groups tend to be studied by scholars with different theoretical perspectives.

The context in which language contact takes place is a macrosocial factor that describes the relation between the learner's ethnolinguistic community of origin and that of the TL community. We adapted the con-textual taxonomy developed by Clément et al. (2007) to describe three aspects of the intergroup context that have implications for motivational variables. These include: (a) the opportunity for immediate contact with members of the TL community (i.e. second language (SL) or foreign lan-guage (FL) contexts); (b) the degree of ancestral relatedness that a person has with the TL community (i.e. whether or not one is a heritage learner

[HL]) and (c) whether the TL is English or not. The most common contact situation was the EFL/ESL (English as a second language) context: 51.3% of the studies were solely based on this situation, and another 12.8% examined the EFL/ESL context and another language. One third of the studies did not include English; 16.7% examined one foreign language, 14.1% examined a second language, and only 3.8% examined multiple languages within one study. HL learning was examined in only 2.5% of the papers. This analysis suggests that greater diversity in the languages represented is needed. As well, more attention could be directed towards HL learning. Although it is important to develop proficiency in the language of the receiving society, maintenance of the HL is also an important issue for immigrants and their offspring.

As noted above, the country in which the data collection takes place has been suggested to make salient different issues in language learning depending on the opportunities available for interaction with the TL group. The country in which the research takes place is also an important consideration because countries potentially differ in their cultural systems in ways that are reflected in motivational processes (see Heine, 2010; Sorrentino & Yamaguchi, 2008). As the Appendix shows, about 70% of the empirical studies using the SEM were carried out in North American or European countries, such as the United States, Canada, Hungary and Spain. In contrast, researchers using SDT or the L2MSS frameworks recruited participants less often in so-called Western societies, but more in East Asian contexts, such as China, Japan and Korea (38.2% and 61.8%, respectively). Given that current research in (cross-) cultural psychology has demonstrated important variations in how people construe their selves, how accepting they are of power hierarchies and how they view their relationships with others, it would seem critical to better understand how these cultural dynamics relate to motivational dynamics involved in LL (see Noels *et al.*, this volume).

Future directions for the self and LLM

In this chapter, we examined the differences and similarities among three theoretical frameworks (SDT, SEM and L2MSS), and highlighted various methodological and contextual trends in the empirical research emanating from these theories. Below, we summarise important issues that we feel merit greater attention in future studies.

First, the researcher's choice of theoretical constructs should be informed by the types of outcome variables that the researcher wishes to understand. Although these theories have conceptual overlap, our review and empirical study findings suggest that if the phenomena we wish to investigate are learning-related (such as motivational intensity, self-evaluation or academic engagement), SDT and L2MSS would be good theoretical choices; however, if we want to look at intercultural and community-related outcomes, it might be useful to incorporate the notion of integrativeness, particularly if there is an identifiable TL group.

Second, the relative absence of studies with longitudinal designs has limited our representations of motivational processes to a static snapshot, even though two of the theories (SDT and L2MSS) have explicitly presented frameworks with a temporal aspect. Longitudinal designs would allow us to better model intra-individual and inter-individual changes in LLM across time. Examinations of short durations provide us with insight into the dynamic interrelations between individual differences and the contextual aspects of LLM (cf. MacIntyre *et al.*, 2010), and investigations of longer durations provide us with a greater understanding of developmental trends and pathways across courses, programmes of study, grade levels and even across the lifespan. Moreover, given that many of the applied questions that LLM researchers ask do not readily lend themselves to experimental examinations in a laboratory setting, longitudinal data would better allow LLM researchers to examine causal relationships between variables of interest (cf. Vargas Lascano & Noels, 2013). There are several developmental approaches that LLM researchers could adopt, including the popular notion of dynamic systems. We maintain that LLM researchers would do well to further explore approaches articulated by developmental scientists (cf. Bornstein, 2009; Zelazo, 2013).

Third, although the three theoretical frameworks appear to be well equipped to explain change over time, researchers must still be attentive to whether the different theoretical frameworks are more or less appropriate for different age groups. For instance, some have argued that L2MSS might be less appropriate for younger age groups because an individual's capacity to think self-reflectively and to envision an ideal self might emerge in adolescence and young adulthood (Dörnyei, 2009). The construct of intrinsic motivation (having fun while learning the language), on the other hand, might be particularly relevant to younger learners. In addition to age, experience with the TL might also moderate motivational processes. For instance, integrated self-regulation might be less relevant to novice language learners who have had limited time and experience to incorporate the TL into their self-concept. One group of (generally) more advanced language learners are HLLs; research suggests that they tend to have a stronger sense of the TL as an integrated part of their self-concept, perhaps due to their more extensive experience with the TL and its community (Comanaru & Noels, 2009). More studies and reviews that compare the empirical data of different age groups by employing cross-grade surveys (cf. Gardner, 2010; Kim, 2012) or meta-analytic reviews (cf. Masgoret & Gardner, 2003), for instance, would be very useful.

Fourth, the increase of studies in EFL contexts, where English represents a global lingua franca rather than any particular TL community, has highlighted many new motivational issues, perhaps the most notable of which is the idea that interactions with the TL community might not carry strong motivational force in some societal contexts. However, this increased interest in English corresponds with the relatively few studies that have been conducted in contexts where learners could readily interact with members of the TL community. This shift in focus raises the question of whether the key concepts in the three theories (integrativeness, ideal L2 self and self-determination) may or may not be relevant in these contexts. Given that some theories, particularly SDT, were not originally developed for the language learning context, they might need to incorporate additional aspects specific to language learning (such as an intercultural aspect) into their formulations to more comprehensively describe and explain LLM.

Fifth, the shift in research focus to the EFL context corresponds with an increased amount of research available across more diverse countries. This increased diversity within societal settings is laudable. However, few studies have explicitly articulated whether and why motivational processes might differ across cultural contexts. Cultural and cross-cultural psychologists, as well as cultural anthropologists and cultural sociologists, have long noted that motivational processes might operate in very different ways depending upon the cultural context. For instance, considerable research suggests that people in East Asian nations tend to hold more collectivistic values and have a sense of self that is more interconnected with other people than do people from North America and some European nations (see Hofstede, 2001; Markus & Kitayama, 2010). Those with more interdependent self-constructs tend to include the considerations of others in their motivated behaviour than do those who have more independent self-constructs (Morling & Kitayama, 2007). Given that the self-related constructs of the three theories originated in Western countries, it is important to address whether and how these constructs might differently account for motivational dynamics and processes across cultures.

Conclusion

These issues we have discussed here make it difficult for us to conclude which theory best describes LLM. Each theory has its own specific perspective, and these perspectives may best explain different populations, different contexts and different outcome variables. If we happen to find ourselves at the stone garden at Ryoanji Temple in Japan, we might choose a particular point of view to experience the garden, but this choice limits the range of what can be seen. If we know which stones we want to look at, we can make an informed choice about what perspective to take while remaining aware of what information we are missing.

Therefore, researchers need to identify what aspect of L2 motivation they want to look at – that is, which theory or theories work best based on their respective research contexts, targeted populations and outcome variables of interest.

That being said, there is clearly an overlap between the three sets of constructs. This might suggest that although each theory takes on somewhat different perspectives, the perspectives they each offer come from one end of the garden alone. Although LLM researchers continue to draw different variables into the realm of investigation (e.g. Mercer *et al.*, 2012), we might wonder how the garden would look from alternative points of view (e.g. Atkinson, 2011). In other words, there may be aspects of language learning experiences that have not been covered by any of these three theories, and some elements would benefit by being re-examined from a new angle.

Acknowledgements

The authors would like to thank Shadi Mehrabi for her research assistance, the Social Sciences and Humanities Research Council of Canada for their research funding and the editors for their constructive comments on earlier versions of this chapter.

Notes

(1) Recent empirical studies submitted to peer reviewed journals were collected through LLBA and PSYCINFO databases and also by directly contacting L2 motivation researchers through e-mail. ERIC administrators took their database offline at the time when the literature review was conducted.

(2) Participants over 18 were identified as post-secondary level learners regardless of their degree information.

(3) It should be noted that several studies conducted before 1990 with the SEM focused on secondary level learners (see Gardner, 1985, for review).

(4) We define the criteria for the SL context as follows: SL context refers to the context in which: (1) the TL is an official or national language and/or (2) the TL is generally spoken, such as in a bilingual context.

(5) The third aspect of the framework of Clément *et al.* (2007) is the relative status or dominance of the TL group compared to the speaker's heritage language group. Because there were relatively few studies of LLM in contexts where inter-ethnic contact between languages other than English was likely, we decided to instead focus on English.

References

Al-Shehri, A.S. (2009) Motivation and vision: The relation between the ideal L2 self, imagination and visual style. In Z. Dörnyei and E. Ushioda (eds) *Motivation, Language Identity and the L2 Self* (pp. 164–171). Bristol: Multilingual Matters.

Anya, U. (2011) Connecting with communities of learners and speakers: integrative ideas, experiences, and motivations of successful black second language learners. *Foreign Language Annals* 44, 441–466.

Atkinson, D. (2011) *Alternative Approaches to Second Language Acquisition*. London: Routledge.

Baker, C., Andrews, H., Gruffydd, I. and Lewis, G. (2010) Adult language learning: A survey of Welsh for adults in the context of language planning. *Evaluation and Research in Education* 24, 41–59.

Bernaus, M. and Gardner, R.C. (2008) Teacher motivation strategies, student perceptions, student motivation, and English achievement. *The Modern Language Journal* 92, 387–401.

Bernaus, M., Masgoret, A.M., Gardner, R.C. and Reyes, E. (2004) Motivation and attitudes towards learning languages in multicultural classrooms. *International Journal of Multilingualism* 1 (2), 75–89.

Boekaerts, M. (1995) *Motivation in Education*. London: British Psychological Society.

Bonney, C.R., Cortina, K.S., Fiori, K.L. and Smith-Darden, J.P. (2008) Understanding strategies in foreign language learning: Are integrative and intrinsic motivation distinct predictors? *Learning and Individual Differences* 18, 1–10.

Bornstein, M.H. (2009) *Handbook of Cultural Developmental Science*. New York: Psychology Press.

Chaffee, K.E., Noels, K.A., Sugita McEown, M., Mizumoto, A. and Takeuchi, O. (2014) Motivation and primary and secondary control: A cross-cultural comparison. Unpublished manuscript, University of Alberta.

Carreira, J.M. (2012) Motivational orientations and psychological needs in EFL learning among elementary school students in Japan. *System* 40, 191–202.

Chen, J.F., Warden, C.A. and Chang, H. (2005) Motivators that do not motivate: The case of Chinese EFL learners and the influence of culture on motivation. *TESOL Quarterly* 39, 609–633.

Clément, R. and Baker, S.C. (2001) Measuring social aspects of L2 acquisition and use: Scale characteristics and administration. Technical Report. Ottawa, Canada: University of Ottawa.

Clément, R., Dörnyei, Z. and Noels, K.A. (1994) Motivation and primary and secondary control: A cross-cultural comparison. *Language Learning* 44, 417–448.

Clément, R., Noels, K.A. and MacIntyre, P.D. (2007) Three variations on the social psychology of bilinguality: Context effects in motivation, usage and identity. In A. Weatherall, B.M. Watson and C. Gallois (eds) *Language, Discourse, and Social Psychology* (pp. 51–77). Basingstoke, UK: Palgrave MacMillan.

Comanaru, R. and Noels, K.A. (2009) Self-determination, motivation, and the learning of Chinese as a heritage language. *Canadian Modern Language Review* 66, 131–158.

Csikszentmihalyi, M. (1990) *Flow: The Psychology of Optimal Experience*. New York: Harper and Row.

Csizér, K. and Lukács, G. (2010) The comparative analysis of motivation, attitudes and selves: The case of English and German in Hungary. *System* 38, 1–13.

Deci, E.L. and Ryan, R. M. (1985) *Intrinsic Motivation and Self-determination in Human Behavior*. New York: Plenum Press.

Dörnyei, Z. (2010) *Questionnaires in Second Language Research: Construction, Administration, and Processing* (2nd edn) London: Routledge.

Dörnyei, Z. (2009) The L2 motivational self system. In Z. Dörnyei and E. Ushioda (eds) *Motivation, Language Identity and the L2 Self* (pp. 9–42). Bristol: Multilingual Matters.

Dörnyei, Z. (2005) *The Psychology of the Language Learner: Individual Differences in Second Language Acquisition*. Mahwah, NJ: Lawrence Erlbaum.

Dörnyei, Z. (2001) *Teaching and Researching Motivation*. Harlow: Longman.

Dörnyei, Z. (1990) Conceptualizing motivation in foreign-language learning. *Language Learning* 40, 45–78.

Dörnyei, Z. and Csizér, K. (2002) Some dynamics of language attitudes and motivation: Results of a longitudinal nationwide survey. *Applied Linguistics* 23, 421–462.

Gardner, R.C. (2010) *Motivation and Second Language Acquisition: The Socio-educational Model*. New York: Peter Lang.

Gardner, R.C. (1985) *Social Psychology and Second Language Learning: The Role of Attitudes and Motivation*. London: Edward Arnold.

Gardner, R.C., Day, J.B. and MacIntyre, P.D. (1992) Integrative motivation, induced anxiety, and language learning in a controlled environment. *Studies in Second Language Acquisition* 14 (2), 197–214.

Gardner, R.C. and MacIntyre, P.D. (1991) An instrumental motivation in language study. *Studies in Second Language Acquisition* 13(1), 57–72.

Gardner, R.C., Tremblay, P.F. and Masgoret, A.-M. (1997) Toward a full model of second language learning: An empirical investigation. *The Modern Language Journal* 81, 344–362.

Goldberg, E. and Noels, K.A. (2006) Motivation, ethnic identity and post-secondary education language choices of graduates of intensive French language programs. *Canadian Modern Language Review* 62, 423–447.

Harter, S. (2012) *The Construction of the Self*. New York: Guilford.

Harwood, J. and Vincze, L. (2011) Mediating second language learning and intergroup contact in a bilingual setting. *Journal of Multilingual and Multicultural Development* 32, 377–386.

Heine, S.J. (2010) Cultural psychology. In D.T. Gilbert, S. Fiske and G. Lindzey (eds) *Handbook of Social Psychology* (5th edn) (pp. 1423–1464). New York: Wiley.

Henry, A. (2009) Gender differences in compulsory school pupils' L2 self-concepts: A longitudinal study. *System* 37, 177–193.

Henry, A. and Apelgren, B.M. (2008) Young learners and multilingualism: A study of learner attitudes before and after the introduction of a second foreign language to the curriculum. *System* 36, 607–623.

Hernández, T.A. (2010) The relationship among motivation, interaction, and the development of second language oral proficiency in a study-abroad context. *The Modern Language Journal* 94, 600–617.

Hernández, T. (2008) Integrative motivation as a predictor of achievement in the foreign language classroom. *Applied Language Learning* 18, 1–15.

Hernández, T. (2006) Integrative motivation as a predictor of success in the intermediate foreign language classroom. *Foreign Language Annals* 39, 605–617.

Higgins, E.T. (1987) Self-discrepancy: A theory relating self and affect. *Psychological Review* 94, 319–340.

Hofstede, G. (2001) *Culture's Consequences: Comparing Values, Behaviors, Institutions and Organizations Across Nations*. 2nd edn, Thousand Oaks, CA: Sage.

Hiromori, T. (2003) Gakushuusha no doukidukeha naniniyotte takamarunoka: jikoketteirironn niyoru koukousei eigogakushuushano doukidukeno kentou [What enhances language learners' motivation? High school English learners' motivation from the perspective of self-determination theory]. *JALT Journal* 25, 173–186.

Humphreys, G. and Spratt, M. (2008) Many languages, many motivations: A study of Hong Kong students' motivation to learn different target languages. *System* 36, 313–335.

Humphreys, G.M. and Miyazoe-Wong, Y. (2007) So what is the appeal? The phenomenon of Japanese as a foreign language in Hong Kong. *Journal of Multilingual and Multicultural Development* 28, 468–483.

Jones, B.D., Llacer-Arrastia, S. and Newbill, P. (2009) Motivating foreign language students using self-determination theory. *Innovation in Language Learning and Teaching* 3, 171–189.

Kiany, G.R., Mahdavy, B. and Ghafar, S. (2013) Motivational changes of learners in a traditional context of English education: A case study of high school students in Iran. *International Journal of Research Studies in Language Learning* 2, 3–16.

Kim, T.Y. (2012) The L2 Motivational Self System of Korean EFL students: Cross-grade survey analysis. *English Teaching* 67, 29–56.

Kim, T.Y. (2009) The sociocultural interface between ideal self and ought-to self: A case study of two Korean students' ESL motivation. In Z. Dörnyei and E. Ushioda (eds) *Motivation, Language Identity and the L2 Self* (pp. 274–294). Bristol: Multilingual Matters.

Kim, Y.K. and Kim, T.Y. (2012) Korean secondary school students' L2 learning motivation: Comparing L2 motivational self system with socio-educational model. *English Language and Literature Teaching* 18, 1–19.

Kimura, Y., Nakata, Y. and Okumura, T. (2001) Language learning motivation of EFL learners in Japan: A cross-sectional analysis of various learning milieus. *JALT Journal* 23, 47–68.

Koga, T. (2010) Dynamicity of motivation, anxiety and cooperativeness in a semester course. *System* 38, 172–184.

Kormos, J. and Csizér, K., (2008) Age-related differences in the motivation of learning English as a foreign language: Attitudes, selves and motivated learning behaviour. *Language Learning* 58, 327–355.

Kormos, J., Kiddle, T. and Csizér, K. (2011) Systems of goals, attitudes, and self-related beliefs in second language learning motivation. *Applied Linguistics* 32, 495–516.

Lamb, M. (2012) A self-system perspective on young adolescents' motivation to learn English in urban and rural settings. *Language Learning* 62, 997–1023.

Lamb, M. (2007) The impact of school on EFL learning motivation: An Indonesian case study. *TESOL Quarterly* 41, 757–780.

Lamb, M. (2004) Integrative motivation in a globalizing world. *System* 32, 3–19.

Landry, R. (2012) Autonomie culturelle, cultures sociétales et vitalité des communautés de langue officielle en situation minoritaire au Canada. [Cultural autonomy, societal cultures and vitality of official language minority communities in Canada]. *Minorités Llinguistiques et Société* 1, 159–179.

Macaro, E. and Wingate, U. (2004) From sixth form to university: Motivation and transition among high achieving state-school language students. *Oxford Review of Education* 30, 467–489.

MacIntyre, P.D., Noels, K.A. and Moore, B. (2010) Perspectives on motivation in second language acquisition: Lessons from the Ryoanji Garden. In M.T. Prior, Y. Watanabe and S.-K. Lee (eds) *Selected Proceedings of the 2008 Second Language Research Forum*. Somerville, MA: Cascadilla Press. http://www.lingref.com/cpp/slrf/2008/paper2381.pdf

Magid, M. (2009) The L2 motivational self system from a Chinese perspective: A mixed methods study. *Journal of Applied Linguistics* 6(1), 69–90.

Magid, M. and Chan, L. (2012) Motivating English learners by helping them visualise their ideal L2 self: Lessons from two motivational programmes. *Innovation in Language Learning and Teaching* 6(2), 113–125.

Mahdinejad, G., Hasanzadeh, R., Mirzaian, B. and Ebrahimi, S. (2012) Motivational orientations and students' English language learning: The case of Iranian EFL learners. *European Journal of Social Sciences* 32, 239–250.

Markus, H.R. and Kitayama, S. (2010) Cultures and selves: A cycle of mutual constitution. *Perspectives on Psychological Science* 5, 420–430.

Markus, H.R. and Nurius, P. (1986) Possible selves. *American Psychologist* 41, 954–969.

Masgoret, A.M., Bernaus, M. and Gardner, R.C. (2000) A study of cross-cultural adaptation by English speaking sojourners in Spain. *Foreign Language Annals* 33(5), 548–558.

Masgoret, A.-M. and Gardner, R.C. (2003) Attitude, motivation and second language learning: A meta-analysis of studies conducted by Gardner and associates. *Language Learning* 53, 123–295.

Masgoret, A.-M. and Gardner, R.C. (1999) A casual model of Spanish immigrant adaptation in Canada. *Journal of Multilingual and Multicultural Development* 20, 216–236.

Mercer, S., Ryan, S. and Williams, M. (2012) *Psychology for Language Learning*. Basingstoke: Palgrave MacMillan.

Mori, S. and Gobel, P. (2006) Motivation and gender in the Japanese EFL classroom. *System* 34, 194–210.

Morling, B. and Kitayama, S. (2007) Culture and motivation. In J.L. Shah and W.L. Gardner (eds) *Handbook of Motivation Science* (pp. 417–433). New York: Guilford.

Nakata, Y. (2006) *Motivation and Experience in Foreign Language Learning*. New York: Peter Lang.

Nishida, R. (2012) An empirical study on L2 ideal self, international posture, intrinsic motivation, willingness to communicate among EFL Japanese university students. Paper presented at the JACET convention 2012. Aichi, Japan.

Nishida, R. and Yashima, T. (2009) The enhancement of intrinsic motivation and willingness to communicate through a musical project in young Japanese EFL learners. Paper presented at the American Association of Applied Linguistics (AAAL), Denver, Colorado. March 21–24, 2009.

Noels, K.A. (2005) Orientations to learning German: Heritage language background and motivational processes. *Canadian Modern Language Review* 62, 285–312.

Noels, K. (2001) New orientations in language learning motivation: Towards a model of intrinsic, extrinsic, and integrative orientations and motivation. In Z. Dörnyei, and R. Schmidt (eds) *Motivation and Second Language Acquisition* (pp. 43–68). Honolulu: University of Hawaii Second Language Teaching and Curriculum Centre.

Noels, K.A., Clément, R. and Pelletier, L.G. (1999) Perceptions of teachers' communicative style and students' intrinsic and extrinsic motivation. *The Modern Language Journal* 83, 23–34.

Noels, K.A. and Giles, H. (2009) Social identity and language learning. In W. Ritchie and T. Bhatia (eds) *The New Handbook of Second Language Acquisition* (pp. 647–670). Bingley, UK: Emerald.

Noels, K.A., Pelletier, L.G., Clément, R. and Vallerand, R.L. (2000) Why are you learning a second language? Motivational orientations and self-determination theory. *Language Learning* 50, 57–85.

Okuniewska, E., Okuniewska, H. and Okuniewski, J. (2010) Motivation and attitudes of Polish students learning Hebrew. *Psychology of Language and Communication* 4, 71–79.

Okuniewski, J. (2012) Polish secondary school students learning German: Motivation, orientations and attitudes. *Psychology of Language and Communication* 16, 53–65.

Otoshi, J., and Heffernan, N. (2011) An analysis of a hypothesized model of EFL students' motivation based on self-determination theory. *The Asian EFL Journal Quarterly* 13, 66–86.

Oxford, R.L. and Shearin, J. (1994) Language learning motivation: Expanding the theoretical framework. *The Modern Language Journal* 78, 12–28.

Papi, M. (2010) The L2 motivational self system, L2 anxiety, and motivated behavior: A structural equation modeling approach. *System* 38, 467–479.

Papi, M. and Abdollahzadeh, E. (2011) Teacher motivational practice, student motivation, and possible L2 selves: An examination in the Iranian EFL context. *Language Learning* 62, 571–594.

Pae, T. (2008) Second language orientation and self-determination theory: A structural analysis of the factors affecting second language achievement. *Journal of Language and Social Psychology* 27, 5–27.

Polat, N. (2011) Gender differences in motivation and L2 accent attainment: An investigation of young Kurdish learners of Turkish. *Language Learning Journal* 39, 19–41.

Ramage, K. (1990) Motivational factors and persistence in foreign language study: A descriptive analysis. *Language Learning* 40, 189–219.

Reinhart, A.L., Haring, S.H., Leven, J.R., Patall, E.A. and Robinson, D.H. (2013) Models of not-so-good behavior: Yet another way to squeeze causality and recommendations for practice out of correlational data. *Journal of Educational Psychology* 105, 241–247.

Ryan, R.M. and Deci, E.L. (2000) Self-determination theory and the facilitation of intrinsic motivation, social development, and well-being. *American Psychologist* 55, 68–78.

Sakai, H. and Koike, H. (2008) Changes in Japanese university students' motivation to learn English: Effects of volunteering in an international event. *Japan Association for Language Teaching* 30, 51–68.

Salmela-Aro, K. and Upadaya, K. (2012) The schoolwork engagement inventory: Energy, dedication, and absorption (EDA). *European Journal of Psychology Assessment* 28 (1), 60–67.

Sampson, R. (2012) The language-learning self, self-enhancement activities, and self perceptual change. *Language Teaching Research* 16, 317–335.

Shaaban, K. and Ghaith, G. (2000) Student motivation to learn English as a foreign language. *Foreign Language Annals* 33, 632–642.

Sorrentino, R. M. and Yamaguchi, S. (eds) (2008) *Handbook of Motivation and Cognition Across Cultures*. San Diego, CA: Academic Press.

Sugita McEown, M., Noels, K.A. and Saumure, K.D. (2014) Students' self-determined and integrative orientations and teachers' motivational support in the Japanese as a foreign language course. Manuscript under review.

Taguchi, T., Magid, M., and Papi, M. (2009) The L2 motivational self system among Japanese, Chinese and Iranian learners of English: A comparative study. In Z. Dörnyei and E. Ushioda (eds) *Motivation, Language Identity and the L2 Self* (pp. 66–97). Bristol: Multilingual Matters.

Tanaka, H. (2009) Enhancing intrinsic motivation at three levels: The effects of motivational strategies. *JALT Journal* 31, 227–250.

Tanaka, H. and Hiromori, T. (2007) The effects of educational intervention that enhances intrinsic motivation of L2 students. *JALT Journal* 29, 59–80.

Taris, T.W. (2000) *A Primer in Longitudinal Data Analysis*. London: Sage Publications.

Tremblay, P.F. and Gardner, R.C. (1995) Expanding the motivation construct in language learning. *The Modern Language Journal* 79, 505–518.

Ueki, M. and Takeuchi, O. (2012) Validating the L2 motivational self system in a Japanese EFL context: The interplay of L2 motivation, L2 anxiety, self-efficacy, and the perceived amount of information. *Language Education and Technology* 49, 1–22.

Vargas Lascano, D. and Noels, K.A. (2013, June) Modeling the motivational dynamics of learning another language. Paper presented at the 5th International Conference on Self-Determination Theory, Rochester, NY, June 27–30, 2013.

Warden, C. and Lin, H.J. (2000) Existence of integrative motivation in an Asian EFL setting. *Foreign Language Annals* 33, 535–547.

Wesely, P. (2009) The language learning motivation of early adolescent French immersion graduates. *Foreign Language Annals* 42, 270–286.

Wesely, P. (2010) Language learning motivation in early adolescents: Using mixed methods research to explore contradiction. *Journal of Mixed Methods Research* 4, 295–312.

Wu, X. (2003) Intrinsic motivation and young language learners: The impact of the classroom environment. *System* 31, 501–517.

Wu Man-fat, M. (2007) The relationships between the use of metacognitive language-learning strategies and language-learning motivation among Chinese-speaking ESL learners at a vocational education institute in Hong Kong. *The Asian EFL Journal* 9, 93–117.

Yang, J.S. and Kim, T.Y. (2011) Sociocultural analysis of second language learner beliefs: A qualitative case study of two study-abroad ESL learners. *System* 39, 325–334.

Yashima, T. (2002) Willingness to communicate in a second language: The Japanese EFL context. *The Modern Language Journal* 86, 54–66.

Yu, B. (2010) Learning Chinese abroad: The role of language attitudes and motivation in the adaptation of international students in China. *Journal of Multilingual and Multicultural Development* 31, 301–321.

Zelazo, P.D. (ed.) (2013) *The Oxford Handbook of Developmental Psychology*. Oxford: Oxford University Press.

Zheng, Y. (2012) Exploring long-term productive vocabulary development in an EFL context: The role of motivation. *System* 40, 104–119.

Appendix A

Table A.1 Methodological and contextual issues in empirical studies by primary theoretical framework

Study by primary theoretical framework	Method		Data	Participants	Context	
	Design				Contact situation	Country
Study by primary theoretical framework	*Cross-sectional/ repeated cross-sectional/ longitudinal/ intervention/ quasi-experimental/ observational*		*Quantitative/ qualitative/ mixed/*	*Elementary (E)/ secondary (S)/ post-secondary (PS)/ teacher (T)*	*HL/SLOE/ESL/ FLOE/EFL*	*Country in which data were collected*
Socio-Educational Model						
1. Baker *et al.* (2010)	Longitudinal		Mixed	PS	SLOE (Welsh)	Wales
2. Bernaus & Gardner (2008)	Cross-sectional		Quantitative	S/T	EFL	Spain
3. Bernaus *et al.* (2004)	Cross-sectional		Quantitative	S	SLOE (Spanish)/ EFL/FLOE (Catalan)	Spain
4. Chen *et al.* (2005)	Cross-sectional		Quantitative	PS	EFL	Taiwan
5. Clément *et al.* (1994)	Cross-sectional		Quantitative	S	EFL	Hungary
6. Dörnyei & Csizér (2002)	Repeated cross-sectional		Quantitative	S	FLOE (German, French, Italian and Russian)/ EFL	Hungary

(continued)

Table A.1 Methodological and contextual issues in empirical studies by primary theoretical framework (continued)

| | Method | | Context | | |
	Design	Data	Participants	Contact situation	Country
7. Dörnyei (1990)	Cross-sectional	Quantitative	PS	EFL	Hungary
8. Gardner (2010)	Cross-sectional	Quantitative	E/S/PS	EFL	Brazil/Japan/Croatia/Poland/Romania/Spain
9. Gardner et al. (1992)	Cross-sectional(experiment)	Quantitative	PS	FLOE (French)	Canada
10. Gardner & MacIntyre (1991)	Cross-sectional(experiment)	Quantitative	PS	FLOE (French)	Canada
11. Gardner et al. (1997)	Cross-sectional	Quantitative	PS	SLOE (French)	Canada
12. Harwood & Vincze (2011)	Cross-sectional	Quantitative	S	FLOE (Swedish)	Finland
13. Hernández (2010)	Longitudinal	Mixed	PS	SLOE (Spanish)	United States
14. Hernández (2008)	Cross-sectional	Quantitative	PS	FLOE (Spanish)	United States
15. Hernández (2006)	Cross-sectional	Quantitative	PS	FLOE (Spanish)	United States
16. Humphreys & Spratt (2008)	Cross-sectional	Mixed	PS	FLOE (Japanese, German and French)/ESL/SLOE	Hong Kong

				FLOE (Japanese, German and French)/ESL/EFL	
17. Humphreys & Miyazoe-Wong (2007)	Cross-sectional	Mixed	PS	FLOE (Japanese, German and French)/ESL/EFL	Hong Kong
18. Koga (2010)	Longitudinal	Quantitative	PS	EFL	Japan
19. Masgoret et al. (2000)	Longitudinal	Quantitative	PS	SLOE (Spanish)	Spain
20. Masgoret & Gardner (1999)	Cross-sectional	Quantitative	PS	ESL/SLOE (Spanish)	Canada
21. Mori & Gobel (2006)	Cross-sectional	Quantitative	PS	EFL	Japan
22. Okuniewska et al. (2010)	Cross-sectional	Quantitative	S/PS	FLOE (Hebrew)	Poland
23. Okuniewski (2012)	Cross-sectional	Quantitative	S	FLOE (German)	Poland
24. Ramage (1990)	Cross-sectional	Quantitative	S	FLOE (French, Spanish)	United States
25. Shaaban & Ghaith (2000)	Cross-sectional	Quantitative	PS	EFL	Lebanon
26. Tremblay & Gardner (1995)	Cross-sectional	Quantitative	S	SLOE (French)	Canada
27. Warden & Lin (2000)	Cross-sectional	Quantitative	PS	EFL	Taiwan
28. Wesely (2009)	Longitudinal	Qualitative	E	SLOE (French)	United States
29. Wesely (2010)	Longitudinal	Mixed	E (Graduates; 6th and 7th graders)	SLOE (French, Spanish)	United States
30. Wu Man-fat (2007)	Cross-sectional	Quantitative	PS	ESL	Hong Kong

(continued)

Table A.1 Methodological and contextual issues in empirical studies by primary theoretical framework (*continued*)

	Method		Context		
	Design	Data	Participants	Contact situation	Country
31. Yu (2010)	Longitudinal	Quantitative	PS	SLOE (Chinese)	China
Self-Determination Theory					
32. Comanaru & Noels (2009)	Cross-sectional	Mixed	PS	HL/FLOE (Chinese)	Canada
33. Hiromori (2003)	Cross-sectional	Quantitative	S	EFL	Japan
34. Carreira (2012)	Cross-sectional	Quantitative	E	EFL	Japan
35. Goldberg & Noels (2006)	Cross-sectional	Mixed	PS	SLOE (French)	Canada
36. Jones *et al.* (2009)	Cross-sectional (intervention)	Qualitative	PS	FLOE (Spanish)	United States
37. Macaro & Wingate (2004)	Cross-sectional	Qualitative	PS	FLOE (German)	England
38. Mahdinejad *et al.* (2012)	Cross-sectional	Quantitative	S	EFL	Iran
39. Nishida & Yashima (2009)	Longitudinal	Mixed	E	EFL	Japan
40. Noels *et al.* (1999)	Cross-sectional	Quantitative	PS	SLOE (French)	Canada

	Design	Method	Level	Language	Country
41. Noels et al. (2000)	Cross-sectional	Quantitative	PS	SLOE (French)	Canada
42. Otoshi & Heffernan (2011)	Cross-sectional	Quantitative	PS	EFL	Japan
43. Polat (2011)	Cross-sectional	Mixed	S	SLOE (Turkish)	Turkey
44. Sakai & Koike (2008)	Longitudinal	Quantitative	PS	EFL	Japan
45. Tanaka (2009)	Longitudinal(intervention)	Quantitative	PS	EFL	Japan
46. Tanaka & Hiromori (2007)	Longitudinal	Mixed	PS	EFL	Japan
47. Wu (2003)	Cross-sectional (intervention:quasi-experimental)	Qualitative	Before E (Age 4–6 years)	EFL	China
L2 Motivational Self System					
48. Al-Shehri (2009)	Cross-sectional	Quantitative	PS	EFL/ESL	Saudi Arabia/United Kingdom
49. Csizér & Lukács (2010)	Cross-sectional	Quantitative	S	EFL/FLOE (German)	Hungary
50. Henry & Apelgren (2008)	Cross-sectional	Quantitative	E	EFL/FLOE (French, Spanish, German and sign language)	Sweden
51. Kiany et al. (2013)	Cross-sectional	Quantitative	S	EFL	Iran

(continued)

Table A.1 Methodological and contextual issues in empirical studies by primary theoretical framework (*continued*)

	Method		Participants	Context	
	Design	Data		Contact situation	Country
52. Kim (2009)	Cross-sectional (observational)	Mixed	PS	ESL	Korea
53. Kormos & Csizér (2008)	Cross-sectional	Quantitative	S	EFL/FLOE (German)	Hungary
54. Kormos, Kiddle & Csizér (2011)	Cross-sectional	Quantitative	S/PS	EFL	Chili
55. Lamb (2012)	Cross-sectional	Quantitative	S	EFL	Indonesia
56. Magid (2009)	Cross-sectional	Mixed	S/PS	EFL	China
57. Magid & Chan (2012)	Longitudinal	Mixed	PS	ESL	England/Hong Kong
58. Papi & Abdollahza-deh (2011)	Cross-sectional (observational)	Mixed	S/T	EFL	Iran
59. Papi (2010)	Cross-sectional	Quantitative	S	EFL	Iran
60. Sampson (2012)	Longitudinal	Qualitative	PS	EFL	Japan
61. Ueki & Takeuchi (2012)	Cross-sectional	Quantitative	PS	EFL	Japan
62. Yang & Kim (2011)	Cross-sectional	Quantitative	S	EFL	China/Japan/Korea/Sweden

63. Zheng (2012)	Longitudinal	Mixed	PS	EFL	China
Socio-Educational Model with L2 Motivational Self System					
65. Anya (2011)	Cross-sectional	Qualitative	PS	ESL/SLOE/FLOE (Spanish, French, Latin, Arabic, Portuguese and Japanese)	United States
66. Henry (2009)	Longitudinal	Quantitative	E/S	EFL/FLOE (French, Spanish, German and sign language)	Sweden
67. Kim (2012)	Cross-sectional	Quantitative	E/S	EFL	Korea
68. Kim & Kim (2012)	Cross-sectional	Quantitative	S	EFL	Korea
69. Kormos & Csizér (2008)	Cross-sectional	Quantitative	S/PS	EFL	Hungary
70. Taguchi, Magid & Papi (2009)	Cross-sectional	Quantitative	S/PS	EFL	Japan/China/Iran
Self-Determination Theory with Socio-Educational Model					
71. Bonney et al. (2008)	Cross-sectional	Quantitative	S	FLOE (French, Spanish, German and Latin)	United States
72. Kimura et al. (2001)	Cross-sectional	Quantitative	S/PS	EFL	Japan
73. Lamb (2007)	Longitudinal	Mixed	S	EFL	Indonesia

(continued)

Table A.1 Methodological and contextual issues in empirical studies by primary theoretical framework (*continued*)

| | Method | | | Context | |
	Design	Data	Participants	Contact situation	Country
74. Sugita McEown et al. (under review)	Cross-sectional	Quantitative	PS	FLOE (Japanese)	Canada
75. Noels (2001)	Cross-sectional	Quantitative	PS	FLOE (Spanish)	United States
76. Noels (2005)	Cross-sectional	Quantitative	PS	HL/FLOE (German)	Canada
77. Pae (2008)	Cross-sectional	Quantitative	PS	EFL	Korea
Self-Determination Theory with L2 Motivational Self System					
78. Nishida (2012)	Cross-sectional	Quantitative	PS	EFL	Japan

HL = heritage language; SLOE = second language other than English; ESL = English as a second language; FLOE = foreign language other than English; EFL = English as a foreign language.

4 Re-imagining the Self as a Network of Relationships

Sarah Mercer

Introduction

Most people intuitively know that their sense of self is complex, multifaceted and dynamic. We are aware of how we feel different in diverse contexts and when together with different people. Although we may have a coherent sense of self that permits us to say, 'this is the real me', we paradoxically also recognise the different sides to ourselves as what we think and feel about ourselves changes across time and in relation to different settings. In this chapter, I seek to envisage a way of conceptualising the self that accommodates the multifaceted, dynamic and situated nature of the self with respect to the domain of foreign language learning (FLL). I outline how contemporary integrative models of the self show how our self is simultaneously composed of personal, social and collective selves. Combining these models with the complexity-related concept of network theory, I propose a conceptual model of the self, which incorporates together in one system personal and social dimensions, as well as contextual and temporal variation. To illustrate this line of thinking, the chapter examines exploratory multimedia data to show how a single female, tertiary-level, English as a Foreign Language (EFL) learner's sense of self can be articulated in terms of her relationships with people, groups, objects, places, contexts, languages and ideas. The chapter concludes by reflecting on the implications for theory, pedagogy and future research of thinking of the self in terms of a network of relationships.

Self-Concept in Second Language Acquisition

Many key developments in second language acquisition (SLA) in recent years such as humanism, learner individual differences, learner-centredness and autonomy have placed the learner more visibly on the centre stage highlighting the crucial role individual characteristics play in language learning. It is now widely acknowledged that if we as researchers and teachers wish to understand how an individual approaches and manages their language learning and their relative success in that undertaking, then we need to more fully appreciate who our individual learners are and how they view themselves in relation to their languages and the learning of them. Essentially, we need to make our learners 'visible' in our understandings and theories of learning processes (Benson, 2005: 5), not as an average prototypical learner (cf. Dewaele, 2005), but as 'real' individuals leading unique and complex lives (cf. Ushioda, 2009: 216).

At the centre of our understandings of truly individual learners lies an appreciation of their unique sense of self and how this mediates all their experiences of language learning and use. The importance of a learner's sense of self in learning processes is indisputable. It lies at the very centre of their psychology bringing together who they believe they are, what they feel, think, want and their strategies for action (Mercer, 2011a: 57–58). With respect to language learning, it is believed that the self could play an especially significant role, given the centrality of self-presentation in foreign language use as well as issues of social and cultural identity and the tight connections between language and the self (ibid: 3).

Within SLA, the self has been drawing increasing attention, particularly with respect to motivation, given the considerable growth of interest generated by Dörnyei's (2005) Second Language (L2) Motivational Self System of motivation. However, whilst the explosion of interest in the self is beneficial for a deeper understanding of learner individuality, there remain difficulties for researchers interested in the self in SLA given the bewildering multitude of self constructs which exist, such as self-efficacy, L2 linguistic self-confidence, identity, self-esteem and self-concept (see, e.g. Mercer & Williams, 2014). As MacIntyre *et al.* (2009: 49) state, 'the vastness of the literature is a double-edged sword. Whereas there is a great deal of prior research on the self, there are also conceptual complications'. Such an array of constructs with respect to the self is understandable as it reflects its inherent complexity and the seeming impossibility of providing a single, neat, all-encompassing definition of such a vast and complex construct (cf. Vallacher & Nowak, 1997: 74).

My own work has been shaped by studies in educational and social psychology on the construct of self-concept. Of all the self constructs, it is one of the most global and least context-bound making it ideally suited to more holistic views of the self. It represents everything a person believes and feels about themselves, and can be conceptualised in global terms or with respect to specific domains. Indeed, a major development in self-concept researching and theorising has been the move from unidimensional conceptualisations to multidimensional models (e.g. Marsh &

Shavelson, 1985). This means that people do not hold a single self-concept but several for different domains. Typically, a domain refers to a subject domain; however, Bong and Skaalvik (2003: 17) explain, 'the term domain-specificity should not be equated to a particular measurement level. Rather, a domain can be represent from (*sic*) relatively limited skill areas such as reading comprehension in English to broader content areas such as social science'. Acknowledging the importance of the domain-specificity of self-concept, self-concept in the domain of FLL has been defined as 'an individual's self-descriptions of competence and evaluative feelings about themselves as foreign language learners' (Mercer, 2011a: 14).

Whilst this definition has proven to be useful in helping to delineate this self construct from other self-related terms, there are some key aspects of the self that it does not accommodate. Firstly, when individuals are asked to describe themselves as language learners, their responses typically encompass much more than simple beliefs of competence or related evaluative feelings (Mercer, 2011a). In addition, learners' self-beliefs often do not fit neatly into specific domain (subject) categories as there appears to be complex interaction and overlap between domains (Mercer, 2011a). This makes defining and delineating domains with respect to data problematic. Finally, there is the question of how more personal individualised views of the self, such as self-concept, are interconnected with and relate to more socially defined constructs such as identity. Consequently, I have been searching for a conceptual model which facilitates a more synthesised view of learners' self systems incorporating personal and social perspectives on the self, as well as taking a broader, more holistic view of the self with a more phenomenologically grounded representation of domains. To this end, two conceptual frameworks have offered useful insights: integrative models of the self and complexity theories.

Integrative models of the self

In psychology-based research, several integrative models of self have been suggested which are intended to capture a multiplicity of perspectives and a more global understanding of the self, as well as providing a degree of conceptual clarity in organising the complex structure that is the self (see, e.g. Allport, 1943; James, 1890/1983; Neisser, 1988). With respect to self-concept, a more recent model that connects various facets of the self is the tripartite model proposed by Sedikides and Brewer (2001). They suggest that 'self-concept consists of three fundamental self-representations: the individual self, the relational self, and the collective self' (Sedikides & Brewer, 2001: 1). They explain how the self can either be formed through processes of individual social comparisons through which one seeks to establish ways in which one is unique and distinguishable to others (the individual self); or in relational terms as one relies on processes of reflected appraisal from significant others in relationships (the relational self); or through processes of identifying with a larger social group and considering ways in which one has the characteristics of the group based on comparisons of one's own group with others (collective self). All three are accepted as co-existing within an individual but perspectives differ about the nature of the interrelationships between these different forms of self-representation. For example, there are those who suggest that one of these facets of the self is primary and thus gives rise to or underlies the other two, whereas others consider all three equally important, although the nature of the relationship can differ by being either complementary, adversarial or independent. The final perspective perceives a form of synthesis between all three forms of the self into a single, more organic, integrative model.

A crucial characteristic of such integrative models is their emphasis on the importance of relationships between the self and others (individually or as groups). As such, they effectively remove the dichotomy between personal, individualistic views of the self and more social views of the self by incorporating both views in one model. A strongly relational view of the self has been proposed by Kashima et al. (2001: 277–278). They argue convincingly that the self can always be conceptualised in relation to something else and is thus determined relationally. For example, they take the view that the personal, individual self represents the self in relation to a goal; the relational self refers to the self in relation to specific other individuals; and the collective self comprises conceptions of the self in relation to a particular group which can also include large scale social categories such as nationality and gender (Kashima et al., 2001: 281).

Forgas and Williams (2003: 2) conclude that 'a proper understanding of the self can only be achieved by considering the interaction of the individual, relational, and collective aspects of the self as a dynamic self-system'. Given my other work on the self as a complex dynamic system (Mercer, 2011b, 2011c), I started to consider how such an integrative approach to the self and complexity perspectives could be usefully combined.

Self from a complexity perspective

There are convincing arguments as to why the self could be conceptualised as a complex dynamic system, such as the interconnection of multiple components and the irreducibility of these, the integration of contexts into the self system (such as in embodied and situated views of the self), the varied forms of dynamism and dynamic stability of the self and the emergent character of the self (Mercer, 2011b, 2011c). Such thinking implies that the self cannot meaningfully be reduced to its component parts such as individual cognitions or emotions or motives or to either solely personal or social self beliefs. Rather it is the emergent, continually ongoing dynamic interaction of all of these aspects of the self across time and place that generates the self as it is experienced and lived.

Traditionally, self-concept has been viewed as a hierarchical, multidimensional model (Marsh & Shavelson, 1985). This conceptualisation has been invaluable in enhancing our understandings of the complexity of the self. It signalled a move away from monolithic, unidimensional models of the self to a recognition of the multiple self-concepts in different domains. However, my own qualitative research questioned the phenomenological validity of the hierarchical structure. Instead, I proposed a three-dimensional, network model of the self (Mercer, 2011a: 68). The network structure was able to show the highly interconnected nature of different self-concept domains, as well as contextual variation in terms of the relative complexity and salience of a domain for an individual at a particular time or in a particular setting. The model also highlighted the potential for overlap and shared commonalities between domains, as well as the differing types of relationships between them.

This network structure was especially useful in conveying the complexity and interrelated nature of domains. It should perhaps, therefore, have come as little surprise to discover that networks are closely related to complex dynamic systems. One of the leading researchers in the field of network theory, Barabási (2003: 238) explains that 'networks are the prerequisite for describing any complex system, indicating that complexity theory must invariably stand on the shoulders of network theory'. A network represents a series of nodes (in my model, nodes stood for domains) which are interconnected in complex multiple ways through pathways. As with complex dynamic systems, networks can be nested within other networks and their boundaries are potentially limitless stretching outward. Networks are often described in terms of their topology, which is the shape and geometry of the network connectivity. Highly connected nodes in a network are known as hubs and these play a more central role in the functioning of the whole network. A characteristic finding of network theory has shown that many real networks display non-random features and patterns, which suggest that behaviour in the system is not entirely random.

In considering the self as a complex dynamic system following a network structure, certain domains (nodes) of particular importance to the individual as a whole can be understood as hubs in the self system. As such, the state of a hub has a greater effect on the whole self network than other less connected, important, nodes. The boundless structure of the self network also helps us to appreciate how the self is continually emerging and never stops forming or building new connections as we continue to experience new things and encounter new contexts and people. It is possible to envisage a network of domain-specific self-concepts interconnected in constellations unique to certain individuals and in ways that enable different patterns of activation depending on the relative saliency or significance of a certain node or pathway in specific contexts. Although such network thinking can effectively convey the complexity of the self, it still implies that contexts exist primarily externally to the self system – influencing its activation, rather than as an integral part of it, as ought to be the case in a complex dynamic system. In integrative models of the self, contexts are embedded in the types of selves included (personal, relational and collective). Therefore, combining both models suggests a network model of relational, thus contextually-defined, selves in which contexts are automatically inherent in the types of relationships of the self.

Exploring a Learner's Self Network

In order to explore this idea of the self as a network of self-related relationships, a small scale qualitative study was conducted with tertiary-level EFL learners at a university in Austria. The study was designed to be exploratory and sought to generate data which would provide details on the self and its possible structure.

In order to make the understanding of domain more phenomenologically valid, the data collection method was deliberately left open to allow learners to include anything that they felt was relevant, although prompts were used to focus the learners' attention on the area of FLL. In this way, what a learner chooses to focus on and report on is what defines the meaningful segment of their self network. As such, the content of a domain is not defined by the researcher, but is instead understood as a functional concept with content defined by learners' own perceptions of relevance and connectedness.

Contexts and participants

Students towards the end of their studies were invited to participate in the exploratory study. It was expected that such learners might have more complex developed self networks with respect to their language learning given that they were somewhat older and had more experience. Volunteers were sought and three female participants agreed to take part in the study. Unfortunately, due to limits of space, I will only report on one of those cases. She was selected from the three on the basis of her rich data and the fact that she was the only one who chose a particular data format. To protect her identity, I will call her Anna. At the time of the study, she was 38 years old and studying English and French. She had previously had various jobs and had completed a full course of studies in law. She had recently returned to study to become a fully qualified teacher and was already working in various contexts teaching both her foreign languages, although primarily English.

Data collection methods

Having conducted many in-depth interviews with participants in the past in order to explore self-concept, I felt that, despite their numerous fine points, I was in some way still only accessing more superficial and less complex aspects of the self. In order to try to elicit more deeply held understandings of the self which might even lie on the periphery of the learner's consciousness, I sought an approach which might help reveal such facets of the self. Inspired by an idea suitable for investigating complexity in Burns (2007: 120), I decided to ask learners to use images and multimedia to make visible deeper-lying aspects of the self with respect to language learning. Burns explains that people have systems in their mind that they may not be conscious of and that these can be uncovered through the use of drawing and images (Burns, 2007). In a short introductory text including an outline of the project and asking for volunteers, the learners were asked to prepare a collage (e.g. a poster – can be a mixture of text, mind-maps, pictures etc.) that they feel represents how they see themselves as language learners and how they experience language learning. The guidelines further explained that my aim as a researcher was to try to better understand the way in which language learners view themselves. No other specific guidelines about relevant content were given. Interestingly, in the session in which I distributed the request for volunteers, we were discussing e-learning and I spontaneously offered an additional alternative choice to create a private blog to be accessed only by me and the respective participant instead of a collage. In the end, Anna chose to do a collage, whereas the other two participants chose to do blogs. As the format of blog data involves specific issues, I have chosen in this chapter to focus exclusively on the collage data.

All of the learners took several weeks to prepare their blogs and collage. When each learner felt their collage/blog was sufficiently complete, they contacted me and we arranged to meet for an interview based on their respective multimedia artefacts. I saw the collage for the first time when Anna and I met for the interview based on it.

We discussed Anna's first collage (see Figure 4.1) in an interview which lasted over an hour and a half. As neither of us felt that we had completely finished our discussion, we agreed on a second follow-up interview to which she also brought unprompted a second additional poster

Figure 4.1 Anna's first collage

Figure 4.2 Anna's second collage

(see Figure 4.2). This second interview lasted a little over an hour. Some weeks later, she again brought a third poster unsolicited; however, as it was unplanned, we did not conduct an interview based on it, although she generously allowed me to use it for my research (see Figure 4.3).

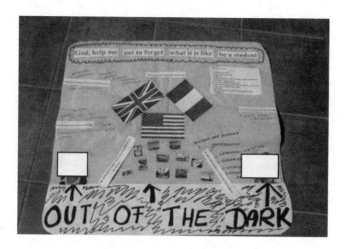

Figure 4.3 Anna's third collage

Analysis

The interviews for each participant were transcribed and coded using ATLAS.ti. Initial waves of coding were grounded in nature. The analytical stage focused explicitly on relationships and interconnections in the self network. The collage was analysed for content using ATLAS.ti and interpreted for meaning based on guidelines from multimodal analysis such as focus on choice of images, colour, layout, format and position of specific content (cf. Machin, 2007).

Both the multimodal data (including both images and text) and the interview data were compared for any potential discrepancies, differences, absences or contradictions. Together their analysis led to the descriptive findings presented below. Finally, in order to make partially visible my interpretation of Anna's data in terms of a network of relationships, a sociogram for her self network related to FLL was generated using specialist sociogram software (Lewejohann, 2005).

Findings and Discussion

Anna's self in relation to FLL

Anna's first collage intended to describe herself as a language learner has three clear sections – on the left her English self, on the right her

French self and in the middle, separating the two distinct halves, is her understanding of language teaching and the kind of language teacher she would like to become. This visual representation of her sense of self in the domain of FLL is a clear expression of the key components of her self-related beliefs and emotions.

For Anna, the division of her FLL self into two halves is a visible indication of her relationship between two languages which she sees as totally separate and distinct. As she explains, 'for me there are no parallels: That's the problem. That's absolutely separated for me'. However, from a structural point of view of the self, these two parts are far from separate. Continually throughout the interviews, she compares her experiences, sense of competence and affective states in relation to the two languages. Research on the Internal/External self reference model (Marsh, 1990) suggests that such internal cross-language comparisons can strengthen and confirm, for example, her positive sense of self in French, whilst simultaneously weakening and reinforcing her negative self-concept in English. Therefore, it is extremely important to understand the relationship between her self-perceptions and experiences in the two languages as part of the overall system, even though she sees them as being totally distinct due to their difference in terms of content and positivity.

Anna has a strongly negative affective relationship with English and lacks confidence in all areas of the language, especially in relation to her speaking skills. Visually this is apparent in both her first and second collages. For English in the first collage, she uses the colour black and portrays her early start in English as a terrible journey with insurmountable obstacles characterised by 'fear' and 'anxiety' leading to a black hole. Despite a stay in New York (positioned within the thick black band), her attitude remains extremely negative towards English and this part of the collage dissolves into a swirling, confused sea of tense forms. She then indicates a turning point which occurs in the top, final quarter of the English half when she meets a new tutor for English who she places in the midst of a yellow sun. This marks for her the starting point of a yellow pathway strewn with more positive words such as 'self-confidence' and 'less nervous' leading to the endpoint labelled 'English is great'. While the relationship with her out-of-school tutor for English has clearly been influential in a positive way as she stresses throughout the interviews, the overall impression of her sense of self in English in the interviews remains distinctly negative. Throughout the first interview, Anna makes clear that she still feels more uncertain and lacks confidence in English. For example, she says, 'I am so afraid of making mistakes in English and not in French'. Thus, although Anna's sense of self in relation to English does appear to have changed since her time in school with her now reporting some more positive associations in relation to her English self, her responses in the interviews make clear that there is still a lot of negativity overshadowing her relationship with English, as she explains, 'I'm still afraid of it [English]'.

Anna attributes her negative self-concept in English as stemming from her bad experiences at school in learning the language. At the top of her first collage she explains, 'I went rather back to a very early stage. I did this by purpose because I think these experiences still influence me today. There is still unease when it comes to speaking or writing English'. Thus, it is apparent that her current sense of self is still strongly affected by her past experiences, and her relationships with those people and events are still of relevance in her self network even now.

In French, Anna has a strong sense of competence and an extremely positive set of relationships with many things and experiences related to the language. On the French side of her first collage, there is a clear starting point. She describes French as 'exploring up to a wonderful new world' and it contains colourful, bright images. This side of the collage does not have an endpoint as is the case for English but is more organic reflecting various real world dimensions of her relationship with French such as literature, food, the country, films and songs. Indeed, this appears to reflect her current sense of self in French which seems to have remained more consistently stable over time. Similarly to her current English self-concept, Anna also attributes her current positive self-concept and affective attitude to French to her extremely positive experiences in school with the language and a very special French teacher with whom she remains in contact many years later. She also reports on the positive group dynamics in her French class at school explaining that it was a good group because, 'Nobody laughed. We didn't correct each other. There was always respect'. Once again, her relationships with past experiences, groups and individuals are still a key part of her present self.

The middle segment of the first collage portrays a key metaphor that reoccurs throughout her interviews, namely, that language learning is like learning to swim. The series of pictures show her son learning to swim from the stage of full dependency on his mother and swim aids to being able to swim alone without support. In the interviews, she emphasises the importance of help and the sense of dependency before you can become autonomous and swim freely under your own agency in your own direction. This implies that without support, you will sink and drown. Indeed, in the midst of the deep black section of the first collage with regard to her experiences of learning English at school, she writes; 'I felt like drowning without any chance to survive'. The role of supportive personal relationships in helping her to become an independent and confident learner is the central concept underlying the swimming metaphor that she returns to repeatedly in the interviews.

In the second collage, Anna again makes a clear distinction between her English and French selves and the affective distinction between the two continues. The French side is written in blue which calls up her positive associations of her summers in France by the sea and contains positive and tranquil colours. She includes words such as 'joy', 'pleasure' and 'easy'. There are no boundaries and it is comprised mainly of photographs of people and places with whom she has a positive relationship and which she associates with French. It culminates at the top in a heart within which she has working, studying and living abroad. She then contrasts this with the English side with an arrow pointing to the heart and writing that this is what she misses for English – again comparing the two languages. The English half is enclosed by a ragged, sharp, aggressive, red edging and contains pictures of grammar books and a dictionary of common errors. The main picture highlighted at the top is a cartoon of Homer Simpson saying 'trying is the first step towards failure'. However, in addition to the predominant negativity, the English side of the collage also includes the statement, 'it's great but it's hard work'. In the interview she explains, 'the longer I do it, the more I like it, so that's okay, so that's why there is this "great" there'. She now begins to describe her relationship with English in a more differentiated way and starts to emphasise the nature of her relationship with English in specific contexts. For example, she explains, 'I love it [*English*], but I don't love it as soon as I am at the university. Then it's gone'. Thus, her relationship with English as a subject in the university context is negative, whereas her relationship with English whilst travelling is gradually becoming more positive.

One specific context in which Anna reports developing a more positive set of relationships towards English is in relation to her two teaching jobs, as a business trainer and a primary school teacher. It becomes apparent in the interviews that her role in these contexts is allowing her to also develop a more positive relationship with English. Of her primary school teaching, she says, 'I enjoy it and I am so happy', and she goes on to explain that her positive experiences of teaching English mean that 'English is coming closer' to her.

This change and contextual variation is most visible in her third and final collage. Anna brought this unsolicited some weeks after the second interview and following a holiday with her son in the United States. We did not discuss it formally in an interview, but she was kind enough to share it with me for research purposes.

This final collage is on bright yellow paper and shows her way 'out of the dark'. Notably, it represents a more balanced view of all her languages together within the context of herself as a language teacher. There is no longer a split into distinct halves but a single shared space for both languages. However, the striking feature of this poster is that it is solely concerned with herself as a teacher and the kinds of things that are important to her in this role. The collage suggests that her changing relationship with English may be driven by her positive experiences and role as an English language teacher. This dynamism in her sense of self is made especially apparent by the movement indicated in the arrows coming out of the dark strip at the bottom with her tutor and another English teacher as well as photographs from her recent trip to the US marked as triggers for change.

Visualising and discussing Anna's self as a network of relationships

As outlined above, the content of Anna's self network in the domain of language learning is self generated. The network is cohesive and represents a meaningful segment of Anna's overall self network from her point of view. It includes various people, contexts, places, experiences and artefacts, as well as more abstract ideas and concepts. It is composed of her relationship with those things which are relevant for her in relation to a more holistically defined domain and it is not temporally bound. It includes relationships with events, people and places in the past, as well as relationships with her goals for the future, particularly in her role as a language teacher.

She mentions many things that contribute to her sense of self. I have chosen to illustrate the relationships that appear to play key roles currently for Anna with respect to the domain of FLL, in order to make clear the thinking underlying this conceptual model. Below I have listed and numbered the most notable relationships and their predominant affective quality. Those relationships marked with a (P) are those which are clearly positive; those which are clearly negative are marked with an (N) and an (M) is used to denote those relationships which are mixed and more ambiguous in affective terms. I have grouped them according to those that are principally associated with French, those with English and those which cover both, albeit not necessarily to equal degrees. I have tried not to overcomplicate the visual but have also included the most salient relationships between elements in the network, mindful that all of the elements are ultimately interconnected as parts of the same network. In my attempt to keep the visual straightforward at this stage, I have not portrayed the relative importance, nature or quality of relationships in the diagram, although this is clearly a potential inherent in the design for the future.

French:

(1) French teacher at school (P)
(2) French class at school (P)

(3) French studies at university (P)

(4) France, the country (P)

(5) French, the subject (P)

(6) French literature, films, songs (P)

English:

(7)   English teacher at school (N)

(8)   English class at school (N)

(9)   English, the subject (N)

(10) English studies at university (M)

(11) America, the country (M – changing towards P)

(12) English tutor in the past (P)

Both languages:

(13) Herself as a future teacher (M)

(14) Herself as a teacher currently (P)

To visualise Anna's sense of self in the domain of FLL, I have generated a network using sociogram software (Lewejohan, 2005) to represent
its key component relationships (Figure 4.4). It depicts Anna as a whole

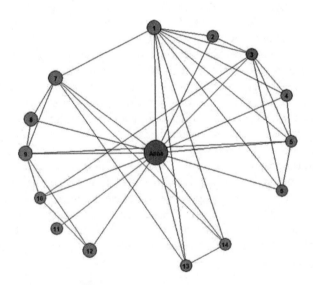

Figure 4.4 Visual representation of Anna's self network using sociogram software
(Lewejohann, 2005). Numbers in the nodes represent the relationships listed above.

embodied being with a core sense of self at the centre and the overall network represents her sense of self as a language learner as comprised of her past, present and future relationships, which she perceives as relevant for this domain. It should be noted that these relationships are also related to each other and not only to Anna, such as is evident from her continual comparison across all aspects of French and English. Together their interaction generates her emergent sense of self as a language learner. As networks do not have boundaries, it must be remembered that this signifies one meaningful segment of her larger entire self network. However, the larger self network is partitioned by Anna herself based on her perception of relevant relationships for the specific domain under investigation. Clearly, although networks hold universal characteristics in terms of how they function, their content and composition can be uniquely individual and varied as every learner's network will be different depending on their own perception of what is relevant for them in this broadly defined area.

Understanding Anna's sense of self as a network of relationships has considerable conceptual potential. Firstly, although this visual here represents a static summative descriptive model of her current self in this domain, the principle of a network model is inherently dynamic and open to change. The relationships are not static and their position, quality and role in the network may change over time as others become more or less relevant. It allows for the self to be dynamic in complex ways as the network and its constituent relationships change. Additionally, a network does not have boundaries and is continually open to change, additions and further developments as new relationships are formed, such as Anna's recent travel experiences in the US. This conveys how the self is continually emerging. It also represents an optimistic view of the self for pedagogical growth and development.

The second point about a network-based relational view of the self concerns the integration of context. Inspired by integrative models, both personal and social relational dimensions of the self can be easily accommodated. Indeed, all of the relationships in the network with people, places, artefacts and the languages themselves are contextualised, so that the context becomes embedded in the network through its inherent presence in the relationships. Nevertheless, it is possible for the learner to also have an explicit relationship with a particular context, such as with a specific class, school, educational institution or culture.

The third key feature of the network concerns its ability to convey temporality. The network of relationships enables past, present and future to be combined as relationships with past people, settings and experiences, as well as relationships with future goals can be included. Portrayed as relationships, this means that it is the learner's interpretation of the past which becomes significant for the current self, and not the past event per se. In other words, it is not simply, for example, the experience of using a language on holiday that is important, but it is how the individual subjectively interprets, evaluates and assigns significance to the experience that matters in terms of the current self. Similarly, in a relational view of personal future goals, the learner's subjectivities, beliefs and motives also play a key role in the kinds of relationships formed with future selves.

Another feature of networks concerns the 'flow' between nodes throughout the network (Kadushin, 2012). The most striking feature of Anna's data is their strongly affective quality. Although the self is comprised of the complex interaction of motives, cognitions and emotions, it is possible that the flow of emotions throughout the network, strengthening the emotional significance of relationships, could be a key facet in understanding the self. The potential for change in the flow of the network can be seen, for example, in the forming of a new relationship, such as Anna's recent trips to America with her son. This has introduced a new positive relationship that flows through the network and may ultimately change the overall positivity of the entire network, especially in connection with other relationships linked to English.

Researching the self

In order to understand the complexity of the self from the learner's perspective, it has been exceptionally useful to use multimedia data. In addition to the invaluable multimedia artefacts themselves, it has also generated particularly rich interview data. In particular, the approach used can perhaps elicit aspects of the self which the learner may not have been immediately conscious of as well as reveal seeming contradictions. Visualising their sense of self may help learners to reach deeper understandings of their relationships surrounding the language. As Anna explains in the second interview, 'I really benefited so much from it [taking part in the research] and things really... I started thinking about it or even just became conscious, and I said "Oh my God", yes... and I think that's so important'. A drawback is the considerable investment in terms of time and energy required to create a collage or a blog. However, as was seen with Anna, for some learners the experience can be rewarding and interesting. In this respect, it is particularly important to allow learners to choose their own preferred form of self expression, whether in the form of a collage, blog, glog (graphical blog) or other type of visual, multimedia artefacts.

Concerning the sociogram, this represents an initial attempt at visualising the self networks of the learners and is by necessity at this stage a rather simplistic visual illustration of the underlying line of thinking. In the future, more sophisticated sociogram or mapping tools could be developed and employed to explore the networks of an individual's sense of self in terms of dynamics and interrelations. Additionally, as more sophisticated network representations of the self become possible, these too could be examined using computer software designed to conduct network analysis and simulations.

Conclusions and Implications

Whilst I have found conceptualising the self as a complex dynamic network of relationships to be extremely useful in describing the data of this learner, it is at this stage merely a theoretical, conceptual proposition. Although it appears to better represent the phenomenological reality and complexity of this learner's sense of self, the challenge now is to explore this hypothetical model of the self and critically evaluate its usefulness in helping us to understand learners' sense of self in relation to their FLL in a wide range of contexts using a range of innovative and diverse research methods. As has been stressed elsewhere (Mercer & Williams, 2014), given the vast complexity of the self construct, we need to be creative and remain open to innovative thinking and a range of research approaches. The puzzle of the self will not be solved through one model or one mode of thinking or researching. Instead, multiple approaches need to be effectively combined together to contribute in complementary ways towards a fuller understanding of the big picture of the self (ibid).

Despite the fact that my own thinking of the self in these terms is very much in its infancy, I have already found this conceptual model to be useful for me as a researcher in order to appreciate the nature, complexity, content, situatedness, interconnectedness and uniqueness of a learner's self in the domain of FLL. I have also found it especially valuable in my role as a teacher. Understanding the self in this way suggests that an accessible way of engendering affirmative change to a person's self-concept is by helping the learner to develop an array of positive, language-related relationships. These may include relationships with traditionally tangible things such as the language itself, the class, peers, teachers, literature, films, songs and target countries, but they can also include ways of interpreting past experiences to create positive relationships with the past, as well as promoting optimistic relationships with future goals. In principle, the more positive relationships and the stronger the connections, the more likely the learner will develop a positive sense of self for that domain. Essentially, if we wish to enhance our learner's sense of self in relation to their foreign language, it is not sufficient to understand what they feel they know and can do now (perceived competence) and how they evaluate that. Their sense of self is much more complex, multifaceted and dynamic than that. Instead, a good place to begin understanding our unique, individual, 'real' learners is by appreciating the nature and positivity of their highly personal, subjective relationships surrounding the language.

References

Allport, G.W. (1943) The ego in contemporary psychology. *Psychological Review* 50 (5), 451–478.

Barabási, A.-L. (2003) *Linked*. New York, NY: Plume Books.

Benson, P. (2005) (Auto)biography and learner diversity. In P. Benson and D. Nunan (eds) *Learners' Stories: Difference and Diversity in Language Learning* (pp. 4–21). Cambridge: Cambridge University Press.

Bong, M. and Skaalvik, E.M. (2003) Academic self-concept and self-efficacy: How different are they really? *Educational Psychology Review* 15 (1), 1–40.

Burns, D. (2007) *Systemic Action Research: A Strategy for Whole System Change*. Bristol: The Policy Press.

Dewaele, J.-M. (2005) Investigating the psychological and emotional dimensions in instructed language learning: Obstacles and possibilities. *The Modern Language Journal* 89 (3), 367–380.

Dörnyei, Z. (2005) *The Psychology of the Language Learner*. Hillsdale, NJ: Erlbaum Associates.

Forgas, J.P. and Williams, K.D (2003) The social self: Introduction and overview. In J.P Forgas and K.D Williams (eds) *The Social Self: Cognitive, Interpersonal, and Intergroup Perspectives* (pp. 1–18). Hove: Psychology Press.

James, W. (1890/1983) *The Principles of Psychology*. Cambridge: Harvard University Press.

Kadushin, C. (2012) *Understanding Social Networks: Theories, Concepts, and Findings*. Oxford: Oxford University Press.

Kashima, Y., Kashima, E. and Aldridge, J. (2001) Toward cultural dynamics of self-conceptions. In C. Sedikides and M.B Brewer (eds) *Individual Self, Relational Self, Collective Self* (pp. 277–298). Philadelphia, PA: Psychology Press.

Lewejohann, L. (2005) Sociogram (Version 1.0). [Computer software]. See http://www.phenotyping.com/sociogram/ (accessed December 2012).

Machin, D. (2007) *Introduction to Multimodal Analysis*. London: Bloomsbury.

MacIntyre, P.D, MacKinnon, S.P. and Clément, R. (2009) The baby, the bathwater, and the future of language learning motivation research. In Z. Dörnyei and E. Ushioda (eds) *Motivation, Language Identity and the L2 Self* (pp. 43–65). Bristol: Multilingual Matters.

Marsh, H.W. (1990) Influences of internal and external frames of reference on the formation of math and English self-concepts. *Journal of Educational Psychology* 82 (1), 107–116.

Marsh, H. W. and Shavelson, R. (1985) Self-concept: Its multifaceted, hierarchical structure. *Educational Psychologist* 20 (3), 107–123.

Mercer, S. (2011a) *Towards an Understanding of Language Learner Self-Concept*. Dordrecht: Springer.

Mercer, S. (2011b) The self as a complex dynamic system. *Studies in Second Language Learning and Teaching* 1 (1), 57–82.

Mercer, S. (2011c) Language learner self-concept: Complexity, continuity & change. *System* 39 (3), 335–346.

Mercer, S. and Williams, M. (eds) (2014) *Multiple Perspectives on the Self*. Bristol: Multilingual Matters.

Neisser, U. (1988) Five kinds of self-knowledge. *Philosophical Psychology* 1 (1), 35–59.

Sedikides, C. and Brewer, M.B (2001) (eds) *Individual Self, Relational Self, Collective Self.* Philadelphia, PA: Psychology Press.

Ushioda, E. (2009) A person-in-context relational view of emergent motivation, self and identity. In Z. Dörnyei and E. Ushioda (eds) *Motivation, Language Identity and the L2 Self* (pp. 215–228). Bristol: Multilingual Matters.

Vallacher, R.R. and Nowak, A. (1997) The emergence of dynamical social psychology. *Psychological Inquiry* 8 (2), 73–99.

Part 2

Self-Concept and Language Learning

5 The Ideal L2 Self, Self-Regulatory Strategies and Autonomous Learning: A Comparison of Different Groups of English Language Learners

Kata Csizér and Judit Kormos

Introduction

Learners' willingness to exercise autonomy and regulate their own learning is intricately linked to motivation. Without a positive attitude to language learning, and the intention to invest effort, energy and persistence when facing difficulties, it is hardly possible for learners to take responsibility for their own second language (L2) acquisition processes. Self-regulation, learner autonomy and motivation dynamically interact with one another and are often described as overlapping concepts. Students' Ideal L2 self, that is, their vision of themselves as successful and competent users of the target language in the future (Dörnyei, 2001), was consistently found to be a highly important determiner of language learning effort (for a review, see Dörnyei & Ushioda, 2009) and has by now been accepted as one of the key factors in L2 learning motivation. A strong future vision of success, which is embodied in the concept of the Ideal L2 self, might not only act as an energiser for learning effort but might also guide students in regulating their learning more effectively and in taking responsibility for their learning.

As we argued in our earlier papers (Kormos & Csizér, 2008; Kormos et al., 2011), the role of the Ideal L2 self in language learning can vary in the case of language learners in different contexts and can largely depend on age. In two successive studies we demonstrated that younger and older students differ from each other in terms of the strength of their future vision of themselves as competent L2 users. The role of the Ideal L2 self in influencing language learning goals and motivated behaviour was also found to be divergent in these groups. In this chapter we report the results of a questionnaire study in which we further investigated the diverse role of the Ideal L2 self among students who differed in age. We were interested in how the Ideal L2 self, self-regulation strategies, autonomous learning behaviour and attitudes towards learner autonomy differed among secondary school students, university students and adult language learners, and how the relationships among these variables varied in these participant groups.

Background

The four main constructs our study set out to investigate are the Ideal L2 self, self-regulatory strategies, autonomous learning behaviour and attitudes towards learner autonomy, which we will briefly describe and define here.

In his L2 Motivational Self System theory, Dörnyei (2005, 2009) argued that the main driving force of language learning is the students' future image of themselves as successful users of the language. His model of motivation contains two self-related components: the Ideal L2 self and the Ought-to L2 self. In this model, the Ideal L2 self is one's ideal self-image expressing the wish to become a competent L2 speaker. The Ought-to L2 self contains 'attributes that one believes one ought to possess (i.e. various duties, obligations, or responsibilities) in order to avoid possible negative outcomes' (Dörnyei, 2005: 106) associated with not being able to speak the L2 in question. A third element of the L2 Motivational Self System is the L2 learning experience, which covers 'situation specific motives related to the immediate learning environment and experience' (Dörnyei, 2005: 106). Previous research that aimed to validate Dörnyei's theory of the L2 Motivational Self System has found unequivocal support for the importance of the Ideal L2 self in various learning contexts (see Dörnyei & Ushioda, 2009).

According to many definitions, self-regulation is a process in which people organise and manage their learning, and this includes learners' control over their thoughts (e.g. their competency beliefs), emotions (e.g. anxiety experienced while learning), behaviours (e.g. how they handle a learning task) and the learning environment (Pintrich & De Groot, 1990; Zimmerman, 1998). These conceptualisations of self-regulation show large overlaps with motivation and autonomy. In order to clearly differentiate the concepts of motivation, learner autonomy and self-regulation, in this research we will understand self-regulation as self-regulatory control that involves the use of strategies which are largely conscious processes that students apply to control their learning.

Dörnyei (2001) proposed a new theoretical conceptualisation of self-regulation in second language acquisition (SLA), for which the empirical study conducted by Tseng *et al.* (2006) provided empirical support. In this taxonomy five main types of control strategies are outlined: commitment control, which regulates goal commitment; metacognitive control, which helps learners maintain focus and concentration; satiation control, with the help of which boredom can be managed and alleviated; emotion control, which is used to manage emotions; and finally environmental control, which assists learners in creating an appropriate study environment. In our study we investigated three of these self-regulatory strategies: commitment, satiation and emotion control.

Learner autonomy in the field of language learning was broadly defined as the learner's ability to exercise control over learning (Holec, 1981). As mentioned above, this definition exhibits a number of similarities with that of self-regulation, and several researchers in educational psychology have equated effective self-regulation with autonomous behaviour. It is important to note, however, that autonomy encompasses control over a wider range of phenomena than self-regulation. Self-regulation in its broad sense entails control over the cognitive, emotional, motivational and behavioural aspects of learning, whereas autonomous learners are also capable of taking responsibility for the content and management of their learning (e.g. course materials) and the social-contextual environment in which learning takes place (Benson, 2001; Oxford, 2003).

Although the potential attributes of autonomous learners might constitute a long list (Benson, 2001; Littlewood, 1996; Oxford, 2003), it is possible to define the crucial elements of the wider concept of learner autonomy, which include learners' control over the affective and cognitive processes of learning, classroom and curriculum decisions, autonomous use of learning skills and the independent use of learning resources and technology (Benson, 2001).

Benson (2001) in his book on learner autonomy lists five important aspects of autonomy, the first of which, called learner-based approaches, involves control over affective and cognitive processes of learning, such as the efficient application of learning strategies, self-regulatory and motivational strategies. The second aspect of autonomy concerns the independent use of learning resources, which can be divided into two important categories: traditional learning resources (e.g. reference and course-books) and resources provided by modern educational technology (e.g. web-based applications, computer programmes, CD-ROMs). Thirdly, classroom-based approaches to autonomy include learner control over classroom decisions and learning materials, whereas the fourth curriculum-based approaches to autonomy allow learners to take an active role in establishing the curriculum. Finally, teacher-based approaches to autonomy highlight the importance of teachers and teacher education in developing learner autonomy.

Benson (2001) further refines the concept of learner control and argues that learner control has three important components: students' ability to take charge of their learning, students' desire to be in control and an environment that allows for learner control. In line with this conceptualisation, in our research, we considered the first two aspects of autonomy: learner autonomy as manifested in actions students take to enhance their learning processes and the views and attitudes students display towards general control over learning.

Based on the above outlined considerations, in this study we set out to investigate the following research questions:

(1) What are the main differences concerning the Ideal L2 self, self-regulatory strategies, autonomous learning behaviour and attitudes to learner autonomy in the three different learner groups?
(2) What is the relationship between the students' Ideal L2 self and self-regulatory strategies, autonomous learning behaviour and attitudes to learner autonomy?

Method

Participants

In our research we surveyed 638 language learners from Budapest, the capital of Hungary. Budapest is the largest city in the country, where one fifth of the total Hungarian population resides. In many respects, Budapest is similar to major metropolitan cities in Europe, with the exception that in Hungary most of the population is monolingual: according to the 2000 census, 92.3% of the population claimed to be ethnic Hungarian and the proportion with Hungarian as their mother tongue was even higher, 98.2% (Demographic Yearbook, 2004). In our research we focused on the three most important language learning contexts in Hungary: secondary schools, universities, colleges and private language schools, and used criterion-sampling.

As for secondary school students, we included three schools that fell into the range of institutions with an average quality of teaching and average student population based on the rank order of schools in terms of the number of students admitted to universities (National Institute of Public Education, Hungary, 2004). Two of the schools were state schools, and in order to represent learners from the private sector of education, we also selected a church-owned school. The three schools were from different geographical locations of the city in order to gather data from students from various social backgrounds. All the students in the second and third year of their secondary education who were studying English were asked to fill in our questionnaires. Altogether 205 learners, 80 males and 125 females, responded to our questions in the secondary school sample. The average age of students was 16 years and 8 months. English is not a compulsory language in Hungarian secondary schools, but it is the most frequently studied language (Halász & Lannert, 2007). When enrolling in a secondary school, students can choose which foreign language they would like to study. The level of students' proficiency in the investigated sample was between pre-intermediate and intermediate.

In selecting the university students, we paid attention to representing the various fields of study one can pursue in Budapest and to including learners from both colleges and universities. One hundred and five college students and 164 university students responded to our questions. Among the participants, there were 163 females and 106 males with an average age of 21.5 years. Studying foreign languages is voluntary at universities, and in most of the institutions students are required to pay for foreign language instruction. Most students in the sample were preparing for one of the accredited intermediate level proficiency exams.

The participating 164 adult language school learners attended private language schools in Budapest. In choosing the language schools, five of the largest language schools in Budapest were approached to allow their students to fill in our questionnaires, and three smaller schools were also invited to participate in the survey. All these schools were well-established and high-quality language schools that won accreditation from the Hungarian Chamber of Language Schools. Among the adult participants, 103 were females and 61 were males with an average age of 35 years. The participants worked in all spheres of life including business, industry, tourism, healthcare, education and the service industry. Adult language learners' proficiency ranged from pre-intermediate to upper-intermediate levels.

Instruments

Our questionnaire consisted of five-point Likert-scale items aimed at measuring the Ideal L2 self as well as self-regulation and specific aspects of learner-autonomy. Three variables were selected to characterise the self-regulation capacity of the learners: emotion control, that is, the ability to control one's feelings and emotions while learning another language; satiation control, in other words, the capacity to overcome boredom and make language learning tasks interesting; and commitment control, which includes strategies to monitor learners' commitment to language learning goals. These variables were adapted from the taxonomy of action control strategies of Corno and Kanfer (1993). A further source of items for these three variables was the Self-Regulating Capacity in Vocabulary Learning scale of Tseng *et al.* (2006), from which questions were reworded to refer to language learning in general. We also measured five aspects of autonomous learner behaviour that were concerned with learners' control over language learning resources (see Benson, 2001). The following are the nine factors that were measured in the questionnaire:

(1) *Ideal L2 self* (6 questions): Students' views of themselves as successful L2 speakers. Example: I like to think of myself as someone who will be able to speak English.

(2) *Emotion control* (4 items): Students' ability to control one's feelings and emotions while learning another language. Example: When I feel stressed about learning English, I can cope with my stress efficiently.

(3) *Satiation control* (4 items): Students' ability to overcome boredom and make language learning tasks interesting. Example: I am confident that I can overcome any sense of boredom when learning English.

(4) *Commitment control* (4 items): Students' ability to monitor their commitment to language learning goals. Example: I have my special techniques to achieve my goals in learning English.

(5) *Autonomous learning skills* (9 items): To what extent students are able to learn and use English on their own. Example: I try to find opportunities to speak English as often as possible.

(6) *Attitudes to autonomy in the language classroom* (7 items): How students relate to making decisions on their own in the classroom. Example: I like it if we can contribute to the planning of the lessons.

(7) *Attitudes to teacher control in the language classroom* (12 items): Learners' disposition towards teacher control and the lack of it. Example: I do not mind if the teacher does not tell us how to solve a task.

(8) *Independent use of learning resources* (7 items): Learners' general capacity to exercise control over learning resources. Example: If there is something that I do not understand in the English class, I make efforts to find out more about it.

(9) *Independent use of technology* (6 items): Learners' general capacity to use learning software and resources from the internet. Example: I use English language-teaching computer programmes.

In the last part of the questionnaire, we asked students background questions concerning what languages they would like to study in the future, when they started learning English, whether they study any other foreign language, what their age and gender are, where and what they study (in the case of university students) and what their job is (in the case of adults).

Procedures

The questionnaire was first administered to 105 undergraduate students studying English language and literature at a university in Budapest. Following the factor and reliability analysis of this pilot run, we omitted or reworded unreliable items. The final version of the questionnaire was personally delivered to the secondary schools, universities, colleges and language schools, where a person who agreed to take charge of the administration of the questionnaires distributed them among teachers and collected the filled in questionnaires. All the questionnaires were computer-coded and SPSS 17.0 was used for analysing the data.

Results

The descriptive statistics for the Ideal L2 self scale suggest that the participants had a positive future image of themselves as successful language learners, but as the ANOVA analysis revealed, the adult group had significantly lower scores on the Ideal L2 self scale than the other two younger groups (Table 5.1). In contrast, the mean values for the scales assessing autonomous learner behaviour and attitudes to learner autonomy in the language classroom were only in the average range of the five-point scale, with the adult group scoring below average. This suggests that the participants did not seek out learning opportunities with high frequency and did not have a highly positive attitude to exercising control in the language classroom. The values for attitudes to teacher control were somewhat higher indicating that the participants, especially the adults, had a stronger desire for teacher control.

The post-hoc Scheffé procedure revealed a number of significant differences in self-regulation strategies, autonomous learning behaviour and attitudes to learner autonomy in the foreign language classroom between the groups. The results indicated that secondary school and university students seemed to be better able to control their boredom than the adult participants. Moreover, the secondary school and university students also made use of technology-based learner approaches more frequently than the adult participants. Adult language learners had a significantly less positive attitude to learner control in the language classroom and demonstrated a stronger desire for the teacher to be in charge than the secondary school and university students.

Table 5.1 Differences in the scales across the three groups

Scales	Sample	Mean	St. Dev.	F	P	Group-based differences*
Independent use of resources	1. Sec. sch. st.	3.01	0.76	1.121	0.327	–
	2. Uni. st.	3.09	0.80			
	3. Adults	3.26	0.77			
Independent use of learning technologies	1. Sec. sch. st.	3.00	0.94	15.995	< 0.001	3 < 1, 2
	2. Uni. st.	3.02	0.92			
	3. Adults	2.53	0.90			
Autonomous learning skills	1. Sec. sch. st.	3.19	0.64	1.514	0.222	–
	2. Uni. st.	3.28	0.59			
	3. Adults	3.28	0.60			
Attitude to autonomy in the classroom	1. Sec. sch. st.	3.03	0.82	9.643	< 0.001	3 < 2, 1
	2. Uni. st.	2.92	0.78			
	3. Adults	2.68	0.81			
Attitude to teacher control	1. Sec. sch. st.	3.62	0.82	17.292	< 0.001	2, 1 < 3
	2. Uni. st.	3.52	0.78			
	3. Adults	3.84	0.81			
Commitment control	1. Sec. sch. st.	3.17	0.78	2.588	0.078	–
	2. Uni. st.	3.26	0.64			
	3. Adults	3.33	0.66			
Satiation control	1. Sec. sch. st.	3.48	0.84	3.532	0.030	3 < 2, 1
	2. Uni. st.	3.46	0.80			
	3. Adults	3.26	0.87			
Emotion control	1. Sec. sch. st.	3.56	0.95	0.594	0.552	–
	2. Uni. st.	3.58	0.85			
	3. Adults	3.49	0.87			

(continued)

Table 5.1 Differences in the scales across the three groups (*continued*)

Scales	Sample	Mean	St. Dev.	F	P	Group-based differences*
Ideal L2 self	1. Sec. sch. st.	4.54	0.61	14.133	< 0.001	3 < 2, 1
	2. Uni. st.	4.50	0.52			
	3. Adults	4.23	0.63			

Notes: *Numbers refer to groups. '<' and '>' denote significant differences. ',' indicates non-significant differences.

Concerning relationships between students' Ideal L2 selves and the various self-regulation-related control scales, we can conclude that future oriented self-guides correlated significantly but only to a moderate extent with both commitment control and satiation control, that is, to what extent students are able to commit to their learning goals and how much they are willing and able to counteract emerging boredom in the learning process (Table 5.2). No significant link between emotion control and the Ideal L2 self was found.

In terms of the correlation between students' autonomous learning behaviour, attitudes to autonomous learning in the classroom and the Ideal L2 self, the results show some significant but moderately strong correlations (Table 5.3). The findings indicate that those students who had strong visions of themselves as successful language users in the future seemed to be more active in using both traditional and technology-based

Table 5.2 Correlation coefficients between participants' Ideal L2 selves and self-regulatory strategies

	Commitment control	Satiation control	Emotion control
Secondary school students			
Ideal L2 self	0.300**	0.302**	0.074
University students			
Ideal L2 self	0.305**	0.226**	0.063
Adult language learners			
Ideal L2 self	0.391**	0.205**	0.116

Notes: ** indicates significance at the $p < 0.05$ level.

Table 5.3 Correlation coefficients between participants' Ideal L2 selves, their autonomous learning behaviour and attitudes to learner autonomy

	Independent use of resources	Independent use of technology	Autonomous learning skills	Attitude to autonomy in the class	Attitude to teacher control
Sec. school students					
Ideal L2 self	0.202**	0.305**	0.225**	0.089	0.166**
University students					
Ideal L2 self	0.274**	0.270**	0.394**	0.095	0.235**
Adult language learners					
Ideal L2 self	0.227**	0.243**	0.357**	0.095	0.190**

Notes: ** indicates significance at the $p < 0.05$ level.

learning resources and tended to have a stronger wish to be in control in the language classroom. Interestingly, there were also positive, albeit relatively weak, correlations between students' Ideal L2 selves and students' attitudes to teacher control.

Discussion and Conclusions

In our study we first addressed the question about the main differences concerning the Ideal L2 self, self-regulation, autonomous learning behaviour and attitudes to learner autonomy in three different learner groups. As in our previous study in a similar context (Kormos & Csizér, 2008), we found that adult language learners had considerably less favourable views of themselves as successful future users of the L2. We can assume that one of the most important reasons for this finding is related to the fact that those studying English as adults either did not succeed in achieving a sufficient level of L2 competence either in secondary or in post-secondary education, or they studied a different foreign language at a younger age. In both cases, acquiring another language as an adult, often parallel to full-time work and family commitments, is a difficult task and possible past failures and the challenges experienced as adult learners might make students more doubtful about the ultimate success of the outcomes of their learning efforts. This finding indicates that in the case of adult language learners, enhancing students' self-confidence and self-efficacy beliefs as well as strengthening their visions of themselves as competent future L2 users is very important. This can be achieved through the teacher's provision of positive feedback, praise and the application of various techniques for enhancing the learners' future vision (Dörnyei & Kubanyiova, 2014).

The adult participants also differed from the younger age groups in their independent use of learning technology, which is understandable given that the younger generation tends to be more familiar with information technology (IT) and the different IT-based resources for finding input in their L2 (e.g. reading texts in English on the internet, watching videos in English) and practising the L2 (e.g. through online chatting or games). The younger generation also displayed more positive attitudes to exercising control over their learning, and they preferred it less when teachers regulated their classroom learning. One of the reasons for this might have been that the secondary school and university student participants were slightly more proficient, and hence, more aware of their learning needs and learning style preferences. Alternatively, as these learners were more autonomous users of learning technology than the adult participants, they had experienced many ways in which they could engage in learning autonomously. Interestingly, the younger participant groups were also more efficient in regulating their boredom in language learning, which might be due to the fact that these students were participating in compulsory language learning programmes. Therefore, no matter how tedious certain language learning tasks seemed to these students, they had to cope with their feelings of boredom as they were formally assessed and could not drop out of the course. In contrast, the adult language learners mostly studied in language schools voluntarily and in these settings formal high-stakes assessment was rare.

In our second research question, we investigated the inter-relationship between the Ideal L2 self and self-regulation strategies on the one hand, and autonomous learning behaviour and attitudes to autonomous learning on the other hand. The results revealed that there was a moderately strong relationship between the Ideal L2 self and commitment control and a significant but somewhat weaker link between the Ideal L2 self and satiation control. The findings indicate that those students who have a strong vision of themselves as successful language users in the future commit themselves more effectively to language learning. This result is similar to the findings of a large number of studies in the field of L2 learning motivation in which a strong link to motivated behaviour, a variable very similar to commitment control, was demonstrated (for a collection of studies, see Dörnyei & Ushioda, 2009). In the field of educational psychology it was also shown that positive self-efficacy beliefs, that is, favourable views about one's own abilities to succeed in the given learning task, are highly important predictors of learning effort (Bandura, 1986, 1997; Mills et al., 2007). As argued by Kormos et al. (2011), the Ideal L2 self shares a number of similarities with self-efficacy beliefs in that without positive views of one's language learning ability it is highly unlikely that one can visualise him/herself as a successful language user in the future. Therefore the self-efficacy component of the Ideal L2 self also contributes to increased control over one's learning processes. It is interesting to note that among the adult participants the Ideal L2 self seems to play a stronger role in commitment control, which might be explained by the assumption that among those learners who study the language voluntarily, and not as part of a compulsory language learning programme, the Ideal L2 self might play a more important role in regulating learning effort.

The correlations between the Ideal L2 self and autonomy-related variables were relatively weak except for the attitudes to learner control scale in the university and adult language learner groups. On the one hand, it might suggest that the Ideal L2 self is only one of the many potential learner-internal and contextual factors that determine learners' autonomous behaviour and attitudes to learner autonomy. Indeed, as described by Benson (2001, 2010), a multitude of factors can contribute to the initiation and maintenance of autonomous learning behaviour and to the formation of attitudes about learner autonomy. On the other hand, the Ideal L2 self might only be indirectly linked to autonomy-related variables and it is with the mediation of other factors that it exerts its effect on autonomous learning and attitudes to learner autonomy. Support for this assumption can be found in our study, in which the relationship between motivational variables, self-regulatory strategies and autonomous learning behaviour was analysed by means of structural equation modelling (Kormos & Csizér, in press). In our research we found that the Ideal L2 self had a strong direct relationship with motivated behaviour, which in turn exerted an effect on the learners' use of self-regulatory strategies. These strategies then influenced the autonomous use of traditional and technology-based learning resources. Based on our structural modelling study and the current investigation, we can hypothesise that students' visions of themselves as competent L2 users might serve as an important foundation and source of energy for effective self-regulation and autonomous learning behaviour, even though its direct link with these variables is moderate or weak.

Our findings highlight the relevance of the Ideal L2 self in self-regulation and learner autonomy and the importance of enhancing learners' self-related views in foreign language learning. This volume includes a number of chapters which address this issue and offer practical suggestions to language teachers and students (see Chapters 18–20).

Acknowledgement

The authors would like to acknowledge that funding for the research reported in this chapter was provided by the OTKA Grant (83243) to the first author.

References

Bandura, A. (1986) *Social Foundations of Thought and Action: A Social Cognitive Theory*. Englewood Cliffs, NJ: Prentice-Hall.

Bandura, A. (1997) *Self-efficacy: The Exercise of Control*. New York, NY: W. H. Freeman.

Benson, P. (2001) *Teaching and Researching Learner Autonomy in Language Learning*. London: Longman.

Benson, P. (2010) Measuring autonomy: Should we put our ability to the test? In A. Paran and L. Sercu (eds) *Testing the Untestable in Language Teaching and Learning* (pp. 77–97). Bristol: Multilingual Matters.

Corno, L. and Kanfer, R. (1993) The role of volition in learning and performance. *Review of Research in Education* 21, 301–341.

Demographic Yearbook (2004) Budapest: Central Statistical Office.

Dörnyei, Z. (2001) *Teaching and Researching Motivation*. Harlow: Longman.

Dörnyei, Z. (2005) *The Psychology of the Language Learner: Individual Differences in Second Language Acquisition*. Mahwah, NJ: Lawrence Erlbaum.

Dörnyei, Z. (2009) *The Psychology of Second Language Acquisition*. Oxford: Oxford University Press.

Dörnyei, Z. and Kubanyiova, M. (2014) *Motivating Learners, Motivating Teachers: Building Vision in the Language Classroom*. Cambridge: Cambridge University.

Dörnyei, Z. and Ushioda, E. (eds) (2009) *Motivation, Language Identity and the L2 Self*. Bristol: Multilingual Matters.

Halász, G. and Lannert, J. (2007) Report on the Hungarian state education, 2006. Budapest: OKI.

Holec, H. (1981) *Autonomy in Foreign Language Learning*. Oxford: Pergamon Press.

Kormos, J. and Csizér, K. (2008) Age-related differences in the motivation of learning English as a foreign language. *Language Learning* 58, 327–355.

Kormos, J. and Csizér, K. (in press) The interaction of motivation, self-regulatory strategies, and autonomous learning behavior in different learner groups. *TESOL Quarterly*.

Kormos, J., Kiddle, T. and Csizér, K. (2011) System of goals, attitudes and self-related beliefs in second language learning motivation. *Applied Linguistics* 32, 495–516.

Littlewood, W. (1996) Defining and developing autonomy in East Asian contexts. *Applied Linguistics* 20, 71–94.

Mills, N.A., Pajares, F. and Herron, C. (2007) Self-efficacy of college intermediate French students: Relation to achievement and motivation. *Language Learning* 57, 417–442.

National Institute of Public Eduction (2004) Rank Order of Secondary Schools. Budapest: OFI.

Oxford, R.L. (2003) Toward a more systematic model of L2 learner autonomy. In D. Palfreyman and R.C. Smith (eds) *Learner Autonomy Across Cultures: Language Education Perspectives* (pp. 75–91). Basingstoke: Palgrave Macmillan.

Pintrich, P.R. and De Groot, E.V. (1990) Motivation and self-regulated learning components of academic performance. *Journal of Educational Psychology* 82, 33–40.

Tseng, W.T., Dörnyei, Z. and Schmitt, N. (2006) A new approach to assessing strategic learning: The case of self-regulation in vocabulary acquisition. *Applied Linguistics* 27, 78–102.

Zimmerman, B.J. (1998) Developing self-fulfilling cycles of academic regulation: An analysis of exemplary instructional models. In D.H. Schunk and B.J. Zimmerman (eds) *Self-regulated Learning: From Teaching to Self-reflective Practice* (pp. 1–19). New York, NY: Guilford Press.

6 EFL Students' L2 Motivational Self System and Self-Regulation: Focusing on Elementary and Junior High School Students in Korea

Tae-Young Kim and Yoon-Kyoung Kim

Introduction

This study investigates the inter-relationship between English as a Foreign Language (EFL) students' Second Language (L2) Motivational Self System (Dörnyei, 2005, 2009), their use of self-regulated learning (SRL) skills and their English test scores in South Korea (henceforth Korea). The L2 Motivational Self System is a useful framework for approaching Korean students' L2 learning motivation.[1] This framework proved to be effective in understanding and explaining the learning motivation and motivated behaviour of Korean learners of English (Kim, 2012; Kim & Kim, 2012). The L2 Motivational Self System includes two types of self-images related to learning and use of an L2: the Ideal L2 self and the Ought-to L2 self. As a positive future self-image, 'if the person we would like to become speaks an L2', the Ideal L2 self can be 'a powerful motivator to learn the L2 because of the desire to reduce the discrepancy between our actual and ideal selves' (Dörnyei, 2009: 29). With regard to the motivational function of the Ideal L2 self, it is important for learners to believe that the gap is not too wide and can be overcome by making conscious academic efforts. The Ought-to L2 self refers to 'the attributes that one believes one *ought to* possess to meet expectations and to *avoid* possible negative outcomes' (Dörnyei, 2009: 29). Those with a high level of Ought-to L2 self would be motivated to learn an L2 because learners feel that they need to live up to the expectations of significant others (e. g. parents).

As for motivated students, one of their characteristics is their active use of SRL skills and strategies (Lens & Vansteenkiste, 2008; Zimmerman & Schunk, 2008). Motivated students see themselves as agents of their own learning process and use skills that enable them to achieve their desired academic outcomes (Torrano Montalvo & González Torres, 2004). Given this, students possessing more vivid L2 selves may have a better chance of demonstrating self-regulated behaviour in their L2 learning. In this paper, we investigate which of the following factors exert a more significant influence on academic achievement in EFL in Korea: (1) the Ideal L2 self, (2) the Ought-to L2 self or (3) SRL skills. It may seem to be the case that students with higher levels of L2 motivation tend to use SRL skills more actively, leading to more successful L2 achievement. However, as Kwaug and Rhee (2009) argued, Korean students' SRL skill use had little impact on or even a negative effect on their EFL achievement. Accordingly, in order to closely examine the relationship between Korean EFL students' L2 selves, SRL skills and English proficiency, this study focuses on how the L2 Motivational Self System and SRL affect students' EFL achievement.

The L2 Selves, SRL and English Proficiency

According to Zimmerman (1990: 4), self-regulated learners are considered to be 'metacognitively, motivationally, and behaviorally active participants in their own learning'. Self-regulated learners monitor their own behaviour in their learning in order to achieve a high level of academic success (Kitsantas et al., 2009; Winne, 2001; Zimmerman, 2002). This process can be facilitated and sustained by learners' motivation to keep pursuing their goals and improve their learning outcomes. Although motivation can play a crucial role in the SRL process, to date it is still unclear if motivation causes SRL or vice versa, and several studies have found that students who were given SRL training displayed a greater increase in their learning motivation (e.g. Schmitz & Wiese, 2006; Stoeger & Ziegler, 2008). However, our stance is that motivation is a prerequisite of SRL. Even if students could initially develop SRL skills through educational training, those with little motivation may hardly maintain it, and thus, the effect of SRL training would diminish. The influence of motivation on SRL has been identified in the study of Wolters and Pintrich (1998) on student motivation and SRL in mathematics, English and social studies. They found that as the case in other studies (Pintrich & De Groot, 1990; Pintrich et al., 1993), students who valued and were interested in the content of the subject area were more likely to employ more self-regulatory strategies. Zimmerman and Schunk (2008: 3) also stated that 'a student can be taught self-monitoring as a cognitive process, but if the student remains motivationally inattentive to his or her feedback, this monitoring is unlikely to be sustained or to enhance learning'.

Besides the relationship between motivation and self-regulation in general, we can find the possible association of the L2 Motivational Self System with self-regulated L2 learning in that the two hinge on the notion of the self. In the L2 Motivational Self System, self-images, in either the Ideal L2 self or the Ought-to L2 self, play a significant role in motivating L2 learners in order to make a conscious effort in L2 learning. In the field of SRL, the self has also drawn attention in that the source of motivation to perform SRL is to improve one's self-concept (McCombs, 2001). Enhancing one's self-concept in L2 learning may be done by actualising one's Ideal L2 self or Ought-to L2 self. That is, the desire to reduce the gap between the perceived L2 proficiency (i.e. what one thinks is his or her current state in L2 learning and use) and future L2-speaking self-images can enable learners to self-regulate in L2 learning. Similarly, Borkowski and Thorpe (1994) stated that possible selves are concerned with SRL. According to their explanation, an essential part of SRL is its goal directedness, and possible selves include goals. Once a learner develops a future goal in order to reach positive possible selves or to avoid negative possible selves, the learner's efforts, which arise as a result of those goals, will be the initial step towards the process of SRL.

In this regard, this study focuses on how influential Korean EFL learners' L2 Motivational Self System is on the extent of their use of SRL skills. In this study, in order to measure the extent to which learners employ SRL skills, we divided SRL skills into three subtypes following Zimmerman's (2002) three-phase model and the classification of Barnard-Brak et al. (2010): forethought, performance and self-reflection phases. The forethought phase of SRL is the process that occurs before the actual enactment of efforts to learn, and Barnard-Brak et al. included the skills of goal setting and environment structuring in this phase. The items for goal setting measure the extent to which students set their standards for assignments and establish short-term goals as well as long-term goals for their own studies. The items for environment structuring indicate how much students are concerned with finding and choosing a place and time for studying efficiently. The performance phase consists of the processes that take place during behavioral implementation, involving task strategies, time management and help seeking. Task strategies include the use of strategies regarding note-taking, reading aloud, questioning and reviewing. Time management is related to students developing a study schedule on their own, and help seeking concerns finding someone to help students with problems that they encounter while studying. The self-reflection phase in SRL occurs after each learning effort and includes self-evaluation when students assess their progress or outcomes, especially comparing themselves with others.

The above three-phase categorisation is also consistent with the Process Model of L2 motivation proposed by Dörnyei and Ottó (1998). The model consists of the following three main phases: (1) the preactional phase, (2) the actional phase and (3) the postactional phase. Since the preactional phase in the Process Model includes three subphases (i.e. goal setting, intention formation and the initiation of intention enactment), in this preactional phase and in the forethought phase of SRL, learners make plans and prepare for making efforts in order to learn and study. The actional phase is concerned with the actual execution of motivational efforts during L2 learning, and therefore, it is associated with the performance phase in SRL. The main process in the postactional phase of the Process Model entails evaluating the action outcomes which is similar to the self-reflection phase in SRL. Given the overlapping domains of the respective three steps in the Process Model of L2 motivation and SRL, it would be worthwhile to examine in which phase the L2 Motivational Self System exerts more of an influence on students' L2 learning.

In addition to the possible relationship of the L2 Motivational Self System with SRL described above, another main focus in this study is to investigate the relationship of academic achievement in English with the L2 Motivational Self System and self-regulated L2 learning. It may seem reasonable to hypothesise a path in which the Ideal and Ought-to L2 selves influence the active use of SRL skills, and then, the activated SRL skills positively affect academic achievement. However, in the Korean context, SRL triggered by vivid Ideal and Ought-to L2 selves may not have a direct impact on students' L2 proficiency. Although private education is a worldwide phenomenon (e.g. Bray, 1999; Silova & Bray, 2006), the Korean educational environment is intensely competitive, represented by a plethora of cram schools and high-stakes college admission tests (Lee, 2006). Students are not used to autonomous learning partly because of their dependency on private education (K.-S. Kim, 2011). In this circumstance, the use of SRL skills may hardly exert a direct influence on the learning process and outcomes as indicated by the following studies. In a cross-cultural comparison of SRL skills between Korean and Filipino students, Turingan and Yang (2009) found that Korean students demonstrated a lower degree of use of SRL skills than their Filipino counterparts. Researchers explained that the results might be attributed to Korean students' excessive reliance on private education. Additionally, in the study of Kwaug and Rhee (2009), Korean students' SRL skills were found to have little or even a negative effect on academic achievement. They added that, for those students, it was perceived as more efficacious to learn passively as planned by their subject teachers.

On the other hand, the L2 Motivational Self System of Korean EFL students proved to have a positive effect on their English proficiency in Kim's (2012) study. He found that the Ideal L2 self and the Ought-to L2 self were statistically significant predictors of EFL proficiency. Given this, in terms of the relationship between L2 selves, self-regulation and academic achievement in English learning among Korean EFL students, our

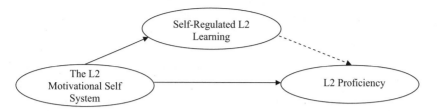

Figure 6.1 The relationship between the L2 selves, SRL and L2 proficiency

assumption is schematised in Figure 6.1. The dotted line indicates a potential, yet limited, effect on L2 proficiency. In order to verify this assumption, we investigate which components of the L2 Motivational Self System and SRL explain our participants' English test scores better.

Also, L2 selves and the self-regulation of elementary (9–12 years old) and junior high school students (13–15 years old) will be compared in this paper. Through a comparative study between elementary and junior high school students, Lee (2001) found that elementary school students demonstrated more positive perceptions and attitudes towards learning English. They possessed higher levels of interest, confidence, expectations and participation. In Kim's (2012) study, it was also found that elementary school students' Ideal and Ought-to L2 selves were more intense than those of junior high school students. Given the results of the studies mentioned above, it would be worthwhile to re-examine if the same pattern is identified in this study. Moreover, since the degree of implementing SRL skills is shown to decrease as Korean students grow older (Park *et al.*, 2007), this study also endeavours to look into the difference in SRL skills. Therefore, this study addresses the following research questions:

(1) Do Korean EFL learners' Ideal L2 self and Ought-to L2 self influence self-regulation in three different phases?
(2) Among the components of the L2 Motivational Self System and SRL of the participants, which component explains their English test scores better?
(3) Are there any differences in the L2 selves and self-regulation between elementary and junior high school EFL learners in Korea?

Method

Participants

A total of 2,625 elementary and junior high school students participated in this study (Table 6.1). They were drawn from 14 different schools across Korea: 10 elementary and 4 junior high schools.

Table 6.1 Participants' profiles

School level	Grade	N	%
Elementary	3	343	13.1
	4	409	15.6
	5	420	16.0
	6	294	11.2
Junior high	7	417	15.9
	8	452	17.2
	9	290	11.0
	Total	2,625	100.0

Among the participants, 1,466 were elementary school students (55.8%) and 1,159 were junior high school students (44.2%). Table 6.1 illustrates the participants' profiles based on their grades, ranging from grades 3–9. A total of 1,380 were female students (52.6%), 1,192 were male students (45.4%), and 53 students did not report their gender (2%).

Data collection

A 36-item questionnaire was employed in this study (see Appendix). The questionnaire items for the Ideal L2 self and the Ought-to L2 self in the L2 Motivational Self System were adopted from the study of Taguchi et al. (2009). Also, goal setting, environment structuring, task strategies, time management, help seeking and self-evaluation were itemised in the SRL scale based on the study of Barnard-Brak et al. (2010). The items were measured by a five-point Likert scale ranging from disagree strongly (1) to agree strongly (5). Moreover, the participants were required to self-report their English test scores.

In order to fine-tune the questionnaire items, 26 elementary and 43 junior high school students were asked to participate in a pilot study in June 2011. They were all excluded from the main survey. The main questionnaire was administered by the English teachers at each school from July to October 2011. Students voluntarily participated in the questionnaire survey after the purpose and instructions on how to respond to the questionnaire were provided to them by their teachers. The participants' anonymity was strictly guaranteed, which was mentioned in the introductory part of the questionnaire.

Data analysis

The collected data were analysed by using three different quantitative methods, utilising SPSS version 18.0. Firstly, descriptive statistics were used to look into the general characteristics of the variables. Secondly, stepwise linear regression analysis was implemented to examine if Korean EFL students' L2 Motivational Self System has an effect on their use of SRL skills. It was also used to investigate the effect of their L2 selves and self-regulation on their English test scores. In this regression analysis, in order to employ English test scores as the dependent variable, we adapted students' self-reported test scores into the z-score, which is the standard score. This was because 14 participating schools had different in-house tests, and as a result, we needed to neutralise the school differences in English test scores. Thirdly, an independent samples *t*-test was carried out in order to determine if there were statistically significant differences in the L2 Motivational Self System as well as in the use of SRL skills between elementary and junior high school students.

Results

This study had eight variables with two from the L2 Motivational Self System and six from SRL skills. As for the general characteristics of the eight variables, the descriptive statistics in Table 6.2 indicate that the participants' Ideal L2 self gained the highest mean score ($M = 3.19$). The other concepts included in the study showed relatively low mean scores, which were less than the 3.0 middle point.

Table 6.2 Descriptive statistics of the L2 Motivational Self System and self-regulation

		M	SD
L2 Motivational Self System	Ideal L2 self	3.19	.99
	Ought-to L2 self	2.80	.81
Self-regulated learning skills	Environment structuring	2.87	.95
	Help seeking	2.86	.98
	Time management	2.79	.96
	Task strategies	2.73	.87
	Self-evaluation	2.61	.91
	Goal setting	2.60	.97

The L2 Motivational Self System and self-regulation

As stated in the previous section, we identified the similarities between the Process Model of Dörnyei and Ottó (1998) and SRL in terms of time sequence. In this section, we endeavour to present the effect of Korean EFL learners' L2 selves on three stages of SRL skills. Table 6.3 exhibits the explanatory power of the L2 selves on SRL skills employed in the forethought phase. This phase is where learners make preparations for self-regulated L2 learning and thus the dependent variable was created from the summed mean score of the items included in goal setting and environment structuring.

Table 6.3 indicates that the participants' Ideal and Ought-to L2 selves had a significant and positive influence on the forethought phase of SRL, explaining 38.7% of the variance. Specifically, the Ideal L2 self was shown to have a considerable explanatory power for this phase, uniquely accounting for 35% of the variance. This finding shows that students with a vivid Ideal L2 self set goals for their English learning or

Table 6.3 Stepwise linear regression analysis for L2 selves predicting SRL in the forethought phase

Model	R	R^2	ΔR^2	R^2 change	t	Collinearity statistics	
						Tolerance	VIF
1. Ideal L2 self	.592	.350	.350	.350	28.868[**]	.804	1.244
2. Ought-to L2 self	.622	.387	.387	.037	12.420[**]	.804	1.244

Notes: [**]$p < .01$; VIF = variance inflation factor.

Table 6.4 Stepwise linear regression analysis for L2 selves predicting SRL in the performance phase

Model	R	R^2	ΔR^2	R^2 change	t	Collinearity statistics	
						Tolerance	VIF
1. Ideal L2 self	.578	.334	.334	.334	27.136[**]	.804	1.244
2. Ought-to L2 self	.619	.384	.383	.049	14.333[**]	.804	1.244

Notes: [**]$p < .01$; VIF = variance inflation factor.

assignments (i.e. goal setting) and arrange time and space that they find most efficient for their learning (i.e. environment structuring).

In the next stage of SRL performance, the dependent variable was the summed mean score of the items in task strategies, time management and help seeking. As shown in Table 6.4, the Ideal L2 self and Ought-to L2 self proved to be influential on the performance phase of SRL. A total of 38.4% of the variance was explained by those L2 selves. The unique explanatory power of the Ideal L2 self was 33.4% and that of the Ought-to L2 self was 4.9%. From this analysis, we can recognise that highly motivated students with a vivid Ideal L2 self have a considerable chance of using SRL skills during their L2 studies.

In the regression analysis for the self-reflection phase, the dependent variable was the mean score of the items in self-evaluation. Table 6.5 shows the significant impact of the L2 selves on the self-reflection phase of SRL. A total of 30.7% of the variance (25.6% of the contribution by the Ideal L2 self and 5.1% by the Ought-to L2 self) was explained. This suggests that evaluating outcomes from SRL can be based on both L2 selves and further, the Ideal L2 self affects the process more substantially.

In sum, the Ideal L2 self and Ought-to L2 self had a statistically significant influence on all of the three stages of SRL. The Ideal L2 self was a more powerful predictor of SRL than the Ought-to L2 self. Considering the effect of the Ideal L2 self on each of the phases, its most powerful effect was identified in the forethought phase ($\Delta R^2 = .350$). With a slight difference in the explanatory power ($\Delta R^2 = .334$), the performance stage of SRL was affected second most highly by the Ideal L2 self. This phenomenon seems related to the three phases of the Process Model of L2 motivation and we will address this issue in the Discussion section in more detail.

Table 6.5 Stepwise linear regression analysis for L2 selves predicting SRL in the self-reflection phase

Model	R	R^2	ΔR^2	R^2 change	t	Collinearity statistics	
						Tolerance	VIF
1. Ideal L2 self	.506	.256	.255	.256	21.528**	.804	1.244
2. Ought-to L2 self	.554	.307	.306	.051	13.731**	.804	1.244

Notes: **$p < .01$; VIF = variance inflation factor.

The L2 Motivational Self System, self-regulation and English test scores

Among the participants' L2 Motivational Self System and SRL skills, the Ideal L2 self, the Ought-to L2 self, time management and self-evaluation exhibited a statistically significant influence on their English test scores, as shown in Table 6.6. A total of 15% of the variance was explained by these four variables. The Ideal L2 self was the most powerful predictor of the participants' English test scores, accounting for 13% of the variance. The unique contribution of the other explanatory variables to the English test scores was around 1% or lower.

The Ideal L2 self and time management positively affected academic achievement in English, suggesting that English test scores would be higher for Korean EFL learners who possess a more vivid Ideal L2 self and who also use time management skills more actively. On the other hand, the Ought-to L2 self and self-evaluation had a negative impact on English test scores. The negative explanatory power of the Ought-to L2 self on the response variable indicates that the more students are concerned about their obligations or the opinions of others, the lower their English test scores become. Similarly, considering the items measuring the skill of self-evaluation, the skill includes a comparison of oneself with others in order to evaluate oneself (e.g. I communicate with my classmates in order to find out how I am doing in studying English; I communicate with my classmates in order to find out the differences between what I have learned and what they have learned). This comparison with others is in line with the self-consciousness of others, denoted in the Ought-to L2 self, which is likely to serve as an obstacle to students' EFL achievement.

Table 6.6 Stepwise linear regression analysis for variables predicting students' English test scores

Model	R	R^2	ΔR^2	R^2 change	t	Collinearity statistics	
						Tolerance	VIF
1. Ideal L2 self	.360	.130	.130	.130	15.494[**]	.625	1.600
2. Ought-to L2 self	.375	.140	.140	.010	−5.734[**]	.752	1.330
3. Time management	.385	.148	.147	.008	5.225[**]	.447	2.237
4. Self-evaluation	.387	.150	.149	.002	−2.442[*]	.470	2.129

Notes: [**]$p < .01$; [*]$p < .05$; VIF = variance inflation factor.

In this regard, it is necessary to help students become aware of the negative consequences of being overly self-conscious in their L2 learning.

Differences between elementary and junior high school students

Table 6.7 demonstrates that there exist statistically significant differences between Korean EFL elementary and junior high school students in their L2 Motivational Self System and SRL. As for the components in the L2 Motivational Self System, elementary school students exhibited stronger Ideal and Ought-to L2 selves than junior high school students, similarly to Kim's (2012) previous study. The Ideal L2 self portrayed a much higher difference ($t = 8.342$), with a significance level of .001 between the two groups, than the Ought-to L2 self ($t = 1.957$; $p = .050$).

Among the SRL skills, significant differences were found in goal setting, environment structuring, time management, help seeking and self-evaluation. With the exception of help seeking, elementary school students demonstrated higher mean scores than their junior high school counterparts in all of the above stated concepts. In order to clarify if this indicates a more effective use of SRL skills among elementary school students, we further examined the different aspects of how influential SRL skills are on English proficiency between the two groups.

As for the effect of elementary school students' SRL on English test scores, only time management had a significant explanatory power of 5.1%, as displayed in Table 6.8. Goal setting, environment structuring, task strategies, help seeking and self-evaluation were excluded from the statistically significant predictors. This suggests that, among elementary school students, using a variety of SRL skills may not lead to more successful EFL achievement.

Table 6.9 exhibits that junior high school students' SRL skills, such as time management, task strategies, goal setting, environment structuring and self-evaluation, had a significant explanatory power on their English test scores. The five variables explained 11.3% of the variance. For junior high school students, a broader range of SRL skills were identified as factors that affect English proficiency with a greater explanatory power, suggesting that junior high school students' SRL skills are implemented more effectively than those of elementary school students in Korea.

Discussion

The Ideal L2 self, self-regulation and academic achievement in English

Zimmerman and Schunk (2008) asserted that motivational processes function as a significant factor in initiating, guiding and sustaining SRL.

Table 6.7 Independent samples *t*-test for the L2 Motivational Self System and SRL

Concepts	School level	M	SD	t	Sig.
Ideal L2 self	Elementary	3.33	.99	8.342**	.001
	Junior high	3.01	.96		
Ought-to L2 self	Elementary	2.82	.85	1.957*	.050
	Junior high	2.76	.76		
Goal setting	Elementary	2.69	1.04	5.457**	.001
	Junior high	2.48	.87		
Environment structuring	Elementary	2.92	1.00	3.045**	.002
	Junior high	2.81	.88		
Task strategies	Elementary	2.76	.94	1.494	.135
	Junior high	2.71	.78		
Time management	Elementary	2.88	1.01	5.385**	.001
	Junior high	2.68	.89		
Help seeking	Elementary	2.81	1.02	-2.786**	.005
	Junior high	2.92	.94		
Self-evaluation	Elementary	2.66	.95	2.899**	.004
	Junior high	2.56	.86		

Notes: N = 2,625; elementary school students = 1,466, junior high school students = 1,159; *$p \leq .05$, **$p < .01$.

In this study, developing Korean EFL learners' L2 selves proved to be an influential motivational process on the forethought, performance and self-reflection phases of self-regulated L2 learning. In particular, students having a more vivid Ideal L2 self can be better at managing SRL skills of the forethought and performance phases. Earlier in this chapter, each of the SRL phases was compared with the Process Model of L2 motivation of Dörnyei and Ottó (1998). We can understand the effects of the Ideal L2 self on the SRL phases, with regard to the pre-actional, actional and post-actional phases in the Process Model of L2 motivation.

In the preactional phase of L2 motivation, motivation needs to be generated; this generated motivation leads learners to select their goal or task which they will pursue (Dörnyei, 2005). From the perspective of the L2 Motivational Self System, the created Ideal L2 self encourages L2

Table 6.8 Stepwise linear regression analysis for elementary school students' SRL predicting English test scores

Model	R	R^2	ΔR^2	R^2 change	t	Collinearity statistics	
						Tolerance	VIF
1. Time management	.225	.051	.050	.051	8.448[**]	1.000	1.000

Notes: [**]$p < .01$; VIF = variance inflation factor.

Table 6.9 Stepwise linear regression analysis for junior high school students' SRL predicting English test scores

Model	R	R^2	ΔR^2	R^2 change	t	Collinearity statistics	
						Tolerance	VIF
1. Time management	.300	.090	.089	.090	4.981[**]	.379	2.636
2. Task strategies	.316	.100	.099	.010	3.895[**]	.309	3.241
3. Goal setting	.326	.106	.104	.006	2.437[*]	.352	2.839
4. Environment structuring	.332	.110	.107	.004	2.431[*]	.378	2.644
5. Self-evaluation	.337	.113	.109	.003	-2.032[*]	.316	3.166

Notes: [**]$p < .01$; [*]$p < .05$; VIF = variance inflation factor.

learners to start self-regulating during their L2 learning. That is, L2 learners set goals and select environments optimal for successful L2 learning, as they wish to actualise their Ideal L2 self. The Ideal L2 self can be helpful for establishing a concrete goal. Borkowski and Thorpe (1994) also stated that possible selves can be a good starting point for self-regulation in learning. Therefore, it is suggested that self-regulation in L2 learning can be elicited by helping learners develop a more vivid Ideal L2 self. After SRL is initiated in the preactional phase, the actional phase is also important for maintaining the learning process even when learners are exposed to a great number of distracting influences (Dörnyei, 2005). A sustained Ideal L2 self would help learners try to protect their focus on studying from distracting influences. That is, in the performance phase of SRL, students with a stronger Ideal L2 self more actively manage their time for studying, use appropriate task strategies and seek help from others. In the postactional phase, evaluating the outcomes can be carried out partly based on the goals, which are derived from the Ideal L2 self, associated with one's own vision for oneself rather than the consideration of others. However, self-evaluation included in the self-reflection phase of SRL entails a comparison with others. As shown in Table 6.6, self-evaluation proved to have a negative influence on students' EFL achievement, and for this reason, although the Ideal L2 self has an influence on the self-reflection phase, the effect is less powerful compared to the forethought and performance phases.

In terms of the relationship between L2 selves, SRL and English proficiency, the research finding highlighted that the L2 Motivational Self System had more of an impact on English proficiency than SRL skills. The use of SRL skills had little influence on learning outcomes, as in the case of the study of Kwaug and Rhee (2009). This result may arise from the characteristics of English learning which have been developed in the Korean context. In Korea, the atmosphere surrounding the English learning environment is intense due to the social pressure for high levels of English proficiency (Yoon, 2007). An eagerness to learn English has been intensified with the social consensus that a high level of English proficiency is a key determinant to upward social mobility (Kim, 2010; Park, 2009). Particularly in Korea, the social consensus of the importance of English has constantly been consolidated due to the close geopolitical ties between Korea and the US after the Korean War in the 1950s. This historically derived social atmosphere obliges students to devote much time and effort to studying English in order to obtain better EFL achievement without paying due attention to autonomous L2 learning or self-regulation. The expansion of private education for English learning is also regarded as one of the reasons why Korean EFL students lack independence in their own L2 learning.[3] In private education, all school subjects are fragmented into chunks of memorisable knowledge, which each student can understand without utilising the necessary learning strategies. Such contextual features as an excessively intense learning environment and an over-reliance on private education for English learning have possibly led students to be passive about their learning, and thus prevented them from developing SRL skills. As a consequence, even if Korean EFL students possess a vivid Ideal L2 self, which exerts a beneficial impact on EFL proficiency, they fail to connect their L2 selves to an enhanced level of SRL skills. This results in the limited influence of SRL skills on EFL proficiency. Their SRL skills rarely serve as a conceptual bridge between L2 learning motivation and academic achievement in English.

Demotivation and SRL skills among elementary and junior high school students

With stronger L2 selves, elementary school students were found to be more motivated than junior high school students. To put it differently, in terms of motivational change over time, elementary school students' L2 motivation is considered to decrease as they become junior high school students. In his cross-grade survey analysis, Kim (2012) demonstrated that Korean elementary school students' motivation consistently decreased until grade 9. Jung (2011) also investigated the change in motivation of Korean EFL learners, asking university students to draw a graph regarding how the degree of motivation changed from when they started to learn English. The students' average pattern of motivational change showed a decrease from grade 7. From these findings, we believe that there exists a demotivational tendency among junior high school students within the Korean context.

In order to explain the possible demotivating factors, education fever, or an excessive obsession with academic degrees, has long been around in the lives of Koreans, deriving partly from the traditional Confucian attitude towards learning (Seth, 2002). Within the tradition, respect for learning is emphasised and education is valued as 'a way of achieving status and power' (Seth, 2002: 9). Korean families 'invest heavily in the education of their children,' and consequently 'children and young adults spend a huge portion of their time studying and preparing for examinations' (Seth, 2002: 2). Although this aspect of education in Korea has led to the expansion of higher education and the growth of the Korean domestic economy, it has also produced problems, one of which is the excessive focus on the college entrance examination. For most Korean high school students and their parents, entering a prestigious university is the most significant issue (Kim, 2006). They consider primary and secondary education as 'a preparatory course for college entrance examinations which focus on a cramming method that emphasises memorization learning' (Lee, 2006: 10). English is one of the four main subject areas in the College Scholastic Ability Test in Korea. English proficiency is considered 'an important tool for obtaining a modern lifestyle and for climbing the social ladder' (Kim, 2010: 212). In these circumstances, many parents believe that they can help their children become more successful by encouraging them, and even requiring them to pursue an English education (Park, 2009). Korean students are urged to follow their parents or social norms, rather than focusing on the future self-images they themselves create. Accordingly, the Ideal L2 self of elementary school students tends to be negatively affected as they become junior high school students.

For five out of six SRL skills, elementary school students showed higher scores than their counterparts. However, it is hard to say that this finding indicates better management of SRL skills among elementary school students. In terms of the standard deviations in the responses for SRL skills, the elementary school student samples showed consistently higher ones with almost one or more than one point, whereas the junior high school samples were all lower than 0.9. That is, the junior high school students' responses are more concentrated towards the mean scores than the elementary school students' responses. This means that junior high school students' use of SRL skills is more selective and focused. They choose more effective SRL skills for their own learning and tend not to use the ineffective ones, whereas elementary school students tend to use a variety of SRL skills without being keenly aware of which ones are more effective for their L2 learning.

Tables 6.8 and 6.9 demonstrate that the SRL skills of junior high school students, including time management, task strategies, goal setting, environment structuring and self-evaluation, had more of an effect on EFL achievement than those of elementary school students. As for elementary school students' SRL, only time management had a significant explanatory power. Accordingly, even though junior high school students' SRL seemed to be less active than elementary school students, we can conclude that junior high school students' eclectic use of effective SRL skills for their L2 learning contributes to achieving higher test scores. Zimmerman (2002: 66) also pointed out that 'self-regulation of learning involves the selective use of specific processes that must be personally adapted to each learning task'. Given this, in training students to utilise SRL skills, they need to be encouraged to find out which specific skills are more efficacious to themselves and to the given tasks, which would eventually result in higher achievement in their English learning.

Summary and Implications

This study investigated Korean EFL students' Ideal and Ought-to L2 selves, their SRL skills and their academic achievement in English. The research findings are summarised as follows:

(1) Two types of L2 selves in Korean EFL learners had a significant explanatory power for all of the three phases of SRL. A vivid Ideal L2 self resulted in the active use of SRL skills in the forethought, performance and self-reflection phases of SRL.

(2) Among the participants' L2 selves and self-regulation, the Ideal L2 self, the Ought-to L2 self, time management and self-evaluation exerted a significant influence on their English test scores, while the Ideal L2 self had the most substantial influence.

(3) Elementary school students had more intense L2 selves. Also, they showed higher mean scores in SRL skills, such as goal setting, environment structuring, time management and self-evaluation. Junior high school students used the skill of help seeking more frequently and SRL skills more efficiently than did their counterparts.

From this study, it was found that SRL skills had less of an influence on English learning than the Ideal L2 self and the Ought-to L2 self. This phenomenon may arise from the Korean educational environment in which English proficiency is considered to be the crucial means of entering prestigious universities and acquiring a secure job. In this social context, students are urged to learn English without focusing much on SRL skills. Instead, they depend on private education (T.-Y. Kim, 2011). Also, despite the significant effect of the L2 Motivational Self System on English proficiency, students' L2 motivation is shown to decrease as they grow older. In the Korean educational system, the demotivational pattern is also attributed to internal student competition. For future research, it would be helpful to focus more closely on how the contextual factors affect individual learners' motivational change in order to better understand the socio-educational environment regarding EFL students' English learning.

Acknowledgment

This work was supported by the National Research Foundation of Korea Grant funded by the Korean Government (NRF-2011-332-B00483).

Notes

(1) In this paper, L2 is interchangeably used to refer to both second and foreign languages.
(2) English education begins from grade 3 in Korea.
(3) Statistics Korea (2012) reported that 71.7% of elementary and junior high school students in Korea had private education, and each of them spent an average of 81,000 Won (approximately 80 US Dollars) per month for private English education.

References

Barnard-Brak, L., Lan, W.Y. and Paton, V.O. (2010) Profiles in self-regulated learning in the online learning environment. *International Review of Research in Open and Distance Learning* 11 (1), 61–80.
Borkowski, J.G. and Thorpe, P.K. (1994) Self-regulation and motivation: A life-span perspective for underachievement. In D.H. Schunk and B.J. Zimmerman (eds) *Self-Regulation of Learning and Performance: Issues and Education Applications* (pp. 45–73). Hillsdale, NJ: Lawrence Erlbaum.

Bray, M. (1999) *The Shadow Education System: Private Tutoring and its Implications for Planners*. Paris, France: United Nations Educational, Scientific and Cultural Organization.

Dörnyei, Z. (2005) *The Psychology of the Language Learner: Individual Differences in Second Language Acquisition*. Mahwah, NJ: Lawrence Erlbaum.

Dörnyei, Z. (2009) The L2 motivational self system. In Z. Dörnyei and E. Ushioda (eds) *Motivation, Language Identity and the L2 Self* (pp. 9–42). Bristol, UK: Multilingual Matters.

Dörnyei, Z. and Ottó, I. (1998) Motivation in action: A process model of L2 motivation. *Working Papers in Applied Linguistics* 4, 43–69.

Jung, S.-K. (2011) Demotivating and remotivating factors in learning English: A case of low level college students. *English Teaching* 66 (2), 47–72.

Kim, K.-S. (2011) Changes in two fifth graders' learner autonomy. *Primary English Education* 17 (1), 357–381.

Kim, T.-Y. (2006) Motivation and attitudes toward foreign language learning as socio-politically mediated constructs: The case of Korean high school students. *The Journal of Asia TEFL* 3 (2), 165–192.

Kim, T.-Y. (2010) Socio-political influences on EFL motivation and attitudes: Comparative surveys of Korean high school students. *Asia Pacific Education Review* 11 (2), 211–222.

Kim, T.-Y. (2011) Korean elementary school students' English learning demotivation: A comparative survey study. *Asia Pacific Education Review* 12 (1), 1–11.

Kim, T.-Y. (2012) The L2 motivational self system of Korean EFL students: Cross-grade survey analysis. *English Teaching* 67 (1), 29–56.

Kim, Y.-K. and Kim, T.-Y. (2012) Korean secondary school students' L2 learning motivation: Comparing the L2 motivational self system with the socio-educational model. *English Language & Literature Teaching* 18 (1), 115–132.

Kitsantas, A., Steen, S. and Huie, F. (2009) The role of self-regulated strategies and goal orientation in predicting achievement of elementary school children. *International Electronic Journal of Elementary Education* 2 (1), 65–81.

Kwaug, S.-L. and Rhee, K.-J. (2009) The analysis of the relationship between students' self-regulated learning skills, teachers' teaching skills and academic achievement. *Educational Research* 29 (1), 35–60.

Lee, J.-K. (2006) Education fever and South Korean higher education. *Revista Electronica de Investigacion Educativa* 8 (1). See http://redie.uabc.mx/vol8no1/contents-lee2.html (accessed July 2012).

Lee, K.-Y. (2001) Comparison of elementary and secondary school students' perceptions about English teachers and English learning: In pursuit of the link between elementary and secondary English education. *Foreign Languages Education* 8 (2), 101–132.

Lens, W. and Vansteenkiste, M. (2008) Promoting self-regulated learning: A motivational analysis. In D.H. Schunk and B.J. Zimmerman (eds) *Motivation and Self-Regulated Learning: Theory, Research, and Applications* (pp. 141–168). New York, NY: Lawrence Erlbaum.

McCombs, B.L. (2001) Self-regulated learning and academic achievement: A phenomenological view. In B.J. Zimmerman and D.H. Schunk (eds) *Self-Regulated Learning and Academic Achievement: Theoretical Perspectives* (2nd edn). (pp. 67–123). Mahwah, NJ: Lawrence Erlbaum.

Park, C., Kim, K.-H., Kim, S.-J., Sohn, W.-S., Song, M.-Y. and Cho, J.-M. (2007) Trends in national assessment of educational achievement (2003–2005). *The Journal of Curriculum & Evaluation* 10 (2), 173–202.

Park, J.-K. (2009) 'English fever' in South Korea: Its history and symptoms. *English Today* 25 (1), 50–57.

Pintrich, P.R. and De Groot, E. (1990) Motivational and self-regulated learning components of classroom academic performance. *Journal of Educational Psychology* 82 (1), 33–40.

Pintrich, P.R., Smith, D.A.F., Garcia, T. and McKeachie, W.J. (1993) Reliability and predictive validity of the Motivated Strategies for Learning Questionnaire (MSLQ). *Educational and Psychological Measurement* 53 (3), 801–813.

Schmitz, B. and Wiese, B.S. (2006) New perspectives for the evaluation of training sessions in self-regulated learning: Time-series analyses of diary data. *Contemporary Educational Psychology* 31 (1), 64–96.

Seth, M.J. (2002) *Education Fever: Society, Politics, and the Pursuit of Schooling in South Korea.* Honolulu, HI: University of Hawaii Press.

Silova, I. and Bray, M. (2006) The hidden market place: Private tutoring in former socialist countries. In I. Silova, V. Būdienė, M. Bray and A. Zabulionis (eds) *Education in a Hidden Marketplace: Monitoring of Private Tutoring* (pp. 71–98). Budapest, Hungary: Education Support Program of the Open Society Institute.

Statistics Korea (2012) Investigation of private education expenses. See http://kostat. go.kr/survey/pedu/pedu_dl/1/index.board?bmode = read&aSeq = 253726 (accessed June 2012).

Stoeger, H. and Ziegler, A. (2008) Evaluation of a classroom-based training to improve self-regulated learning: Which pupils profit the most? *Metacognition and Learning* 3 (3), 207–230.

Taguchi, T., Magid, M. and Papi, M. (2009) The L2 motivational self system among Japanese, Chinese, and Iranian learners of English: A comparative study. In Z. Dörnyei and E. Ushioda (eds) *Motivation, Language Identity and the L2 Self* (pp. 66–97). Bristol: Multilingual Matters.

Torrano Montalvo, F. and González Torres, M.C. (2004) Self-regulated learning: Current and future directions. *Electronic Journal of Research in Educational Psychology* 2 (1), 1–34.

Turingan, J.P. and Yang, Y.-C. (2009) A cross-cultural comparison of self-regulated learning skills between Korean and Filipino college students. *Asian Social Science* 5 (12), 3–10.

Winne, P.H. (2001) Self-regulated learning viewed from models of information processing. In B.J. Zimmerman and D.H. Schunk (eds) *Self-Regulated Learning and Academic Achievement: Theoretical Perspectives* (2nd edn). (pp. 153–189). Mahwah, NJ: Erlbaum.

Wolters, C.A. and Pintrich, P.R. (1998) Contextual differences in student motivation and self-regulated learning in mathematics, English, and social studies classrooms. *Instructional Science* 26 (1–2), 27–47.

Yoon, J.-K. (ed.) (2007) *Yongeo, Nae Maeumae Sicminjooui [English, Imperialism in My Heart].* Seoul, Korea: Dangdae.

Zimmerman, B.J. (1990) Self-regulated learning and academic achievement: An overview. *Educational Psychologist* 25 (1), 3–17.

Zimmerman, B.J. (2002) Becoming a self-regulated learner. *Theory into Practice* 41 (2), 64–70.

Zimmerman, B.J. and Schunk, D.H. (2008) Motivation: An essential dimension of self-regulated learning. In D.H. Schunk and B.J. Zimmerman (eds) *Motivation and Self-Regulated Learning: Theory, Research, and Applications* (pp. 1–30). New York, NY: Lawrence Erlbaum.

Appendix

Questionnaire items

(1) The Ideal L2 self ($\alpha = .936$)

- I can imagine myself living abroad and having a discussion in English with the locals.
- I can imagine myself speaking English with foreigners.
- I can imagine myself speaking English with foreign friends or acquaintances.
- I imagine myself as someone who will be able to speak English fluently.
- I can imagine myself speaking English as if I were a native English-speaking teacher.
- Whenever I think of my future career, I imagine myself using English.
- I can imagine myself living abroad and speaking English with the locals.
- I can imagine myself studying in a university where all of my courses are taught in English.

(2) The Ought-to L2 self ($\alpha = .846$)

- I study English because close friends of mine think it is important.
- I have to study English because if I do not study English, my parents will be disappointed with me.
- Learning English is necessary because people around me expect me to do so.
- I consider learning English important because the people I respect think that I should do it.
- Studying English is important to me in order to gain the approval of my peers/teachers/family.
- Studying English is important to me in order to bring honour to my family.
- Studying English is important to me because most of the educated people are able to speak English.
- Studying English is important to me because other people will respect me more if I have good knowledge of English.

(3) Goal setting ($\alpha = .860$)

- I set my own standards for English assignments.

- I set short-term (daily or weekly) goals, as well as long-term goals (monthly or for the semester) for studying English.
- I set goals to help me manage my time for studying English.

(4) Environment structuring ($\alpha = .788$)

- I find a comfortable place to study English.
- I know where I can study English most efficiently.
- I choose the location where I study English in order to avoid too many distractions.
- I choose a time with few distractions for studying English.

(5) Task strategies ($\alpha = .666$)

- I try to take thorough notes for my English classes.
- I read aloud what I am studying in order to fight against distractions when I study English.
- I prepare questions about what I have learned before English classes.
- I study more than what I have learned in English classes.

(6) Time management ($\alpha = .778$)

- I allocate extra studying time for English because I know it is time-consuming.
- I schedule the same time every day or every week in order to study English, and I observe the schedule.
- I try to distribute my studying time evenly across days for studying English.

(7) Help seeking ($\alpha = .736$)

- I find someone who is knowledgeable in English when I need help for studying English.
- I share my problems in studying English with my classmates so that we can solve the problems together.

(8) Self-evaluation ($\alpha = .770$)

- I summarise what I have learned in order to examine my understanding of it after English classes.
- I ask myself a lot of questions when studying English.
- I communicate with my classmates in order to find out how I am doing in studying English.
- I communicate with my classmates in order to find out the differences between what I have learned and what they have learned.

7 The L2 Self-Concept in Second Language Learning Motivation: A Longitudinal Study of Korean University Students

David Lyons

Introduction

Second language (L2) motivation has long been regarded as an important component in L2 acquisition, dating back to the seminal work of Gardner and Lambert (1959, 1972). Their ideas, particularly the concept of the integrative motive, dominated thinking in the field of L2 motivation for several decades. However, the idea of integrativeness came under increasing criticism, especially in English as a Foreign Language (EFL) and classroom learning contexts where a salient first language (L1) community could rarely be said to exist. In addition, the increasing globalisation of English (Crystal, 2003) made it ever more difficult to conceive of any one community laying claim to the language. As such, theories of L2 motivation have moved away from the social-psychological perspective of Gardner and Lambert to encompass a broader range of ideas.

Various theories of L2 motivation have been proposed, such as Dörnyei's (1994) three-level framework and the social constructivist model of Williams and Burden (1997). Ideas such as these drew from the fields of educational and cognitive psychology. They were followed by a period characterised by more process approaches to L2 motivation, such as the work of Dörnyei and Ottó (1998), and now, according to Ushioda and Dörnyei (2012: 396), we have reached yet another stage in the evolution of L2 motivation research, a 'socio-dynamic period', which recognises the socially constructed and dynamic nature of motivation.

Intimately connected with modern motivation theory is the notion of the self-concept, that is, the knowledge, ideas, feelings, hopes and fears that the individual possesses in relation to him or herself (Cantor et al., 1986).

These conceptions are important in that, as Williams and Burden (1999) point out, they have a large impact not only on the way we view ourselves but also on how we approach learning and indeed on our attitudes towards that learning. In addition, self-concepts include both a personal and a social component (Oyserman *et al.*, 2006), meaning that a person's self-concept is not dependent just on his or her perceptions, but is also potentially substantially influenced by the immediate environment. Most modern researchers have placed the self-concept firmly at the center of understanding what drives individuals and directs their actions. Some researchers have gone even further, suggesting that 'the self lies at the very core of human experience and must be part of any theoretical formulation in the field of human motivation' (Weiner, 1986: 286).

The research reported in this chapter takes cognizance of some of the most recent advances in L2 motivation theory and seeks to investigate the concept with reference to these developments. However, the research did not set out to validate any particular theory. It sought instead to apply an inductive approach to the collection and analysis of data and on the basis of this analysis to formulate hypotheses on the factors influencing the participants' motivation to learn an L2. To achieve this, the researcher investigated the motivational orientations (e.g. reasons for studying English, their goals in the language and the influences on their attitudes to learning the language) of a group of 33 South Korean university students through a longitudinal qualitative study. The research involved both focus group and individual interviews, while data analysis involved both the construction of individual student profiles and the qualitative coding of data sets to determine common themes.

This chapter will begin by outlining some of the most pertinent developments in modern L2 motivation theory before moving on to the development of the research design. It will then present some of the findings of the research and discuss their significance in relation to both the Korean context and our understanding of L2 motivation in general.

Recent Developments in L2 Motivation

By the end of the 1990s, there was an increased emphasis among researchers on the cognitive aspects of learners' motivational orientations. Ushioda (1996) applied Attribution Theory (Weiner, 1986) to the question of how learners perceived success and failure and how this affected their motivation. In addition, the advent of process approaches led to the recognition that motivation can and does change dramatically over time. This new focus also led to the beginning of a change in research methodology in the L2 motivation field, a field that had been dominated by the quantitative methodology of social psychology. There now began to appear a number of studies following more qualitatively based lines of enquiry (e.g. Ushioda, 1998). As the 1990s came to an end, and as research such as the longitudinal studies of Dörnyei and Csizér (2002) in Hungary highlighted problems with traditional conceptions of integrativeness, the field began to move into a period characterised by an increased focus on learners' concepts of themselves as language learners, their interactions with their learning contexts and the dynamic nature of motivation.

Developments in L2 motivation theory have been greatly influenced by theoretical constructs from the field of psychology. One of the best known of these is Self-Determination Theory (Deci & Ryan, 1985, 2002). This theory takes cognizance of individuals' desire to construct a self that is both integrated within itself and also with the environment and those within it. It thus deals with the concepts of intrinsic and extrinsic motivation. It further posits that human beings have particular basic psychological needs, labeled as autonomy, competence and relatedness, and that these are intricately related to the self-concept and by extension a learner's motivation (Deci & Ryan, 1985). Among those who have been greatly influenced by the ideas inherent in Self-Determination Theory is Kimberley Noels. Noels et al. (2000) began to apply Self-Determination Theory in an effort to identify L2 learners' orientations and how these potentially affected both their initial approach to language learning and the path they might follow in their learning. Noels sees Self-Determination Theory and its ideas of intrinsic and extrinsic motivation as useful predictors of individuals' attitudes towards and persistence in particular activities. She also sees in the fostering of the basic needs of autonomy, competence and relatedness a means of helping learners develop more intrinsic forms of L2 motivation. Through this, the learner's engagement in L2 learning, including 'effort (i.e., motivational intensity), persistence in learning, and willingness to communicate' (Noels, 2001: 60), can be enhanced.

Another researcher in the vanguard of recent theoretical developments in L2 motivation is Zoltán Dörnyei. In particular, Dörnyei (2009) has recently proposed the L2 Motivational Self System as a way of making sense of the complex relationship between motivation, the learner's concept of self and the learning context. Basing his ideas on possible selves (Markus & Nurius, 1986; Markus & Ruvolo, 1989) and Self-Discrepancy Theory (Higgins, 1987, 1996), Dörnyei identifies two aspects of the learner's self-concept, the Ideal L2 self and the Ought-to L2 self, the first corresponding to the person the learner personally aspires to be and the latter to the person the learner feels an obligation to become. Dörnyei postulates that a vivid conception of an Ideal L2 self can act as a powerful motivator in learning a language by providing a clear image for the learner to strive for. This in turn can act as a guide for the setting of intermediary goals. The Ought-to L2 self, on the other hand, is more to do with the vision others, be they teachers, family or society, have of the learner. Although these visions may not be closely related to the learner's ideal self-concept, they can have a considerable influence on the learner's motivation (Boyatzis & Akrivou, 2006), given the social, educational and familial obligations to which people have to conform.

Ushioda (2011a) offers modern global identity perspectives as a means of linking present experience and motivation to the future direction that motivation can take, the vehicle for this being possible future selves. Ushioda (2009: 215) further calls for a 'person-in-context relational view' of motivation. She argues that learners are individuals with unique identities, experiences and goals who interact with their context in unique and meaningful ways. Drawing on ideas from educational psychology (Brophy, 2009; Kaplan & Flum, 2009), Ushioda (2011b) claims that identity and L2 motivation are intricately linked and that for students to maximise their motivation and create genuine possible selves, their identities must be involved. She advocates the engagement of learners' 'transportable identities' and allowing them to 'speak as themselves' (Ushioda, 2011b: 17) in the target language. By so doing, not only will students be more motivated as they engage their real selves in genuine communication, but also they can formulate a more vivid image of themselves as users of the language (i.e. a possible future self). She further refers to Brophy (2009) and the crucial role of 'socialisers' (teachers, parents, peers) in the support and encouragement of healthy identities which 'can solidify and develop into core values and more long-term stable identities' (Ushioda, 2011b: 21).

Ushioda is not the only researcher working with the concept of identity in L2 motivation. Ryan and Mercer (2011) propose that the inability of a learner to construct an identity as an autonomous learner can have negative effects on motivation, effort and self-esteem. Lamb (2011) has added weight to the consideration of identity and autonomy in L2 motivation research. In a longitudinal study of a group of learners in Indonesia from 2002 to 2004, he found that the highly motivated learners were also those who exhibited the most autonomous learning behaviour, linking this to their ability to visualise a clear future self (Lamb, 2007).

With the increasing acceptance and use of theories from a variety of branches of psychology, research into L2 motivation has moved far beyond the original conception of integrativeness and has entered a phase characterised by 'a focus on the situated complexity of the L2 motivation process and its organic development in interaction with a multiplicity of internal, social and contextual factors' (Ushioda & Dörnyei, 2012: 398). Ideas related to the self and identity are crucially relevant to any enquiry into L2 motivation within this paradigm, and it is with this in mind that the present research study was developed. It sought to answer the following two questions:

(1) How important are learners' self-concepts in terms of their motivation to study an L2?
(2) What role do external factors play in their motivation?

The following section details the context in which the research took place, the development of the research method and the data collection and analysis procedures utilised.

Methods

The research context

The university where the research took place has an undergraduate population of some 25,000 spread throughout 19 colleges and 97 majors. There is quite an international presence with over 100 non-Korean academic staff as well as over 100 exchange students from various parts of the globe and almost 900 Chinese students. As in most universities in Korea, there is a considerable emphasis on English, with specified Test of English for International Communication (TOEIC) scores being a graduation requirement for many majors. Although the concentration on English varies according to the department, four departments (English, American Studies, European Studies and Hotel and Tourism Management) offer English conversation classes, while the International College conducts all classes solely in English. The Department of English Language and Literature is the single largest department in the university with over 600 students.

Data collection procedures

After a thorough survey of the literature in both L2 motivation and related psychological fields (e.g. Higgins, 1987; Markus & Nurius, 1986; Ryan & Deci, 2002), it was felt that a quantitative approach would not be effective in looking at L2 motivation in this context. Researchers such as Ushioda (2001) and Lafford (2007) have criticised the quantitative paradigm for its narrow focus on cause and effect in relation to motivation. In addition, according to Dörnyei and Ushioda (2011: 198), motivation 'is not stable but changes dramatically over time as a result of personal progress as well as multi-faceted interactions with environmental and other individual difference variables'. Furthermore, as Richards (2003: 11) points out, 'Qualitative research is multimethod in focus, involving an interpretive, naturalistic approach to its subject matter'. As such, it is eminently suited to the study of a phenomenon such as L2 motivation, which in many respects implies a longitudinal interpretive study.

Rather than approaching data collection with a preconceived set of concepts, the research sought to adopt a more grounded approach and 'to allow theory to develop from the data' (Richards, 2003: 17). As Lincoln and Guba (1985: 208) state, a research design that seeks to investigate a phenomenon in this way 'must be emergent rather than preordained'. The rationale for a longitudinal qualitative enquiry was thus clear. Given that the academic year in Korea runs from March to December, it seemed appropriate to use this as the timeline for data collection. Attempting to retain the participants over two consecutive years risked a higher level of attrition due to factors such as students taking time off or potentially securing employment. However, as the largest group of participants consisted of freshman students, recruitment of participants did not begin until April, thus giving them some time to adapt to university life and to overcome any potential reluctance to getting involved in the project. However, once participants were recruited, data collection began as soon as it was feasible. The project then ran from May 2012 until January 2013. The initial round of data collection (May 2012) involved focus group interviews with groups of between four and six students. These interviews were then followed by three rounds of individual interviews in September, November and December/January.

Research participants

Given the longitudinal nature of the research and to reduce the possibility of attrition, it was important that all participants were volunteers. As such, a series of class visits was conducted to recruit participants. This resulted in 41 students originally volunteering for the project: 21 freshmen, 11 sophomores and 9 juniors/seniors. Unfortunately, it proved extremely difficult to entice male students into the project, and only two sophomores actually volunteered. The other 39 original participants were female.

The participants predominantly came from English-related majors, with English Language and Literature (14), English Education (12), European Studies (5) and American Studies (4) comprising the majority. Although their language learning experience varied, with a low of six years and a high of 17, the average participant had been studying English for 11 years. Participants were also asked to self-report on their perceived level of English. Of those who responded, only one characterised himself as upper-intermediate, while 17 indicated that they were of intermediate level. Eight reported a level of lower-intermediate, with the same number choosing beginner. In addition, participants were asked to report any standardised test scores that they had achieved. Eighteen reported having taken the TOEIC, scores ranging from a low of 370 to a high of 900, with an average score of 695. Only two indicated having taken the Test of English as a Foreign Language (TOEFL), one scoring 55 and the other 107.

For a variety of reasons, eight of the participants (five freshmen and three juniors) dropped out of the project. However, 33 completed four interviews each between May 2012 and January 2013.

Interviews

Focus group interviews

Focus group interviews were conducted during the first phase of the project. These have the advantage of 'generating ideas to inform the development of [...] subsequent deep interviews' (Dörnyei, 2007: 146). In addition, it was felt that the group format was potentially a more secure and comfortable environment for the participants than a one-on-one interview. As Miller and Glassner (1997, cited in Richards, 2003: 88) point out, 'how interviewees respond to us [is] based on who we are – in their lives, as well as the social categories to which we belong, such as age, gender, class and race'. Participants were grouped according to age and, where possible, major, so that they would feel less inhibited in their responses and more comfortable expressing their personal ideas. In addition, they had the choice of speaking in either English or Korean. The interviews took place in May 2012.

In preparation for the interviews, six general categories were formulated which illustrated the participants' attitudes towards learning English and their conceptions of themselves as language learners. The categories chosen were language-learning experience, immediate environment, learning environment, attitude to English/English-speaking cultures, autonomy and identity and self. In each of these areas, several potential interview questions were then formulated which could promote genuine student responses. In formulating the questions, a variety of qualitative studies from L2 motivation research were consulted (Campbell & Storch, 2011; Gan et al., 2004; Ushioda, 2001). The following are examples of the questions that were used in the interviews.

(1) Please describe your language-learning experience up to now.
(2) Tell me about the people who are important/influential in your life.
(3) Do you ever lose interest in English? Can you tell me about something that made you lose interest in English?
(4) How do you feel about people who speak English/English-speaking cultures?
(5) How do you plan your learning? Do you feel you need guidance in what to study?
(6) What are your goals in English? How did you choose these goals?
(7) How important to you is succeeding in English? How do you define success?

Follow-up interviews

In September 2012, a second round of interviews was conducted. These interviews were conducted in a one-on-one format and allowed the researcher to more deeply investigate themes that had emerged in the first interviews. In preparation for these interviews, participant profiles were constructed based on the transcripts from the initial interviews. From these, a list of personalised questions was drawn up focusing on ideas that each participant had brought up. In addition, the transcripts were manually analysed for common themes. Among those themes emerging as potentially influential were the previous language-learning experience of the participants; the role played by significant others, be they parents, teachers or other students; the participants' goals and visions of themselves as future users of English; how they monitored their progress and how they felt speaking English to both Koreans and non-Koreans. On the strength of these emerging themes, common questions to supplement the questions for each individual were then developed. Examples of these included:

(1) Your teacher seems to have been quite important to you. Why is this?
(2) What are your goals in English this semester?
(3) Do you have a picture of yourself using English in the future?
(4) How do you assess your progress in English?
(5) You talked about wanting to be fluent in English. Why is this important to you? Why do you think this is necessary?
(6) How do you feel speaking English in front of other Koreans/ foreigners?

In November 2012, based on an analysis of the transcripts from the previous round, a third round of interviews was held. In preparation for this round, the questions were again refined, keeping a mixture of both individualised and common questions. The questions at this stage became more focused on identifying any changes in the participants' attitudes or behaviours and what may have caused these changes. As such, common questions asked included:

(1) Has your feeling about English changed this semester?
(2) What are your goals in English at the moment?
(3) Do you have many opportunities for communicating in English these days?
(4) How do you feel about your English classes this semester?
(5) Do you think your English has improved this semester?
(6) What will be your major use of English in the future?

In preparing questions such as these, care was taken to both refine the areas under investigation and differentiate the questions from those asked in the previous round of interviews. This was done in an attempt to avoid panel conditioning (Dörnyei, 2007) and to elicit the most genuine responses possible from the participants.

The final round of interviews took place in December 2012/January 2013, just after the end of the semester. Once again, the previous round of interviews was transcribed and analysed and both individual and common questions were prepared. Although the ideas investigated in this round of interviews were in many ways similar to those in the third round, once again questions were formulated in a slightly different fashion. Among the questions asked were:

(1) How would you describe this semester in terms of your English learning?
(2) Do you think you have changed as a person this semester?
(3) Who or what has influenced you in terms of learning English this semester?
(4) What is your main reason for studying English these days?
(5) In terms of your English proficiency, what do you think is important to focus on?
(6) Do you think that your attitude towards English has changed this semester? What has influenced this?
(7) What are your short-term/medium-term/long-term goals in English?

In total, the data collected amounted to approximately 70 hours of interviews.

Quality control and triangulation of the data

As Dörnyei (2007) points out, the face validity of any study will be enhanced when it can be demonstrated that the researcher has spent a considerable amount of time in the research context. At the time of data collection, the researcher had been living in Korea for 12 years and had worked at the university for 10. As such, it can be said with confidence that he had an intimate knowledge of the research context. In addition, the longitudinal nature of the project was a means of ensuring that the participants were actually behaving in a natural fashion and were not in some way modifying their behaviour due to the researcher's presence (Mackey & Gass, 2005).

The data collection procedures themselves also ensured the quality of data for analysis. The participants were given the choice of speaking in either English or Korean, and the same interpreter was present for all of the interviews. The interpreter had prior experience of conducting interviews in a doctorate-level research project. Each interview was recorded using multiple devices and later translated and transcribed by the same interpreter. These transcripts were then proofread and any issues arising from the translation were discussed. In an attempt to ensure the quality of the translations, opinions were sought from a variety of perspectives, heeding Davis (1995), who recommends consulting researchers from both within and outside the context under investigation, thus guarding against cultural biases from either perspective. As such, independent translations of a particular interview were made by two different translators and then compared by a Korean academic with considerable experience in the field. On the basis of this comparison and meetings with the primary translator, strategies were developed for dealing with issues such as vagueness of language, interpretation of interviewees' utterances versus faithfulness to the words spoken and the translation of Korean idioms. These strategies were then discussed with an expert in translation studies from outside the Korean context before completion of the transcription of the first round of interviews.

In coding the data and identifying common themes, the researcher enlisted the assistance of another academic from outside the Korean context. The same interview was coded by both researchers and codes were then compared. Any discrepancies in coding were then discussed and codes were agreed upon. The longitudinal nature of the project also made it possible to check interpretations with the participants themselves. Each follow-up interview included questions based on the answers received in the previous interview. This allowed the researcher to check not only the facts of the interview but also the participants' impressions of any interpretations made, what Lincoln and Guba (1985: 109) term 'member checks'.

Results

Throughout the course of the research, six general themes emerged. These relate to the participants' concept of self, goal-directed behaviour, monitoring of progress, the educational context, willingness to communicate and external factors. The following section will outline the findings in these areas.

Ideal vs. 'idyllic' self

One of the findings of the research relates to Dörnyei's (2009) concept of the Ideal L2 self. This implies a vision of oneself as a future user of a language and is theorised to promote goal-directed behaviour. However, many of the participants in this study display more of what might be termed an 'idyllic' self. As the term implies, these learners seem to have an almost utopian future view of themselves as users of English. However, rather than being a desire, this seems more of a wish or indeed wishful thinking. It seems that these learners do not actually see either a need for such a facility in English or indeed the possibility of achieving it. In describing their hopes for the future, many of the participants refer to a desire to 'speak English fluently' or to 'speak English like Korean'. However, when asked whether they have a distinct vision of themselves as future users of the language, many have difficulty in elaborating one. For example, one female freshman stated, 'I want to speak like that, but I'm not sure about the situation'. In addition, a considerable number of the participants have difficulty elaborating why such a level of proficiency is important to them or indeed necessary. A response such as the following by a female sophomore was not atypical: 'Because I studied for a long time. And I wanna get a job in other countries, and I think it is very important'. This lack of a clear future possible self seems linked to a general lack of clear goal-directed behaviour on the part of some participants. This finding in many ways echoes the findings of Williams and Burden (1999), who found a lack of learning strategies among some of their subjects despite professed self-involvement in their learning.

Goal-directed behaviour

In some cases, the participants did exhibit a clear sense of themselves as future users of English. An example of this is a freshman student who seems to have determined a clear future for herself as either a journalist or a translator. With this as her end goal, she has developed a series of intermediate goals. These include getting a high TOEIC score, becoming an exchange student, studying in a foreign university and gaining work experience abroad. This would seem to suggest the advantage of constructing a vivid future possible self.

Another example of this ability to construct a vivid possible self is a sophomore student who appears to have a quite definite sense of where he is going and what he will need English for. His professed goal is to attend graduate school abroad:

> I want to study abroad, so my view ... my vision for my English using English ... like reading English journals and writing English essays of journal and speak in English with other people about something scholaric [sic] fluently.

This vision seems to be quite vivid as he professes to being able to imagine and hear conversations with his future peers in English: 'I can't say the conversation now, but I can imagine "Blah, blah, blah," or something very difficult word or ... '. As the interviews progressed, it seemed that this vision was strengthened and became even more focused. He found a way to combine his major, English Education, with his interest in psychology and began to visualise himself in the role of an industrial psychologist. On the strength of this, he secured a place on an overseas experience programme during winter vacation 2012/13, his professed goal being to 'Visit many company, HP, Symantec, and other' and get some insight into human resources development and industrial psychology. The trip very much focused him on working on his communicative facility in English:

> I want to gain some information about graduate school in America. So, I have three or four time for meeting English ... some professors in university in US. So, I want to ask them how and what do I need to prepare for entering graduate school, and there, what kind of support do they have. Actually, it is the most important thing.

The ability of these two learners to create quite vivid future selves that are clearly linked to the use of English seems to have had a marked effect on their ability to formulate clear goals for themselves. By extension, the formulation of these goals seems to have facilitated the construction of relevant strategies directly linked to the achievement of these goals, a clear sign of genuinely motivated behaviour. This seems to suggest a clear link between L2 self-concept, goals and motivation.

Monitoring progress

An aspect of language learning that is intricately linked to goals is the monitoring of progress. Indeed, one could also claim that this speaks to the level of autonomy of the learners in question. Some of the participants seem to have developed quite clear monitoring strategies with the potential to provide positive and motivating feedback. The following are two examples:

> Last semester, I took Professor W's class. At that time, I understand her about 60%, but this semester I take another class with Professor W. Now, I think I understand her 80% so I feel get better. (Sophomore, female)

> When I speak English ... when I realised I don't hesitate when I speak English and I don't really afraid of making mistakes, because I know that I am better now because I am not afraid just speaking English and then I feel like yeah, I got better. (Senior, female)

Other students appear to have developed the ability to look at their long-term language progress and to assess this by reference to, for example, their ability to write effectively in English.

We have a course called Academic English. We're given writing assignments. The first time I was doing it, when I went through it, it looked like an elementary student wrote it ... the expressions that were used and all ... but I did 6-7 similar assignments. The topic was similar. I saved them on a USB drive at the time, and I went through them again recently. I was able to see that I was improving when I compared the first assignment to the second, and the second assignment to the third. Others may not be able to notice the difference, but in my perspective, the vocabulary I used changed, and the contents improved as well. I felt that I have improved by looking at that kind of thing. (Freshman, female)

Here, we have examples of learner strategies with the potential to produce not just the affective benefits of perceived improvement but also a focus on particular aspects of linguistic performance. This suggests that the participants in question have internalised their learning and become more autonomous learners. In addition, the ability to critique their performance can lead to motivated behaviour through the formation of clear learning goals.

For many of the participants in this sample, the most common means of monitoring progress in the language was test scores, especially TOEIC: 'English score [TOEIC] ... I can measure my English ability, and also I just use score as the measurement of my English ability' (Freshman, female). Not surprisingly, good performance had positive effects on the participants' attitude. However, poor scores, although somewhat disheartening, did not seem to have profoundly negative effects. Most participants attributed these scores to a lack of effort, rather than any lack of ability on their part ('I think the score is from my effort' Sophomore, male; 'When score goes down and my English speaking gets stuck, I think I don't study' Freshman, female). Even in situations where poor performance could not be ascribed to lack of effort, participants found other external factors to rationalise their grade. Most common among these was blaming the grading curve at the university ('I didn't get a good grade because of the relative evaluation system' Sophomore, female).

Another common means of monitoring progress was through an enhanced ability to understand English, often illustrated by the ability to watch US dramas without subtitles or to understand the content of English-medium classes ('I feel I have listening ability when I watch the dramas' Freshman, female). However, somewhat interestingly, only a small number of students made mention of monitoring their performance in communicative encounters. Although some participants made reference to perceived improvements in communicative ability ('While I said almost nothing and passed by when I met foreigners before, now I can say hello to them and do basic conversation' Junior, female), cultural understanding

('My first impression was that they are footloose and fancy free when I came across their media. However, I realised they are not that footloose and fancy free when I met foreigners personally' Freshman, female) and confidence ('I can get confidence and I learn more when I talk with native speakers in English' Senior, female), this was not typical of the majority.

Educational context

An overwhelming number of the participants refer to their middle and high school period in a negative sense. They speak of the unfulfilled desire they had for more communicative opportunities and the stress and anxiety they experienced in high school. It appears that the entire high school environment with its heavy focus on reading, grammar and test preparation has a pronounced negative effect on students' attitudes to English. More than one participant speaks in terms of hating English at this time, while others speak of an inability to see the relevance of what they had to study. According to one sophomore, the system 'brainwashes you ... we're just forced to go along with it ... without any sense of purpose ... I just didn't have a dream ... You find yourself frustrated and lost without any sense of motivation'.

On the other hand, a considerable number of participants speak much more positively about their experiences of learning English in university. Many of them refer to English classes being more 'fun' or 'relaxed'. They feel less pressure in studying the language as opposed to high school where 'I had a lot of stress because of mock exams. I did like English but I didn't want to take the exams many times' (Freshman, female). Others speak of their changing view of English in university. One female sophomore described the difference quite elegantly: 'Unlike the English in high school, which felt like decoding a password, in university, it feels more like English functions as a medium'. Perhaps most importantly, there is evidence to suggest that for at least some of the learners, university has for the first time given them the opportunity to follow their own interests, develop their own path and engage their own identities in their learning. A perfect example of this is the following freshman:

> In high school, I would just sit at the desk and be spoon-fed grammar and vocabulary. I memorised as a habit. I used to learn English because it was a compulsory subject, but after I came to university, I was allowed to study in my own way.

The clear dichotomy between the participants' views of their secondary and tertiary educational experiences strongly suggests the considerable influence that the educational context can have on a learner's self-concept and motivation.

Willingness to communicate

An interesting finding of the research has been the participants' attitudes to communicating with different interlocutors. Although they confess to a degree of anxiety when speaking to foreigners, the majority often feel far more intimidated speaking with or in front of other Koreans ('I squirm when I use English to Koreans' Sophomore, female). There is a belief that their speech and proficiency are being evaluated, and this has an especially negative effect when speaking with other learners who they perceive as being better or with Korean professors.

When I speak with English, they checked my corr … my mistake. And then, I'm … this is why I'm very anxious about speaking English because they check my mistake one, two, three in my sentence. They just … they don't do that but … just my thinking. So, this is very anxious to me. (Sophomore, female)

The effects of feelings such as this were perfectly illustrated by one participant who spoke of having a conversation with a previous foreign teacher of hers. However, once she noticed some Korean women observing her, she was unable to speak and quickly ended the conversation.

Among many of the participants, there is a genuine desire to have relationships with and experiences of English speakers and other cultures. Interactions with English speakers seem to have a wide variety of positive effects ranging from increased pride and self-esteem to a perceived improvement in communication skills and cross-cultural understanding ('getting lower anxiety is a big thing' Sophomore, male). Several of the students in the sample actively seek opportunities to interact with English speakers, taking advantage of the large number of exchange students on campus or frequenting spots where foreigners are known to congregate. However, a not insignificant number of students do not take advantage of such opportunities, despite a professed desire to do so. Although intimidation does seem to be a factor here, more commonly cited reasons include not knowing how to approach people from other countries, a lack of common topics, fear of being misunderstood and not wanting to offend the English speaker: 'When I speak to a foreigner, I think to myself if I say something wrong and if he or she doesn't understand what I'm saying' (Freshman, female).

External factors

A variety of external factors seem to be influential in the participants' attitudes towards English. Among the strongest of these is the social and institutional emphasis on the TOEIC. All the participants recognise the importance of this in terms of employment in Korea, although few of them view it as anything other than a pathway to employment. In addition, they are heavily influenced by the university's emphasis on the test. More than half spent considerable time devoting themselves to studying for this test both during the semester and vacation periods. However, it is clear that this focus on getting a good score does not seem to promote positive motivation or learning behaviours on the part of many of the participants. As previously mentioned, considerable numbers of them use the test as their own barometer of progress in English, while others are negatively influenced by having to focus on it. One senior student is a clear illustration of this:

> I succeed [in TOEIC], but I don't feel anything. I should have felt like 'I did it,' but no. Just I'm exhausted, and I have been lost. I forgot how did I study English. All I remembered about English is TOEIC.

It is also clear that significant others have a considerable influence on both the participants' decision to study English and how they choose to study. Many chose English-related majors on the advice of their teacher or through the intervention of parents ('... my parents wanted me to major English education so I came here. Actually what I wanted to is international trade and economics' Freshman, female). A considerable number of them are also still in contact with old teachers or mentors and regularly contact them for advice ('about studying, I depend on him most' Freshman, female). These individuals thus have a considerable effect on the participants' perceptions of language study and the direction they take in it.

Discussion

The findings to date suggest that the ability of a learner to create a vivid possible self is an important component in motivated, self-directed learning. The participants who exhibited such an ability were able to not only clearly describe their future visions of themselves but also seemed to be able to use these visions as the foundation of genuine goal-directed behaviour. This included the ability to identify specific areas on which to focus their learning and to formulate both short-term and medium-term goals based on these. This is in many ways consistent with Dörnyei's (2009) concept of the Ideal L2 self and the effect it can have on learners' behaviour. However, the evidence here also suggests that a professed desire to learn the language is only a small part of what constitutes an ideal self. 'Igniting the vision' (Dörnyei, 2009: 33) entails learners being able to visualise concrete reasons for learning the language and contexts in which they will later use the language. Without clear self-guides, the learner seems unlikely to exhibit motivated learning behaviours. Jeon (2010) has noted that difficulty visualising either situations where learners may need English or a specific, well-defined need for the language appears to feed into a lack of goal-directed behaviour on the part of many learners. This suggests the vital importance of helping them discover the personal relevance of their language learning.

The results also suggest that an important component of motivated, goal-directed learning is the ability to monitor one's progress towards a desired end state. Higgins (1996: 1063), in fact, refers to a 'monitored self' as one of the three components of his self digest, '... the idea that self-knowledge summarises information about oneself as an object in the world in order to serve self-regulatory functions'. It seems clear that the ability of learners to assess their progress towards a specific goal is an important component of them actually achieving that goal. A number of the participants in this study appear to have developed a range of strategies to aid them in this endeavour. These strategies provide them with information on how they are progressing towards the achievement of their goals and the specific aspects of their learning that are improving or are in need of attention. Not only is this important in terms of goal achievement but also the results show that it is closely tied to the participants' motivation and their developing self-concept. The ability of learners to detect specific instances of progress in their learning seems likely to lead to more motivated behaviour as well as indicating an increased level of autonomy.

On the other hand, ascriptions of progress or lack thereof to test scores seem unlikely to lead to purposeful changes in behaviour or focused learning. The motivational impacts of test scores seem to have been neither substantial nor long-lasting. In addition, a simple test score is unlikely to provide learners with the information necessary to enhance their learning. This reliance also seems to suggest a lack of autonomy and that such learners do not have a well-developed concept of themselves as L2 users. This may be related to what Yang and Kim (2011: 147) call 'a widespread utilitarian belief among Korean L2 learners that English is important for career development', leading to a major focus on achieving high test scores rather than monitoring their own development in the language. However, without a clear perception of a definite L2 self, it is difficult for a learner to formulate standards against which to measure his or her progress. In addition, the motivation to actually achieve personal progress in the language may also be affected. This is in some ways supported by the relatively small number of participants who reported monitoring their progress through communicative encounters. It would thus seem evident that there is an important link between an active L2 self-concept and motivated, autonomous behaviours.

The attributions of success and failure apparent in the data also have potential implications for the participants' concept of self and motivation. The results obtained here in many ways reflect Weiner's (1986, 2005) concept of Attribution Theory. The general ascription of successes and failures to degree of effort is positive in that it allows the learner to feel a level of control over his or her performance and does not necessarily, therefore, negatively affect the perceived competence of the learner. However, as Williams and Burden (1999: 200) point out, such ascriptions 'may not foster in learners an ability to make sense of their own language learning in the most helpful way'. By focusing purely on the level of performance on set tasks (generally tests), the participants may not be developing a useful or usable conception of themselves, a self-guide that could direct their learning and provide overt standards to aim for. Although the potential for expectancy of success may remain, without such a self-guide, the ability of the learner to pursue an autonomous path in his or her learning may be considerably restricted, with potentially negative effects for that learner's long-term language learning motivation.

One negative finding of the research was that the middle and high school experiences of these learners have a negative effect on their L2 self-concepts. The data clearly show an overwhelming desire on the part of many of the participants for communication. However, not only do the participants not seem to have received this but also their attitudes towards English seem to have been negatively affected. There seems to be a clear disjunction between what many parents and teachers focus on (reading and grammar) and what the students think they need. As Ushioda (2011b: 22) notes, 'classroom practices that promote autonomy are likely to contribute to socialising and consolidating adaptive values, identities and motivational trajectories'. However, in the absence of these, it seems highly unlikely that learners will be able to construct a sustainable L2 self-concept, retarding their ability to visualise themselves as users of the language and negatively impacting their motivation to learn the language. This also points out the importance of an 'individual's immediate social experiences' (Markus & Nurius, 1986: 954) in constructing a healthy L2 self-concept. As Ushioda (2001: 122) emphasises, these experiences have an ongoing effect on learners' beliefs about themselves and their learning, and these 'cognitions and beliefs then shape subsequent involvement in learning'.

Another finding with obvious classroom implications is the anxiety that many learners feel speaking in front of their peers, a finding in line with Edwards (2006) and Kang (2005). Although this anxiety is perhaps understandable in contexts where the interlocutors do not know each other well, the learners in this study suggested that a more important factor was their perception of the ability of their interlocutors and the belief that their English proficiency was being judged. This in turn suggests that the participants often evaluate themselves negatively in relation to their peers, which has obvious implications for their self-concept. Given that the majority of opportunities that Korean students have to use English are in the classroom, such beliefs are a clear impediment to their progress in the language and the construction of a positive L2 self-concept. This emphasises the vital importance of constructing an atmosphere of trust and safety within the language classroom. On the other hand, the difficulties that many learners seem to have in interactions with foreigners would seem to stem not so much from fear but rather a lack of understanding of how to interact with them. This suggests perhaps a re-emphasis on the teaching of cultural aspects of communication and the development of strategic competence.

It seems clear that external and social factors play a considerable role in the participants' concepts of language learning and indeed of themselves as language learners. The heavy emphasis on the TOEIC in Korean society is directly implicated in the type of language study that learners undertake. For some learners, especially those who seem to lack a clear L2 self-concept, the test appears to condition their learning behaviours. Booth (2012) has shown that the TOEIC has significant washback effects on how students study English, and it is clear from this study that the test occupies a considerable amount of the participants' focus and time. However, it seems that this focus is potentially retarding the development of an L2 self-concept in many of these learners. As demonstrated by one participant, her focus on the TOEIC seems to have prevented her from setting individual goals or formulating a vision of herself as a future user of English. In addition, some participants seem to use the test as their only real monitoring strategy. However, it is questionable whether the feedback that a simple test score provides can aid in the formulation of a useful L2 self-concept. In addition, the TOEIC, with its heavy emphasis on reading and listening comprehension, seems unlikely to provide the kind of feedback necessary for students to achieve a goal such as expressing themselves in English.

Significant others are also clearly influential both in the participants' choice of language study and the direction they take in it. This is undoubtedly important in that, as LaGuardia (2009: 93) shows, the influence of these 'relational partners ... informs one's self-concept, goals, and identity-related behaviors'. Looking at this from Dörnyei's (2009) perspective, we might conclude that such influences may lead to the development of more of an Ought-to L2 self. Although this can still lead to motivated behaviour, in the case of the participant mentioned earlier, the abandonment of her own dream in favour of her parents' desires led to quite a serious crisis within the student, so much so that she contemplated leaving the university. On the other hand, the support and advice of an old teacher seem to be key factors in sustaining and validating one participant's path in her language learning. As such, one can clearly see the potentially crucial role of those around the learner in developing and sustaining an L2 self-concept.

For learners to develop healthy L2 identities and a sense of autonomy, these external factors need to be balanced by personal self-awareness, goals and needs. To achieve this, learners need 'to engage with their future possible selves as proficient users of the language' (Ushioda 2011a: 206) and be able to visualise both the contexts in which they will use the language and the importance of doing so. Given the learning context of the learners in this study, teachers play a vital role in this process. The challenge, of course, is to find ways to help students formulate and achieve their visions within the societal and institutional constraints that are clearly in operation.

Conclusion

The research reported in this chapter has identified a number of important influences on the development of an L2 self-concept and its relationship to L2 motivation. In particular, there seems to be little doubt that the ability of a learner to formulate a definite future possible self has a direct influence on the path language learning takes and the learner's persistence along that path. In addition, a learner's willingness to communicate, both with fellow L2 learners in his or her own learning context and with English speakers from outside this context, is clearly affected by the learner's capacity to maintain his or her L2 self-concept in the face of perceived threats. This finding also has clear implications for classroom practice and the importance of nurturing and maintaining students' developing conceptions of themselves. The data also show that the self-concept indeed plays a crucial role in students' L2 motivation, and that it is clearly affected by students' learning contexts, significant others and societal norms.

While this chapter has focused more on the 'socio' than the 'dynamic', in terms of the characterisation of the present period of L2 motivation research by Ushioda and Dörnyei (2012), further analysis will shed light on the changing nature of motivation among this group of learners. In addition, ongoing data collection from a select group of the original participants will allow for more in-depth analyses and comparisons of the learners, both with themselves at different stages of their development and with other learners in, for example, different age groups. As such, it will add to what is as yet, unfortunately, a relatively small number of qualitative studies into the L2 self-concept and motivation. There is thus a clear need for similar studies to be undertaken in different contexts in order to fine-tune analyses and see if the findings presented here are replicated. Such studies would add greatly to our ability to both investigate and understand how L2 learners perceive themselves and their learning.

References

Booth, D. (2012) Exploring the washback of the TOEIC in South Korea: A sociocultural perspective on student test activity. PhD thesis, University of Auckland.

Boyatzis, R.E. and Akrivou, K. (2006) The ideal self as the driver of intentional change. *Journal of Management Development* 25 (7), 624–642.

Brophy, J. (2009) Connecting with the big picture. *Educational Psychologist* 44 (2), 147–157.

Campbell, E. and Storch, N. (2011) The changing face of motivation: A study of second language learners' motivation over time. *Australian Review of Applied Linguistics* 34 (2), 166–192.

Cantor, N., Markus, H., Niedenthal, P. and Nurius, P. (1986) On motivation and the self-concept. In R.M. Sorrentino and E.T. Higgins (eds) *Handbook of Motivation and Cognition. Foundations of Social Behavior* (pp. 96–121). New York, NY: The Guildford Press.

Crystal, D. (2003) *English as a Global Language*. Cambridge: Cambridge University Press.

Davis, K. (1995) Qualitative theory and methods in applied linguistics research. *TESOL Quarterly* 29 (3), 427–453.

Deci, E.L. and Ryan, R.M. (1985) *Intrinsic Motivation and Self-determination in Human Behavior*. New York, NY: Plenum.

Deci, E.L. and Ryan, R.M. (2002) *Handbook of Self-determination Research*. Rochester, NY: The University of Rochester Press.

Dörnyei, Z. (1994) Motivation and motivating in the foreign language classroom. *The Modern Language Journal* 78 (3), 273–284.

Dörnyei, Z. (2007) *Research Methods in Applied Linguistics*. Oxford: Oxford University Press.

Dörnyei, Z. (2009) The L2 motivational self system. In Z. Dörnyei and E. Ushioda (eds) *Motivation, Language Identity and the L2 Self* (pp. 9–42). Bristol: Multilingual Matters.

Dörnyei, Z. and Csizér, K. (2002) Some dynamics of language attitudes and motivation: Results of a longitudinal nationwide survey. *Applied Linguistics* 23, 421–462.

Dörnyei, Z. and Ottó, I. (1998) Motivation in action: A process model of L2 motivation. *Working Papers in Applied Linguistics* 4, 43–69.

Dörnyei, Z. and Ushioda, E. (2011) *Teaching and Researching Motivation* (2nd ed.). Harlow: Pearson Education Ltd.

Edwards, P.A. (2006) Willingness to communicate among Korean learners of English. PhD thesis, University of Nottingham.

Gan, Z., Humphreys, G. and Hamp-Lyons, L. (2004) Understanding successful and unsuccessful EFL students in Chinese universities. *The Modern Language Journal* 88 (2), 229–244.

Gardner, R.C. and Lambert, W.E. (1959) Motivational variables in second language acquisition. *Canadian Journal of Psychology* 13 (4), 266–272.

Gardner, R. C. and Lambert, W.E. (1972) *Attitudes and Motivation in Second Language Learning*. Rowley, MA: Newbury House.

Higgins, E.T. (1987) Self-discrepancy: A theory relating self and affect. *Psychological Review* 94 (3), 319–340.

Higgins, E.T. (1996) The "self-digest": Self-knowledge serving self-regulatory functions. *Journal of Personality and Social Psychology* 71 (6), 1062–1083.

Jeon, J. (2010) Issues for English tests and assessments: A view from Korea. In Y. Moon and B. Spolsky (eds) *Language Assessment in Asia: Local, Regional or Global?* (pp. 53–76). Seoul: Asia TEFL.

Kang, S.-J. (2005) Dynamic emergence of situational willingness to communicate in a second language. *System* 33 (2), 277–292.

Kaplan, A. and Flum, H. (2009) Motivation and identity: The relations of action and development in educational contexts – An introduction to the special issue. *Educational Psychologist* 44 (2), 73–77.

Lafford, B.A. (2007) Second language acquisition reconceptualized? The impact of Firth and Wagner (1997). *The Modern Language Journal* 91 (5 (Focus Issue)), 735–756.

La Guardia, J.G. (2009) Developing who I am: A self-determination theory approach to the establishment of healthy identities. *Educational Psychologist* 44 (2), 90–104.

Lamb, M. (2007) The impact of school on EFL learning motivation: An Indonesian case-study. *TESOL Quarterly* 41 (4), 757–780.

Lamb, M. (2011) Future selves, motivation and autonomy in long-term EFL learning trajectories. In G. Murray, X. Gao and T. Lamb (eds) *Identity, Motivation and Autonomy in Language Learning* (pp. 177–194). Bristol: Multilingual Matters.

Lincoln, Y.S. and Guba, E.G. (1985) *Naturalistic Enquiry*. Newbury Park, CA: Sage.

Mackey, A. and Gass, S.M. (2005) *Second Language Research. Methodology and Design*. New York, NY: Routledge.

Markus, H. and Nurius, P. (1986) Possible selves. *American Psychologist* 41 (9), 954–969.

Markus, H. and Ruvolo, A. (1989) Goal concepts in personality and social psychology. In L.A. Pervin (ed) *Possible Selves: Personalized Representations of Goals* (pp. 211–241). Hillsdale, NJ: Lawrence Erlbaum.

Miller, J. and Glassner, B. (1997) The "inside" and the "outside": Finding realities in interviews. In D. Silverman (ed) *Qualitative Research: Theory, Method and Practice* (pp. 99–112). London: Sage.

Noels, K. (2001) New orientations in language learning motivation: Towards a model of intrinsic, extrinsic, and integrative orientation and motivation. In Z. Dörnyei and R. Schmidt (eds) *Motivation and Second Language Acquisition* (pp. 43–68). Honolulu, HI: University of Hawaii Second Language Teaching and Curriculum Center.

Noels, K., Pelletier, L.G., Clément, R. and Vallerand, R.J. (2000) Why are you learning a second language? Motivational orientations and self-determination theory. *Language Learning* 50 (1), 57–85.

Oyserman, D., Bybee, D. and Terry, K. (2006) Possible selves and academic outcomes: How and when possible selves impel action. *Journal of Personality and Social Psychology* 91 (1), 188–204.

Richards, K. (2003) *Qualitative Inquiry in TESOL*. Basingstoke: Palgrave Macmillan.

Ryan, R.M. and Deci, E.L. (2002) Overview of self-determination theory: An organismic dialectical perspective. In E.L. Deci and R.M. Ryan (eds) *Handbook of Self-Determination Research* (pp. 3–36). Rochester, NY: University of Rochester Press.

Ryan, S. and Mercer, S. (2011) Natural talent, natural acquisition and abroad: Learner attributions of agency in language learning. In G. Murray, X. Gao and T. Lamb (eds) *Identity, Motivation and Autonomy in Language Learning* (pp. 160–176). Bristol: Multilingual Matters.

Ushioda, E. (1996) Developing a dynamic concept of L2 motivation. In T. Hickey and J. Williams (eds) *Language, Education and Society in a Changing World* (pp. 239–245). Clevedon: Multilingual Matters.

Ushioda, E. (1998) Effective motivational thinking: A cognitive theoretical approach to the study of language learning motivation. In E.A. Soler and V.C. Espurz (eds) *Current Issues in English Language Methodology* (pp. 77–89). Castelló de la Plana: Universitat Jaume I.

Ushioda, E. (2001) Language learning at university: Exploring the role of motivational thinking. In Z. Dörnyei and R. Schmidt (eds) *Motivation and Second Language*

Acquisition (pp. 93–125). Honolulu, HI: University of Hawaii Second Language Teaching and Curriculum Center.

Ushioda, E. (2009) A person-in-context relational view of emergent motivation, self and identity. In Z. Dörnyei and E. Ushioda (eds) *Motivation, Language Identity and the L2 Self* (pp. 215–228). Bristol: Multilingual Matters.

Ushioda, E. (2011a) Language learning motivation, self and identity: Current theoretical perspectives. *Computer Assisted Language Learning* 24 (3), 199–210.

Ushioda, E. (2011b) Motivating learners to speak as themselves. In G. Murray, X. Gao and T. Lamb (eds) *Identity, Motivation and Autonomy in Language Learning* (pp. 11–24). Bristol: Multilingual Matters.

Ushioda, E. and Dörnyei, Z. (2012) Motivation. In A. Mackey and S.M. Gass (eds) *The Routledge Handbook of Second Language Acquisition* (pp. 396–409). New York, NY: Routledge.

Weiner, B. (1986) Attributions, emotion, and action. In R.M. Sorrentino and E.T. Higgins (eds) *Handbook of Motivation and Cognition: Foundations of Social Behavior* (pp. 281–312). New York, NY: The Guildford Press.

Weiner, B. (2005) Motivation from an attribution perspective and the social psychology of perceived competence. In A.J. Elliot and C.S. Dweck (eds) *Handbook of Competence and Motivation* (pp. 73–104). New York, NY: The Guildford Press.

Williams, M. and Burden, R.L. (1997) *Psychology for Language Teachers*. Cambridge: Cambridge University Press.

Williams, M. and Burden, R.L. (1999) Students' developing conceptions of themselves as language learners. *The Modern Language Journal* 83 (2), 193–201.

Yang, J.-S. and Kim, T.-Y. (2011) The L2 motivational self system and perceptual learning styles of Chinese, Japanese, Korean, and Swedish students. *English Teaching* 66 (1), 141–162.

8 Culture, Autonomy and the Self in Language Learning

Kimberly A. Noels, Kathryn Everhart Chaffee, Megan Michalyk and Maya Sugita McEown

> *You can't walk alone. Many have given the illusion, but none have really walked alone. Man is not made that way. Each man is bedded in his people, their history, their culture, and their values.*
> Peter Abrahams, 1953, *Return to Goli*

Introduction

In recent years much second language acquisition (SLA) research on motivation has centred on the learning and use of English around the world. This focus has heightened researchers' and teachers' awareness of important language issues concerning globalisation, colonisation and immigration, and has contributed to the development of new conceptual frameworks in which the self and identity figure prominently (e.g. Block, 2007; Dörnyei, 2005; Norton, 2000). Although this research has been carried out internationally, there has been little discussion and less empirical examination of the role of culture in motivational processes. This lacuna is important to address, since many motivational models that are widely used were developed in Western countries, and their applicability across cultures is not certain.

This chapter explores this issue with particular attention to autonomy as it is defined by Self-Determination Theory (Deci & Ryan, 1985; Ryan & Deci, 2002). We begin with a definition of culture and its relation with communication. We then examine the link between autonomy and the self, particularly as it is described in Self-Determination Theory. We consider three ways in which autonomy has been construed to vary across cultures, and we argue that each of these approaches emphasises that autonomy's importance for motivated learning operates in concert with other fundamental needs, particularly a sense of competence and relatedness with significant others in the learners' social world.

Culture and Communication

There are numerous definitions of culture, each stressing different aspects of this complex concept (Baldwin *et al.*, 2006; Kroeber & Kluckhohn, 1952). For the present purpose, culture is defined as the systems of meaning (i.e. representations, beliefs, rituals, and other symbols and symbolic practices) that are 'shared' in two senses: first, they are co-constructed by interlocutors, and second, they become the conventions and mores that are more or less distributed among members of a social network (cf. Chiu & Hong, 2006). Although there are many kinds of meanings that can be shared, anthropologists, psychologists and others have focused on some aspects more than others, including notions of the self, values and cognitive styles (e.g. Hofstede, 2001; Markus & Kitayama, 1991; Nisbett, 2004).

Culture, then, is the intersubjective or normative 'web of belief' distributed among members of a social group. This definition does not suggest that all individuals within a given group (national or otherwise) share homogeneous meaning systems with impermeable boundaries between them. Some knowledge and/or practices may be more or less widely understood, endorsed, embodied and enacted among members of a social network, and this diversity is amplified by the fact that different subsystems (e.g. family, religion and education) intersect in different ways for each person in each social interaction. Moreover, a person may belong to multiple social networks with different meaning systems (e.g. multiple ethnocultural groups).

Furthermore, this conception does not suggest that cultural meaning systems are static and unchangeable. Psychologically, cultural understandings and practices can be construed as mental habits that are the default manner in which thought, emotion and action are framed (Bourdieu & Passeron, 1990). However, these normative, habitual frames of reference are not fixed, but rather are mindsets that can become salient in different situations and may be intentionally overridden (cf. Oyserman, 2011). Because each interaction involves the construction of common ground between individuals who each bring different assumptions, goals and interpretations to each interaction, culture is contextually and temporally dynamic. Although culture and psyche are mutually constituted (cf. Markus & Kitayama, 2010), shared cultural systems do not determine any individual person's thoughts, emotions or actions; neither do interlocutors have free will to construct completely idiosyncratic meanings with each new encounter. Propensities can be questioned or challenged, and accepted, resisted or stylised to suit, as human needs warrant.

Culture is intricately tied to communication. We define communication similarly to Carey (1992), such that it refers not simply to the transmission of information between sender and receiver (cf. Shannon & Weaver, 1949), but more fully as the symbolic practices whereby culture is created and maintained, transmitted and transformed. As stated above, culture derives from patterns of interactions between members of a group, and these patterns establish a common system of coding and decoding information about the world specific to those people. To the extent that these communicative interactions are repeated, a culture develops which is the 'sum of the consensuses of the individual communication patterns manifest by the way of life' (Kim, 1988: 46; see also Kim, 2008). Although meaning is also constructed through the communicative moves of paralinguistic and non-linguistic acts, language has a special status as a communicative and cognitive tool that is particularly well adapted to orienting interlocutors' attention to aspects of their shared physical and psychological worlds (cf. Tomasello, 2011). An implication of this assumption is that when new communication practices are adopted and a new communication system is acquired, as happens when one learns a new language, one potentially has access to a new meaning system (Kim, 1988, 2008; Kramsch, 2013).

Autonomy, Self-Determination and Motivation across Cultures

Within language learning research, autonomy has many definitions and its study has been informed by technical, social psychological, sociocultural and critical approaches (Benson, 1997; Oxford, 2003). Benson (2011: 58) offers a broad definition of autonomy, as 'the capacity to take control of one's own learning'. One theory in which autonomy plays a central role is Self-Determination Theory (Deci & Ryan, 1985; Ryan & Deci, 2002). This theory narrows the definition to 'being the perceived origin or source of one's own behavior, … [and] acting from interest and integrated values' (Ryan & Deci, 2002: 8). Although it is argued to be the key to motivated engagement, autonomy works in concert with two other fundamental needs: competence, which refers to 'feeling effective in one's ongoing interactions with the social environment and experiencing opportunities to exercise and express one's capacities' (Ryan & Deci, 2002: 7), and relatedness, which involves 'feeling connected to others, to caring for and being cared for by those others and to having a sense of belongingness both with other individuals and with one's community' (Ryan & Deci, 2002: 7). To the extent that these needs for autonomy, competence and relatedness are fulfilled, language learners could be expected to experience greater enjoyment and stimulation in learning and using the target language (TL), and would be likely to report that they are learning the language because they see it as personally important and possibly central to their sense of self (termed 'intrinsic motivation', 'identified regulation' and 'integrated regulation', respectively), rather than that they are learning the language because they feel situational circumstances or other persons are deciding and directing their involvement in language learning (termed 'external regulation' and 'introjected regulation', respectively). Greater self-determination is associated with better psychological well-being (Deci & Ryan, 2000), as well as a host of educationally relevant attitudes and behaviours, including more positive attitudes towards the learning situation, more engagement and persistence in learning, increased creativity and stronger academic success (see Noels, 2009, for a review of research on language learning).

The centrality of autonomy as a motivational construct seems appropriate when discussing motivation in Western societies, where individualism is a strongly held cultural value. However, it might be argued to be less important for motivation in other societies, notably Asian societies. According to cross-cultural psychologists (e.g. Hofstede, 2001; Triandis, 1995), people from Western societies tend to hold relatively individualistic values, which emphasise the importance of self-determination and achieving personal goals, along with independent self-construals, which involve a sense of oneself as autonomous and separate from the social context (Markus & Kitayama, 1991). In other cultures, particularly in East Asian nations, people purportedly emphasise more collectivistic values, which prioritise the harmony and structure of interpersonal and group relationships, along with interdependent self-construals, in which one's sense of self is construed as connected with others and the broader context. In a related vein, researchers have claimed that Western and East Asian cultures have different cognitive styles, such that Western cultures are more analytic and East Asian cultures are more holistic (Nisbett, 2004). These cognitive styles are linked to different educational ideologies. According to Tweed and Lehmann (2002; see also Kühnen et al., 2012), the Western Socratic educational tradition emphasises the questioning of knowledge (including one's own); the value of self-generated knowledge and the search for true knowledge, not just true belief. The East Asian Confucian educational tradition emphasises respect for teachers, effort and high fidelity in the mastery of course materials. Rather than being solely a search for truth, learning is linked to the moral and social development of a more virtuous person by dedicating oneself to the process of learning.

Consistent with these observed broad tendencies, several researchers have argued that the social and psychological dynamics of language learning and teaching in East Asian societies may be quite different from North America. Some argue that traditional East Asian pedagogical approaches that include teacher-focused instructional styles, form-focused content and exacting assessment criteria are detrimental to students' sense of competence and autonomy (e.g. Yang, 1998). Others argue that stressing autonomy in language education may be inappropriate in Asian contexts where social interconnectedness and respect for authority are emphasised (Farmer, 1994; Ho & Crookall, 1995; Jones, 1995; Riley, 1988). Still others suggest that autonomy may take different forms depending upon the cultural context (Littlewood, 1999).

Proactive and Reactive Autonomy: An Empirical Investigation

Several frameworks attempt to articulate how autonomy might differ qualitatively across cultures. Littlewood (1999) distinguishes between proactive and reactive autonomy. Proactive autonomy refers to an experience of autonomy in which the learner sets the direction of learning, regulates the activity and self-evaluates his/her progress independently of the teacher. The focus is on volition, choice and actions that affirm one's individuality and separateness from the group. In contrast, reactive autonomy refers to a form of autonomy in which the learner regulates their own learning once direction has been set by the teacher. Once this direction is articulated, learners are able to autonomously organise their resources to achieve the goals they choose from among those suggested by the teacher. Littlewood argues that language learners in Western contexts prefer teaching approaches that promote proactive autonomy, but East Asians prefer an approach that fosters reactive autonomy. He links these broad preferences to differences in self-construals, the value accorded to power differentials and ideologies regarding education, such that greater interdependence, greater regard for authority, and Confucian (vs. Socratic) approaches to education would predict greater preference for reactive autonomy, and the converse would predict proactive autonomy.

As a first step in examining whether there are ethnocultural group differences in preferences for these two forms of autonomy, we asked Euro-Canadian and Asian-Canadian students registered in university language classes to complete a questionnaire. Large-scale surveys point to the particularly strong value that Chinese immigrant families in North America place on education compared to non-Asian families (e.g. PEW Research Centre, 2013). These patterns complement findings from cross-cultural comparisons that show that families in East Asia conceptualise education differently than those in North America (e.g. Fryberg & Markus, 2007; Stevenson & Stigler, 1992). Thus, although participants in this study were educated in Canadian schools, we hypothesised that there would still be differences between groups on some education-relevant variables.

Method

The 63 Euro-Canadian students were registered primarily in European-language courses (85.4%; 7.9% in Asian-language courses); the 60 Asian-Canadian students were registered primarily in Asian-language courses (70%; 20% European-language/English classes). Chi-square tests showed that there were no differences between the groups in the distribution across gender (31.4% male), heritage language status (23.7% heritage language learners), nor the level of the language class (beginner: 77.1%; advanced: 17.9%). The results of t-tests indicated that the groups were of the same age ($M = 19.16$ years, SD = 1.82), had studied the language for an equal duration ($M = 24.61$ months) and expressed the same degree of TL competence in reading, writing, speaking and understanding ($M = 4.48$, SD = 1.17). Thus, the groups were similar on a number of dimensions other than ethnic background that might affect their feelings of self, autonomy and motivation.

The participants completed a questionnaire that assessed the aspects of cultural belief systems that Littlewood (1999) suggested predict differences in preferences for proactive and reactive autonomy. Drawing from Tweed (2000), various measures indexed students' endorsement of a Socratic learning approach, including public and private questioning, generating ideas, as well as a learning style that emphasises judging and evaluating things and ideas (i.e. Sternberg & Wagner's (1992) judicial thinking style). Another set of indices assessed aspects of a Confucian learning approach, including a preference for structured problems and 'getting things done' (i.e. Sternberg & Wagner's (1992) executive thinking style) and a pragmatic desire for structured knowledge (adapted from Wilkinson & Migotsky's (1994) naïve realism scale; see Table 8.1 for a summary of these indices). As well, the questionnaire indexed students' independent and interdependent self-construals (Leung & Kim, 1997), and beliefs regarding instructor authority (adapted from Earley & Erez, 1997). Lastly, we assessed motivational intensity (Gardner, 2010) and students' endorsement of external, introjected and identified regulation and intrinsic motivation. We weighted the scores for each type of regulation from −2 to +2, such that the summed score provided an index of how self-determined the students' motivational orientations were, such that negative scores indicated more controlled and positive scores indicated more autonomous motivational orientations (Ryan & Connell, 1989).

As well, we developed a nine-item instrument to assess proactive autonomy (e.g. 'In my second language class, I prefer setting my own goals for what I hope to accomplish') and reactive autonomy (e.g. 'In my second language class, I prefer to choose my goals for what I hope to accomplish from those that my teacher identifies as important') based on Holec's (1981) discussion of autonomy in setting learning objectives;

Table 8.1 Examples of instrument items and Cronbach alpha indices of internal consistency

Instrument	Number of items	Cronbach Alpha	Item example
Independent self-construal	15	.85	My personal identity independent of others is very important to me
Interdependent self-construal	14	.85	My relationships with others in my group are more important than my personal accomplishments
Acceptance of teacher authority	8	.71	In education-related matters, instructors have a right to expect obedience from their students
Desire to evaluate and compare ideas	8	.78	I like projects where I can study and rate different points of view or conflicting ideas
Generating ideas	5	.80	I try to invent my own theories relating to topics we study
Public questioning	4	.75	I've been known to publicly disagree with instructors
Private questioning	4	.65	I tend to be somewhat sceptical in my thinking regarding the material taught in textbooks
Desire for structured knowledge	3	.55	I prefer that teachers simply tell me the facts
Desire for structured tasks	7	.73	I like to follow clear rules and directions when doing a task
Motivational intensity	10	.77	I really work hard to learn my second language

determining the content, format and pace of learning activities; and evaluating progress and achievement (see Appendix). We also created an index of abdicated autonomy, which indicated the extent to which the student desired the teacher to take control over the learning process (e.g. 'In my second language class, I prefer for my teacher to determine the goals that I should try to accomplish'). Students indicated which of these three possibilities they preferred and a summed score for each form of autonomy was computed.

Results

Was there any evidence that self-construals, cognitive style and beliefs about instructor authority were interrelated in a 'web of beliefs'? As hypothesised, the more students reported independent self-construals, the more they endorsed public questioning of the instructor and a preference for comparing and evaluating ideas ($r = .28$ and $r = .20$, respectively, $p < .05$). Also consistent with expectations, the more students endorsed an interdependent self-construal, the more they endorsed a desire for structured knowledge and structured tasks ($r = .23$ and $r = .20$, respectively, $p < .05$), but also a preference for private questioning, comparing and evaluating ideas, and generating ideas ($r = .23$, $r = .23$, and $r = .36$, respectively, $p < .05$). Stronger endorsement of instructor authority in the classroom was also related to the desire for structured knowledge and structured tasks ($r = .23$ and $r = .22$, respectively, $p < .05$). Thus, with some exceptions, there is general support for the idea that different types of self-construals and power values relate to distinct cognitive styles, reflecting a system of cultural beliefs regarding self-construals, power hierarchies and cognitive styles.

Did these indicators of cultural belief systems differ across ethnic groups? A 2×2 mixed model ANOVA compared the Asian and Euro-Canadian groups (i.e. the between-subjects factor) on independent and interdependent self-construals (i.e. the within-subjects factor), and showed a significant interaction effect ($F(1,120) = 18.83$, $p < .01$, $\beta^2 = .14$). The results of post-hoc Tukey tests showed that both groups endorsed independent self-construals (Asian-Canadians: $M = 5.11$, SD = .72; Euro-Canadians: $M = 5.68$, SD = .71) more than interdependent self-construals (Asian-Canadians: $M = 4.52$, SD = .83; Euro-Canadians: $M = 4.26$, SD = .86), but the difference was larger for the Euro-Canadians such that they scored significantly higher on independent self-construals than did Asian-Canadians. Thus, consistent with expectations, Euro-Canadians more strongly endorsed independent relative to interdependent self-construals than did Asian-Canadians.

Further evidence of ethnic group differences came from a series of t-tests, which showed that the Asian-Canadian students scored significantly higher

Table 8.2 Means, standard deviations and t-values for cognitive and motivational values as a function of ethnic group

Variables	Ethnocultural Groups				t-value
	Asian-Canadian		Euro-Canadian		
	M	SD	M	SD	
Generating ideas	3.93	1.06	3.96	1.21	0.14
Desire to evaluate and compare ideas	4.13	0.77	4.22	0.84	0.59
Public questioning	3.12	1.21	3.29	1.29	0.78
Private questioning	3.63	1.06	3.47	1.12	0.80
Desire for structured knowledge	5.32	0.78	5.06	0.84	1.79[†]
Desire for structured tasks	4.49	1.10	4.00	1.10	2.59*
Acceptance of teacher authority	2.96	0.91	2.89	0.72	0.50
Self-determination index	0.42	3.60	2.23	4.02	2.61*
Motivational intensity	4.92	0.82	5.19	0.90	1.74[†]
Proactive autonomy	2.13	2.11	2.24	1.77	0.30
Reactive autonomy	4.42	2.06	4.92	1.73	1.47
Abdicated autonomy	2.45	2.00	1.84	1.64	1.85[†]

$*p < .05$; $^{†}p < .08$.

on the two indicators of Confucianist cognitive style including a preference for structured tasks and (marginally) structured knowledge than did the Euro-Canadian students (see Table 8.2). The Asian-Canadian students also scored lower on self-determination and marginally lower on motivational intensity than did their Euro-Canadian counterparts. There was no difference between groups on the Socratic indices, nor on their acceptance of teacher authority. Perhaps because both groups were enrolled in the Canadian secondary and post-secondary school system, they were similar in their endorsement of these Western educational norms and practices. The groups differed, therefore, only in terms of self-construals and the beliefs indexing Confucian learning approaches.

Our third question was whether there was a difference in the patterns of endorsement of the three autonomy categories as a function of participants' ethnocultural background. Based on Littlewood's (1999) discussion,

Table 8.3 Distribution of participants and adjusted standardised residuals as a function of autonomy form and ethnocultural group

Item number	Autonomy form	Ethnocultural group				Chi-squared (with 2 df)
		Asian-Canadian (N = 60)		Euro-Canadian (N = 63)		
		%	Adj. SR	%	Adj. SR	
1.	Proactive	43.3	0.4	39.7	-0.4	
	Reactive	36.7	-1.4	49.2	1.4	2.79
	Abdicated	20.0	1.4	11.1	-1.4	
2.	Proactive	43.3	1.0	34.9	-1.0	
	Reactive	31.7	-1.8	47.6	1.8	3.35
	Abdicated	25	1.0	17.5	-1.0	
3.	Proactive	25.0	0.0	25.4	0.1	
	Reactive	61.7	-0.6	66.7	0.6	0.97
	Abdicated	13.3	1.0	7.9	-1.0	
4.	Proactive	15.0	1.2	7.9	-1.2	
	Reactive	31.7	-0.7	38.1	0.7	1.71
	Abdicated	53.3	0.0	54.0	0.1	
5.	Proactive	10.0	-2.4	27.0	2.4	
	Reactive	26.7	0.0	27.0	0.0	6.43*
	Abdicated	63.3	1.9	46.0	-1.9	
6.	Proactive	13.3	-1.3	22.2	1.3	
	Reactive	53.3	-0.8	60.3	0.8	4.69
	Abdicated	33.3	2.0	17.5	-2.0	

(continued)

Table 8.3 Distribution of participants and adjusted standardised residuals as a function of autonomy form and ethnocultural group (*continued*)

Item number	Autonomy form	Ethnocultural group				Chi-squared (with 2 df)
		Asian-Canadian (N = 60)		Euro-Canadian (N = 63)		
		%	Adj. SR	%	Adj. SR	
7.	Proactive	20.0	0.1	19.0	-0.1	
	Reactive	65.0	-1.0	73.0	1.0	1.65
	Abdicated	15.0	1.2	7.9	-1.2	
8.	Proactive	30.0	0.0	30.2	0.0	
	Reactive	58.3	0.0	58.7	0.0	0.01
	Abdicated	11.7	0.1	11.1	0.0	
9.	Proactive	13.3	-0.6	17.5	0.6	
	Reactive	76.7	0.7	71.4	-0.7	0.49
	Abdicated	10.0	-0.2	11.1	0.2	

*$p < .05$; Adj. SR = adjusted standardised residual; df = degree of freedom

we hypothesised that there would be a difference between Euro- and Asian-Canadians in their endorsement of proactive and reactive autonomy, such that Euro-Canadians would more strongly endorse proactive autonomy than Asian-Canadians, and conversely Asian-Canadians would endorse reactive autonomy more than Euro-Canadians. The results of chi-squared analyses, however, showed that there were no differences in the distribution of student responses across cultural groups. As seen in Table 8.3 (see Appendix for items), both groups of students preferred to set goals by themselves or with the instructor's help (items 1–3); they preferred to choose content with the help of the teacher or have the teacher do it (items 4–6) and they preferred to work with the teacher to monitor their pace and assess their achievement (items 7–9). One exception concerned decisions about assignment topics, such that fewer Asian-Canadian students chose the proactive autonomy response and more

Euro-Canadian students chose the proactive autonomy item than would be expected by chance ($\chi^2(2) = 6.43$, $p = .04$; see item 5 in Table 8.3).

A second analysis approached this question from another angle. Summed scores for each autonomy score were computed and these were compared across the two groups using a 2×3 mixed model ANOVA, with group (Asian- vs. Euro-Canadian) as the between-subjects factor and autonomy form (proactive vs. reactive vs. abdicated autonomy) as the within-subjects factor. The results yielded neither an interaction effect between the group and the form of autonomy nor a main effect for the group; however, a main effect for autonomy form showed that both Euro- and Asian-Canadians preferred reactive autonomy to proactive and abdicated autonomy ($F(2,242) = 47.91$, $p < .001$; see Table 8.2). Moreover, reactive autonomy was marginally correlated with greater self-determination and more motivational intensity ($r = .15$, $p = .09$ and $r = .15$, $p = .09$, respectively) and abdicated autonomy was linked marginally to less motivational intensity ($r = -.16$, $p = .09$). Proactive autonomy was unrelated to either motivational index, indicating that reactive autonomy was the more motivating form of autonomy.

Discussion

We can draw two general conclusions from these findings. Consistent with the claims of Markus and Kitayama (1991) and Tweed and Lehman (2002), we can see that beliefs about the self and ideologies of education (to a lesser extent) differentiate ethnocultural groups, but inconsistent with the claims of Littlewood (1999) there is little evidence that the groups differ in their preferred forms of autonomy in the language classroom. There are certainly limitations to this small study, notably that both groups originate from Canada and have experience with the Canadian educational system, and so it is not surprising that there are relatively few differences between groups, particularly with regard to their teacher authority and Socratic beliefs. That said, it would seem that these Asian-Canadian students nonetheless hold beliefs about education based to some extent on Chinese cultural traditions, perhaps instilled by their parents. More substantial group differences due to differences in educational ideologies could possibly be evident in comparisons of students in China and other parts of the world, where there is likely to be less influence from Western cultural traditions.

Perhaps the more interesting, if somewhat counter-intuitive, finding was that both groups, regardless of their cultural background, preferred reactive to proactive autonomy. This contrasted with the expectation that North American students would prefer proactive autonomy, that is, the opportunity to set the goals, pace and evaluation in as independent a manner as possible. Instead, students from both backgrounds generally preferred to work collaboratively with their teacher across most aspects of the learning process. As reactive autonomy is framed in this study, the teacher is the 'expert' in the area, and so can offer constructive guidance, but the learner must follow through with the hard work of learning the material and acquiring the skills. Reactive autonomy would seem to have some motivational force, as evidenced by its positive (although weak) correlations with greater self-determined orientation and motivational intensity.

This finding that students prefer the guidance of the teacher in helping them to make decisions in their learning instead of complete independence is consistent with the observation that autonomy is not equivalent to independence (Chirkov et al., 2003). Moreover, it is also consistent with the observation that autonomy support does not only imply providing choices to students so that they can act according to their own wishes, but also providing informative instruction and feedback on their learning progress and establishing a secure, involved connection between teacher and student (Reeve et al., 2004). Stated otherwise, autonomy support does not function in isolation, but in concert with competence and relatedness-support.

Personal and Relational Autonomy

The importance of interconnectedness with others is highlighted in other frameworks that claim there are differences in the forms of autonomy across culture. For example, Yeh and Yang (2006; see also Yeh et al., 2007) maintain that individuating autonomy refers to an intrapersonal domain of individuation and volitional agency, and relating autonomy refers to an interpersonal domain of interdependence and volitional agency in accordance with the surrounding context and others participating in the interaction. Similarly, Rudy et al. (2007) differentiate between individual and inclusive autonomy, and report results showing that a sense of individual autonomous motivation is predictive of the well-being of European Canadians, but a sense of inclusive autonomous motivation (particularly relating to family members) is also predictive of well-being for Chinese Singaporeans. Gore and Cross (2006) have framed this distinction as one reflecting reasons for pursuing a task that relate to one's personal goals and reasons for pursuing a task that take into account close relationships. Both personal and relational reasons can be more or less autonomous, depending on the extent to which they are consistent with the person's choices and values. Gore and Cross found that both personal reasons and relational reasons that were autonomous predicted American students' effort and progress in achieving a variety of goals. They further maintain that people with stronger interdependent self-construals endorse more relationally autonomous reasons for their goals.

These perspectives emphasise that close relationships and social obligations are not necessarily opposed to individual preferences and wishes, particularly in collectivistic societies (Miller *et al.*, 2011). SDT claims that 'autonomy' refers to 'a sense of endorsement and initiation with regards to one's own behavior' (Deci & Ryan, 1991: 272). This definition does not imply that people must choose individualistic courses of action that are distinct from or run contrary to the expectations of others. Rather, persons may feel autonomous while meeting social expectations if they have internalised and identify with those expectations. Thus, it would be expected that in societies where interdependent self-construals are fostered, expectations from family and friends would be associated with better well-being. This hypothesis has been supported in comparisons of American and Indian participants (Gore & Cross, 2006; Miller *et al.*, 2011). In the context of language learning, then, it might be expected that relationally autonomous reasons (e.g. 'I am learning English because it is important to someone close to me') might be at least as important as personally autonomous reasons (e.g. 'I am learning English because I really believe it is an important goal to have') for predicting engagement and satisfaction in the language classroom, whereas controlled reasons of both kinds would undermine these behaviours and feelings (e.g. 'I am learning this language because I would feel guilty, ashamed or anxious if I did not' or 'I am learning English because I would let someone else down if I did not').

When considered in connection with the findings regarding reactive autonomy, these frameworks raise questions about how we should consider autonomy across cultural contexts. Is it of greater theoretical and applied value to frame cultural variations in terms of qualitatively different forms of autonomy, as these models do? Or should we assume that the two dimensions of autonomy and relatedness play greater or lesser roles depending upon the cultural group (cf. Bao & Lam, 2008; Hui *et al.*, 2011; Iyengar & Lepper, 1999)? The answer to this question could have important implications for how we understand culture, autonomy and the self, and also how we develop and deliver language courses in different cultural and educational contexts.

Primary and Secondary Control

The preceding discussion of forms of autonomy has the overarching premise that cultural groups differ in the emphasis placed on defining autonomy in terms of one's unique interests and in terms of one's interests that are consistent with important others in their social and educational ecologies, largely because differences in self-construals have different implications for how distinct the self is from construals of significant others. This perspective allows us to reconcile the universality of autonomy as fundamental to human motivation, as long as we simultaneously recognise the importance of relatedness. Another approach to understanding how culture is tied to the relation between autonomy and the self is to consider how people react to situations where their autonomy is constrained. According to Self-Determination Theory (Ryan & Deci, 2002), controlling forces in the environment that limit an individual's freedom of choice should hamper one's sense of autonomy and thereby decrease intrinsic motivation. Cross-cultural research indicates that North Americans are particularly sensitive to perceived constraints compared to members of other cultural groups. Factors like having a choice made for them by others, feelings of social obligation and even having to make a choice in front of a picture of eyes have been shown to decrease North Americans' sense of autonomy and reduce the motivational benefits they gain from having choices; for members of other cultures these conditions have a neutral or even a positive effect (Iyengar & Lepper, 1999; Miller et al., 2011; Na & Kitayama, 2011).

To understand how some people manage to maintain a sense of autonomy and well-being even in controlled environments, we consider a distinction that has been drawn between primary and secondary control strategies (Rothbaum et al., 1982). Through primary control, individuals achieve a sense of control through actions that influence the environment or the other people around them. Secondary control has been defined as a more internally targeted, accommodative strategy through which individuals achieve control by adjusting some aspect of themselves to better fit the environment. This can include adjusting their perspective on a situation to accept things as they are, termed 'positive reappraisals' (Morling & Evered, 2006: 282). To illustrate these strategies, consider the example of a student who is enrolled in a language class with an instructor who uses a teacher-centred, authoritarian style, including choosing the topics that will be discussed during conversation sessions. This student could engage in a primary control strategy by visiting the instructor's office hours to argue for more opportunities to do projects that reflect individual class members' interests, or she/he could use a secondary control strategy by deciding to look at this situation as an opportunity to learn new things that perhaps she/he might not have considered otherwise. Depending on the situation, either of these reactions could be adaptive, and she might even pursue both types of control at the same time.

The results of a study of 100 university students registered in various language classes show that students in authoritarian situations can effectively deal with pressure and control by adapting their own approach to the learning situation (Chaffee, Noels & Sugita McEown, in press). This study looked mainly at secondary control in terms of positive reappraisals (e.g. 'I find I usually learn something meaningful from a difficult situation in my [TL] studies'; four Likert-type items; Cronbach alpha = .62) (some items adapted from Wrosch, Heckhausen & Lachman, 2000). We assessed students' use of primary control strategies (e.g. 'When faced with a bad situation in my [TL] class, I do what I can to change it for the better'; five Likert-type items; Cronbach alpha = .79), and whether participants perceived their TL instructor to be relatively autonomy-supportive or controlling using 23 Likert-type items based on the Learning Climate Questionnaire (LCQ) (Williams et al., 1994) and Assor et al. (2002; e.g. 'I feel that my [TL] instructor provides me with choices and options'; 'My [TL] instructor tells me what to do all the time.'; Cronbach alpha = .90). We also measured students' motivational orientation along the SDT continuum (i.e. amotivation, external, introjected, identified and integrated regulation, and intrinsic motivation; adapted from mean Cronbach alpha = .81), anxiety using the TL in the classroom (adapted from Gardner, 1985); 10 Likert-type items, Cronbach alpha = .86), academic engagement (Salmela-Aro & Upadaya, 2012; three-item subscales measured energy; 'I am enthusiastic about my [TL] studies', absorption; 'Time flies when I am studying [the TL]', and dedication; 'I find my [TL] coursework full of meaning and purpose'; mean Cronbach alpha = .76).

The results of regression analyses showed that both primary control and secondary control were associated with high levels of academic engagement and self-determined motivational orientations, and low levels of amotivation and anxiety. Unlike primary control, however, secondary control also moderated the effect of a controlling instructor on many of these outcomes. As shown in Figure 8.1, for students low in secondary control, anxiety was high when the instructor was controlling but moderate when the instructor was autonomy-supportive. However, students high in secondary control experienced only moderate levels of anxiety regardless of the instructor's style. Students high in secondary control also had high intrinsic and self-determined extrinsic motivation when the teacher was controlling compared to students who did not use the internally targeted, secondary control strategy. It appears that a students' capacity to reappraise the learning situation positively does protect them against the negative, demotivating effects of a controlling teacher.

Secondary control, then, has an important effect on a range of affective and motivational factors that are important for language learning. It has been argued that secondary control may be an adaptive strategy in some collectivistic societies, including East Asian contexts, where social harmony and authority are valued (Ashman et al., 2006; Morling, 2000;

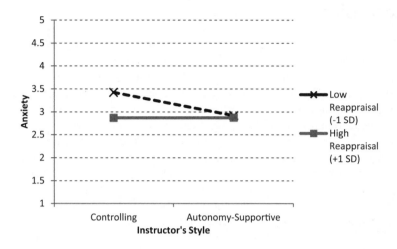

Figure 8.1 Interaction of secondary control and instructor's style on anxiety

Morling *et al.*, 2002; Weisz *et al.*, 1984). Morling and her colleagues (2002) found that situations that evoked stronger feelings of relatedness were linked to secondary control for Japanese, but less so for Americans, which suggests that East Asians maintain motivation especially well when using this form of control. Moreover, Rothbaum and his colleagues (1982) argue that there may be other ways to assert secondary control, including illusory secondary control, predictive secondary control and vicarious secondary control. Although Chaffee, Noels and Sugita McEown (in press) found that vicarious and predictive secondary control were not particularly helpful to Canadian students, these other aspects of secondary control may be associated with positive outcomes outside North America if these strategies are encouraged and positively viewed. For instance, North American students are often encouraged to 'aim high', so it is easy to see why exerting control by lowering one's aspirations (i.e. predictive secondary control) might not be an effective motivational strategy. However, if revising one's goals or expectations is viewed as realistic rather than unambitious, this control strategy might be adaptive. Similarly, in East Asia, where interdependence and collectivism are emphasised, we speculate that vicarious secondary control (i.e. through associating with others) may be more effective than it would be in Canada. We are currently conducting a study to examine these possible cultural differences in Canada and Japan (see Chaffee, Noels, Sugita McEown, Mizumoto & Takeuchi, in preparation).

Conclusion

In this chapter, we examined the relation between autonomy and the self, and considered how culture might be implicated in this relation. We feel that a valuable perspective is one which incorporates Deci and Ryan's (2000) claim that autonomy works in concert with other fundamental needs to sustain motivated action and bring about well-being and other positive outcomes in the learning environment. Regardless of the cultural context, the needs for autonomy, relatedness and competence are intertwined, and it remains for researchers to sort out how these needs are fulfilled in different contexts. The research reported here suggests that promising avenues include examinations of different conceptualisations of autonomy as more personally and relationally oriented, as well as potential moderating factors such as secondary control.

We think it is important for future research in this area to take a dialectical perspective, such that the person and the social ecology are viewed as an interactive phenomenon. Consistent with sociocultural scholars (e.g. Lantolf & Pavlenko, 2001; Norton & Toohey, 2004), agency and autonomy are not simply characteristics of a person, but rather a relational phenomenon that is subject to the constraints and affordances of one's sociocultural and physical worlds. We maintain that the shared ideologies related to notions of the self, power relations, cognitive styles and many other cultural beliefs interact with motivational processes within and outside the classroom.

We have shown that there are empirical grounds for construing culture as a web of meaning, including relations between the ways in which the self is construed, acceptance of power relations and ideologies regarding education, and such a web might meaningfully differentiate groups with different ethnic backgrounds. This set of beliefs is only one aspect of our definition of culture, and a more complete analysis of the relation between culture, the self and language learning must focus on communicative practices as they relate to culture. We need to examine the intersubjective construction and distribution of beliefs and practices throughout a given group, as well as the manner through which these shared beliefs are internalised, stylised and resisted. For instance, work in conversation analyses demonstrates how beliefs are constructed and shared (cf. Kramsch, 2011), and we need to further investigate how teachers, classmates, family members, members of the TL community and others communicate with learners in a manner that facilitates or undermines the internalisation of the language (and relevant sociocommunicative representations and practices), and the emergence of a sense of self that incorporates a sense of ownership of that language. We also need to better understand how sociocultural meanings become distributed throughout a classroom, a school, a community and even broader social networks and communities, such that they become the normative, intersubjective 'reality' that forms the common ground for that group's members. Given the current international interest in language learning, as a field we are well poised to contribute substantially to understanding these and other issues concerning culture, autonomy and the self.

Authors' Note

The authors would like to thank Kristie Saumure for her help with various aspects of the research reported in this chapter, and Shadi Mehrabi for her editorial assistance. The authors would also like to acknowledge that funding for the research reported in this chapter was provided by a standard research grant from the Social Sciences and Humanities Research Council of Canada to the first author.

References

Abrahams, P. (1953) *Return to Goli*. London: Faber and Faber.

Ashman, O., Shiomura, K. and Levy, B.R. (2006) Influence of culture and age on control beliefs: The missing link of interdependence. *The International Journal of Aging and Human Development* 62 (2), 143–157.

Assor, A., Kaplan, H. and Roth, G. (2002) Choice is good, but relevance is excellent: Autonomy-enhancing and suppressing teacher behaviours predicting students' engagement in schoolwork. *British Journal of Educational Psychology* 72 (2), 261–278.

Baldwin, J.R., Faulkner, S.L., Hecht, M.L. and Lindsley, S.L. (eds) (2006) *Redefining Culture: Perspectives across the Disciplines*. Mahwah, NJ: Lawrence Erlbaum.

Bao, X.-H. and Lam, S.-F. (2008) Who makes the choice? Rethinking the role of autonomy and relatedness in Chinese children's motivation. *Child Development* 79 (2), 269–283.

Benson, P. (1997) The philosophy and politics of learner autonomy. In P. Benson and P. Voller (eds) *Autonomy and Independence in Language Learning*. London: Longman.

Benson, P. (2011) *Teaching and Researching Autonomy in Language Learning*. Harlow: Pearson Education.

Block, D. (2007) *Second Language Identities*. London: Continuum.

Bourdieu, P. and Passeron, J.C. (1990) *Reproduction in Education, Society and Culture*. London: Sage.

Carey, J. (1992) *Communication as Culture: Essays on Media and Society*. New York, NY: Routledge.

Chaffee, K.E., Noels, K.A. and Sugita McEown, M. (in press) Learning from authoritarian teachers: Controlling the situation or controlling yourself can sustain motivation. *Studies in Second Language Learning and Teaching*.

Chaffee, K.E., Noels, K.A., Sugita McEown, M., Mizumoto, A. and Takeuchi, O. (2014) Motivation and primary and secondary control: A cross-cultural comparison. Unpublished manuscript, University of Alberta.

Chirkov, V., Ryan, R.M., Kim, Y. and Kaplan, U. (2003) Differentiating autonomy from individualism and independence: A self-determination theory perspective on internalization of cultural orientations and well-being. *Journal of Personality and Social Psychology* 84 (1), 97–110.

Chiu, C.Y. and Hong, Y.Y. (2006) *Social Psychology of Culture*. New York, NY: Psychology Press.

Deci, E.L. and Ryan, R.M. (1985) *Intrinsic Motivation and Self-determination in Human Behavior*. New York, NY: Plenum.

Deci, E.L. and Ryan, R.M. (1991) A motivational approach to self: Integration in personality. In R. Dienstbier (ed.) *Nebraska Symposium on Motivation: Perspectives on Motivation*, Vol. 38 (pp. 237–288). Lincoln, NE: University of Nebraska Press.

Deci, E.L. and Ryan, R.M. (2000) The "what" and "why" of goal pursuits: Human needs and self-determination of behavior. *Psychological Inquiry* 11 (4), 227–268.

Dörnyei, Z. (2005) *The Psychology of the Language Learner*. Mahwah, NJ: Lawrence Erlbaum.

Earley, P.C. and Erez, M. (1997) *The Transplanted Executive*. New York, NY: Oxford University Press.

Farmer, R. (1994) The limits of learner independence in Hong Kong. In D. Gardner and L. Miller (eds) *Directions in Self-access Language Learning*. Hong Kong: Hong Kong University Press.

Fryberg, S.A. and Markus, H.R. (2007) Cultural models of education in American Indian, Asian American and European American contexts. *Social Psychology of Education* 10 (2), 213–246.

Gardner, R.C. (1985) *Social Psychology and Second Language Learning: The Role of Attitudes and Motivation*. London: Edward Arnold.

Gardner, R.C. (2010) *Motivation and Second Language Aquisition*. New York, NY: Peter Lang.

Gore, J.S. and Cross, S.E. (2006) Pursing goals for us: Relationally autonomous reasons in long-term goal pursuit. *Journal of Personality and Social Psychology* 90 (5), 848–861.

Ho, J. and Crookall, D. (1995) *Breaking with Chinese cultural traditions: Learner autonomy in English language teaching*. System 23 (2), 235–243.

Hofstede, G. (2001) *Culture's Consequences: Comparing Values, Behaviors, Institutions, and Organizations Across Nations*. Thousand Oaks, CA: Sage.

Holec, H. (1981) *Autonomy in Foreign Language Learning*. Oxford: Pergamon.

Hui, E.K.P., Sun, R.C.F., Chow, S.S.-Y and Chu, M.T.-T. (2011) Explaining Chinese students' academic motivation: Filial piety and self-determination. *Educational Psychology: An International Journal of Experimental Educational Psychology* 31 (3), 377–392.

Iyengar, S.S. and Lepper, M.R. (1999) Rethinking the value of choice: A cultural perspective on intrinsic motivation. *Journal of Personality and Social Psychology* 76 (3), 349–366.

Jones, J.F. (1995) Self-access and culture: Retreating from autonomy. *ELT Journal* 49 (3), 228–234.

Kim, Y.Y. (1988) *Communication and Cross-cultural Adaptation*. Clevedon: Multilingual Matters.

Kim, Y.Y. (2008) Intercultural personhood: Globalization and a way of being. *International Journal of Intercultural Relations* 32 (4), 359–368.

Kramsch, C. (2011) Language and culture. In J. Simpson (ed.) *Routledge Handbook of Applied Linguistics* (pp. 305–317). New York, NY: Routledge.

Kramsch, C. (2013) Culture in foreign language teaching. *Iranian Journal of Language Teaching Research* 1, 57–78.

Kroeber, A.L. and Kluckhohn, C. (1952) *Culture: A Critical Review of Concepts and Definitions*. Cambridge, MA: Peabody Museum.

Kühnen, U., van Egmond, M.C., Haber, F., Kuschel, S. Özelsel, A., Rossi, A.L. and Spivak, Y. (2012) Challenge me! Communicating in multicultural classrooms. *Social Psychology of Education* 15 (1), 59–76.

Lantolf, J.P. and Pavlenko, A. (2001) (S)econd (L)anguage (A)ctivity theory: Understanding second language learners as people. In M. Breen (ed.) *Learner Contributions to Language Learning: New Directions in Research* (pp. 141–158). Harlow: Longman-Pearson.

Leung, T. and Kim, M.S. (1997) A Revised Self-construal Scale. Unpublished manuscript. Honolulu, HI: University of Hawaii at Manoa.

Littlewood, W. (1999) Defining and developing autonomy in East Asian contexts. *Applied Linguistics* 20 (1), 71–94.

Markus, H.R. and Kitayama, S. (1991) Culture and the self: Implications for cognition, emotion, and motivation. *Psychological Review* 98 (2), 224–253.

Markus, H.R. and Kitayama, S. (2010) Cultures and selves: A cycle of mutual constitution. *Perspectives on Psychological Science* 5 (4), 420–430.

Miller, J.G., Das, R. and Chakravarthy, S. (2011) Culture and the role of choice in agency. *Journal of Personality and Social Psychology* 101 (1), 46–61.

Morling, B. (2000) "Taking" an aerobics class in the U.S. versus "entering" an aerobics class in Japan: Primary and secondary control in a fitness context. *Asian Journal of Social Psychology* 3 (1), 73–85.

Morling, B. and Evered, S. (2006) Secondary control reviewed and defined. *Psychological bulletin* 132 (2), 269–296.

Morling, B., Kitayama, S. and Miyamoto, Y. (2002) Cultural practices emphasize influence in the United States and adjustment in Japan. *Personality and Social Psychology Bulletin* 28 (3), 311–323.

Na, J. and Kitayama, S. (2011) Trait-based person perception is culture-specific: Behavioral and neural evidence. *Psychological Science* 22 (8), 1025–1032.

Nisbett, R. (2004) *The Geography of Thought: How Asians and Westerners Think Differently and Why.* New York, NY: Free Press.

Noels, K.A. (2009) Identity and the internalization of language learning into the self-concept. In Z. Dörnyei and E. Ushioda (eds) *Motivation, Language Identity and the L2 Self.* (pp. 295–313). Bristol: Multilingual Matters.

Norton, B. (2000) *Identity and Language Learning: Gender, Ethnicity and Educational Change.* Harlow, UK: Longman/Pearson Education.

Norton, B. and Toohey, K. (eds) (2004) *Critical Pedagogies and Language Learning.* Stuttgart: Ernst Klett Sprachen.

Oxford, R.L. (2003) Toward a more systematic model of L2 learner autonomy. In D. Palfreyman and R.C. Smith (eds) *Learner Autonomy across Cultures: Language Education Perspectives* (pp. 75–91). New York, NY: Palgrave MacMillan.

Oyserman, D. (2011) Culture as situated cognition: Cultural mindsets, cultural fluency, and meaning making. *European Review of Social Psychology* 22 (1), 164–214.

PEW Research Centre (2013) *Second Generation Americans: A Portrait of the Adult Children of Immigrants.* Washington, DC: Pew Research Centre. See http://www.pewsocialtrends.org/files/2013/02/FINAL_immigrant_generations_report_2-7-13.pdf (accessed May 2013).

Reeve, J., Deci, E.L. and Ryan, R.M. (2004) Self-determination theory: A dialectical framework for understanding sociocultural influences on student motivation. In D. M. McInerney and S. Van Etten (eds) *Big Theories Revisited: Volume 4: Sociocultural Influences on Motivation and Learning* (pp. 31–60). Greenwich, CT: Information Age Publishing.

Riley, P. (1988) The ethnography of autonomy. In A. Brookes and P. Grundy (eds) *Individualization and Autonomy in Language Learning* (pp. 12–34). London: Modern English Publications and British Council.

Rothbaum, F., Weisz, J.R. and Snyder, S.S. (1982) Changing the world and changing the self: A two process model of perceived control. *Journal of Personality and Social Psychology* 42 (1), 5–37.

Rudy, D., Sheldon, K.M., Awong, T. and Tan, H.H. (2007) Autonomy, culture, and well-being: The benefits of inclusive autonomy. *Journal of Research in Personality* 41 (5), 983–1007.

Ryan, R.M. and Connell, J.P. (1989) Perceived locus of causality and internalization: Examining reasons for acting in two domains. *Journal of Personality and Social Psychology* 57 (5), 749–761.

Ryan, R.M. and Deci, E.L. (2002) Overview of Self-Determination Theory: An organismic dialectical perspective. In E.L. Deci and R.M. Ryan's (eds) *Handbook of Self-Determination Theory* (pp. 3–33). Rochester, NY: University of Rochester Press.

Salmela-Aro, K. and Upadaya, K. (2012) The schoolwork engagement inventory: Energy, dedication, and absorption. *European Journal of Psychological Assessment* 20, 60–67.

Shannon, C.E. and Weaver, W. (1949) *The Mathematical Theory of Communication*. Urbana, IL: University of Illinois Press.

Sternberg, R.J. and Wagner, R.K. (1992) Thinking Styles Inventory. Unpublished test, Yale University.

Stevenson, H.W. and Stigler, J.W. (1992) *The Learning Gap: Why our Schools are Failing and what we can Learn from Japanese and Chinese Education*. New York, NY: Summit Books.

Tomasello, M. (2011) Human culture in evolutionary perspective. In M. Gelfand, Y.-Y. Hong and C.Y. Chiu (eds) *Advances in Cultural Psychology* (pp. 5–51). Oxford: Oxford University Press.

Triandis, H.C. (1995) *Individualism and Collectivism*. Boulder, CO: Westview.

Tweed, R.G. (2000) Learning considered within a cultural context: Confucian and Socratic approaches. Unpublished dissertation. Vancouver, BC: University of British Columbia.

Tweed, R.G. and Lehman, D.R. (2002) Learning considered within a cultural context: Confucian and Socratic approaches. *American Psychologist* 57 (2), 89–99.

Weisz, J.R., Rothbaum, F.M. and Blackburn, T.C. (1984) Standing out and standing in: The psychology of control in America and Japan. *American Psychologist* 39 (9), 955–969.

Wilkinson, W.K. and Migotsky, C.P. (1994) A factor analytic study of epistemological style inventories. *The Journal of Psychology* 128 (5), 499–516.

Williams, G.C., Wiener, M.W., Markakis, K.M., Reeve, J. and Deci, E.L. (1994) Medical student motivation for internal medicine. *Journal of General Internal Medicine* 9 (6), 327–333.

Wrosch, C., Heckhausen, J. and Lachman, M.E. (2000) Primary and secondary control strategies for managing health and financial stress across adulthood. *Psychology and Aging* 15 (3), 387–399.

Yang, N.D. (1998) Exploring a new role for teachers: Promoting learner autonomy. *System* 26 (1), 127–135.

Yeh, K.H. and Yang, Y.J. (2006) Construct validation of individuating and relating autonomy orientations in culturally Chinese adolescents. *Asian Journal of Social Psychology* 9 (2), 148–160.

Yeh, K.H., Liu, Y.L., Huang, H.S. and Yang, Y.J. (2007) Individuating and relating autonomy in culturally Chinese adolescents. In J. Liu, C. Ward, A. Bernardo, M. Karasawa and R. Fischer (eds) *Casting the Individual in Societal and Cultural Contexts* (pp. 123–146). Korea: Kyoyook-Kwahak-Sa Publishing.

Appendix

Items to assess proactive, reactive and abdicated autonomy

Note: In each set of items, the first option indexes proactive autonomy, the second indexes reactive autonomy and the third indexes abdicated autonomy.

(1) In my second language class, I prefer:
   - (a) setting my own goals for what I hope to accomplish.
   - (b) to choose my goals for what I hope to accomplish from those that my teacher identifies as important.
   - (c) for my teacher to determine the goals that I should try to accomplish.

(2) In my second language class, I prefer
   - (a) to have specific goals in mind for what I want to learn.
   - (b) to develop my goals for what I want to learn with my teachers.
   - (c) for my teacher to provide me with goals.

(3) In my second language class, I prefer
   - (a) to not rely on anyone to provide me with goals for what I want to accomplish in my second language class.
   - (b) to create my own goals once my teacher has provided examples of several goals for the class.
   - (c) for my teacher to identify goals for what I want to accomplish.

(4) In my second language class, I prefer
   - (a) to be able to choose the order in which I learn new concepts.
   - (b) to work with my language teacher to select the order in which new concepts are presented.
   - (c) for my language teacher to choose the order in which new concepts are presented.

(5) In my second language class, I prefer
   - (a) to create an assignment that I can tailor to my own interests.
   - (b) to work with my teacher in deciding the topics of assignments.
   - (c) to complete an assignment created by my teacher.

(6) In my second language class, I prefer
   - (a) assignments where I decide the form and topic by myself (e.g. a poster of a country's traditional dances).

(b) having options to choose from when deciding the form and topic of an assignment (e.g. a poster of a country's traditional dances or a video presentation of the same topic).

(c) assignments that are clearly planned out by my teachers.

(7) In my second language class, I prefer

(a) to be the one to monitor my progress.

(b) to work with my teacher in monitoring my progress.

(c) for my teacher to be completely responsible for monitoring my progress.

(8) In my second language class, I prefer

(a) to rely on myself to determine whether or not I am keeping pace.

(b) to take into account both my teacher's opinion and my own in determining whether or not I am keeping pace.

(c) to rely on my teacher to inform me of whether or not I am keeping pace.

(9) In my second language class, I prefer

(a) to decide for myself if I have performed well.

(b) to use feedback I have received from my teacher to decide if I have performed well.

(c) to wait to know how well I have performed until my teacher tells me.

9 Investigating Adult Migrant ESL Learners' Language Learning Motivational Profile in Australia: Towards a Bicultural Identity

Elke Stracke, Jeremy Jones
and Nicolette Bramley

Introduction

'I want to go anywhere [...] just myself for example hospital and bank'. So says Jihye, a young Korean migrant to Australia and a participant in the study from which the research in this chapter draws its data. Her words illustrate the gulf that adult migrant English as a Second Language (ESL) learners feel between their competence now and in the imagined future, between their actual self and their ideal self (Dörnyei, 2005). The broad topic of the present chapter is this gulf, and in particular the self-perception of these ESL migrant learners in Australia as they seek to realise their Ideal second language (L2) selves. Since the Ideal L2 self is a potent factor in improving one's language competence, the study thus illuminates the motivational profile of these learners.

A great deal of research has been conducted on motivation in language learning, and since Dörnyei and his colleagues introduced the concept of the Ideal L2 self (Csizér & Dörnyei, 2005; Dörnyei, 2005), the quantum of research on this dimension of motivation has steadily grown. However, the focus of studies on the L2 self has to date largely been in English as a Foreign Language (EFL) contexts, where students are usually learning a foreign language in their home countries. The present study shifts the focus to the ESL environment in which adult migrants live in an English-speaking community, intend to spend the rest of their lives there and as a result need the language for employment, educational and social purposes.

One strong characteristic of the research participants that we have had to accommodate is the fact that they are all in transition from one culture and language to another. They are not settled. In the case of some participants who came as refugees, the transition has taken place against a background of trauma. But all of them are struggling between languages and cultures – with greater or lesser degrees of success. The vast majority do not shed their original identity, yet they seek a new and additional layer of identity in the new country. Following Hornberger and Wang (2008: 6), we take an 'ecological perspective [...] and use the terms self-concept or self system interchangeably with identity, a hierarchical and multidimensional construct involving the perceptions, descriptions, and evaluations of one's self in relation to significant others, the social environment, and specific contexts [...]'. We acknowledge in this self a natural tension, a bicultural identity, and explore the extent of the migrants' attachment to the culture and language of their home and of Australia.

Conceptual Background

Beyond doubt, motivation is essential to success in language learning. Without it learners are not likely to reach high proficiency; further, 'even individuals with the most remarkable abilities cannot accomplish long-term goals, and neither are appropriate curricula and good teaching enough on their own to ensure student achievement' (Dörnyei, 2005: 65). It is no surprise then that a huge amount of research has been conducted on the nature of L2 motivation and of motivated L2 learners over recent decades (Gardner, 1985; Gardner & Lambert, 1972; Lamb, 2009; Masgoret & Gardner, 2003; Noels et al., 2003).

Dörnyei's particular contribution has been to reconceptualise past approaches to language learning motivation into the framework of the L2 Motivational Self System. The three components of the model are now well known:

- The Ideal L2 self 'is one's ideal self-image expressing the wish to become a competent L2 speaker' (Csizér & Kormos, 2008: 331)
- The Ought-to L2 self contains 'attributes that one believes we ought to possess to avoid negative outcomes – this motivational dimension may therefore bear little resemblance to our own wishes and desires' (Dörnyei et al., 2006: 145)
- The L2 learning experience covers 'situation specific motives related to the immediate learning environment and experience' (Dörnyei, 2005: 106).

In sum, the concept entails how one views oneself in the L2 and in the community of its speakers. Applied, as it is most often, to foreign language contexts (like the EFL context), the concept takes this community as imagined, since the learners are studying the language at a distance from the place or places where it is natively spoken. Our project, however, places the learners in the real community and studies their lived experience as migrants. Their L2 learning experience involves struggling with linguistic and cultural demands outside the classroom, and the Ideal L2 self involves hopes and aspirations about reaching a point where they feel confident in the language and settled in the culture.

The transitional status of the migrants is a very important consideration for the present research, and it suggests a shift from a monocultural identity towards a bicultural identity. To account for this shift, we expanded the instruments that we used in this study (see Methodology section) by adding items and questions to our instruments that allowed us to explore these migrant learners' identification with their first language (L1) and/or L2 language and culture.

Bicultural identity, first advanced by Arnett (2002), thus becomes a key concept for the research. It recognises that a vast number of learners of English across the globe view that language as a means of access to the world rather than to the language of a particular English-speaking country. Bicultural identity theory may be seen as a challenge to the traditional theory of motivation advanced by Gardner (1985) that bases the concept of integrative motivation on a specific target language community. However, Dörnyei's theory of the L2 Motivational Self System embraces motivation as a pathway to both global English and a specific community through the construct of the Ideal L2 self. It helps to explain the nature of motivation in an EFL situation where English is not commonly spoken, is mainly confined to school learning and is considered the global language; and it may (as proposed in the present research) explain motivation in an ESL situation where English is the local and national language, and learning it is essential in order for one to play a role in society.

Therefore, in a sense, any motivated learner has a bicultural identity, and any theory of the L2 self must come to terms with the L1 self or, to use Syed's (2001) term, heritage identity. This includes 'those attributes of the self that are linked with one's race, language, religion, and ethnicity' (Syed, 2001: 129). The L2 self, as conceived in this research on migrant learners in Australia, does not deny heritage identity and is premised on an acceptance of two identities of the aspiring migrant. That said, an understandable tension between the two has to be appreciated: this study probes, among other things, the extent to which a given respondent is attached to her or his home culture and whether perhaps this attachment is so strong that it may weaken the L2 self and reduce the possibility of satisfactory settlement.

This research seeks answers to the following two research questions:

(1) How do the ESL adult migrants perceive themselves (now) in terms of their L1 and L2 language and culture?
(2) What is their Ideal L2 self?

This research will make a contribution to current motivation theory by expanding it into the ESL context, studying the learners' actual and Ideal L2 selves, and taking into account their bicultural identity. Thus, it is hoped that the study will allow for a better understanding of new migrants' identity and their motivation to learn English. Ultimately, this research will create knowledge in the fields of motivation research, ESL education and migration policy in Australia as well as in comparable immigrant contexts around the world.

Methodology

In this study we used a mixed-method research design consisting of a motivation questionnaire that provides an overview of the motivational profile of the ESL adult migrant learners, and semi-structured interviews that offer information on individual motivational profiles and individual learners' dynamic development over time.

Participants

Our research participants were learners of English and adult migrants to Australia attending one of three adult migrant English language programmes. These English language programmes are designed to assist with their settlement in Australia. All three programmes are located in Canberra, Australian Capital Territory. Students hold permanent residency or Australian citizenship.

The average level of English proficiency of our research participants was approximately intermediate, that is, somewhere between International Second Language Proficiency Ratings (ISLPR) 1, Basic Transactional Proficiency (able to satisfy basic everyday transactional needs) and 1 + Transactional Proficiency (able to satisfy everyday transactional needs and limited social needs). The research participants ($N = 82$) came from 29 countries, ranged in age from 20 to 65 years, and their duration of residence in Australia was between two and 32 years.

Instruments

Questionnaire

The questionnaire comprised three main groups of scales (expanded from Csizér & Dörnyei, 2005; Ryan, 2008): (1) self and the target language and culture; (2) self and the language community and (3) self and non-language specific attitudes. In the light of our ESL context, it was necessary to revise some of the original constructs. The most important change is the shift from a monocultural identity towards a bicultural identity and the development of two new scales, 'Regard for L1 and culture' and 'Regard for non-L1 cultures' (please refer to Tables 9.2, 9.3 and 9.4 for all items and scales analysed in this paper). We also had to take into account, in the question design, the respondents' range of English proficiency and show sensitivity to their psychological and cultural circumstances.

There were two parts to the questionnaire. Part 1 included 71 five-point Likert scale items and one final open-ended question; Part 2 elicited information about the research participants' background and included seven questions about gender, age, country of origin, L1, length of residence in Australia, permanent residency or citizenship status.

Interview

An interview guide was developed from the questions from the three main groups of scales used in the questionnaire. The questions in the interview guide were made open-ended in order to elicit in-depth answers. We grouped our questions around seven topics: (1) language learning experience (for instance, 'Have you had any good/bad experiences in your learning? What are the best/worst ones?'); (2) attitudes to English ('What does English mean to you?'); (3) attitudes to speakers of English ('When you imagine a competent speaker of English, what does he or she look like?'); (4) goals and orientations ('Do you have clear learning goals?'); (5) obligations and needs to learn English ('Have other people ever pushed you to learn English?'); (6) Ideal L2 self; ('Can you imagine a clear situation when you are a successful speaker of English? Who would you be speaking to?' and (7) identification with L1 and/or L2 language and culture ('How do the Australian and your culture/language go together for you?'). Interviews were conducted in English.

Data collection

Initially we collected questionnaire data from 84 intermediate proficiency ESL learners. Students were also asked if they would like to participate in the subsequent qualitative phase of the study (i.e. the interview). Of the students who indicated their willingness to

participate in an interview, we selected 15 students, choosing five participants from each of the three programmes. We selected as diverse a sample as possible, accommodating a range of ages, genders, countries of
origin and length of residence in Australia. Only one interviewee (Leslie)
held Australian citizenship. Interviews were between 30 and 45 minutes
in length and were conducted by the authors of the study. This qualitative phase of the data collection allowed for a more complete and
deeper understanding of the motivational profile of selected learners
($N = 14$; one interview recording was unsuccessful). Please refer to
Table 9.1 for details. All names are pseudonyms to ensure anonymity.

Data analysis

All the data from the questionnaire were put into an SPSS database in
order to carry out descriptive statistics. Mean, Standard Deviation,

Table 9.1 Background of research participants in interview ($N = 14$) (names are
pseudonyms)

Interviewee	Gender	Age	Country of origin	Duration of residence in Australia (in months)
Fadwa	F	47	Lebanon	24
Giuseppe	M	43	Italy	5
Ibrahim	M	23	Egypt	16
Jihye	F	29	South Korea	12
Jimmy	M	37	China	48
John	M	39	South Korea	12
Leslie	M	45	China	60
Mahmoud	M	36	Afghanistan	12
Maria	F	32	Colombia	6
Mira	F	25	South Korea	18
Neda	F	33	Iran	42
Paitaya	F	34	Thailand	24
Sadiq	M	65	Iraq	48
Sangeetha	F	28	India	12

Minimum and Maximum were calculated for each item in order to gain an initial picture of the motivational profile of the research participants.

The interviews were recorded and then transcribed verbatim. The transcripts from the interviews were analysed in negotiation between the three authors of the study looking for common themes in response to the two research questions mentioned above. The major themes in response to these two guiding questions are presented in the following section.

Results

In this section we present the results of the study by addressing the two research questions. For each research question we refer firstly to the relevant items and/or scale in the questionnaire. Then we present the main themes that emerged from the interviews.

ESL adult migrants' regard for L1 and L2 language and culture

Overall, the participants in this study showed a high regard for both their heritage language and culture as well as for other cultures including the ones in Australia. Whereas the questionnaire data could only indicate that most participants have a comparable level of respect for customs and traditions of Australia (and beyond) and of their heritage culture, the interview data shed more light on these participants' perceptions of merging (or not) their respective heritage language and culture with Australian language and culture. With regard to the first research question, we firstly highlight the importance of the participants' high regard for their L1 language and culture as well as for non-L1 cultures. Secondly, we turn our attention to these migrant learners' development of a bicultural identity in the new country, which was a salient theme in all of the interviews.

High regard for L1 language and culture

In the questionnaire we probed five items to explore these adult migrants' regard for their respective L1 language and culture (please refer to Table 9.2). Item 53 (I am proud of my home language and culture and wish to keep them) indicates the participants' overall pride in their first language and culture and their desire to keep them alive (mean = 4.4). At the same time, there are mixed responses with regard to these migrants' possible concerns about losing their home language and culture (items 42 and 45) and to a potential preference for their L1 (items 59 and 68) over other languages.

Table 9.2 Regard for L1 language and culture

Question	Mean*	SD	Min	Max
Q42 It worries me that people from other countries like me may forget the importance of their own culture.	2.6	0.9165	1	5
Q45 I worry that if I learn more English I will lose something of my culture.	1.7	0.6860	1	4
Q53 I am proud of my home language and culture and wish to keep them.	4.4	0.7310	2	5
Q59 I would like to use my own language in my work.	2.5	1.1308	1	5
Q68 My first language is the best language in the world.	2.9	1.1154	1	5

*Rounded to one decimal point.

High regard for non-L1 cultures

Another five items in the questionnaire provide insight into these migrants' regard for cultures other than their own, also in relation to the Australian culture (please refer to Table 9.3). Participants express an overall high level of respect for other cultures (items 39, 48 and 56) and an equal respect for L1 and Australian cultures (items 50 and 64).

In the interviews, we explored the participants' regard for their L1 and Australian language and culture further to understand how these adult migrant learners perceived themselves with respect to the 'old' and 'new' language and culture. The main theme, Development of a bicultural

Table 9.3 Regard for non-L1 cultures

Question	Mean*	SD	Min	Max
Q39 I respect the values and customs of other cultures.	4.6	0.6333	2	5
Q48** I don't trust people with different customs and values to myself.	4.0	0.7635	2	5
Q50 Both the customs and traditions of my culture and the customs and traditions of Australia are good.	4.3	0.7252	2	5
RQ56 I am not very interested in the values and customs of other cultures.	3.9	0.9796	1	5
Q64 I respect Australian customs and traditions in the same way as I respect my own.	4.5	0.6717	2	5

Notes: *Rounded to one decimal point; **we reversed the scoring for this negatively worded item.

identity, that emerged from the interview data clearly indicates that (most of) these migrants are in transition: they are, to a greater or lesser extent, developing a bicultural identity.

Development of a bicultural identity

Participants' development of their bicultural identity can best be described as a continuum between a strong identification with L1 language and culture on the one end and a strong identification with L2 (Australian) culture on the other. Due to space constraints, in this section we focus on three of our interviewees who represent typical positions on that continuum. Neda represents a migrant whose development of a bicultural identity is only just beginning. Sadiq, on the other hand, represents the other pole of the continuum due to his almost complete disconnection from his heritage language and culture. Fadwa, with a balanced embrace of heritage and Australian language and culture, is the most representative participant for the complete group of migrants interviewed for this study.

Neda's identity is strongly anchored in her L1 culture, especially for religious reasons: 'I would say I am a Muslim [...] Iranian ah Turkish woman'. Clearly, her strongest identification is with her religion. Australian citizenship will also have an influence in due course: 'I think after getting citizenship I will be Australian as well (laughs)'. The interviewer's question about how she would feel when she becomes an Australian citizen seems too early for Neda. She admits that she has not considered this: 'I haven't ever thought about it'. Later on in the interview she also indicates that due to her lack of Australian friends, she has not really taken up Australian customs or traditions. However, she does not exclude this possibility for the future: 'Ah because I don't have too much friends Australian friends here. Maybe in the future'. It is interesting to note that Neda's interest in learning English is by no means negatively affected by her somewhat distant attitude towards Australian culture in general (see also Discussion section).

In contrast to Neda, Sadiq has developed a very solid attachment to the Australian culture and language. He considers it the 'best country' and is looking forward to becoming an Australian citizen. He wants to shed his Iraqi origin after the discrimination he endured: 'I will be Australian and this is an honour for me [...] because [...] when er you face discrimination in your country [...] of course [...] this is my great day [...] when I will be I have the citizenship'. He has a 'bad memory [after] [...] two or three wars', subsequently forgot the happy memories from his childhood, and now detaches himself from his L1 identity. Neda's identity, in contrast, even though she also has clearly distanced herself from the political situation in her country of origin, Iran, is so strongly determined by her religious identity that for her, her heritage identity is very strong. Sadiq's detachment from his heritage culture is mirrored in his giving up of his L1: 'when my I left my country I left the Arabic away [...] because Arabic it doesn't going to help me anymore', even though he admits that he and his wife still speak Arabic. However, in general and with regard to his sons, he thinks 'the best way is to learn English and to not connect it with mother language', which means, for instance, that he does not want his sons to listen to television news in Arabic: 'as we are here in Australia [...] we need to hear the news from your TV'.

Fadwa is very typical of most of the 14 interviewees in this study. For her, Arabic and English languages and cultures go well together. She uses her L1 or English according to the circumstances. While she speaks Arabic with older members of her family living in Australia, she needs English for the younger members: 'they speak English so the daughter and the granddaughter, the kids they speak English, but the old (laughs), my sister-in-law and brother-in-law, they speak Arabic with me but when I speak with the nephew and the niece in English'. She does not express any concern about losing her L1. Interestingly, she makes very conscious use of English when she wishes to talk about her L1 culture with Australians: 'when I speak English I can if one, someone ask me about my culture so in English I can explain it clearly for him'. For her, her heritage culture and Australian culture have a lot in common. When asked whether she thought that her culture and the Australian culture can go together, Fadwa does not hesitate to express her belief that they have many similarities, like having a barbecue with family and friends on the weekend or fundraising events, like a marathon: 'yeah they go together very easy [...] sometime I found the same culture'. When asked how she feels about her potential Australian identity, similarly to Neda, she expresses awareness that she might need more time: 'it's early to say (laughs)'. She sees herself as 'a little bit Australian', whereas she refers to her husband, who has lived in Australia now for 43 years, as an Australian.

The following section will now focus on how these participants' Ideal L2 self expresses itself as part of their developing bicultural identity. All participants are very much aware of their ongoing English language learning needs that will allow them to fully develop as individuals, now living in a non-L1 environment.

Ideal L2 self: English as a gateway to life goals

With regard to our second research question, both the questionnaire data and the interview data indicate plainly that all participants in this study conceive of themselves as L2 speaking selves. The interview data highlight the importance of English for these migrant learners' life goals and their ongoing learning needs.

The questionnaire data, in particular the items that probed the participants' Ideal L2 self, show high scores on all items on this scale (please refer to Table 9.4 for details).

Participants' strong agreement with all items on this scale indicates their awareness of the link between good English proficiency, communication with Australians and people from other countries (Q16, Q41), work (Q70) and, most importantly, their vision of their future life (Q14, Q22, Q34, Q69).

The questionnaire also contained a final open-ended question where we asked the participants whether there was anything else that they would like to tell us about why they were learning English. The analysis of all answers to this item (40 out of 82 participants responded to this item) likewise shows a strong link between English competence, work (and study) and these migrants' future life. Certain significant words and ideas are repeated through the answers with such regularity that they cannot be ignored. These words are *life, job, social, family, children* and *independence*. The common reference to life underlines the huge importance of English for the respondents' present and future to the extent that they cannot separate life from English. One respondent, for example, says, 'If I don't have

Table 9.4 Ideal L2 self

Question	Mean*	SD	Min	Max
Q14 I need to speak English for the things I want to do in the future.	4.8	0.4165	4	5
Q16 I can imagine speaking English with people from other countries.	4.0	0.6009	2	5
Q22 When I think about my future, it is important that I use English.	4.7	0.5530	2	5
Q34 I often imagine myself as someone who is able to speak English.	4.3	0.7112	2	5
Q41 In the future I really would like to talk more with English-speaking people in the Australian community.	4.6	0.5687	1	5
Q69 If my dreams come true, I will speak very good English in the future.	4.5	0.7896	2	5
Q70 To have the job I want in the future, I must speak English very well.	4.5	0.7403	1	5

*Rounded to one decimal point.

English I can't settle my life in Australia'. Life includes the hope for 'a better future in my live [sic]'. All other significant ideas from these answers in a sense fall under the heading of 'life'. Another recurrent idea is job or work, which is no surprise since all of the participants seek a livelihood and financial security. A respondent confides, 'I'm learning English because I want to learn a job and work in Australia'. English for social interaction arises as a further preoccupation in the minds of these migrants, 'to communicate with people around' and to be 'social with English speakers'. It is interesting that references to family and children recur, correlating with the sentiments of a number of interviewees who spoke of learning English for the sake of their family and even their unborn children. One participant writes, 'It's very important for me to help my kids when they go to school'. Finally, an important motif seems to be independence; indeed, one participant, for instance, insists that she wants to do everything for herself and not be dependent on her son, who acts as her interpreter. This topic of independence probably emerges because participants regard becoming competent in English as a pathway to it.

The interviews contain further numerous examples of how these participants perceive the extent to which they are competent speakers of English in their present and, most importantly, their future. Participants realise that English competence will allow them to achieve their life goals. The goals are work and study, social interaction within the family, the local and global community, all of which match the significant words and ideas that emerged from the open-ended question. They can be seen in the following quotations from Ibrahim, Jihye and Fadwa that show these recurrent goals expressed throughout the interviews:

> I think it be perfect English because I'm learning quickly and I would be married (laughter). I'm get a good job here in ah Egyptian ah sorry in Australian I hope so but I'm strongly believe I will get it. (Ibrahim)

> I have big goals. I want to speak like Australian people because I want to go to [mentions two universities in town]. My major was childhood education in South Korea. I was a teacher in preschool. I loved my job so I want to continue in here but education is very high level in here is right? (Jihye)

> I feel happy when I just start to study these things and have some knowledge about English [...] so I'm happy now I feel independent. I can do anything by myself. I feel English is the best way for people with second language [...] in five years I see myself good education [...] speak English well [...] have my own business and I success in my life [...] yeah I see myself as better than now yeah [...] more successful person I hope so [...] (Fadwa)

Perhaps Neda says it best: 'English in a country which English is the first language is everything I think, work communicating life'. Learning English is vital 'for returning to the life here'.

Participants in this study show high awareness of their ongoing language learning needs to achieve their goals in life. English language learning has a high priority for them. Fadwa knows that she needs to further improve her English proficiency, particularly in writing, when she says, 'yeah it's affect me a lot because if I finish studying and I have good knowledge in English I have open my own business in future'. Jimmy insists that English is important in Australia if you 'want to get really get future'. This means that he 'want[s] to study English anytime if possible. I will use any method to study English not only from the TV or some book or some internet. I just try to study from everywhere'.

Discussion

Reviewing the results, we may identify a number of clear trends in the data. These may be readily aligned with the research questions: the first one about how the participants perceive themselves now in terms of L1 and L2 language and culture, and the second one asking about their Ideal L2 self. The broad key concepts imparted by the results are heritage identity, bicultural identity and transition, notions already signalled in the conceptual background.

Overwhelmingly, the participants affirm the great value of their heritage language and culture, thus their heritage identity (Syed, 2001). With regard to their L1, they do not feel that they are losing it. They do not generally feel self-conscious when using it in front of Australian native English speakers. In general, they manage to practise their customs in Australia. Does this adherence to L1 language and culture produce a conflict with L2 language and culture? There appears in general to be no such conflict. If there had been a conflict, their enthusiasm for learning English and for Australian culture, as demonstrated in both the questionnaire and interview, would not have been so evident. Even Neda, who asserts that she would have preferred to live in her own country if she had had the chance and choice, agrees that English is crucial for her and more significantly, is able at least to tolerate the existence of two cultures in her life. Sadiq, at the other end of the scale from Neda, is adamant that he is trying to relinquish his culture, as a result of traumatic experiences in Iraq, and claims that he is using his L1 as little as possible. All other migrants in the survey, to various degrees, show a commitment and willingness to participate in Australian culture.

It may therefore be said that they possess a bicultural identity (Arnett, 2002) that is balanced and well-established. They place a high value on their L1 and are committed to improving their L2. They maintain their heritage culture in Australia to an extent that satisfies them, are interested in Australian culture and see no contradiction between their two cultures. A caveat here is that, while they all feel the need to improve their English skills, most recognise that the journey is slow and difficult. The language itself is usually not easy, may cause frustration – even humiliation, as Giuseppe complains – and they have to find the time and energy to study, a particular consideration if they have a job and/or a family.

Furthermore, despite the harmony that they see between the two cultures in their lives, they do not all necessarily 'feel Australian' yet. The more fluent and relatively confident Maria, for example, says that she 'sometimes' feels Australian but at this stage is simply comfortable in the environment. Perhaps our interview question (whether the interviewee felt somewhat Australian) was premature. These migrants are, after all, to repeat a phrase from the introduction, in transition. 'Now is a moment of passage', says Giuseppe.

With the above conditions in mind it may be said then that the general response to the first research question is that our ESL migrants overwhelmingly have a positive and balanced self-perception now in terms of their L1 and L2 language and culture. With regard to the second question, the results speak of a robust Ideal L2 self among the participants. Naturally, the ideal is more tangible for some than for others, but all have goals. They are unanimous in their desire to reach a high enough competence and confidence in English to do things such as getting a good job, communicating easily in the workplace and helping their children with their English educational needs. Indeed, this is their English for 'life', as referred to in the Results section. For some the goals are quite specific, whereas for others they are not as detailed. On the one hand, for example, Mahmoud clearly imagines himself 'enjoying television', speaking 'idiomatic English' and participating in business. On the other hand, Mira claims to have no specific goals but merely hopes to be 'a successful person' and a 'good mother'. As underlined earlier, with respect to their present self-perception, the participants are in transition towards an ideal status in Australia and they have a vision of the future that incorporates their L2 speaking selves.

Conclusion

This research supports the generalisation made by Marginson *et al.* (2010) that language is an extremely important factor in migrants' whole intercultural experience. The migrants in our study are learners of both language and culture, the two being indissolubly connected. Journeying from present self-perception to their Ideal L2 self, they are not found to be in a linguistic and cultural limbo. In their transition, they take with them their first language and culture and look forward to assimilating much more English and much more of Australian culture. Their bicultural identity, reinforced by the competence in English that they have achieved so far, seems to offer them – in the great majority of cases – a pleasing measure of independence and freedom; they suffer from no particular discomfort.

There are limitations to the research. It has concentrated on one small region of Australia and the sample size is modest. Yet we believe that we have captured some significant truths about the language and culture learning of migrants in Australia as well as about their lives. This is a solid basis for further research, with a larger sample. Also, since the world is now one of enormous movements of emigrants and immigrants, the study and its findings may well influence other research on migrant L2 motivation far beyond Australia.

Acknowledgements

We would like to express our sincere thanks to Victor Surkus for assisting us with the data analysis. We would also like to thank the reviewers and editors for their insightful comments and suggestions on earlier drafts of this paper. Our thanks also go to the University of Canberra for providing funding to support this research.

References

Arnett, J.J. (2002) The psychology of globalization. *American Psychologist* 57 (10), 774–783.
Csizér, K. and Dörnyei, Z. (2005) Language learners' motivational profiles and their motivated learning behavior. *Language Learning* 55 (4), 613–659.
Csizér, K. and Kormos, J. (2008) The relationship of intercultural contact and language learning among Hungarian students of English and German. *Journal of Multilingual and Multicultural Development* 29 (1), 30–49.
Dörnyei, Z. (2005) *The Psychology of the Language Learner: Individual Differences in Second Language Acquisition*. Mahwah, N.J.: L. Erlbaum.
Dörnyei, Z., Csizér, K. and Németh, N. (2006) *Motivation, Language Attitudes and Globalisation: A Hungarian Perspective*. Clevedon: Multilingual Matters.
Gardner, R.C. (1985) *Social Psychology and Second Language Learning: The Role of Attitudes and Motivation*. London: Edward Arnold.
Gardner, R.C. and Lambert, W.E. (1972) *Attitudes and Motivation*. Rowley, M. A.: Newbury House.
Hornberger, N.H. and Wang, S.C. (2008) Who are our heritage language learners? Identity and biliteracy in heritage language education in the United States. In D. M. Brinton, O. Kagan and S. Bauckus (eds) *Heritage Language Education: A New Field Emerging* (pp. 3–35). New York and London: Routledge.

Lamb, M. (2009) Situating the L2 Self: Two Indonesian school learners of English. In Z. Dörnyei and E. Ushioda (eds) *Motivation, Language Identity and the L2 Self* (pp. 229–247). Bristol: Multilingual Matters.

Marginson, S., Nyland, S., Sawir, E. and Forbes-Mewett, H. (2010) *International Student Security*. Cambridge: Cambridge University Press.

Masgoret, A. and Gardner, R. (2003) Attitudes, motivation and second language learning: A meta-analysis of studies conducted by Gardner and associates. *Language Learning* 53 (1), 123–163.

Noels, K.A., Pelletier, L.C., Clément, R. and Vallerand, R.J. (2003) Why are you learning a second language? Motivational orientations and self-determination theory. *Language Learning* 53 (1), 33–63.

Ryan, S. (2008) The ideal L2 selves of Japanese learners of English. PhD thesis, University of Nottingham. See http://etheses.nottingham.ac.uk/550/ (accessed October 2010).

Syed, Z. (2001) Notions of self in foreign language learning: A qualitative analysis. In Z. Dörnyei and R. Schmidt (eds) *Motivation and Second Language Acquisition* (pp. 127–148). Honolulu: Second Language Teaching & Curriculum Center University of Hawaii at Manoa.

10 Investing in Experiential Capital: Self-efficacy, Imagination and Development of Ideal L2 Selves

Kay Irie and Damon R. Brewster

Introduction

Where do learners come up with their future self-images? How do they come to envision themselves as effective users of the target foreign language? How do fantasies and wishes to successfully acquire a language become more concrete self-guiding images?

Ever since Dörnyei (2005) proposed the Second Language (L2) Motivational Self System in 2005, much attention has been given to the validation of the theoretical model and the construction of instruments to assess its various components (i.e. Dörnyei & Ushioda, 2009; Nakahara & Yashima, 2012; Papi, 2010). While the motivational capacity of the Ideal L2 self, the image of being a successful L2 learner or user, as a self-guide that encourages effort to learn the target language, has been empirically examined and demonstrated (Csizér & Kormos, 2009; Nakahara & Yashima, 2012; Ryan, 2009; Taguchi *et al.*, 2009), the emergence of such images and how they alter over time have not, with a few exceptions (i.e. Lamb, 2011; Kim, 2009), been investigated as extensively. In this chapter, we explore the development and changes of the Ideal L2 self as a self-guide towards L2 mastery in one exceptional student, focusing particularly on two elements: (1) self-efficacy, an individual's perception of his or her ability to successfully complete a specific task and (2) imagination, which contributes to the emergence of hoped-for future self-images, including a robust L2 self.

We first encountered Makio as a freshman in a longitudinal multi-case study we began in Tokyo in 2010 (Irie & Brewster, 2013). His story highlights the significance of investment in a wide range of life experiences, as this investment enhanced his self-efficacy, fostered a positive outlook, as well as stimulated his imagination of positive future selves, including the image of himself as a fluent speaker of English. Through this qualitative inquiry, we propose that investment in and reflecting on experiences inside and outside the classroom, what we refer to as experiential capital, play a powerful role in promoting self-efficacy and provide a fertile ground for imagining future possible selves, both important factors if an effective Ideal L2 self is to be realised.

Key Concepts

The L2 Motivational Self System

Building on work on possible self-concepts in psychology, particularly the work of Markus and Nurius (1986) and Higgins (1987), Dörnyei developed the L2 Motivational Self System that encompasses previously proposed L2 motivational concepts such as Gardner's integrative and instrumental orientations to explain the more dynamic and idiosyncratic nature of L2 motivation (For an overview of the L2 Motivational Self System, see Dörnyei & Ushioda, 2009, 2011). This theoretical model consists of three components: the Ideal L2 self, the Ought-to L2 self and the L2 learning experience. The first two, the Ideal L2 self and the Ought-to L2 self, are in a sense domain-specific iterations of the possible selves forwarded by Markus and Nurius (1986) and Higgins (1987). That is, they refer more narrowly to possible selves specifically as a language learner. These researchers argue that ideal images of our future selves can be powerful motivating forces when allied with other considerations (see Dunkel & Kerpelman, 2006 for a collection of research on possible selves). These possible selves are future-oriented, multi-faceted conceptualisations (Oyserman & Fryberg, 2006) that can act as roadmaps and motivators, in the case of this research, for language learning. The third component of the L2 Motivational Self System is the L2 learning experience, which refers to the immediate learning environment, such as the impact of teachers, curriculum, peer groups and class dynamics. Students may have favourable experiences in a particular English teacher's class, and these positive feelings may encourage a desire to do well in the subject and an association of English with enjoyment. Dörnyei and Ushioda put it this way:

> For some language learners the initial motivation to learn a language does not come from internally or externally generated self-images but rather from successful engagement with the actual language learning process, for example because they discover they are good at it. (2011: 86)

Critically, for desired self-images to be effective in instigating motivated behaviour, Dörnyei emphasises that they must be vivid and elaborately imagined in such a way that the future self-images are tangible (Dörnyei & Ushioda, 2011). The more concrete they are, the more likely they will be successful in 'directing purposeful behavior' (Dörnyei, 2005: 101).

The L2 Motivational Self System was a means to explore how our university students may navigate their L2 learning from their first year to graduation by looking at the developmental process of their Ideal and Ought-to L2 selves, partly in interaction with changing L2 learning experiences and other contextual factors, and how Ideal L2 selves might function as future guides in their L2 learning at university.

Self-Efficacy

Bandura's (1977, 1986) concept of self-efficacy, the way an individual reflects on their experiences and actions, provides a sense of whether or not instigated actions and planned undertakings will succeed or fail, and plays an important role in supporting future self-images. This concept is important in gaining an understanding of how learning and other experiences are assimilated into an individual's concept of self and utilised in the development of hoped-for future self-images.

One of our initial research goals was to consider why it is that one English learner may maintain the motivation to become a competent English user and regulate his/her own English language studies, while another starting at the same skill level struggles to engage in his/her L2 learning. Research shows that other variables being equal (Schunk, 1989), self-efficacy is a strong predictor of an individual's likelihood of success in a variety of settings: from achievement in academic life and career choices to pain management and recovery rates from heart attacks (e.g. Bandura, 1986; Schunk, 1991). It is described by Bandura as, 'the belief in one's capabilities to organise and execute the courses of action required to manage prospective situations' (1994: 2). Our actions are regulated by forethought, which is born out of the examination and appraisal of our performances in similar situations or tasks from our past experiences. Although in second language acquisition (SLA), self-efficacy is still an under-studied concept, Raoofi et al. (2012) identified and reviewed 32 studies published between 2003 and 2012, finding that these studies, on the whole, reinforce the more general findings and provide compelling evidence that this learner variable can be of key importance to how learners proceed in their language learning lives (2012: 66).

Self-Efficacy Theory proposes that individuals 'are active, thinking, self-reflective creatures that change, create, and manipulate their environments, and respond to environmental events emotionally, cognitively, and behaviorally' (Riggio, 2012: 1). Those with high self-efficacy tend to persevere longer in the face of difficulty, approach difficult tasks as ones that need to be mastered, attempt more ambitious tasks and exhibit higher motivation (Bandura, 1994). Students assess their own potential and make judgments about their capabilities utilising information gained primarily from reflecting on mastery experience in the past, the observation of peers' performance, allied with social persuasion, such as the encouragement of others to overcome their self-doubt. When this judgment is positive with agentic self-belief in a perceived capability to attain positive outcomes, self-efficacy is considered to be high (Bandura, 1986). This sense of feasibility in turn facilitates possible L2 self-images to evolve into Ideal L2 selves or Ought-to L2 selves that encourage learners to exert effort to realise these images.

Experiential capital

We live and act in social networks and to a greater or lesser extent the options for actions open to us, the resources we can draw upon, and the chances of succeeding in our goals and undertakings are reliant on social capital (Coleman, 1988). These networks – initially our families, neighbourhood and school communities, and later in life, networks we create ourselves – support and invest in us and give us opportunities to develop as individuals. As Sandefur et al. stress, 'families provide a variety of resources to adolescents that can prove instrumental in their educational attainment' (2006: 547). However, the benefits of these structures are not limited to scholastic achievement: they also provide chances to explore experiences that are similar to those we imagine or to observe other people's experiences. This is vital when considering the development of possible selves, as it is difficult to appraise how challenging a course of action will be against our perceived capability with no actual or vicarious experience. This judgment of plausibility is considered to be critical in influencing whether a particular possible self will develop into an ideal self or whether it will exert a motivating capacity and function as a self-guide (MacIntyre et al., 2009: 197). It also differentiates possible selves from mere implausible fantasy, as not all mental simulations lead to the regulation of goal-directed behaviour (Ryan & Irie, 2014).

As we have outlined above, the L2 Motivational Self System's L2 learning experience is concerned only with the immediate learning environment and its influence on executive motivation. However, the experiences we have in our lives can positively or negatively influence us and shape our possible selves. As Barreto and Frazier (2012) suggest, integration of salient life events into possible selves can contribute to the articulation of images and increase self-regulatory power (2012: 1778–1779). These experiences, from our childhood to more immediate domain specific memories, are what we call experiential capital. This capital could be a rich bank of experiences to draw from or more limiting portfolios of episodes.

Table 10.1 Summary of data collection

Interview	Location	Date	Academic calendar	Participant's location/status
1.	Tokyo	Jul 2010	End of Spring Semester	First year at university in Tokyo
2. (Email)	Texas	Oct 2010	Beginning of Autumn Semester	First year at university in Tokyo on study-abroad programme
3.	Tokyo	Jan 2011	End of Autumn Semester	First year at university in Tokyo
4.	Tokyo	Aug 2011	End of Spring Semester in Japan	Second year at university in Tokyo
5. (Online – Skype)	Boston	Nov 2011	Autumn Semester in Boston	First year at community college in Boston
6.	Tokyo	Jan 2012	Break between Autumn and Spring Semester	First year at community college in Boston
7. (Online – Skype)	Boston	Aug 2012	Summer session I in Boston	Taking summer sessions at another university in Boston
8. (Email)	Boston	Oct 2012	Autumn Semester in Boston	Second year at community college in Boston

Note: The Japanese academic year starts in April. Spring semester is from April to July. Autumn semester is from September to January.

After the first interview with Makio in July 2010 (see Table 10.1), the uniqueness of his experiential capital compared with the other students in the study stood out. The story we tell in this chapter will discuss some atypical experiences that he had, compared to his peers, illustrating his Ideal L2 self, as part of a larger hoped-for future self, and how he has incorporated some of these salient life events, including his trip to India when he was very young, the catching of an arsonist and an unexpectedly forced cramming for entrance exams.

Case Study

Context and participant

The longitudinal multi-case study, planned for four years, began in April 2010 at a mid-size Japanese university in Tokyo. For students not making it into top-ranked universities, this university enjoys a reputation for its English programme, 360 minutes of compulsory English spread over four classes every week for first-year students, as well as its study abroad programmes and a wide variety of foreign languages offered. Students are streamed into three proficiency bands after taking an online English proficiency test. Classes cover the four skills and are taught in English.

Makio was one of the participants selected for this study. He was admitted to the university's Liberal Arts Department through the entrance examination and is from a financially secure family with four younger siblings, who all go to private schools. At the beginning of the study, his proficiency could be considered average for Japanese university students, around 500 on the Test of English for International Communication (TOEIC), based on his initial placement test. After considering his responses to an L2-self discrepancy survey, Makio was chosen for the study from 45 students we were teaching in two of the top-level classes. On this survey, he indicated that he considered many of the successful L2 learner attributes mentioned to be relevant to him at the time and would be even more so in the future.

Data collection and analysis

After the initial selection process but still in the first semester, we started collecting data on Makio from classroom observation of motivated behaviour, the reports of other English teachers he had and our own field notes. However, starting at the end of his first semester at the university in Tokyo, the bulk of our data came from interviews. We held seven semi-structured interviews with Makio and sent two questionnaires in place of a face-to-face interview, with the last being a questionnaire, which was sent just after he had started his second year of studies at a college in Boston. These interviews were conducted in Japanese, typically lasted between 40 minutes and an hour, and were transcribed. They focused on Makio's L2 learning experience, future goals, any pressures he was experiencing and any short or long-term plans for his language learning. We then, separately, coded the interviews for elements that were felt to be pertinent to the research questions before we compared our choices. Points of congruence were discussed and codes were selected to describe themes (see Irie & Brewster, 2013, for the details).

Makio's story: Developing Ideal L2 selves

I'd like to start my own business. So I want to get some ideas for it on the GO Program (a study-overseas programme for first-year students). If I'm going to do business, I want to succeed, of course. I want to be successful enough to establish a system that supports people in developing countries in Central and South America or Africa: a business that can last for a long time. It's great to support individuals but volunteer workers (from NGOs) get tired and cannot stay there long, and the fundamental issues are not resolved. So my goal is to fix those problems. [...] That's right. It is highly likely that I would be talking to people and government officials overseas about the business. I would like to attain a level of English communication ability that I can use in such meetings and discussions. (Excerpt 1, Interview 1, July 2010).[1]

This extract highlights Makio's unusually, for a first-year Japanese student, clear description of a successful future self-image, including an Ideal L2 self. Not only did he imagine himself succeeding in creating a sustainable business in a developing country, he was already making plans to study abroad and improve his English proficiency. The short-term study-abroad programme he mentioned (in Texas) was known to have the most demanding course of all the study-abroad programmes on offer, and would stretch him the furthest. Makio already had a lot to say about how he would go about realising his successful future L2 self and was convinced that it would be vital for him to become a functional user of English.

With his first semester barely finished, Makio started to critically evaluate the compulsory English classes and his teachers as to how meaningful or not the experiences in class were for him. This is in contrast to the majority of first-year students, who seem satisfied just surviving the English-only classes for the entire semester, coming, as most do, from teacher-centred, exam-oriented English classes in high school. Just surviving was not good enough for Makio:

Makio: We do discussions in class, right? Well, something like discussion...

Interviewer: You mean the activities you do in Mr W's class?

Makio: They have become like skits. There are scripts prepared in advance. [...] I think it's better to have an environment where everybody can participate more actively. Not letting them sit at the desk passively but encouraging them to engage in conversation. (Excerpt 2, Interview 1, July 2010)

We were intrigued to find out where this vivid future self-imagery, self-efficacy and proactive approach to academic work, including analysing the effectiveness of his English classes, came from. In order to do so, we need to visit what we consider to be critical events in his life.

One event that stands out in Makio's childhood was his vacation trip with his parents to India before he was in elementary school – an unusual destination for a Japanese family with a young child. This response gives an insight into his family's international attitude:

> My father was interested in finding a religion for himself and meeting with all kinds of people. He also wanted to show me the plight of parts of the world outside Japan. (Excerpt 3, Interview 1, July 2010)

Although we cannot say that this trip in Makio's childhood was the source of his future self as a benevolent entrepreneur in a developing country, the seed might have been sown and nurtured by the constant encouragement from his parents to do something helpful and valuable for others rather than to simply focus on doing well at school.

Makio has shown himself at university to be an eager student. However, throughout his high school life, he did not do so well in school and was neither particularly enthusiastic about English nor studying in general. In fact, he had serious behavioural issues at a public junior high school and was, in effect, forced to transfer to a private school when he was 14. Even then, his parents did not demand that Makio study.

Interviewer: Have you ever been told to study? Study English?

Makio: They never really told me to study. (Excerpt 4, Interview 1, July 2010)

A second major setback in school came when Makio was in the final year of senior high school at the age of 17. Again, due to poor grades and attitudinal problems, the school decided not to recommend Makio to its affiliated university, to which he assumed he would be granted automatic admission. Unlike after his first setback at a public junior high school, this time Makio decided himself to take control. After studying intensively over a short period of time for the entrance exams, he was accepted to all three colleges he applied for. He reflected on this experience, noting that studying was revenge to show the high school what he was capable of.

Makio's growing confidence in himself can be detected also in a high school graduation trip alone to Italy. It is common for Japanese high school students to go on a graduation trip, but most often with a group of close friends and usually to a place within Japan. Makio said that he simply could not find anyone to go to Italy with. When we asked whether he was afraid of going to a country alone where he did not speak the language, he told us about a dramatic experience that put travelling alone abroad into perspective. While he was in the second year of high school, he had apprehended an arsonist in his neighbourhood by using the skills and confidence his karate lessons had given him. He described the experience of subduing the arsonist to be extremely frightening but that it made a trip to Italy and other physical and mental challenges since then seem manageable. Significantly, for his L2 future self-image, on this trip to Italy, he realised the usefulness of English and, for the first time, thought English might be worth studying.

Makio: That's right. I just knew phrases that you use for daily survival or sightseeing, such as buongiorno, il conto, per favore. Before I went, I had thought you could use Italian only in Italy. But when I got there, you could use English and communicate without any problem. I thought it was useful. I got lost so many times but I tried really hard and spoke English and made it to the hotel.

Interviewer: So English is useful.

Makio: Yeah, it's useful. You can talk to all kinds of people. So I started to think about studying it. (Excerpt 5, Interview 1, July 2010)

The biggest decision Makio made on his own with regards to his academic career and studying English was to transfer to a college in Boston in September 2011. This decision was preceded and inspired by the experience of the short-term study-overseas programme in his second semester. He decided to pursue this experience in Texas as it would be a more 'efficient' way to get closer to his Ideal L2 self as a functional user of English than staying in Japan and finishing his compulsory courses.

While in Texas, Makio's determination was demonstrated through his decision not to use Japanese, despite the fact that this somewhat unyielding attitude inevitably caused friction with other Japanese students on campus. His decision paid off, as it led to opportunities to meet and discuss issues, such as culture, religion and politics, with people of different nationalities, an experience that he found refreshing and stimulating.

After a heated discussion, they [students at the university in Texas] would just say, 'okay, let's go eat!' ... I was confused at first but I started to like the way in which people can differentiate [opinions and friendship] or maybe it's better to say not mix the two up? I was really impressed by that. I thought I would like to be at a place like that again. That's why I want to study overseas. (Excerpt 6, Interview 3, January 2011)

After being inspired by his experiences, on his return to Japan in December 2010, Makio began to make arrangements to re-start his tertiary education in the US. He succeeded in these plans and is currently in his second year (as of November 2012) at a college in Boston. At the time of writing, he is planning to transfer to a larger university in the academic year of 2013, where he hopes to major in quantum physics and possibly pursue a career as an academic. This is a drastic change from the successful future self that led him to go on the short-term study overseas programme and to strive to master English in the first place. How did this change come about?

Makio's interest in particle and quantum physics emerged following the nuclear accidents caused by the tsunami after the Great East Japan Earthquake in March 2011. He had just applied to colleges in Boston and was about to begin his final semester in Japan in April when this unforeseen event affected Makio deeply. Instead of attending classes, Makio felt compelled to engage in volunteer work in the disaster-stricken areas, becoming keenly aware of the danger posed by the meltdown in Fukushima and feeling the need to understand the risk the country was facing. He purchased a radiation measuring device, checked data presented by the government, organised a radiation measuring event on campus, started reading the literature and even contacted some experts to clarify his doubts and questions. Thus, Makio's interest drastically shifted away from the international relations and current affairs that he had enjoyed so much only a few months prior to the earthquake to radioactive substances, particles and eventually quantum physics. With his parents' consent, Makio withdrew from the university in April. He admitted himself that this was an unexpected turn of events:

Interviewer: So about when did you decide not to attend or enroll any more at the university?

Makio: Yes, in the second half of March. While I was doing various things, I learned about radiation. Well, I hate to say it, but... understanding the problem seemed...

Interviewer: More important than studying other things?

Makio: Yeah, that's how I began to feel.

Interviewer: So if it wasn't for the earthquake, do you think you would have attended classes as expected?

Makio: I might have been studying English if the disaster hadn't occurred. But there were two totally unexpected turning points [applying to colleges in the US and the earthquake]. I'm surprised too. It's interesting how it's turned out. (Excerpt 7, Interview 4, July 2011)

Along with this sudden shift in interest came modifications to his Ideal L2 self, and Makio became much more focused on attaining a higher Test of English as a Foreign Language (TOEFL) score to be eligible to apply for the undergraduate programme in quantum physics. Yet, while he was keeping himself busy with his studies, he did not stop making investments in experiences. For instance, he took a course on leadership for scientists and engineers at the Massachusetts Institute of Technology while he was taking summer courses in physics at another university in Boston. Moreover, after the summer, with encouragement from one of his professors back at his own college, Makio started organising weekly discussion circles on campus. He was realising his Ideal L2 self as a functional user of English at the same time as moving towards his larger ideal self goal.

The story of Makio and the development of his Ideal L2 self is ongoing. His successful future self-image will further develop and change. The story so far reveals some key elements in the process of developing his future self-image that exert motivating influences on his self-regulatory behaviour, which seem to be carried over from one ideal future self to another.

Discussion

Experiential capital and self-efficacy

Based on their study to determine the types of life experiences in adulthood that are integrated into possible selves, Barreto and Frazier (2012) argue that possible selves are susceptible to life experiences, and self-efficacy and self-regulation were higher for people who have successfully integrated critical experiences into their possible selves. What seems to set Makio apart from the majority of students we encounter at Japanese universities is the richness of his experiential capital – the wide range of experiences his parents and Makio himself invested in. Makio's ideal self-images and the self-efficacy that are required to envisage the future as plausible seem to have emerged out of his various momentous and life-changing experiences, particularly those outside the classroom.

Until around the time that Makio had to make a decision about university, the opportunities to gain such experiences were provided primarily by his parents and local structures. In particular, the training in karate gave him self-confidence, and a connection that he could use to widen his network in Texas. Furthermore, Makio's inquisitiveness and pro-activeness seem to be nurtured, at least partially, by his parents, particularly his father, who appears to have an international outlook and the financial power to invest in expanding the children's experiences by taking Makio to India, sending three of his siblings to study English in Switzerland for a summer, and paying for Makio's education overseas.

After Makio succeeded in the university entrance exams, he became the primary decision maker for his own course of action, beginning to make investments in himself: the graduation trip alone to Italy, the short-term study-overseas programme, applying for colleges in the US, doing volunteer work, following up on the effect of the accidents in

Fukushima and making a plan to transfer to another university to study physics. Through reflecting on earlier experiences, Makio confirmed that his own efforts brought success when faced with challenges: his hard work in the karate dojo resulted in enough confidence to tackle a danger-ous and potentially violent person; his decision to study intensively after setbacks at high school saw him ultimately pass all the university entrance exams. It seems that such stressful or life-changing experiences became a chance for Makio to confirm and develop his agency and build his self-efficacy by integrating these experiences into his self. This seems to be in line with Erickson's view that agency is a distinctive feature of possible selves and self-efficacy can be considered a measure of people's confidence in their personal agency to influence outcomes (2007: 352). Therefore, it is possible to say that the richer the experience, the more resources and chances people have to become aware of their agency.

For example, through internalising the experience of the stress, intense studying and success in university entrance exams, Makio gained self-effi-cacy, allowing him later to imagine the possibility of becoming a physi-cist: he perceives he has the ability to carry out the tasks necessary to succeed. Studying for the entrance exams was the first time he worked seriously for something that was externally imposed on him. It is ironic that he developed his self-regulation and self-efficacy in academic per-formance from this, as success in entrance exams is what is required to earn the right to pursue what he is truly interested in doing. His self-efficacy in academic work in general now supports his struggle to achieve the prerequisites to take the higher level physics classes, as this comment illustrates:

> I hate to be so confident, but to be honest, I would have no problems [in school] if I only had English ability. So the question is how am I going to improve my English... (Excerpt 8, Interview 7, August 2012)

Despite the fact that he is struggling to attain the TOEFL score that is required for the transfer, his motivation to improve his English has not diminished. The Ideal L2 self part of his hoped-for future self and the self-efficacy he has gained from his critical experiences are being applied to maintain his continuous effort for L2 learning.

Experiential capital and imagination

In addition to self-efficacy, experiential capital provides crucial ingre-dients for the development of possible selves – ideas and imagination. Makio's earlier ideal self-image, to start his own business in a developing country, did not emerge overnight. Unlike his ideal self-image of becom-ing a physicist, Makio does not recall any one particular incident that triggered this goal. It was shaped through various experiences, such as the trip to India and seeing how his father started and managed his own business. These experiences may not have immediately brought about changes as did the catching of an arsonist or the desperate studying for high-stakes exams, but they provide ideas and tangible images that Makio could slowly work on over the years. Communicating successfully in English during his trip to Italy showed him the usefulness of the language, a part of his possible L2 self of becoming a functional user of English. This was an important experience, which he might not have noticed at the time, yet certainly changed his perception of English from a school subject he always avoided to a tool he could use in his future, as Excerpt 5 indicates. Without this experience, it might have taken him much longer to realise or imagine the L2-self component in his future.

Another return Makio has received from his investment in widening his experience may be the emergence of an imagined community of practice (Anderson, 1991; Norton, 2001). It is an imagined community of physics majors at a reputable undergraduate programme, those who are earnest about physics and other related subjects and willing to share their knowledge and opinions and engage in debate. This imagined community has been developed out of two sets of experiences. One is the experience on the short-term study-abroad programme in which he was inspired by the educational culture of discussion and debate. Makio's desire to experience this again led him to Boston and the summer course at a prestigious east-coast science and research-oriented university and to start and manage a discussion group at the college in Boston. Another experience was the summer course in physics he took at a university in Boston. This was the first time he met with others who were interested in the subject he was so passionate about. At the beginning of the summer, Makio expressed his frustration at not having anybody to talk to about physics at his college.

> I'm making friends. But our attitudes towards physics are different. For them it is a set of knowledge that is necessary for engineering. But I'm interested in how what the study of physics reveals affects our lives...I want to be able to refine my thinking by talking to others. I feel like I'm going around in circles thinking by myself. It's really difficult without having anybody to talk to. (Excerpt 9, Interview 8, August 2012)

Makio's comment in the email after the summer seems to indicate that meeting other students who are interested in physics stimulated his imagination for a future ideal community of learning and strengthened his desire for a transfer to become a member of the community.

The summer session was fun. That's because I was able to study all day and every day with only those students who are really motivated [about studying physics]. I'm very excited to think I'll get to meet more people like them as I move up to the advanced levels. (Excerpt 10, Interview 8, October 2012)

The concept of an imagined community was introduced by Norton (2001) into SLA and its motivating capacity has been discussed by various L2 motivation researchers (Murphey *et al.*, 2012; Murray, 2011; Pavlenko & Norton, 2007; Ryan & Irie, 2014; Yashima, 2013b). Makio seems to have partially experienced and confirmed the existence of the community he had been imagining based on past experiences, which then further expanded to the more advanced and serious community of physics major students that he is imagining joining at his target university. His experiential capital is shaping his ideal self and imagined community, the latter requiring English proficiency, a certain level of understanding of physics, and most importantly passion for the subject to qualify for its membership. These, in turn, are exerting their self-regulatory power on his studies for the TOEFL and the other required courses for the transfer.

Transferable Ideal L2 self

One of the most fascinating moments for us in this longitudinal study was when Makio's future self-image of starting a business in a developing country, which was motivating him to regulate his actions and learning of English, and was so clear and stable for the first year of our research, shifted so dramatically. The total overhaul of the hoped-for future self, brought about by the earthquake, was such a surprise that we began to doubt the stability of the ideal self-concept. The change in Makio's ideal self developed between Interview 3 and Interview 4 and when we saw him nearly five months after the earthquake, his mind was no longer set on establishing a sustainable business in a developing country – the ideal self he had so vividly described in his first and subsequent interviews. Boyatzis and Akrivou (2006) call such an emergence of new future aspirations as a phase change, borrowing a term from complex theory (2006: 628). Their point is that a small noticing of desires can bring about changes in people's ideal self, tremendously impacting their views and behaviours. Makio's noticing of his desire to understand the situation in Fukushima led him to develop his ideal self as a physicist and drove him to study harder for a transfer to a more suitable and advanced environment.

However sudden and unforeseeable the trigger may be, the adaptation of the new ideal self is undoubtedly influenced by self-efficacy and imagination that are already part of the current self. While Makio had not focused on studying science before, after he became interested in nuclear physics, he started to review mathematics and physics using high school textbooks that he borrowed from the local library. Makio's self-efficacy in school gained from the university entrance exam experience has been transferred to help him be optimistic about his success in a new academic field, as he sees that his ideal self is attainable and plausible.

Makio's Ideal L2 self has been transferred to his new ideal self. He now imagines himself as researching, presenting or teaching using English, rather than talking to government officials in a developing country. The durability, with slight modifications, of his Ideal L2 self is necessary and inevitable because it continues to be an integral part of Makio's successful future. His image of being an effective user of English is already a well-established part of his self-concept and provides continuity over various hoped-for futures selves, affecting the selection and construction of possible selves to pursue.

Final Thoughts

We have looked into one student's trajectory of his Ideal L2 self as part of a changing ideal self. Makio is neither exceptionally gifted in learning a language nor a typically good student. In fact, he can deal only with matters that inspire his interests, a fact that has caused difficulties for him in formal educational settings. However, at least in the part of his life that we are observing, Makio's vivid hoped-for future self-images, that include his Ideal L2 self as an effective user of English, are motivating him to learn English and regulating his plans and actions for L2 learning.

We identified experiential capital as a seedbed for the development of the ideal self and its L2 component. These experiences range from instantly life-changing, such as natural disasters, to the seemingly inconsequential, such as having problems arriving at a hotel on an overseas trip, or those that take a long period of time to have an impact, such as going to a karate school for over 15 years. How these experiences are internalised and become part of the self play a key role in the formation of hoped-for future selves.

The pre-condition for the L2 Motivational Self System is that learners have successful future self-imagery in the first place. The vast majority of first-year Japanese university students that we have met do not have these images, or at most, they are vague and hopeful rather than tangible and seen as achievable (Irie & Brewster, 2013). The majority of adolescents in Japan typically spend their time in class, club activities after school and cram schools for university entrance exams (Fukuzawa & LeTendre, 2001; Johnson & Johnson, 1996). They have a limited range of experiences, which do not stimulate their curiosity and imagination, preventing them from developing vivid future self-images. This lack of imagination seems to be connected, at least partially, to a tendency among Japanese university students to be inward looking (Yashima, 2013a). The fact that many students cannot imagine themselves as functional users of English, particularly in the current climate, in which there is an abundant discourse on the value of becoming global citizens, is something to be taken seriously by language educators. To practically address this, several researchers have started to focus on imagination and visualisation, which are now increasingly recognised as useful resources in language learning (Dörnyei & Kubanyiova, 2014; Murray, 2011; Magid & Chan, 2012; Ryan & Irie, 2014). This interest in stimulating learners' imagination and visualisation of future selves has led to specific intervention programmes (Magid & Chan, 2012, see also this volume chapters 18, 19 and 20) and practical teaching suggestions (Dörnyei & Kubanyiova, 2014).

Perhaps more of a challenge is that, in addition to the lack of imagination, having to spend six years in high school studying English as a school subject that is ultimately assessed by the receptive skills and explicit knowledge of grammar and vocabulary in exams is not conducive to the development of a successful image as a functional user of English. In this environment, students often lack the opportunities to build the self-efficacy required to see the possibility of realising goals. Researchers such as Yashima and Zenuk-Nishide (2008) suggest fostering an imagined community that, in the future, students can envision taking part in. This may be an effective way to start the positive self-regulating motivational cycle that we have seen Makio has developed for himself. If we are to believe in the power of the Ideal L2 self as a motivator for language learners in Japan, we must encourage an educational system that inspires students to invest in gaining experiences that may not have immediate goals but may help them gain self-efficacy in foreign language learning and use, enabling them to incorporate into a hoped-for possible self an L2 self-image as an effective user of the target foreign language.

Note

(1) The original transcriptions in Japanese are available upon request.

References

Anderson, B. (1991) *Imagined Communities: Reflections on the Origin and Spread of Nationalism*. London: Verso.

Bandura, A. (1977) Self-efficacy: Toward a unifying theory of behavioral change. *Psychological Review* 84 (2), 191–215.

Bandura, A. (1986) *Social Foundations of Thought and Action*. New York, NY: Prentice-Hall.

Bandura, A. (1994) Self-efficacy. In V.S. Amachaudran (ed.) *Encyclopedia of Human Behavior*, Vol. 4 (p. 71). New York, NY: Academic Press.

Barreto, M.L. and Frazier, L. (2012) Coping with life events through possible selves. *Journal of Applied Social Psychology* 42 (7), 1785–1810.

Boyatzis, R. and Akrivou, K. (2006) The ideal self as the driver of intentional change. *Journal of Management Development* 25 (7), 624–642.

Coleman, J.S. (1988) Social capital in the creation of human capital. *The American Journal of Sociology* 94, 95–120.

Csizér, K. and Kormos, J. (2009) Attitudes, selves and motivated learning behaviour: A comparative analysis of structural models for Hungarian secondary and university learners of English. In Z. Dörnyei and E. Ushioda (eds) *Motivation, Language Identity and the L2 Self* (pp. 98–119). Bristol: Multilingual Matters.

Dörnyei, Z. (2005) *The Psychology of the Language Learner: Individual Differences in Second Language Acquisition*. Mahwah, NJ: Lawrence Erlbaum.

Dörnyei, Z. and Kubanyiova, M. (2014) *Motivating Learners, Motivating Teachers: Building Vision in the Language Classroom*. Cambridge: Cambridge University Press.

Dörnyei, Z. and Ushioda, E. (eds) (2009) *Motivation, Language Identity and the L2 Self*. Bristol: Multilingual Matters.

Dörnyei, Z. and Ushioda, E. (2011) *Teaching and Researching Motivation* (2nd edn). Harlow: Longman.

Dunkel, C. and Kerpelman, J. (eds) (2006) *Possible Selves: Theory, Research and Applications*. New York, NY: Nova Science.

Erickson, M.G. (2007) The meaning of the future: Toward a more specific definition of possible selves. *Review of General Psychology* 11 (4), 348–358.

Fukuzawa, R.E. and LeTendre, G.K. (2001) *Intense Years: How Japanese Adolescents Balance School, Family, and Friends*. New York, NY: Routledge Falmer.

Higgins, E.T. (1987) Self-discrepancy: A theory relating self and affect. *Psychological Review* 94 (3), 319–340.

Irie, K. and Brewster, D. (2013) One curriculum, three stories: Ideal L2 self and L2-self-discrepancy profiles. In M. Apple, D. Da Silva and T. Fellner (eds) *Language Learning Motivation in Japan* (pp. 110–128). Bristol: Multilingual Matters.

Johnson, M.L. and Johnson, J.R. (1996) *Daily Life in Japanese High Schools*. ERIC Clearinghouse for Social Studies/Social Science Education Bloomington. ED406301.

Kim, T. (2009) The sociocultural interface between ideal self and ought-to self: A case study of two Korean students' ESL motivation. In Z. Dörnyei and E. Ushioda (eds) *Motivation, Language Identity and the L2 Self* (pp. 274–294). Bristol: Multilingual Matters.

Lamb, M. (2011) Future selves, motivation and autonomy in long-term EFL learning trajectories. In G. Murray, X. Gao and T. Lamb (eds) *Identity, Motivation, and Autonomy in Language Learning* (pp. 177–194). Bristol: Multilingual Matters.

MacIntyre, P.D., Mackinnon, S.P. and Clément, R. (2009) Toward the development of a scale to assess possible selves as a source of language learning motivation. In Z. Dörnyei and E. Ushioda (eds) *Motivation, Language Identity and the L2 Self* (pp. 193–214). Bristol: Multilingual Matters.

Magid, M. and Chan, L.H. (2012) Motivating English learners by helping them visualise their Ideal L2 Self: Lessons from two motivational programmes. *Innovation in Language Learning and Teaching* 6 (2), 113–125.

Markus, H.R. and Nurius, P. (1986) Possible selves. *American Psychologist* 41 (9), 954–969.

Murphey, T., Falout, J., Fukada, Y. and Fukuda, T. (2012) Group dynamics: Collaborative agency in present communities of imagination. In S. Mercer, S. Ryan and M. Williams (eds) *Psychology in Language Learning: Insights from Research, Theory and Practice* (pp. 220–238). Basingstoke: Palgrave Macmillan.

Murray, G. (2011) Imagination, metacognition and the L2 self in a self-access learning environment. In G. Murray, X. Gao and T. Lamb (eds) *Identity, motivation and autonomy in language learning* (pp. 75–90). Bristol: Multilingual Matters.

Nakahara, S. and Yashima, T. (2012) *Toward the development of instruments to assess motivation based on the L2 motivational self system.* JACET Journal 55, 31–48.

Norton, B. (2001) Non-participation, imagined communities and the language classroom. In M. Breen (ed.) *Learner Contributions to Language Learning: New Directions in Research* (pp. 150–171). Harlow: Pearson Education.

Oyserman, D. and Fryberg, S. (2006) The possible selves of diverse adolescents: Content and function across gender, race and national origin. In C. Dunkel and J. Kerpelman (eds) *Possible Selves: Theory, Research, and Applications* (pp. 17–39). New York, NY: Nova Science Publishers, Inc.

Papi, M. (2010) The L2 motivational self system, L2 anxiety, and motivated behavior: A structural equation modeling approach. *System* 38 (3), 467–479.

Pavlenko, A. and Norton, B. (2007) Imagined communities, identity, and English language learning. In J. Cummins and C. Davison (eds) *International Handbook of English Language Teaching* (pp. 669–680). New York, NY: Springer.

Raoofi, S., Tan, B. H. and Chan, S. H. (2012) Self-efficacy in second/foreign language learning contexts. *English Language Teaching* 5 (11), 60–73.

Riggio, H. R. (2012) The psychology of self-efficacy. In S. L. Britner (ed.) *Self-efficacy in School and Community Settings* (pp. 1–18). New York, NY: Nova Science Publishers, Inc.

Ryan, S. (2009) Self and Identity in L2 Motivation in Japan: The Ideal L2 Self and Japanese Learners of English. In Z. Dörnyei and E. Ushioda (eds) *Motivation, Language Identity and the L2 Self* (pp. 120–143). Bristol: Multilingual Matters.

Ryan, S. and Irie, K. (2014) Imagined and possible selves: Stories we tell ourselves about ourselves. In S. Mercer and M. Williams (eds) *Multiple Perspectives on the Self in SLA* (pp. 109–123). Bristol: Multilingual Matters.

Sandefur, G.D., Meier, A. and Campbell, M. (2006) Family resources, social capital and college attendance. *Social Science Research* 35 (2), 525–553.

Schunk, D.H. (1989) Self-efficacy and cognitive skill learning. In C. Ames and R. Ames (eds) *Research on Motivation in Education: Vol. 3. Goals and Cognitions* (pp. 13–44). San Diego, CA: Academic.

Schunk, D.H. (1991) Self-efficacy and academic motivation. *Educational Psychologist* 26 (3–4), 207–231.

Taguchi, T., Magid, M. and Papi, M. (2009) The L2 motivational self system among Japanese, Chinese, and Iranian learners of English: A comparative study. In Z. Dörnyei and E. Ushioda (eds) *Motivation, Language Identity and the L2 Self* (pp. 66–97). Bristol: Multilingual Matters.

Yashima, T. (2013a) Imagined L2 selves and motivation for intercultural communication. In M. Apple, D. Da Silva and T. Fellner (eds) *Language Learning Motivation in Japan* (pp. 35–53). Bristol: Multilingual Matters.

Yashima, T. (2013b) Individuality, imagination and community in a globalizing world: An Asian EFL perspective. In P. Benson and L. Cooker (eds) *The Applied Linguistic Individual: Sociocultural Approaches to Identity, Agency and Autonomy* (pp. 46–58). Sheffield: Equinox Publishing.

Yashima, T. and Zenuk-Nishide, L. (2008) The impact of learning contexts on proficiency, attitudes, and L2 communication: Creating an imagined international community. *System* 36 (4), 566–585.

11 Self-Constructs in Language Learning: What is their Role in Self-Regulation?

Janina Iwaniec

Background

In 2005, Dörnyei proposed a tripartite model of language learning motivation, the Second Language (L2) Motivational Self System consisting of the Ideal L2 self, the Ought-to L2 self and the language learning experience. The proposition instigated a plethora of research to confirm the motivational properties of the model. In particular, the Ideal L2 self has been found to have a positive influence on language learning motivation (Al-Shehri, 2009; Csizér & Kormos, 2008a, 2008b, 2009; Kim, 2009; Kormos et al., 2011; Lamb, 2009; Lyons, 2009; Ryan, 2009; Segalowitz et al., 2009; Taguchi et al., 2009; White & Ding, 2009). However, there has been relatively little investigation into how other self-constructs, such as self-efficacy beliefs and English self-concept, influence self-regulatory behaviours of Polish students. Neither has there been enough examination of the extent to which these are related to the Ideal L2 self.

The Ideal L2 self is an image of oneself as a proficient speaker of an L2. It subsumes positive attitudes towards the members of the L2 community and includes the promotion aspects of instrumentality – motives related to career enhancement (Dörnyei, 2009: 29). In line with Markus and Nurius (1986), the Ideal self is a future self representing possible positive outcomes. In other words, language learners create a vision of themselves as successful L2 users. According to Higgins (1987), the motivational power of the Ideal self originates from the discrepancy between the future self and the present self that causes discomfort. To minimise the unpleasant experience, the individual attempts to diminish the existing gap; for example, by investing effort in language learning.

Other self-constructs that are frequently used in educational psychology include Bandura's (1977) self-efficacy beliefs and self-concept

(Shavelson *et al.*, 1976). Self-efficacy can be defined as an individual's perceptions of their ability to successfully complete a particular task (Bandura, 1977, 1997). In the case of language learning, it could be conceptualised as the learner's perceptions of their ability to complete various tasks connected with language learning, such as writing an e-mail in English or being able to give a short presentation. Bandura (1997) proposes that self-efficacy beliefs usually originate from one's previous experience of completing a task. However, they can also be modelled by verbal persuasion from significant others, observing others with a similar level of skill performing a task and even affective and physiological states experienced while completing a task. Schunk (1989, 2008) explains that high levels of self-efficacy beliefs enhance motivation as individuals believe in a positive outcome of their learning. Motivation, in turn, aids effort and persistence at the task. In this way, individuals can improve their performance while maintaining their self-efficacy beliefs. One of the few studies examining the role of self-efficacy beliefs in the domain of language learning is by Hsieh and Kang (2010), who reported a positive correlation between self-efficacy beliefs and language learning proficiency.

Self-concept is 'a person's perception of himself' (Shavelson *et al.*, 1976: 411). Self-concept is differentiated for different domains (e.g. maths self-concept, English self-concept) and is hierarchically organised. For example, maths self-concept and English self-concept can be organised under a more general academic self-concept (Shavelson *et al.*, 1976). Whereas self-efficacy beliefs are concerned with specific tasks and are fairly malleable, self-concept is theorised to be a rather stable perception of one's abilities at a more general level, such as at the level of a school subject (Bong & Skaalvik, 2003). Although self-concept, just like self-efficacy beliefs, is derived from personal experience, it is also heavily influenced by social comparison and comparisons across domains (Shavelson *et al.*, 1976). Unlike the Ideal L2 self and self-efficacy beliefs, self-concept is past oriented (Bong & Skaalvik, 2003) (see Table 11.1 for comparison of the main characteristics of the three self-constructs). Similarly to other self-constructs, self-concept is considered to influence motivation and achievement (Bong & Skaalvik, 2003) as people who have a positive self-concept are more likely to engage in an action to maintain its high levels. In contrast, individuals with low self-concept are not likely to pursue an action, which does not allow them to improve their performance or boost their levels of self-concept. For the purpose of this study, self-concept in the domain of English as a foreign language, later referred to as English self-concept, is investigated.

Macaro (2001: 264) claims that 'across learning contexts, those learners who are pro-active in their pursuit of language learning appear to learn best'. In other words, students who self-regulate achieve better outcomes than those who do not. It seems worthwhile to examine to

Table 11.1 Characteristics of the three self-constructs

	English self-concept	Self-efficacy beliefs	Ideal L2 self
Time orientation	Past-oriented (Bong & Skaalvik, 1993)	Future-oriented (Bong & Skaalvik, 1993)	Future-oriented (Dörnyei, 2005)
Temporal stability	Stable (Bong & Skaalvik, 1993)	Malleable (Bong & Skaalvik, 1993)	Malleable (Markus & Nurius, 1986)
Judgment specificity (within the domain)	General (Bong & Skaalvik, 1993)	Specific (Bong & Skaalvik, 1993)	General
Key antecedents	Frames of reference, causal attributions, reflected appraisals from significant others, mastery experiences, psychological centrality (Shavelson et al., 1976)	Mastery experience, verbal persuasion, vicarious experience, affective and physiological states (Bandura, 1997)	Aspirations (Ruvolo & Markus, 1992), real-life experiences of L2 community members (Dörnyei, 2005), personal goals (Dörnyei, 2005)

what extent self-regulation can be influenced by other variables, such as self-constructs. Self-regulation is defined as 'the degree to which individuals are metacognitively, motivationally, and behaviourally active participants in their own learning process' (Zimmerman, 1989: 4). Self-regulation is not, however, a skill or ability but rather a cyclical process, in which learners plan and set their goals, perform activities and reflect on the efficiency of the learning techniques they use (Zimmerman, 2000). As a result, self-regulated students can be described as intrinsically motivated, aware of their preferred learning styles and persistent in pursuing their goals (Zimmerman, 1994).

The study described in this paper is part of a larger research project that seeks to establish what motivates young Polish language learners. However, in this paper, I outline methods and results pertinent to the research questions specified below:

(1) What is the influence of the Ideal L2 self, self-efficacy beliefs and English self-concept on the self-regulation of Polish students?
(2) What is the relationship between the three self-constructs, the Ideal L2 self, self-efficacy beliefs and English self-concept, in a population of Polish learners?
(3) What are the sources of English self-concept, and to a certain extent, self-efficacy beliefs of Polish language learners?

The choice of population, Polish teenage language learners enrolled in compulsory English language courses, is not accidental. To date, there have been few studies into language learning motivation in the Polish context (see Gardner, 2012; Pawlak, 2012), despite the fact that Poland is one of the biggest European countries with a relatively large number of language learners. Poland is largely a monolingual country with Polish as the dominant language of its population. Polish is one of the most frequently spoken Slavonic languages. It does not exist in isolation as other Slavonic languages are spoken south and east of Poland (Lewis, 2009), which to a certain extent, might facilitate acquisition and communication in these languages. Belonging to the Indo-European family, Polish shares a substantial number of similarities with other European languages, including English (Lewis, 2009).

Methods

In the current study, I employed a mixed-method approach to investigate the relationships between the Ideal L2 self, self-efficacy beliefs and English self-concept and to examine their influence on self-regulation. Firstly, I used semi-structured interviews to obtain qualitative data about the three self-constructs and self-regulation of Polish students. These data were also used to prepare a motivational questionnaire appropriate for young Polish learners of English. Secondly, I administered the motivational questionnaire to obtain the quantitative data to illustrate the trends in the population and establish significant relationships between the variables.

Interviews

Nine (five female, four male) middle school students aged 15–16 years, characterised by their teachers as motivated language learners, took part in the interviews. From private conversations with the teachers involved, it became clear that they concurrently understood the term 'motivated language learners' in two ways. The first understanding involved students who were successful language learners in that their level of English was higher than that of their peers, their grades were very good or even excellent and they tended to participate in various competitions testing their English proficiency and knowledge of the cultural heritage of English native speakers. The second definition referred to students whose proficiency was not necessarily above average. Nevertheless, they demonstrated interest in language learning, positive language learning attitudes and clearly invested effort in the study of English.

Six of the interviewees came from two schools located in rural areas, whereas the other three studied in an urban school. English was a compulsory course for all of the participants. The interview lasted 35 minutes on average. As the interviews were part of a larger study, the questions elicited data about a number of topics confirmed to be relevant in the language learning motivation literature; namely, language learning goals, beliefs about one's ability to study English, contact with English (direct and indirect), effort invested in language learning and its manifestations, the influence of 'important others', such as parents and peers, on language learning behaviour, language learning attitudes and experience and views on the role of gender in language learning. However, in this paper, I will focus on the data on beliefs about one's ability to study English as well as their sources and effort invested in language learning.

All of the interviews were conducted by the researcher in Polish, the native language of the participants. Before the interview data were transcribed, the participants had been assigned pseudonyms, which are used in the latter parts of this paper, to ensure anonymity. The data analysis was a cyclical process. In the first step, utterances concerning similar topics were grouped together. The themes that emerged in this way were then defined into categories and subcategories and ascribed an appropriate code. The process was repeated until all definitions were precise and all utterances were coded accurately.

The questionnaire study

The participants

Two hundred and thirty-six students aged 15–16 years, enrolled in a compulsory English course in their schools as part of the national curriculum, completed the motivational questionnaire. Similarly to the interviewees, the language learners came from three schools, two of which were located in rural areas and one in the city. In total, 171 students came from rural schools and 65 came from the urban one. One hundred and twenty-two participants were females, 112 were males and two participants failed to provide data on their gender. Most of the participants (162) had been studying English for more than six years prior to the completion of the questionnaire, with the second largest group (61) attending an English course for three to six years. Only eight participants had less than three years of English language experience and five failed to provide the appropriate data. The differences can be accounted for by two explanations. Firstly, until recently, foreign language education was compulsory from the age of 11 only. However, head teachers could use the available teaching hours at their discretion to provide extra language tuition earlier. In many cases, additional language courses (paid for by parents) were available at schools to younger students. Secondly, whereas foreign language education is compulsory, different languages such as English, German, Russian or French can be provided in different schools. Therefore, some students may have studied a foreign language other than English before they joined middle school.

The motivational questionnaire

Since the data were collected as part of a larger study, the questionnaire included 12 scales but only 4 of them are reported in this chapter; namely, self-regulation, the Ideal L2 self, self-efficacy beliefs and English self-concept. The overall number of items, including items about the students' background information, was 103. The motivational scales were measured using a five-point Likert scale. The answers ranged from 'I strongly agree' coded later as (5) to 'I strongly disagree' (1). The conceptualisation of the scales that the questionnaire set out to measure is provided below:

(1) Self-regulation (11 items) – the degree to which students are motivationally, metacognitively and behaviourally active participants in the process of learning English (adapted from Zimmerman, 1989: 4). Self-regulation involves taking responsibility for the learning process and developing learning strategies that are most effective for the

individual. For example, *I have my own techniques that help me focus on studying English*. The scale was developed based on the conceptualisation of self-regulation. However, a number of items were adapted from the Self-regulating Capacity in Vocabulary Learning Scale of Tseng *et al.* (2006). In particular, I used reworded items addressing satiation control, environmental control, metacognitive control and commitment control.

(2) Ideal L2 self (six items) – students' vision of themselves using English successfully in the future. For example, *I imagine myself speaking English abroad*. The scale was designed to target four main language skills; namely reading, writing, speaking and listening. Some items from this scale were adapted from the motivational questionnaire used by Csizér and Kormos (2009).

(3) Self-efficacy beliefs (eight items) – students' beliefs in their skills and ability to be able to use English successfully in the future. For example, *I am certain that I will be able to watch TV in English*. Similarly to the Ideal L2 self scale, the items targeted reading, writing, speaking and listening comprehension skills.

(4) English self-concept (seven items) – students' perceptions of themselves as learners of English based on their past experiences and social comparison. For example, *In comparison with other students in my class, I am good at English*. This scale was adapted from Marsh's (1990) Academic Self-description Questionnaire.

Procedures

The motivational questionnaire was prepared in Polish based on the results of the interview part of the study. It was then piloted by asking nine students aged 15–16 years to complete it while thinking aloud. The items that were found to be problematic were subsequently reworded or dispensed with. The final version of the questionnaire was administered in schools during English classes. The researcher was present at the time of administration and explained to the participants that their participation in the study was entirely voluntary and that the data were strictly confidential and anonymous. This was done in order to ensure that the students felt free to answer the items truthfully. The completion of the questionnaire took 20 minutes on average. However, the students were allowed to finish completing the questionnaire at their own pace, even if it took substantially longer.

The data were analysed using SPSS version 18.0. Factor analysis (Maximum Likelihood with Direct Oblimin rotation) was conducted to confirm that the items measured the intended variables. Subsequently, correlational analysis was run to identify the relationships between variables, and a series of regression analyses was carried out to find out how well self-constructs predict self-regulation and to what extent English self-concept and self-efficacy beliefs can contribute to the Ideal L2 self.

Results and Discussion

The factor analysis revealed that the items measured four separate concepts. In the case of the English self-concept and self-regulation, some items had to be dropped as they did not seem to measure the intended variables well. The final scales consisted of either six items, as in the case of English self-concept and the Ideal L2 self, or eight items (self-regulation and self-efficacy beliefs). The reliability of the scales was high with all values above 0.8. For more details, see Table 11.2.

The mean scores in Table 11.2 demonstrate that the students scored highest on the self-efficacy beliefs variable, followed by English self-concept and self-regulation. The participants scored lowest on the Ideal L2 self scale. The scores of above three on the five-point scale on English self-concept and self-efficacy beliefs suggest that, on the whole, Polish students tended to have a rather positive view of their language learning skills. Nevertheless, there was a degree of variation between students as expressed by the standard deviation, which might mean that some students might hold highly positive beliefs, whereas others exhibit negative beliefs.

The interview data seem to provide support for the claim that there is variation within the population, with some students exhibiting a positive English self (and, to some extent, self-efficacy beliefs) and others displaying a negative self-concept. The interviewees, described as motivated language learners by their teachers, reported having at least moderately positive views of their language learning skills. As many as five out of

Table 11.2 The composition, reliability and mean scores of the final scales

Variable	No. of final items	Reliability	Eigenvalue	% of variance explained	Mean score	Standard deviation
English self-concept	6	.892	3.54	58.99	3.13	.97
Ideal L2 self	6	.860	2.66	44.30	2.72	.93
Self-efficacy beliefs	8	.910	4.45	55.61	3.23	.88
Self-regulation	8	.809	2.79	34.88	2.95	.79

nine students claimed to have strong beliefs in their abilities. One of them was Kasia, who noted 'to be honest, it (language learning) doesn't cause me any trouble; I learn it easily so it doesn't take much time' (Kasia). The other students reported that their English self-concept to learn foreign languages was average. For example, Monika appeared to believe that she was an average language learner and that her higher than average language proficiency was the result of hard work. She said 'I don't think I have a gift. I think I'm like the others but I put more effort into it. I know there are people who have a knack for it and I admire them, but it's definitely not me' (Monika). Some students went into more detail when describing their language learning abilities. Magda first noted 'I'm a person who, in general, finds it easy to study'. Then she added 'I don't have problems with grammar. Tenses are very easy, but if I have to learn very difficult words, many of which start with the same syllable, it is rather hard' (Magda). As seen in the quote above, whereas Magda's English self-concept was high, her self-efficacy beliefs for different sub-skills involved in language learning varied. Magda was confident about studying grammar but believed that memorising vocabulary was more difficult.

To be able to successfully influence students' positive thinking about their language learning abilities, it is important to know how their English self-concept and self-efficacy beliefs are constructed. The interview data provided useful insights into this matter. When asked about the sources of beliefs in their language ability, the interviewees named a number of predecessors of their English self-concepts, such as positive language learning experiences (eight students), grades (five), comparison with their peers (five), appraisals from important others (one), emotional cues (five) and even comparisons to their progress in other subjects (1). All the determinants are in line with the predictions of Bandura (1997) and Shavelson et al. (1976) as specified in Table 11.1.

In all cases students mentioned more than one antecedent of their positive English self-concept. For example, Gosia reported:

> We get reports from my language school. Last year I had very good results and a very high average from tests. When I compare that to what it was like when I was ten, I can see I have made a lot of progress. Also from the praise from my tutors, although they always praise me, looking at my final mark and my results, I can see it's good. (Gosia)

Apart from grades, progress and the appraisal of tutors, later on Gosia listed positive language experiences and emotional clues, and compared English to chemistry and physics, the two subjects that she found difficult. The sources of English self-concept and self-efficacy beliefs seem abundant and readily available to language learners.

Whereas self-concept is 'a person's perception of himself' (Shavelson *et al.*, 1976: 411), the interview data suggest that it is, at the same time, socially constructed. Firstly, students tend to obtain information from social comparisons between group members. Therefore, students in mixed-level groups might draw starkly different conclusions regarding their self-concept, with some considering themselves talented and others believing themselves to be inept at languages. Secondly, students derive information from important others, such as teachers, and their evaluations of their abilities. Finally, teachers and learners co-construct self-concepts by providing positive or negative language learning experiences. Consequently, the levels of English self-concept are not only dependent on the individual but also on the whole learning environment, including other learners and teachers.

Whereas the overall score for self-efficacy beliefs and English self-concept was above the middle point of the scale, the means for the Ideal L2 self and self-regulation were lower (i.e. 2.75 and 2.95 respectively). The results suggest that a typical Polish student does not have a well-established Ideal L2 self. However, the interview data reveal that motivated learners have developed visions of their success. Piotrek described what he wanted to achieve by comparing himself to his language teacher:

> I know for sure that my teacher is better at it (English) than me, but I can sometimes hear that, I suppose, she makes a mistake. I doubt that it is because of lack of knowledge. Everyone makes mistakes, don't they? But I think that if I study, I will have a chance to speak better (than my teacher). (Piotrek)

When asked about what she wanted to achieve in English, Ania briefly but resolutely replied 'The maximum'. For Irek, who did not know what he would like to be in the future, English was so important that his future profession would definitely be linked to it. It seems then that, for many of the participants who were interviewed, the Ideal L2 self is a vision of what they will be like when they have achieved their language learning goals.

Whereas the questionnaire results implied that Polish students rarely self-regulate, the interviews with motivated learners revealed a different picture. As Table 11.3 demonstrates, the interviewees tended to engage in additional language activities. Four out of nine students were enrolled in additional language classes, two attended language schools, one had private tuition and one attended extracurricular classes provided by the school. Seven students used the Internet, in particular to read the news, to prepare for tests and to find explanations to problems that they did not understand. Pastime activities involving the use of English were also popular, such as watching films, listening to

Table 11.3 Additional language learning activities endorsed by interviewees

Activity	No. of students
Watching films	5
Music	5
Computer games	2
Internet	7
Language school	2
Private tuition	1
Extracurricular classes	1
Language learning programmes	1
Reading books	2

music and, to a lesser extent, playing computer games and reading books in English. One student also reported using a computer program to study English vocabulary.

Motivated language learners invested time and effort in studying English and exhibited a number of self-regulatory strategies. They tended to have preferred language learning methods. As Kasia said:

> The best way to study is not to memorise because you can forget what you've learnt quickly, but to understand. But when you've got vocabulary, it is not possible to do it this way. I like it when words are in groups according to a topic, for example, house. I find it easier to study. (Kasia)

Kasia first strove to understand how the language worked. When memorisation of vocabulary was required, she used categorisation to make it more efficient. The students realised in what environments they learnt best and tried to avoid possible distractions. For example, Magda tended to study at seven because at this time there was nothing interesting on the news that could distract her. Once again, the interview data pointed to the variation among language learners.

Correlations

The correlational analysis revealed a number of positive relationships between variables that ranged in strength from medium to large.

Table 11.4 Correlations between the variables

	Self-regulation	Ideal L2 self	Self-efficacy beliefs
Self-regulation			
Ideal L2 self	.657*		
Self-efficacy beliefs	.547*	.744*	
English self-concept	.407*	.602*	.719*

Note: *Correlation is significant at the .01 level (two-tailed).

Table 11.4 shows that all the correlations between the three self-constructs were large. However, the Ideal L2 self was more closely related to self-efficacy beliefs than to English self-concept. When self-regulation was taken into account, it correlated most strongly with the Ideal L2 self, followed by self-efficacy beliefs. The correlation between self-regulation and English self-concept was the lowest among the variables.

Of the three-self constructs, self-regulation turned out to be associated most strongly with the Ideal L2 self. The strength of this correlation was large. Similar results were reported by Csizér and Kormos (Chapter 5, this volume) who found positive correlations between the Ideal L2 self and two out of three aspects of self-regulation, commitment control and satiation control, in three student populations: secondary school students, university students and adult language learners.

The results of the correlational analysis revealed that the three self-constructs tended to be more closely related to each other than to self-regulation. This finding confirms that the three are similar constructs, whereas the self-regulation scale subsumes items expressing language learning behaviours rather than self-beliefs. The only exception was the correlation between the Ideal L2 self and English self-concept as the Ideal L2 self correlated better with self-regulation than English self-concept. However, the difference was not large (.657 and .602). The explanation for this could be found in the differences between the two self-constructs. Whereas the Ideal L2 self embodies a future vision of oneself speaking English successfully (Dörnyei, 2005), English self-concept is an actual self representing the current beliefs and feelings of the individual (Higgins, 1987). In view of Higgins's (1987) self-discrepancy theory, English self-concept might be considered the benchmark to which the Ideal L2 self is compared and from which it derives its motivational force. The bigger the gap between the two, the more unpleasant the feelings the individual experiences, which results in a stronger motivational force to minimise the tension. This, in turn, can be done by actively putting effort into language learning.

Regression analyses

To find out to what extent the variables contribute to each other, I carried out regression analyses. Firstly, self-regulation was regressed on all self-constructs (Table 11.5). Despite the relatively high correlations with the variables, only the Ideal L2 self was found to be a direct predictor of self-regulated behaviour. The regression analysis of the Ideal L2 self (Table 11.6) revealed that both self-efficacy beliefs and English self-concept significantly contributed to the variable. However, like the results of the correlational analyses, the impact of English self-concept was much weaker than that of self-efficacy beliefs.

The regression analysis of self-regulation confirmed the vital role of the Ideal L2 self in motivating language learners (Dörnyei, 2009). As Csizér and Kormos (2009) explained, the Ideal L2 self subsumes intrinsic interest together with a powerful self-concept, both of which have been reported to predict the amount of effort expended on a particular action. The regression analysis of the Ideal L2 self confirmed this proposition as self-efficacy beliefs and, to a lesser extent, English self-concept were found to be its direct predictors. It appears unlikely that it is possible to create an image of oneself as a successful language learner without the actual beliefs in one's ability to fulfil the vision. Dörnyei asserted that while drawing on 'hopes, wishes, and fantasies' (Dörnyei, 2009: 11), the Ideal

Table 11.5 Regression analysis of self-regulation

Model	B	SE B	Beta	R^2	F for change in R^2
1. Ideal L2 self	.502	.070	.606*	.428	47.847
2. Self-efficacy beliefs	.055	.086	.062		
3. English self-concept	.000	.062	.000		

Note: *$p < .001$.

Table 11.6 Regression analysis of Ideal L2 self

Model	B	SE B	Beta	R^2	F for change in R^2
1. Self-efficacy beliefs	.666	.070	.632*	.572	134.069
2. English self-concept	.150	.062	.161*		

Note: *$p < .001$.

L2 self is a possible self that can one day become reality, provided that the necessary amount of effort is invested.

The results of the regression analyses showed that English self-concept and self-efficacy beliefs did not predict self-regulation directly. Nevertheless, their influence was mediated by the Ideal L2 self. While they seem to be prerequisites of self-regulation, they do not guarantee that self-regulatory behaviour will take place. This was illustrated by one of the interviewees, Tomek, who reported no difficulties in studying English and declared that he found it much easier than his colleagues. However, at the same time, Tomek admitted that he often put minimal effort into his class and test preparation by either learning the necessary things by heart or not studying at all. He claimed, 'I remember more quickly what our teacher says in class. I don't have to study'. Tomek's case shows that high self-concept and self-efficacy beliefs might sometimes have an adverse effect on the amount of effort learners make.

Despite the fact that self-efficacy beliefs, together with English self-concept are both actual selves (Bong & Skaalvik, 2003), self-efficacy beliefs predicted the Ideal L2 self more closely than English self-concept. The reason for such close proximity could be the fact that both the Ideal L2 self and self-efficacy beliefs refer to the future (Bong & Skaalvik, 2003; Dörnyei, 2009). Self-efficacy beliefs are beliefs about the individual's ability to successfully complete a specific task connected with language learning (Bandura, 1997). Therefore, they are a form of prediction of what may happen in the near future. Similarly, the Ideal L2 self represents the future, although this vision is more distant. On the other hand, English self-concept refers to the past (Bong & Skaalvik, 2003). The interviewees not only reflected on whether they had successfully completed a task but also compared their results with those of their colleagues and, in many cases, received feedback on their performance from others. Therefore, in many ways, English self-concept draws on another part of Dörnyei's (2005) L2 Motivational Self System, which is the language learning experience.

Conclusion

In this mixed-methods study, I attempted to find answers to the three following research questions: (1) to what extent do self-constructs predict the self-regulation of Polish students, (2) what is the relationship between self-constructs and (3) what are the antecedents of English self-concept and self-efficacy beliefs?

The results of correlational and regression analyses suggest that the Ideal L2 self is the best predictor of self-regulatory behaviour in the population of Polish teenage language learners. This confirms previous research findings (see Dörnyei & Ushioda, 2009). The strong motivational power of the Ideal L2 self can be ascribed to its intrinsic values, inclusion of a powerful self-concept and visualisation of language learning goals. Additionally, the results of the interviews suggest that motivated learners who reported self-regulation tended to display positive English self-concept and self-efficacy beliefs.

The Ideal L2 self is closely related to self-efficacy beliefs, and to a lesser extent to English self-concept, suggesting that it is necessary to hold positive beliefs towards language learning tasks in order to be able to visualise oneself as a successful language learner. A strong positive link was also found between self-efficacy beliefs and English self-concept, both of which are concerned with the actual evaluation of one's own language skills.

The results of the interviews suggest that English self-concept is socially co-constructed. Students receive information about their language learning abilities from the following types of sources: their own experiences, comparisons with their peers, feedback from their teachers and their grades.

The findings point to an important role of positive language learning beliefs that support the creation and endorsement of the Ideal L2 self and enable self-regulation. As Bandura (1997) explained, self-efficacy beliefs might affect not only motivation but also thought processes. People who are equally skilful may differ in their performance on the same task according to their levels of self-efficacy beliefs. Similarly, promoting high levels of self-concept could be beneficial for language achievement, as students who consider themselves good language learners tend to be more likely to engage in language learning behaviours (Bong & Skaalvik, 2003). To stimulate positive self-efficacy beliefs and self-concept, teachers need to adjust the level of activities to the abilities of students in order to create successful language learning experiences. Constructive feedback is also essential, as focusing on the negative aspects only might have a negative impact on students' self-beliefs.

References

Al-Shehri, A. (2009) Motivation and vision: The relation between the ideal L2 self, imagination and visual style. In Z. Dörnyei and E. Ushioda (eds) *Motivation, Language Identity and the L2 Self* (pp. 164–171). Bristol: Multilingual Matters.

Bandura, A. (1977) Self-efficacy: Toward a unifying theory of behavioral change. *Psychological Review* 84 (2), 191–215.

Bandura, A. (1997) *Self-Efficacy: The Exercise of Control*. New York, NY: W.H. Freeman and Company.

Bong, M. and Skaalvik, E.M. (2003) Academic self-concept and self-efficacy: How different are they really? *Educational Psychology Review* 15 (1), 1–40.

Csizér, K. and Kormos, J. (2008a) An overview of Hungarian secondary school students' foreign language motivation. In H.V. Knudsen (ed.) *Secondary School Education* (pp. 65–87). Hauppauge, NY: Nova Science Publishers.

Csizér, K. and Kormos, J. (2008b) The relationship of intercultural contact and language learning motivation among Hungarian students of English and German. *Journal of Multilingual and Multicultural Development* 29 (1), 30–48.

Csizér, K. and Kormos, J. (2009) Motivation, language identity and the L2 self. In Z. Dörnyei and E. Ushioda (eds) *Motivation, Language Identity and the L2 Self* (pp. 98–119). Bristol: Multilingual Matters.

Dörnyei, Z. (2005) *The Psychology of the Language Learner: Individual Differences in Second Language Acquisition.* Mahwah, NY: Erlbaum.

Dörnyei, Z. (2009) The L2 motivational self system. In Z. Dörnyei and E. Ushioda (eds) *Motivation, Language Identity and the L2 Self* (pp. 9–43). Bristol: Multilingual Matters.

Dörnyei, Z. and Ushioda, E. (2009) *Motivation, Language Identity and the L2 Self.* Bristol: Multilingual Matters.

Gardner, R.C. (2012) Integrative motivation and global language (English) acquisition in Poland. *Studies in Second Language Learning and Teaching* 2 (2), 215–226.

Higgins, E.T. (1987) Self-discrepancy: A theory relating self and affect. *Psychological Review* 94 (3), 319–340.

Hsieh, P.P.H. and Kang, H.S. (2010) Attribution and self-efficacy and their interrelationship in the Korean EFL context. *Language Learning* 60 (3), 606–627.

Kim, T. (2009) The sociocultural interface between ideal L2 self and ought-to self: A case study of two Korean students' ESL motivation. In Z. Dörnyei and E. Ushioda (eds) *Motivation, Language Identity and the L2 Self* (pp. 274–295). Bristol: Multilingual Matters.

Kormos, J., Kiddle, T. and Csizér, K. (2011) Systems of goals, attitudes, and self-related beliefs in second-language-learning motivation. *Applied Linguistics* 32 (5), 495–516.

Lamb, M. (2009) Situating the L2 self: Two Indonesian school learners of English. In Z. Dörnyei and E. Ushioda (eds) *Motivation, Language Identity and the L2 Self* (pp. 229–248). Bristol: Multilingual Matters.

Lewis, P. (2009) *Ethnologue: Languages of the World* (16th edn). Dallas, TX: SIL International.

Lyons, Z. (2009) Imagined identity and the L2 self in the French Foreign Legion. In Z. Dörnyei and E. Ushioda (eds) *Motivation, Language Identity and the L2 Self* (pp. 248–274). Bristol: Multilingual Matters.

Macaro, E. (2001) *Learning Strategies in Foreign and Second Language Classrooms.* London: Continuum.

Markus, H. and Nurius, P. (1986) Possible selves. *American Psychologist* 41 (9), 954–969.

Marsh, H.W. (1990) The structure of academic self-concept: The Marsh/Shavelson model. *Journal of Educational Psychology* 82 (4), 623–636.

Pawlak, M. (2012) The dynamic nature of motivation in language learning: A classroom perspective. *Studies in Second Language Learning and Teaching* 2 (2), 249–278.

Ruvolo, A.P. and Markus, H.R. (1992) Possible selves and performance: The power of self relevant imagery. *Social Cognition* 10 (1), 95–124.

Ryan, S. (2009) Self and identity in L2 motivation in Japan: The ideal L2 self and Japanese learners of English. In Z. Dörnyei and E. Ushioda (eds) *Motivation, Language Identity and the L2 Self* (pp. 120–144). Bristol: Multilingual Matters.

Schunk, D.H. (1989) Self-efficacy and cognitive skill learning. In C. Ames and R. Ames (eds) *Research on Motivation in Education: Vol. 3. Goals and Cognitions.* (pp. 13–44). San Diego, CA: Academic Press.

Schunk, D.H. (2008) *Motivation and Self-Regulated Learning: Theory, Research, and Applications.* New York, NY: Lawrence Erlbaum Associates.

Segalowitz, N., Gatbonton, E. and Trofimovich, P. (2009) Links between ethnolinguistic affiliation, self-regulated motivation and second language fluency: Are they mediated by psycholinguistic variables? In Z. Dörnyei and E. Ushioda (eds) *Motivation, Language Identity and the L2 Self* (pp. 172–193). Bristol: Multilingual Matters.

Shavelson, R.J., Hubner, J.J. and Stanton, G.C. (1976) Self-concept: Validation of construct interpretations. *Review of Educational Research* 46 (3), 407–441.

Taguchi, T., Magid, M. and Papi, M. (2009) The L2 motivational self system among Japanese, Chinese, and Iranian learners of English: A comparative study. In Z. Dörnyei and E. Ushioda (eds) *Motivation, Language Identity and the L2 Self* (pp. 66–97). Bristol: Multilingual Matters.

Tseng, W.T., Dörnyei, Z. and Schmitt, N. (2006) A new approach to assessing strategic learning: The case of self-regulation in vocabulary acquisition. *Applied Linguistics* 27 (1), 78–102.

White, C. and Ding, A. (2009) Identity and self in e-language teaching. In Z. Dörnyei and E. Ushioda (eds) *Motivation, Language Identity and the L2 Self* (pp. 333–350). Bristol: Multilingual Matters.

Zimmerman, B.J. (1989) Models of self-regulated learning and academic achievement. In B.J. Zimmerman and D.H. Schunk (eds) *Self-regulated Learning and Academic Achievement: Theory, Research, and Practice* (pp. 1–25). New York, NY: Springer-Verlag.

Zimmerman, B.J. (1994) Dimensions of academic self-regulation: A conceptual framework for education. In D.H. Schunk and B.J. Zimmerman (eds) *Self-Regulation of Learning and Performance: Issues and Educational Applications* (pp. 3–21). Hillside, NJ: Lawrence Erlbaum Associates.

Zimmerman, B.J. (2000) Attaining self-regulation: A social cognitive perspective. In M. Boekaerts, P.R. Pintrich, and M. Zeider (eds) *Handbook of Self-Regulation* (pp. 13–39). San Diego, CA: Academic Press.

12 Emerging Self-Identities of Second Language Learners: Emotions and the Experiential Profile of Identity Construction

Masuko Miyahara

Introduction

The growing body of interest among theorists and practitioners to examine the relationship between language acquisition and identity from a sociocultural perspective stems largely from what Block (2003) identifies as the social turn in second language acquisition (SLA). This phenomenon has inevitably created opportunities to move beyond the essentialist view of identities as static, unitary and fixed, towards a more social constructivist and post-structuralist understanding where identities are viewed as multifaceted, fluid and emerging in interactions with others in a range of contexts. However, I problematise the current dominant emphasis on the social dimension of the post-structuralist understanding, and call for a more balanced approach between the social domain and the psychologically oriented aspects of a language learner's identity. I maintain that identities are not merely products of one's response to the environment, but that they are conditioned by and from what the individual brings into their interactions within a certain discourse. Grounded in the concept of situated learning (Lave & Wenger, 1991) and imagined communities (Anderson, 1991; Norton, 2000), the study explores ways to close the gap between the social and the psychological dimensions of identity construction by focusing on emotions and the experiential profile of the learners. In particular, I draw on Dörnyei's notion of the Ideal Second Language (L2) self (2009) to examine how learners in this context construct their identity through imagining their future selves participating in communities of English users and how emotions are implicated in the process. Past studies have centred mainly on what kind of identities develop, but in this study, I focus on how and why, and in what contexts the students construct their identities, and how the affective dimensions are implicated in this process. I approach this subject by taking a participant-relevant perspective in the form of a narrative where the aim is to investigate learners' language experiences from their perspective (Casanave, 2009). It traces the identity development of learners studying English at a liberal arts college in Tokyo by obtaining first-hand accounts of their language learning experiences mainly through talks with the participants. The study reports how learning a language can often turn into subjective experiences by focusing on the following three research areas that were based on the findings of the pilot study:

(1) The learners and their past English language learning experience
(2) The learners' relationships with and orientations to English, and their views of themselves as English users in the past, present and future context
(3) The learners' views of themselves as English users in the past, present and future context

These three broad areas of inquiry serve as guidelines to address the main question of this study: how and in what ways is the affective dimension implicated in the construction of the identity of a language learner?

Theoretical Foundations

Identity and Dewey's notion of experience and learning

The key concept in the post-structuralist notion of identity is that meaning and identity are not fixed, but are created through social discourses and practices. They understand identity as contextually situated, relational and discursively produced. Identities are constructed and co-constructed through activities in which individuals engage in interactions with the environment. However, the understanding of self as in constant flux and transition has been regarded as one of the perplexing issues of the post-structuralist account of identity (Block, 2007; Norton, 2000). Academics have attempted to provide an explanation of this issue by proposing that change could be understood in terms of continuity or what Giddens (1991) terms as a biographical continuity: an ongoing narrative project in which we tell stories of ourselves by weaving events from the past and present with projected events from the future to create an array of possible stories.

Such a view of continuity and interaction in the post-structuralist account of identity resonates well with Dewey's concept of experience and learning, and it is for this very reason that I adopt Dewey's (1938, 1997) notion of experience to explore my research inquiries. Dewey's experience is based on the two following intertwining principles: interactions and continuity. Interaction refers to the transaction between the individual and the environment. To Dewey, experience is not merely a mental phenomenon of the individual, but one that emerges from one's interactions with the environment. Furthermore, referring to educational experience in particular, he emphasises that nothing can exist in isolation and that everything is relational, and very often is in co-existence with something else (Dewey, 1997). Dewey also emphasises the discriminatory nature of experience. Not all experiences are educative. One important aspect is that influence experience has upon later ones: 'every experience takes up something from those which have gone before and modifies in some way the quality of those which come after' (Dewey, 1997: 35). Here, Dewey flags elements such as growth, reflexivity and transformation. In other words, for Dewey, learning is the result of what one learns from experience. The quality of that experience depends on the process of giving meaning to what is experienced and to making connections with the future. As Dewey (1938: 111) affirms 'teaching and learning are continuous processes of reconstruction of experiences'. Experience and learning are thus regarded as essentially a continuous interactive process with one's social context.

Points of convergence: Situated learning, imagined communities and the Ideal L2 self

The view of learning a language as a social phenomenon acknowledges that learning a language is not merely a process of acquiring knowledge, but that it often involves a discoursal reconfiguration of one's identity (e.g. Lantolf, 2000; Pellegrino, 2005). A sense of self is closely tied with language learning where learning is contingent on the interplay of various forces that emerge from the individuals themselves as well as from their external framework.

Learning understood in terms of identification and participation is central to the concept of situated learning of Lave and Wenger (1991). Learning occurs in relation to the community of practice whereby learners gradually shift from a legitimate peripheral position towards a more fuller participation through aligning practices with those who are considered as experts in that particular community of practice. Here, with new forms of participation comes a transformed identity.

Having its roots in the workplace, applications of the theory of situated learning and community of practice in educational settings have apparently not come without criticism (Jewson, 2007). One of the notable arguments has been to enrich the concept of community by extending the idea of community especially with reference to language learning in a foreign language context (Haneda, 2006). The construct of imagined community of Kanno and Norton (2003) allows us to extend the idea of community both spatially and temporally. The central tenet here is how imagination mediates agency in constructing learners' identities as learners strive to come in alignment with their imagined communities. As Dörnyei explains, the crucial aspect here is that imagined communities are 'constructed by a combination of personal experiences and knowledge (derived from the past) with imagined elements related to the future' (2005: 98). Quite a number of studies have explored how future visions of learners participating in imagined communities can have considerable influence on learners' learning trajectories (e.g. Murphey & Arao, 2001; Ryan, 2006). Murray's (2011) recent study with Japanese college students learning English as a foreign language and how imagination plays a role in the development of their future selves serves to add yet another dimension to further the studies in this area. However, few studies have focused on the discursive space that is created as an individual moves towards his/her attempt in coming to alignment with one's imagined communities, and how emotions and the experiential are intertwined in the process. For this purpose, I now turn to another complementary source to this study, the Ideal L2 self as proposed in Dörnyei's theory of the L2 Motivational Self System.

Dörnyei's L2 Motivational System (2009) is based on the theoretical notion of possible selves introduced by Markus and Nurius (1986) and Higgins (1987) in the field of psychology. It is composed of three dimensions, the Ideal L2 self, the Ought-to L2 self and the L2 learning experience. The Ideal L2 self is the image of who we wish to become as an L2 user; the Ought-to L2 self is the 'attributes that one believes one ought to possess to meet expectations and to avoid possible negative outcomes' (2009: 29) and, finally, the L2 learning experience relates to motives generated as a result of the learning environment. By imagining a desired future self, visions of their ideal self images are realised by alignment to their aspired selves. An interesting aspect of this research is how emotion appears to be a critical component in understanding the motivational properties of the possible L2 selves. For instance, Dörnyei postulates that one's motivation to learn a language stems out of the discrepancies between one's current L2 self and the future L2 self that one aspires to achieve. The discomfort caused as a result of the gap forces an individual to take action in order to reduce that feeling of discomfort.

Another important aspect in Dörnyei's model is how the future self-guides act as motivators. Dörnyei (2009) discusses provisional prerequisites for an Ideal L2 self. Most important is apparently the need for an existence of a successful possible self, but Dörnyei also identifies several other conditions that might be necessary for future self-guides to act as motivators depending on one's past and their learning context. For instance,

(1) Construction of the Ideal L2 self.
(2) Strengthening the vision of the Ideal L2 self.
(3) Making the Ideal L2 self plausible.
(4) Activating the Ideal L2 self.

However, how do learners form their ideal self in the first place? Do all learners possess images of their Ideal L2 self? Can learners' future images change over time? If so, why? Is there a learning environment conducive to the formation of ideal possible selves? How are emotions and the experiential profile factored into the process?

To explore these questions, I underscore the relevance of the third component, the L2 learning experience. In my view, what occurs in this discursive space is the most distinctive feature of Dörnyei's L2 Motivational Self System (2009). The L2 learning experience is concerned with the actual learning process (e.g. positive learning histories, language-related enjoyment or liking, personal satisfaction, language learning activities inside or outside of the classroom, etc.). It is based on the premise that a learner's initial desire or motivation 'to learn a language does not come from internally or externally generated self images, but rather from successful engagement with the actual learning process' (Dörnyei, 2009: 29). As MacIntyre et al., point out, the L2 learning experience is 'related to motivation inspired by prior experience interacting with the present environment' (2009: 49). In this respect, the L2 learning experience is redolent of Dewey's (1997) notion of experience in that experience propels us not to question the immediate context, but to draw on connections among experiences that encompass both past and present for the future. It suggests that there is a temporal, developmental and transformative element inherent in the process of learners' active engagement with their own learning. This calls for a more detailed examination of this component since it will be useful in offering an account of what actually takes place in the discursive space as learners strive towards their Ideal L2 selves as well as providing us with helpful insights as to how the emotional dimension could be implicated in the process of the formation of the self. In this chapter, this study will show how an individual's past L2 learning experience to date can factor into their short or long-term perspective in their language learning processes.

Situating emotions

Pavlenko (2005) argues to redirect the current trend on studies of emotions in language learning research by suggesting that we understand emotions from a wider perspective and take on board a more interdisciplinary and integrated approach. In a similar vein, Imai (2010) also criticises the traditional assumptions of the affective domain in SLA where a major 'affective domain can be characterised as individualistic, cognitive, dichotomous, and product-oriented in its assumptions and foci' (2010: 280), and suggests understanding emotions as a social phenomenon. Understanding emotions as a social construct suggests that it can mediate language learning and participation in various ways. For example, emotions such as embarrassment may be the same for all, but how those emotions are acknowledged or recognised is different across cultures or the specific social context in which an individual is situated (Swain *et al.*, 2011). Furthermore, how an individual perceives one's position within a certain social environment has a tremendous impact on how one can flexibly and creatively respond to the possibilities in that environment, which in turn, can have grave implications in terms of one's participation. Emotions can thus be both individually experienced and, at the same time, socially or culturally shaped. For the participants in this study, the narrative accounts of their experiences can entail reflections on their states of feeling that are not generally perceived by others. Moreover, their stories also have the potential to reveal how their feelings can be shaped by concepts specific to a particular language or medium that they share with others. By bringing together stories of my participants' introspective reports on their language learning experience, and conceptualising emotions as socially constructed, this study will focus on the learners' emotional experiences of their L2 learning, and ways in which emotions mediate the transitions in their experiential worlds.

The Context

Six students, all volunteers, going through their first year of their two-year English language curriculum participated in the study (Table 12.1). The research site, a private university located in the suburbs of Tokyo, aims to build a global community where a diversity of people from various ethnic and religious backgrounds gather together. This institution is also famous for its bilingual identity, and, in Japan, the graduates and alumni are regarded by the general public as being fluent and well-versed in the English speaking language and culture. English is used on a daily basis as a means of communication not only in classes but also in the daily lives of the students and faculty alike.

The university has several college-wide courses that are required components for all students, and the English Language Programme (ELP) is one of them. Students for whom English is a second language must study English intensively for the first two years. The main focus of the programme is

Table 12.1 Participants' profiles (names are pseudonyms)

Name	Gender	Past English language learning experiences	Experiences abroad episodes before college
Sayaka	F	From Pre-K	Yes (two-week study abroad programme)
Maki	F	From Pre-K	Yes (international school in Bangladesh for three years)
Megumi	F	From Pre-K	No
Yui	F	From elementary school	No
Hinako	F	From junior high school	No
Takehiro	M	From junior high school	Yes (two-week study abroad programme)

designed to teach English for academic purposes with a focus on critical thinking. The curriculum is further complemented by a study abroad programme referred to as the Study English Abroad (SEA) Programme. The first and second year students are able to take part in the six-week programme during the summer break at various universities located in the United States, the United Kingdom, Canada, New Zealand and Australia.

The Study

Methodology: Narratives

The nature of my research inquiry requires me to examine the experiences of my participants and listen to their voices from their perspective. This called for a methodology that would allow me to be sensitive to the learners' account of their experience. A narrative approach appeared to be particularly suited to probe into the inner complexities of my research participants. Following Bruner (1990) and Clandinin and Connelly (2000), narratives are fundamentally stories of experiences. In the experience-centred approach, narratives are the means of human sense-making: human beings create meaning from their experiences both individually and socially. Life is storied in a way that people make sense of who they and others are as they interpret their past in terms of their current lives and self as well as their future lives. Most important though is the fact that narratives are not only about people telling their past experience but also how individuals understand those experiences, and how they ascribe meanings to those actions (Clandinin, 2007). Understanding narrative as experience also implies that narratives are not simply individual productions, but also include a social dimension. Personal experiences need to be grounded in the light of the participants' wider social and historical context (Riessman, 2008). There is an implicit parallel here to Dewey's (1997) ontology of experience discussed earlier.

Data collection design and methods

The principle way of collecting the main data was via a series of interviews with my participants over a period of approximately one year. The data are complemented by other tools such as the participants' weekly reflections and weekly e-mail exchanges during their six-week study abroad programme in the summer. My reason for opting to focus on oral interviews was because my participants' descriptions of their language learning trajectory were not only based on retrospective after-the-fact accounts but also on their experiences as they took part in their university's first year English language programme. The research design was thus ongoing, which permitted me to evaluate and adjust the tactics during the months in which the fieldwork was carried out.

The form of interviews employed in this study was semi-structured in the sense that the researcher had a range of topics/issues to be covered and the language used in conducting the interviews was Japanese. The participants were given choices, but none opted for English. All of the interviews were audio-taped and transcribed in their entirety using a simplified transcription style. In terms of practicality, translations from Japanese to English were prepared for selected sections during the course of the analysis. The transcripts were translated by the researcher. In order to increase accuracy, these transcriptions were reviewed and cross-checked by a bilingual colleague for any errors or omissions. Discrepancies were discussed, and a more accurate translation was presented as the final product.

Data analysis

In analysing data, the common trend in much of the recent narrative-based research is its heavy reliance on thematic analysis. Critics such as Pavlenko (2007) point out the absence of transparency and rigour in analysing narratives by presenting major problems that appear to dominate the thematic approach to narrative analysis. On the other hand, as Riessman (2008) forcefully contests, there is a general misconception that the thematic approach appears to be rather simple, intuitive and straightforward.

Using Riessman's (2008) typology of four different ways of dealing with narrative analysis (i.e. thematic analysis, structural analysis, dialogic/performative analysis and visual analysis), Block (2009) contends that there is a need to 'negotiate an appropriation of Riessman's thematic and structural approach as they move towards a dialogic/performative approach' (2008: 342). It is necessary to examine what is said against how participants position themselves and how they are positioned in the course of interaction, which should then be considered at a broader level where the what is related to larger social constructs such as identities or social groups (Block, 2009). For this purpose, I found it helpful to combine Riessman's approach to narrative analysis with Ollerenshaw and Creswell's Three-Dimensional Space Narrative Structure (2002), and developed a six-step procedure for analysis (Miyahara, 2012). The guiding principle throughout is that data are a product of interaction between the participants and myself, their interlocutors or the social milieu. The process presented here did not always occur in a linear fashion as the steps overlap. Quite often I found myself moving back and forth in a cyclical manner.

Findings and Discussion: Weaving the Stories of the Six Participants

In this section, I first present an overview of the stories of the participants in line with the three core questions that address the overarching question of this study:

(1) What are their English language learning experiences? What kind of emotional relationship have learners formed in the process of their language learning experience?
(2) How do learners regard the English language (e.g. as a language of work and leisure)? Do learners see themselves as learners of the language or users or both? What kind of emotional state do learners ascribe to learning English?
(3) How do learners view themselves as English users over time and in different contexts? What are the affective factors that have shaped their views?

While the individual's learning trajectory of each of the six participants was unique, three distinct patterns emerged in the way that their past experiences and, in some cases, the future visions of themselves interacted with their current learning environment that influenced the formation of their Ideal L2 selves:

Pattern 1: Learners who have already established their Ideal L2 self prior to entering college (Sayaka and Yui).

Pattern 2: Learners who formed their Ideal L2 self in their new college environment (Megumi and Maki).

Pattern 3: Learners who were not able to generate a substantial image of their Ideal L2 self prior to entering college nor in their new English-mediated learning environment (Hinako and Takehiro).

In what follows, I attempt to weave together the main findings that emerged in the course of this research. I will discuss the stories of my participants that appear to exhibit similar themes and show how their narratives contribute to the formulation of responses to the three areas of inquiry guiding this research.

Learners' past English learning experience

The six diagrams that follow attempt to highlight the significance of how past language learning experiences factor in with their present learning environment to authenticate, reinforce, transform, develop or generate images of the learners' future selves. In general, one's past learning has been considered to be an influential factor in one's learning process, but there has been little research done as to how, why and in what manner past learning impacts on language learning as a whole.

Sayaka's and Maki's stories

Figures 12.1 and 12.2 exemplify Sayaka's and Maki's stories in terms of their Ideal L2 selves. Both Sayaka and Maki had clear visions of becoming active participants in an international community of English speakers prior to entering college that were created largely by what their contextual resources, particularly their immediate family background and their educational resources offered them.

However, it is necessary for individuals to strengthen the visions of their successful L2 selves as realistic and attainable in order to activate the desired self and also for the future self to serve as an impetus for learning. The English-medium tertiary institution had no doubt contributed to sharpening the visions of Sayaka's and Maki's Ideal L2 selves (Extract 1), but the affordances and the resources that were provided to substantiate or personalise their possible selves were quite different.

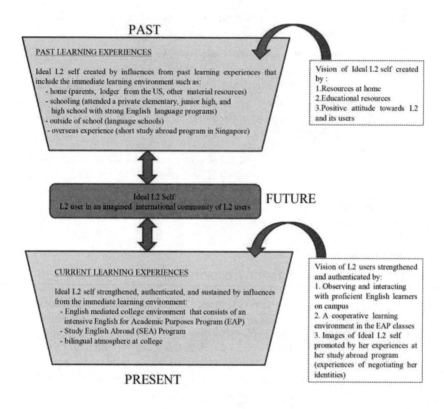

Figure 12.1 Pattern 1. Sayaka's language learning experience

Extract 1

> With foreign students coming in from various countries, on campus, I could talk to them in English. I really felt that here I am, using English! It was a great sense of accomplishment! (Maki)

For instance, in Sayaka's case, the bilingual and bicultural learning environment at college had strengthened her vision of her Ideal L2 self, but nevertheless, on several occasions, she developed ambivalent feelings towards her language learning in her new surroundings. The most prominent examples are Sayaka's experiences of setbacks during her six-week summer study abroad programme when her identity clashed with her Columbian peers. However, she turned linguistic constraints into a facilitative learning environment by revealing her agency (Extract 2). In an attempt to negotiate her position in class with her Columbian peers, she relied on her Japanese identity. By drawing on her personal experiences of

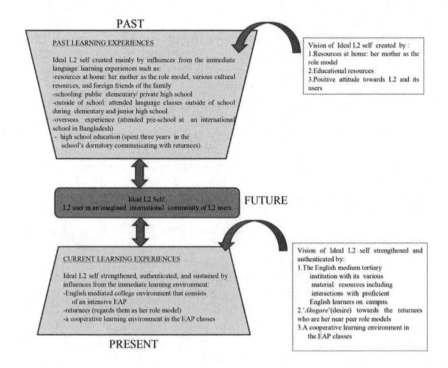

Figure 12.2 Pattern 1. Maki's language learning experience

the Japanese culture, she tried to open and maintain a conversation with her peers during breaks and after classes. The rapport that she was able to build with her peers contributed to creating a favourable position in the classroom.

Extract 2

> I talked to them outside of class. I knew that if the topic was different I could express myself, so we talked about Japan. You know, Japanese customs and food. I wanted to be acknowledged and accepted by them. I didn't want them to think I was an invalid with nothing to say. We got along very well. I thought this made a difference in class. They started to ask me questions in group discussions. I was happy. Even after returning to Japan, I communicate with them through Facebook or emails. (Sayaka)

A crucial feature of Sayaka's episode above is the link she makes to her identity and to her emotional disposition. Her story is a forceful example that illustrates the interrelationship between emotions and identity in the formation of her Ideal L2 self. It shows how both positive and negative emotions can contribute to forming learners' future selves. In other words, not only do positive emotions impel learners to take actions but also negative emotional experiences such as frustration could become psychological resources for development.

As for Maki, the conception of her Ideal L2 self as a competent English user in an international community was also sharpened by her new environment. Maki actively engaged with her new learning context that provided abundant social learning resources (e.g. overseas students, returnees and proficient language users). Providing models for learners to emulate is an effective way to authenticate or substantiate their future possible selves (Higgins, 1998). Maki's role models were, for one, her mother who is a global professional involved in developmental work in developing countries, and two, the returnees. Returnees are sons and daughters of Japanese governmental officials and businessmen who have lived abroad for a certain period of time during their childhood and adolescence before returning to Japan (Kanno, 2003). Both were very influential near peer role models (Murphey & Arao, 2001) who contributed to the co-construction of Maki's visions of her future desired self (Extract 3). Exposure to English from an early age and meaningful interactions in an English using environment developed at the interface of the past and present allowed her to authenticate her future possible self.

Extract 3

I have a strong akogare (desire) (Piller & Takahashi 2006) for English, and the returnees. I see them talk in English like native speakers on the trains and in town. I tried to mimic their pronunciations. They are cool! I try to even dress and act like them sometimes....I want to major in international studies. I am particularly interested in development work for NGO, and perhaps, someday, hope to go to developing countries to help out as my mother does. (Maki)

Megumi's and Yui's Stories

Meanwhile, by focusing on the stories of Megumi and Yui, we witness how they generate or develop their future visions of their desired L2 self. The following two diagrams of their learning trajectories, Figures 12.3 and 12.4, represent how past learning experiences build up to create images of a desired future self. Here, again we observe how the past could function as an impetus for the present and future.

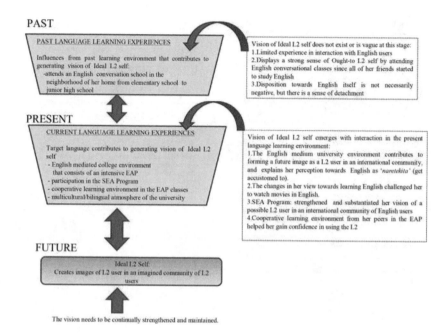

PAST

PAST LANGUAGE LEARNING EXPERIENCES

Influences from past learning environment that contributes to generating vision of Ideal L2 self:
-attends an English conversation school in the neighborhood of her home from elementary school to junior high school

Vision of Ideal L2 self does not exist or is vague at this stage:
1.Limited experience in interaction with English users
2.Displays a strong sense of Ought-to L2 self by attending English conversational classes since all of her friends started to study English
3.Disposition towards English itself is not necessarily negative, but there is a sense of detachment

PRESENT

CURRENT LANGUAGE LEARNING EXPERIENCES

Target language contributes to generating vision of Ideal L2 self
- English mediated college environment that consists of an intensive EAP
- participation in the SEA Program
- cooperative learning environment in the EAP classes
- multicultural/bilingual atmosphere of the university

Vision of Ideal L2 self emerges with interaction in the present language learning environment:
1.The English medium university environment contributes to forming a future image as a L2 user in an international community, and explains her perception towards English as 'naretekita' (get accustomed to).
2.The changes in her view towards learning English challenged her to watch movies in English.
3.SEA Program: strengthened and substantiated her vision of a possible L2 user in an international community of English users
4.Cooperative learning environment from her peers in the EAP helped her gain confidence in using the L2

FUTURE

Ideal L2 Self:
Creates images of L2 user in an imagined community of L2 users

The vision needs to be continually strengthened and maintained.

Figure 12.3 Pattern 2. Megumi's language learning experience

Like Sayaka and Maki, both Megumi and Yui had received early English education by attending classes at local English conversation schools. However, there is an overall tone of detachment as Megumi and Yui talk about their English learning experiences. For instance, they started to learn English at private language schools largely in line with the vast majority of their friends. The fear of being left out by their peers appears to have threatened them (Extract 4). There is a strong sense of obligation to study English for both participants here as they are told, especially by their parents, that English will be an effective instrumental tool for their future life.

Extract 4

A foreigner would come to our pre-school and we would sing songs and play games. Learn words by repeating after the teacher like 'fish, fish, fish'. I don't think I could speak English, but that was OK for me. I just wanted to be there because it was a way to be with my friends. We all took the same English lessons. (Megumi)

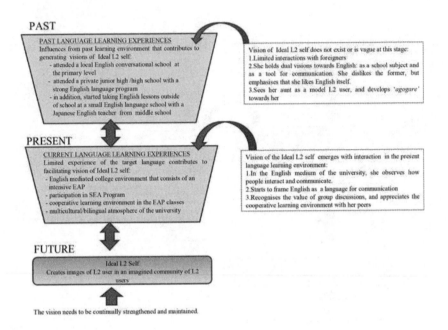

PAST

> PAST LANGUAGE LEARNING EXPERIENCES
> Influences from past learning environment that contributes to generating visions of Ideal L2 self:
> - attended a local English conversational school at the primary level
> - attended a private junior high /high school with a strong English language program
> - in addition, started taking English lessons outside of school at a small English language school with a Japanese English teacher from middle school

> Vision of Ideal L2 self does not exist or is vague at this stage:
> 1.Limited interactions with foreigners
> 2.She holds dual visions towards English: as a school subject and as a tool for communication. She dislikes the former, but emphasises that she likes English itself.
> 3.Sees her aunt as a model L2 user, and develops 'agogare' towards her

PRESENT

> CURRENT LANGUAGE LEARNING EXPERIENCES
> Limited experience of the target language contributes to facilitating vision of Ideal L2 self:
> - English mediated college environment that consists of an intensive EAP
> - participation in SEA Program
> - cooperative learning environment in the EAP classes
> - multicultural/bilingual atmosphere of the university

> Vision of the Ideal L2 self emerges with interaction in the present language learning environment:
> 1.In the English medium of the university, she observes how people interact and communicate.
> 2.Starts to frame English as a language for communication
> 3.Recognises the value of group discussions, and appreciates the cooperative learning environment with her peers

FUTURE

> Ideal L2 Self
> Creates images of L2 user in an imagined community of L2 users

The vision needs to be continually strengthened and maintained.

Figure 12.4 Pattern 2. Yui's language learning experience

However, a major transformation towards their learning occurs when they become immersed in the English-medium university environment. The presence of returnees and the international students provided ample opportunities for them to interact in a meaningful manner with their peers and teachers. In the bilingual and multicultural learning environment of this institution, Megumi and Yui gradually start to perceive themselves as English users. It is also possible that this new environment revived the enjoyable memories of using English that they had previously experienced outside of their formal school contexts. In particular, Megumi's developing sense of affinity towards English and learning English as well as her increased perception of herself as an English user made her more agentive in her behaviour. This is exemplified by the fact that she starts to challenge herself by watching foreign movies in English, and applying for the SEA Programme (Extract 5).

Extract 5

I am trying to watch foreign movies without subtitles. I'm sort of interested in acting, so it's also good for my acting. I think watching

American movies is good for language learning. You watch it many times, and after a while, you start to feel you are a part of it. ... My first month here has prompted me to apply for SEA Programme. (Megumi)

As for Yui, the new learning environment has enabled her to consolidate the image of her English using self. This increased sense of herself as an English user in a bilingual and multicultural context has enabled her to become more tolerant of her perceived limited English, and she feels that she is now able to contribute more to class discussions (Extract 6). By reframing her perception of herself as an English user, Yui is able to interpret her past learning experiences and find potential abilities with and uses of English in the future. The account suggests the developmental and transformative nature of the future possible self that is context dependent. The Ideal L2 self is not a stable entity, but it has the potential to change or develop over time.

Extract 6

It was a surprise to find out that there are a lot of variations in English. When you listen to overseas students talking to each other or amongst themselves, there are different kinds of pronunciation. But the most interesting point for me was it was OK – fine to have a different pronunciation. Communicating was more important than speaking with native like pronunciation. (Yui)

Hinako's and Takehiro's stories

At the opposite end of the spectrum are the stories of Hinako and Takehiro. Figures 12.5 and 12.6, respectively, outline Hinako's and Takehiro's learning trajectories. Contrary to Sayaka and Maki, they lacked any clear visions of their future L2 selves prior to entering college, and more importantly, forming their desired L2 self did not come as easily as it did for Megumi and Yui.

The striking difference in Hinako's and Takehiro's past learning experiences compared to the other four participants is that neither Hinako nor Takehiro received early language education to the same extent as the other four participants. With limited exposure to English and fewer opportunities for interactions with its users, it was difficult for them to visualise their L2 using self. As far as Hinako was concerned, the only opportunity to interact in English with non-Japanese nationals was the weekly English class with the Assistant Language Teachers (ALTs) at her school. With minimal exposure to English and fewer opportunities to see

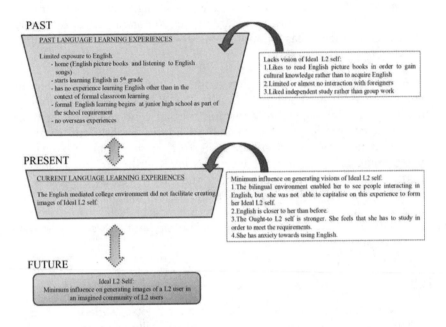

Figure 12.5 Pattern 3. Hinako's language learning experience

English used or to use or communicate in the language themselves, it was apparent that they did not have sufficient past learning experiences with which to capitalise on or utilise English in order to build their ideal future L2 selves. The capacity to visualise a possible self depends largely on the extent to which individuals are able to associate themselves with the English using world (Ushioda & Dörnyei, 2009; Ushioda, 2011). This, in turn, is dependent on the learner's past learning experiences (regardless of whether these are positive or negative) with the target language and how learners are able to relate to the language. This brings us to the second research question, which focuses on the learners' relationship with English and how it contributes to their learning, the formation of their L2 self and their identities.

Learners' relationship and orientations to English

Next, I will discuss the participants' stories in terms of their relationship and orientation to English. English in Japan is still very much perceived as a foreign language where the Japanese language prevails virtually in all domains of life. In spite of the current trend of globalisation, visualising an active self in an international community does not come easily. It is now an

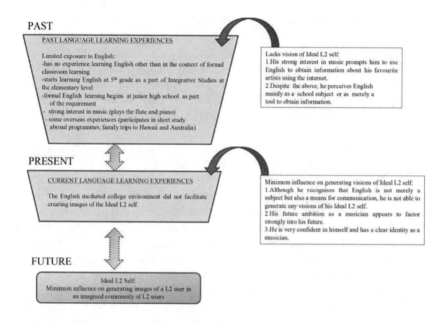

PAST

PAST LANGUAGE LEARNING EXPERIENCES

Limited exposure to English:
-has no experience learning English other than in the context of formal classroom learning
-starts learning English at 5ᵗʰ grade as a part of Integrative Studies at the elementary level
-formal English learning begins at junior high school as part of the requirement
- strong interest in music (plays the flute and piano)
- some overseas experiences (participates in short study abroad programmes; family trips to Hawaii and Australia)

Lacks vision of Ideal L2 self:
1.His strong interest in music prompts him to use English to obtain information about his favourite artists using the internet.
2.Despite the above, he perceives English mainly as a school subject or as merely a tool to obtain information.

PRESENT

CURRENT LANGUAGE LEARNING EXPERIENCES

The English mediated college environment did not facilitate creating images of the Ideal L2 self.

Minimum influence on generating visions of Ideal L2 self:
1.Although he recognises that English is not merely a subject but also a means for communication, he is not able to generate any visions of his Ideal L2 self.
2.His future ambition as a musician appears to factor strongly into his future.
3.He is very confident in himself and has a clear identity as a musician.

FUTURE

Ideal L2 Self:
Minimum influence on generating images of a L2 user in an imagined community of L2 users

Figure 12.6 Pattern 3. Takehiro's language learning experience

established notion that how learners conceptualise the target language has major implications for the entire language learning process (Ushioda, 2011; Ushioda & Dörnyei, 2009; Yashima, 2009). Whether learners see themselves as merely learners studying the target language as a school subject or regard themselves to be language users interacting with English speakers in a global community becomes a crucial issue. As we can observe from the stories of the participants, the views that they hold towards English are in line with Yashima's concept of international posture (2009), where learners desire to integrate into the global society that uses English and other languages as a medium for communication rather than identifying with the target culture.

The stories of Sayaka and Maki show that they had access to a variety of learning resources both inside and outside of formal schooling including abundant contextual support, which were all instrumental in imagining themselves as future users of English. Moreover, the emotional disposition towards English and learning English was overall positive for both Sayaka and Maki. This is illustrated by their display of strong affinity for the target language as well as their identification as English users functioning in global contexts, where English is perceived as a lingua franca rather than as a language belonging to a particular Anglophone community.

By contrast, Megumi's and Yui's conception of English, and their understandings of themselves as English users were quite the opposite from that of Sayaka's and Maki's at the outset of the academic year. It was not until their experiences in the English medium environment at college that they were finally able to see themselves as English users. By broadening their perception of English to include the Outer Circle Norm (Kachru, 1985), they realised that the English which they strive for does not necessarily have to be characterised by a certain Anglophone community.

Conceptualising English in this manner increased the learners' potential to develop and sharpen their vision of their Ideal L2 self. Images became more realistic and more achievable, and, in turn, prompted them to become more proactive in their learning. For instance, as we have observed in the previous section, they encouraged Yui to take a more active part in the discussions with her peers in the classroom. She realised that she did not need native-like fluency for the content of her opinions to be valued. Repositioning herself in this alternative discourse of English increased her participation in group discussions, which also led to the sharpening of her emergent Ideal L2 self.

Let us now turn to the central concern of this study, which is the subject of how emotions are implicated in the process of the emerging L2 possible self. How a person sees herself emotionally in relation to the social environment has a great impact on her ability to respond flexibly to the possibilities of the environment (Imai, 2010; Swain et al., 2011). Both Megumi and Yui reframed themselves positively as English users in the discourse of English as an international language in a global community. Here, native speaker norms were not a prerequisite. Becoming active participants in an international community of English speakers was their aspiration. To draw a conclusion such as positive emotions lead to successful learners would obviously be too simplistic, but the stories of my participants highlight one important feature: positive emotions allow learners to become proactive learners and also respond flexibly to their social environment at any given moment.

As for Hinako and Takehiro, it was difficult for them to form visions of their Ideal L2 selves. Both participants appear to recognise the value of English and view mastery of English as a valuable goal as there is a strong sense of obligation to study English here. For them, success in English equates with obtaining good marks at school. Although their conceptualisation of English somewhat alters as they become exposed to the all English medium of the university instructional practices, and also as they engage in meaningful interactions with their peers and teachers, these interactions did not appear to have influenced the emergence of their future L2 selves (Extract 7).

Extract 7

On campus, I meet many non-Japanese people talking to one another in English on the subjects like what to have for lunch or where to go after classes. I hear people answering their mobiles in English, joking in English, and even quarrelling in English. In classes, we have to discuss in English, we listen to lectures in English, we take notes in English, and write papers in English. It's a totally different ball game for me. You find yourself almost on a different planet. It is sort of refreshing to see English used this way. But at the same time, I was afraid whether I would able to survive in a place like this. (Hinako)

The notion of affordances (Gibson, 1977) is helpful in providing us with some insights here. It is clear from the findings from this study that, for participants who represent Patterns 1 and 2, the learning environment at this college provided the necessary affordances for realising their identities and their future selves as English language users. However, for Hinako and Takehiro, who represent Pattern 3, the same environment did not necessarily lead to the realisation of themselves as possible users of English. What is highlighted most from these three diagrams is the difference in their past language learning experiences. Particularly, for learners in Patterns 1 and 2, they were exposed to English language education at an early stage. Of course, although this does not indicate that only those who have received early meaningful contact with the target language have an advantage of mastering that language, the findings of this study suggest that early exposure appears to provide learners with more favourable conditions to perceive and recognise the possibilities presented to them. It is therefore reasonable to speculate that learners with more experience with the language tend to possess higher levels of language awareness. A higher level of language awareness, and the more experience learners have with the language (either learning or using or observing how it is used), the better equipped they become in exploiting the possibilities offered to them. Clearly, the participants represented in Patterns 1 and 2 had an advantage in terms of using the possibilities made available to them compared to learners featured in Pattern 3.

Learners' views of themselves as English users over time and in different contexts

As the findings related to the third research question overlap in certain respects with those for the first and the second questions, my discussion here is brief. The main theme underlying all three questions is how learners' language learning trajectories intersect with their current learning as they strive towards their future desired selves. We have observed how individual past language learning experiences influence the present and visions for the future. We have also seen that the present and the future can have an impact on the past. Emotions are intricately implicated in the way that learners perceive their experiences and how these perceptions have an effect on their experiences of their self-concept. Struggles and negotiations may also guide emerging dispositions and the affective state of the learner since they promote particular response patterns, which express or inform their identities (McCaslin, 2009). Conflicts are always a part of an emerging self. The stories of the six participants reflect how the socially mediated nature of emotions emerges through complex interactions among social, individual and contextual processes. By linking identity formation and emotions, we are able to bring into focus more long-term developmental processes and personal trajectories of learners' language experiences to the fore.

Proposing a model

The three distinct patterns of the participants' trajectory towards forming (or the opposite) their Ideal L2 selves bring me to propose two models, Model A and Model B.

Model A

Model A is representative of the first pattern (Sayaka and Maki) where learners already have a clear vision of their Ideal L2 selves. Having been exposed to the bilingual college environment, their new learning experiences interacted with their previous learning experiences to reinforce, enhance and maintain their visions of their L2 selves. Since learners have their own unique learning histories with their particular biographical background, the manner in which they perceive their affordances as well as how they personalise them in response to their learning opportunities vary from learner to learner. Both Sayaka and Maki raised their consciousness in learning English in their English medium college environment. This promoted and strengthened the images of their English using self. The focus of this study was to investigate how emotions factor into this process and to examine the implications that they have on one's identity formation. The stories of my participants revealed that both positive and negative emotions contributed to enhancing the images of their Ideal L2 selves.

Model B

Model B illustrates the second and the third patterns where learners do not yet have a clear image of their Ideal L2 selves prior to entering their new learning context. The obvious difference between the second and the third patterns is that while learners in the former group were able to generate their Ideal L2 selves in response to their new language learning environment with learners in the latter group, their visions of their Ideal L2 selves were minimised and appear to have functioned only to support a different, more dominant self. What then are the main factors that appear to contribute to the differences between these two patterns? One interesting feature that emerged was how previous learning experiences could affect learners' views and attitudes towards their subsequent learning.

Patterns 2 and 3 shed light on this issue. Megumi and Yui, representatives of learners of Pattern 2, with a history of learning English in childhood, were apparently helped by this experience in forming their identities as L2 users. Prior to entering college, English was learned mainly in the context of formal schooling, where learners' views about English were more as a school subject or for exams. However, the English-mediated college environment revived their awareness of English as a means of communication as they learned the language through using it. Learners' perceptions of the target language changed as they had more opportunities to interact with others in the language being learned. This enabled them to develop more readily a sense of their English using selves and to find the link between the real world and their learning.

On the other hand, with the participants represented in Pattern 3, the L2 self is minimised to the point that the learners are not able to form clear visions of their Ideal L2 selves. As is evident in the stories of Hinako and Takehiro, learning the target language by using it in a meaningful manner in their new college environment raised their awareness of English as a tool for communication and increased their sense of an English using self to a certain extent, but it was nevertheless not enough to influence their capacity to visualise their L2 possible selves. This leads me to suggest that there may be a threshold in learners' capacity to generate or form substantial images of their Ideal L2 selves.

In other words, foreign language learners all do, at one time or another, have visions of their successful English using selves, but how and when and in what manner those visions become clear images that would be necessary to form future images of their Ideal L2 selves can be largely influenced by the extent and nature of their previous language learning histories. For instance, let us examine Takehiro's case. Through his new learning experience, Takehiro's perception of English does change from English as a school subject to English as means of communication. However, Takehiro had future visions of himself in other areas (as a musician), which hindered (or slowed down) the formation of clear images of his Ideal L2 self. In addition, his limited exposure to the target language in early childhood did not appear to play a major role in supporting or accelerating the creation of his Ideal L2 self as it did for my participants in Pattern 2 (Extract 8).

Extract 8

We aren't studying English per se, but we are learning a lot of things through English. We listen to lectures in English and we have to use English to talk about things in group discussions. In order to discuss things, we need to have information, and understand that information. I guess, we have to check things on our own....

I'm interested in music. I especially like playing the flute. I am also interested in philosophy. This is one of the few colleges in Japan, as far I know, that offers courses in theology in music. So, I didn't come here to study English, as many around me presumed I did. (Takehiro)

Hinako's stories provide additional insights into the developmental process involved in the construction of the L2 possible selves above. What is of most interest to us is her two years of withdrawal from formal schooling while in high school. It appears that in those two years (and also, for that matter, during her early childhood), she was exposed to quite a large amount of written English, mainly through sources from the Internet. In her new learning environment at college, it was quite a challenge for her to get back into the swing of learning in collaboration with others in an institutional setting of a formal classroom where group work was the main pedagogical approach. By learning English through using it in the new college learning environment, Hinako has evidently begun to form visions of her English using self, but since her priority to develop her identity as a learner in a certain community of learning (i.e. her new formal learning environment is more dominant) visions of her Ideal L2 self were minimised. Hinako's case is significant in that it clearly shows the learners' developmental process of forming future visions of their Ideal L2 selves.

Taking into account the transformative and developmental nature of the Ideal L2 selves, this does not mean that Hinako or Takehiro do not have the capacity to develop images of their L2 possible selves. In fact, if we were to follow these two participants for an extended period of time, there is a strong possibility of the emergence of their Ideal L2 selves in the future. The findings of this research indicate that early English education does appear to have a strong influence on one's subsequent foreign language learning, but this does not indicate that only those learners who have learned English in their childhood can form their Ideal L2 selves. English learning in the early years, however, appears to be conducive to setting the stage for forming learners' Ideal L2 selves. Childhood language education appears to facilitate the process of generating images of learners' L2 selves more readily.

Concluding Remarks

In its attempt to unravel the role of emotions and experiential profiles of learners studying English as a foreign language, the study provided empirical evidence for Dörnyei's construct of the Ideal L2 self. By exploring the discursive space that constitutes the L2 learning experience, the study illustrates the transformative and developmental nature of the Ideal L2 self where both positive and negative emotions can affect learners' responses and ability to negotiate their social environment. The Ideal L2 self is generated by the past, present and future where emotions and the experiential are intertwined in the process. The important point is, however, not how one constructs, maintains or realises one's Ideal L2 self, but how visions of the future are used in the construction of oneself.

References

Anderson, B. (1991) *Imagined Communities: Reflections on the Origin and Spread of Nationalism.* (Rev. Ed). London: Verso.

Block, D. (2003) *The Social Turn in Second Language Acquisition.* Edinburgh: Edinburgh University.

Block, D. (2009) Second language learner identities. Current and future angles of interest. In L. Wei and V. Cook (eds) *Contemporary Applied Linguistics. Volume 1 on Language Teaching and Learning* (pp. 215–232) London: Continuum.

Bruner, J. (1990) *Acts of Meaning.* Cambridge, MA: Harvard University Press.

Casanave, C. P. (2009) *Perspective Taking.* Keynote Speech presented at JALT Annual Convention 2009. Shizuoka, Japan.

Clandinin, D.J. (ed.) (2007) *Handbook of Narrative Inquiry.* Thousand Oaks, CA: Sage.

Clandinin, D.J. and Connelly, F.M. (2000) *Narrative Inquiry: Experience and Story in Qualitative Research.* San Francisco, CA: Jossey-Bass.

Dewey, J. (1938) *Experience and Education.* New York: Macmillan.

Dewey, J. (1997) *Experience and Education* (First Touchstone edition). New York: Touchstone.

Dörnyei, Z. (2009) The L2 Motivational Self System. In Z. Dörnyei and E. Ushioda (eds) *Motivation, Language Identity and the L2 Self* (pp. 9–42). Bristol: Multilingual Matters.

Gibson, J.J. (1977) The theory of affordances. In R. E. Shaw and J. Brasford (eds) *Perceiving, Acting and Knowing* (pp. 67–82). Hillsdale, NJ: Lawrence Erlbaum Associates.

Haneda, M. (2006) Classrooms as communities of practice: A reevaluation. *TESOL Quarterly* 40 (4), 807–816.

Higgins, E.T. (1987) Self-discrepancy: A theory relating self and affect. *Psychological Review* 94 (3), 319–340.

Higgins, E.T. (1998) Promotion and prevention: Regulatory focus as a motivational principle. *Journal of Personality and Social Psychology,* 30, 1–46.

Imai, Y. (2010) Emotions in SLA: New insights from collaborative learning for an EFL classroom. *The Modern Language Journal* 94 (2), 278–291.

Jewson, N. (2007) Cultivating network analysis: Rethinking the concept of community within communities of practice. In J. Hughes, N. Newson and L. Unwin (eds) *Community of Practice: Critical Perspectives*. New York: Routledge.

Kachru, B.B. (1985) Standards, codification and sociolinguistic realism: The English language in the outer circle. In R. Quirk and H.G. Widdowson (eds) *English in the World: Teaching and Learning the Language and Literatures* (pp. 11–30). Cambridge: Cambridge University Press.

Kanno, Y. (2003) *Negotiating Bilingual and Bicultural Identities: Japanese Returnees Betwixt Two Worlds*. Mahwah, N.J.: Lawrence Erlbaum.

Kanno, Y. and Norton, B. (2003) Imagined communities and educational possibilities: Introduction. *Journal of Language, Identity and Education* 2 (4), 241–249.

Giddens, A. (1991) *Modernity and Self-Identity: Self and Society in the Late Modern Age*. Cambridge: Polity.

Lantolf, J.P. (2000) Introducing sociocultural theory. In J.P. Lantolf (ed.) *Sociocultural Theory and Second Language Learning* (pp. 1–26). Oxford: Oxford University Press.

Lave, J. and Wenger, E. (1991) *Situated Learning: Legitimate Peripheral Participation*. Cambridge: Cambridge University Press.

MacIntyre, P., MacKinnon, S. and Clément, R. (2009) The baby, the bathwater and the future of language learning motivation research. In Z. Dörnyei and E. Ushioda (eds) *Motivation, Language Identity and the L2 Self* (pp. 43–65). Bristol: Multilingual Matters.

Markus, H. and Nurius, P. (1986) Possible selves. *American Psychologists* 41 (9), 954–969.

McCaslin, M. (2009) Co-regulation of student motivation and emergent identity. *Educational Psychologist* 44 (2), 137–146.

Miyahara, M. (2012) Evolving Self-Identities of Second Language Learners in Japanese Higher Education. PhD thesis. Institute of Education, University of London.

Murray, G. (2011) Imagination, metacognition and the L2 Self in a self-access learning environment. In G. Murray, G. Xuesong and T. Lamb (eds) *Identity, Motivation and Autonomy in Language Learning* (pp. 75–90). Bristol: Multilingual Matters.

Murphey, T. and Arao, H. (2001) Reported belief changes through near peer role modeling. *TESL-EJ* 5(3). See http://tesl-ej.org/ej19/al.html (accessed October 2007).

Norton, B. (2000) *Identity and Language Learning: Gender, Ethnicity and Educational Change*. London: Longman/Pearson Education.

Ollerenshaw, A.J. and Creswell, J. (2002) Narrative research: A comparison of two restorying data analysis approaches. *Qualitative Inquiry* 8 (3), 329–347.

Pavlenko, A. (2005) *Emotions and Multilingualism*. Cambridge: Cambridge University Press.

Pavlenko, A. (2007) Autobiographic narratives as data in Applied Linguistics. *Applied Linguistics* 28 (2), 163–188.

Pellegrino, A. (2005) *Study Abroad and Second Language Use*. Cambridge: Cambridge University Press.

Piller, I. and Takahashi, K. (2006) A passion for English: Desire and the language market. In A. Pavlenko (ed.) *Bilingual Minds: Emotional Experience, Expression, and Representation* (pp. 59–83). Clevedon: Multilingual Matters.

Riessman, C. (2008) *Narrative Methods for Human Sciences*. Newbury Park, CA: Sage.

Swain, M., Kinnear, P. and Steinman, L. (2011) *Sociocultural Theory in Second Language Education: An Introduction through Narratives*. Bristol: Multilingual Matters.

Ushioda, E. (2011) Motivating learners to speak as themselves. In G. Murray, X. Gao, and T. Lamb (eds) *Identity, Motivation and Autonomy in Language Learning* (pp. 11–24). Bristol: Multilingual Matters.

Ushioda, E. and Dörnyei, Z. (2009) Motivation, language identities and the L2 Self: A theoretical overview. In Z. Dörnyei and E. Ushioda (eds) *Motivation, Language Identity and the L2 Self* (pp. 1–8). Bristol: Multilingual Matters.

Yashima, T. (2009) International posture and the Ideal L2 Self in the Japanese EFL context. In Z. Dörnyei and E. Ushioda (eds) *Motivation, Language Identity and the L2 Self* (pp. 44–163). Bristol: Multilingual Matters.

13 Fear of the True Self: Social Anxiety and the Silent Behaviour of Japanese Learners of English

Jim King

I would come around ((the class)) and ask if anyone had any problems or questions or knew what they needed to do. This would often be returned with not a look at me but a look towards their immediate left or right to somebody else as if I'd just disappeared from the conversation and it was amazing...I'd ask 'are there any problems?' and it was as if they took that as a stimulus to then ignore me...So more often than not they wouldn't ↑ respond and it would piss me off and I'd walk away. (Jack, English instructor at a Japanese university)

Introduction

Feelings of frustration, like those described by Jack in the extract above, appear to be quite common for educators encountering silent, unresponsive students (e.g. Korst, 1997). However, what lies beneath this puzzling avoidance of talk? Although it is true that silence can be a positive phenomenon in some classroom contexts (e.g. when accompanying reading and writing tasks or during activities which require extended periods of reflection), in the language classroom a lack of oral production represents a serious barrier to a learner's target language development (see Long, 1996; Swain, 2005). In previous work (King, 2013a, 2013b), I have demonstrated that there is a significant trend towards silence within the foreign language classrooms of Japanese universities and that this silence emerges through multiple, complex routes. The current chapter is an attempt to highlight just one of these routes, one which is characterised by the avoidance of talk by the socially anxious. Structuring my arguments around the seminal model of social anxiety of Clark and Wells (1995) and using data garnered from a series of interviews and classroom observations, I will discuss the self-focused attention, social fear beliefs and in-class safety behaviours of English learners in Japan and will relate how these issues appear to significantly impact upon their second language (L2) oral performance. While there already exists a significant body of research into the issue of anxiety and language learning (e.g. Aida, 1994; Hewitt & Stephenson, 2012; Horwitz *et al.*, 1986; Liu & Jackson, 2008; MacIntyre & Gardner, 1994; Woodrow, 2006; Young, 1999), serious discussion focusing on the ways in which classroom silence may be related to the cognitive processes and skewed self-concepts of socially anxious Japanese learners of English is notably absent from the literature. By the end of this chapter I hope the seemingly perplexing behaviour displayed by students like Jack's will be better understood, and perhaps be the cause for less frustration and irritation for those educators encountering it.

What is Social Anxiety?

Characterised by a marked or persistent fear of specific social situations in which one is under the scrutiny of others (American Psychiatric Association, 2000), social anxiety (sometimes referred to as 'social phobia' – see Kring & Johnson, 2012, for more on terminology) differs from other anxiety conditions due to its emphasis on concerns regarding evaluation by others. These concerns are associated with the heightened processing of the social self and a preoccupation with self-focused attention (McManus & Hirsch, 2007). People who suffer from social anxiety excessively self-monitor during social performance situations and focus on the impression they are making on others, fearing that their true self may be revealed at any moment. They typically hold false assumptions about their perceived inability to behave in an appropriate manner in front of others and tend to be highly critical of their social performance, believing it will be negatively evaluated and will ultimately lead to embarrassment and humiliation (Clark & Wells, 1995). In addition to emotional discomfort, somatic symptoms include blushing, trembling, a dry mouth, sweating and heart palpitations (Blackmore *et al.*, 2009). A socially anxious person may endure an anxiety-provoking situation in discomfort, flee from it prematurely or actively try to avoid the situation in the first place. If the situation happens to be a classroom, then the potential for disengagement from learning is clear (see Purdon *et al.*, 2001; Topham & Russell, 2012).

Research into social anxiety has received some criticism in the past for suggesting that shyness is a form of mental illness requiring treatment. I should make clear at this point therefore that it is not my intention in this chapter to engage in the over-medicalisation (see Lane, 2008; Scott, 2006; Wakefield *et al.*, 2005) of what might be perfectly normal human emotions experienced by language learners during classroom instruction. Indeed, it would be quite wrong to assume that all learners who experience some form of social anxiety are ill. McManus and Hirsch (2007) rightly remind us that an individual's experience of social anxiety exists on a continuum. Some people may experience the anxiety only occasionally during the most demanding social performance situations, such as attending a job interview or giving a speech in public, while at the other end of the scale, others may be distressed by all of the social situations they encounter. However, if a socially anxious learner is not able to function effectively within a classroom setting over a prolonged period, then a working knowledge of the phenomenon is likely to be of great value to language practitioners because it can aid in better understanding how a skewed self-concept may impact upon the cognitive processes and in-class behaviours of inhibited students.

Social Anxiety and Culture

A number of studies (e.g. Essau *et al.*, 2012; Heinrichs *et al.*, 2006; Kleinknecht *et al.*, 1997; Schreier *et al.*, 2010; Stein, 2009) have explored the intriguing relationship between cultural factors and social anxiety. Socio-cultural values, norms and expectations all help to shape anxiety within social situations, and this appears to be particularly true within Japanese contexts where socially reticent, reserved behaviour is culturally acceptable and, indeed, positively regarded. Add to this the relatively high positive value that the Japanese tend to place on silence in comparison to overt verbalisation (see Ishii & Bruneau, 1994; Lebra, 1987) and we can see that conditions appear ripe for individuals to engage in withdrawn behaviour during social situations which require participants to talk to others, such as in a language classroom. Even so, it is interesting to note that while some researchers (e.g. Essau *et al.*, 2012) report that levels of social anxiety are relatively high in samples from East Asian nations, others (e.g. Hofmann *et al.*, 2010; Ramsawh *et al.*, 2010) report that prevalence rates within these countries are actually significantly lower in comparison to those found within Western countries, such as the United States. Low reporting rates may be explained by the fact that countries like Japan view reserved and withdrawn behaviour as being 'socially syntonic' (Rapee *et al.*, 2011: 486) meaning the behaviour might not cause distress for some individuals. Furthermore, Kawakami *et al.* (2004)

highlight the social desirability bias of many Japanese who tend to deny psychological problems because of the stigma and loss of face that is connected to admitting to a mental disorder.

An intriguing variant of social anxiety associated primarily with Japan is *taijin kyofusho*. Literally meaning 'fear of interpersonal relations disorder', *taijin kyofusho* is experienced by sufferers during social encounters which require face-to-face contact and is characterised by a fear that one's 'inappropriate' appearance or behaviour will offend or embarrass others (Essau *et al.*, 2012; Kleinknecht *et al.*, 1997). Note that the emphasis here is on the embarrassment of others rather than oneself. Kasahara (1986) points out that individuals experiencing *taijin kyofusho* typically develop a dread of being watched, particularly when contact situations involve acquaintances rather than strangers or significant others. This level of intimacy, of course, perfectly describes most classroom environments. Even though my own study did not uncover any data specifically relating to the allocentric concerns of *taijin kyofusho* amongst its participants, I include this brief description of the phenomenon in order to provide a more rounded account of social anxiety as it exists within the Japanese context.

Cognitive-behavioural model of Clark and Wells (1995)

The model of Clark and Wells (1995) provides us with one of the best known experimentally supported explanations of social anxiety. The model focuses on how the socially anxious have a distorted self-concept (related to their supposed inability to make a favourable impression on others), which contributes to excessively negative interpretations of social situations. These negative appraisals (also termed feared predictions or social fear beliefs) are maintained by four dynamically connected processes: (1) an increase in self-focused attention at the expense of observing the behaviour of others; (2) the use of erroneous feelings and self-images to infer how one appears to others; (3) the use of safety behaviours (see Salkovskis, 1991) which, while employed in order to lessen the risk of negative evaluation, actually work to maintain negative beliefs and anxiety and (4) negatively biased thinking about one's performance prior to entering a situation, followed by further biased post-event reflections (Clark, 2001; Clark & Wells, 1995; Hodson *et al.*, 2008; McManus & Hirsch, 2007).

The cognitive-behavioural processes described in the model of Clark and Wells (1995) are dynamically connected meaning that, for example within a language classroom, a socially anxious learner's feared predictions that her performance will be embarrassing cause her to engage in excessive self-focused attention as she monitors how she is coming across to others as the class progresses. This all-consuming self-focused attention, along with a strong desire to avoid negative assessment by the instructor and peers, contributes to the learner interacting only very minimally with classmates. Such safety seeking behaviour, working in tandem with her social fear beliefs, causes the student to feel tense and to become flustered when asked a question in the target language. Thinking she looks like a fool, her discomfort, in turn, leads to yet further worry over her inept image or behaviour and these concerns extend to after the lesson has ended, therefore feeding the cycle of negative self-beliefs for the next class. While this outline nicely illustrates the way in which a socially anxious learner's pre-, post- and in-situation cognitive processes are dynamically connected, I would now like to focus on how findings from my mixed methods research into the silent behaviour of Japanese students of English relate to the various components of the model of Clark and Wells (1995).

Data Collection and Analysis

An interview approach was utilised in order to uncover students' fundamental beliefs about classroom silence and to explore their individual experiences of the phenomenon. This qualitative phase of the study was essentially exploratory in nature and involved 11 participants who were each interviewed twice in sessions lasting approximately 45 minutes. While all the interviewees discussed the issue of social anxiety and language learning to some extent, this chapter presents testimony from six participants for whom the issue appeared to be of particular consequence. Sampling was based on teacher and student recommendations in order to ensure that interviewees met a number of set criteria to create a diverse sample, thus reflecting the broad range of learners currently studying English within Japan's university system. This strategy successfully produced a cohort which consisted of both language and non-language majors who were at various points of their university education (from first-year undergraduate through to second-year postgraduate), and whose L2 proficiency levels were similarly varied (despite the fact that everyone in the sample had received at least eight years of English language instruction). To help counter this inconsistency in L2 abilities, participants were able to choose whether their interviews were conducted in English, Japanese or a mixture of both languages. After gaining the participants' consent, all interview sessions were audio recorded and later transcribed in full using a relatively detailed transcription convention (see below) based on recommendations made by Richards (2003). Data analysis took the form of an iterative, unfolding process during which the significant theme of social anxiety and learner silence emerged. Following repeated coding of the data, strong resonances and similarities with the cognitive model of social anxiety of Clark and Wells (1995) quickly became apparent in the interviewees' testimony. Thus, the following discussion is organised into separate sections which explore the language classroom as a social situation; learners' social fear beliefs; the issue of self-focus image; learners' in-class safety behaviours; and the somatic and cognitive symptoms associated with the socially anxious.

Results and Discussion

The language classroom as a social situation

In order to reflect the variety of universities that exist in Japan, over the course of my research I visited nine institutions and observed 30 different class groups, encountering a diversity of classroom contexts. This ranged from an intimate seminar-style lesson for just nine learners at an elite metropolitan university, through to a massive communicative English class at a private institution containing 103 students. All of the classes I observed represented public social performance situations for the learners attending them as they were expected to perform tasks such as verbally interacting with their instructors, giving presentations, performing role plays, drills and dialogues, and engaging in discussions – all of which took place in front of others.

Indeed, the language classroom represents a social situation in which a complex array of forces are at work influencing the behaviour of participants. Dörnyei (2009) underlines this point when he notes that within educational psychology the classroom environment has been variously defined, and includes not only the dimensions of an 'instructional context' relating to the teaching method, curriculum and learning tasks but also a '"social context", which is related to the fact that the classroom is also the main social arena for students, offering deeply intensive personal experiences such as friendship, love, or identity formation' (237). This last point is especially significant when we consider the unstable self-concept of some language learners whose silence emerges during the precarious process of moving between their first language (L1) and fledgling L2 selves (see Granger, 2004).

As classrooms and the students who inhabit them are themselves embedded within much broader social systems (see Breen, 1985; Holliday, 1994), we can also add macro concerns, such as socio-cultural values, norms, attitudes and beliefs, to the already dynamic mix of situational and learner-internal forces which play a role in shaping language learner behaviour. However, in order to avoid generalisations involving national traits, it is advisable to treat these macro issues more as an informative conceptual background whilst paying close attention to the immediate situational and individual features of a learner's silent behaviour.

Feared predictions

Clark and Wells (1995) highlight that the socially anxious tend to interpret social situations negatively because they hold erroneous beliefs about themselves and how they should act during the situation. These dysfunctional self-concept and social action beliefs fall into three categories: (1) excessively high standards for social performance; (2) conditional beliefs concerning social evaluation and (3) unconditional beliefs about the self. With regard to the first of these categories, a strong theme in the interview phase of my own study was related to the belief that it was essential for students to use 'perfect English' when speaking in front of others. Interviewees spoke of their worries concerning issues connected to the pronunciation, word order, grammatical correctness and relevance of their utterances in the target language. Mistakes were viewed with dread; with some believing that their English language errors might potentially lead to rejection by peers. Discussing her fears of what would happen if she spoke out in class, one learner revealed:

> I'm worried about whether the grammar is correct and there's no end of those kinds of things. But there are some people who are brighter than me (...) so I'd feel embarrassed if they thought my question wasn't relevant or was off the point. I'd also feel humiliated if my poor English ability was exposed.

Note how this student assesses her target language ability. This is a good example of a negatively biased self-concept in that she believes her linguistic capabilities to be wholly inadequate. In reality, the learner was an English language major who had been chosen to study at a United States university for a year because of her excellent language skills. Clark and Wells (1995) make the point that setting oneself excessively high standards for social performance actually generates anxiety because such standards (e.g. appearing witty and intelligent in class whilst speaking perfect, error-free English) are extremely difficult to achieve. As a consequence of this difficulty, socially anxious learners may become preoccupied with the fact that they are failing to convey a favourable impression to classmates.

In addition to the concern that making mistakes while speaking in English would result in being rejected by peers, some interviewees spoke about other feared predictions which were related to social evaluation in their classrooms. For example, one fourth-year non-language major described how he was afraid that his voice would become weak and his mind would go blank as a result of the embarrassment of being called on to talk in English in front of the rest of the class. Yet other learners recounted how they avoided interacting with instructors because of worries that they would be labelled as being 'stupid' if they did. Describing a classroom scenario in which she is unable to understand a point during the lesson, one interviewee explained how she would be reluctant to ask for help and that she believed she would be evaluated if she did speak up:

> but you think (.) maybe <u>all</u> the other students know the answer and I will be (.) the only student who can't understand so that if I say- if I ask a question, that is showing that I'm the idiot in the class.

It seems that learners' social fears do not just involve conditional beliefs like the one in the extract above. Indeed, Clark and Wells (1995) draw attention to the dynamism of the social phobic's self-schemata. With this in mind, we can see that sometimes a socially anxious learner's feared predictions involve unconditional beliefs about the self which only come to the fore during social situations. The person may have a negative view of his/her classroom self, believing they are different, strange, inadequate, boring or stupid, but this unconditional belief does not necessarily extend into situations in which the individual perceives there to be no evaluation, for example settings involving family, friends or being alone.

Self-focused attention

McManus and Hirsch (2007) note that the socially anxious become preoccupied with how well they are coming across during social situations and this self-focused attention interferes with social performance, making it less effective. Heightened processing of the social self encourages a preoccupation with impression management (see Leary, 1995; Tedeschi, 1981), feelings of inhibition and the use of silence as a defensive strategy. During my own research, students frequently related how they felt they were being observed and judged during their English lessons, making repeated references to the inhibiting 'eyes' that were around them. As one postgraduate student put it, 'when I speak out, I can feel people are watching me and judging me'. Another learner, who was highly proficient in English, also spoke about her preoccupation with her classroom self-image, stating that, 'I always look at people around me and I always search (.hhh) what they think (.) about me- how I look- I'm <u>very</u> careful'. Her concerns centred more around the appeal of her utterances, rather than their lexico-grammatical accuracy, disclosing that 'when I speak, when I say something I always care what other people think and then I care if they are interested in what I'm talking about'. It would seem that such a hypersensitivity to others is supported at a societal level by the enculturated notion of an ever-present and ever-watching 'other' which exists within Japanese society (see Greer, 2000; Lebra, 1976, 1993;

McVeigh, 2002). Writing about the socialisation of communicative style in Japan, Clancy (1990) argues convincingly that a concern for others' reactions is inculcated into Japanese infants from an early age by caregivers who employ it as a control strategy, teaching children to fear the criticism and disapproval of those around them.

According to Clark and Wells (1995), when a socially anxious individual faces a situation in which there is the potential for negative evaluation, a significant amount of the person's attention is shifted towards monitoring his/her self-generated image. This shift in attention inwards towards the self feeds a heightened awareness of anxiety responses, diverts attention away from the objective interpretation of external information and therefore helps to distort how the individual thinks he/she is coming across to others. Let us consider, for example, the cognitive processes of a socially anxious learner during a whole-class discussion – a daunting activity for many Japanese students and one that I rarely observed to work well over the course of the 48 classroom observations I conducted. As the discussion progresses, our socially anxious learner fears becoming the centre of everyone's attention if called upon to express an opinion. As one student put it, 'I think you might feel embarrassed when your opinion is kind of rejected in some way or- or part of you is kind of rejected, you know like, you are different from others'. This fear triggers a focus on how the learner feels and she assumes that her anxious feelings are relevant to how others perceive her. Thus, if the learner senses she is, say, blushing, she assumes that everyone can clearly see her bright red face and will consequently form a negative impression of her; even though in actual fact she may have only flushed barely noticeably. In addition to adopting silence as a defensive strategy in order to avoid attracting attention or to avoid causing offence by expressing an opinion which others in the class might disagree with, concentrating more on internal matters would make it that much more difficult for the learner to attend to the actual points of the discussion as they arose and her attention would be further diverted from the tricky process of forming a contribution in the target language. Immediate contextual factors, such as the topic under discussion, level of self-disclosure required (see Barnlund, 1974), size of the class and nature of the learner's interpersonal relationships with classmates/instructor, would all play a role in shaping the cognitive processes and level of oral participation of this socially anxious learner.

Safety behaviours

Safety behaviours are strategies that the socially anxious employ so as to prevent or minimise a feared event from occurring (Salkovskis, 1991). Clark and Wells (1995) point out that individuals tend to engage in multiple safety-seeking behaviours in order to minimise the risk of negative evaluation. In the context of Japan's language classrooms, these strategies primarily involve the ways in which learners avoid or minimise the chance of having to speak English in front of others. Not asking questions, not initiating discourse and providing monosyllabic answers are all effective ways of achieving this. On occasion during classroom observations I was able to observe learners performing such strategies and also a number of interviewees provided testimony about their own safety-seeking behaviours. One of the most common strategies involved the learner's seating position within the classroom. One fourth-year student explained how he would:

> usually sit at the back. Nobody goes to the front, they sit at the back instead. I don't have any other plan, I just sit at the back to avoid being asked a question in English, like translate something into Japanese.

Another student, who spoke extensively about her fear of negative evaluation, also related how she invariably made a beeline for the back of the language classroom because, 'I won't be noticed and when there are lots of people, if I sit at the back, as I'm small, I can occasionally hide myself in the shadow of someone sitting in front'. This fourth-year human sciences student went on to recount how, when entering the room, she would avoid eye contact with her teacher and would not greet her either. Once sitting, her gaze would remain lowered throughout the class. Through these safety behaviours, the student believed she would become less memorable and noticeable to the instructor and this would consequently reduce the likelihood of being nominated to speak during the lesson, thus allowing her to maintain her silence.

Of course, avoiding nomination is not always possible and interviewees also described some safety behaviours that they performed in the event of being called on to speak in the target language. One postgraduate student revealed:

> I was strongly concerned about 'what if I made a mistake?' ((spoken while laughing)). So I think when I was invited to speak, first of all, (1.5) I would make sure my answer was right. I would check with the person next to me before I spoke.

This strategy of consulting a partner before speaking was something I observed numerous times during my classroom research. While the intention may be to avoid the feared prediction of making a mistake and being negatively evaluated, what actually happens is the long, silent pause for peer consultation has the effect of slowing the pace of interaction right down, and consequently target language talk becomes further restricted. A similar scenario occurs when a student mentally rehearses a response or spends an extended interval translating their utterance (safety behaviours may also involve internal mental processes (Clark, 1999; Clark & Wells, 1995)). Hinting at an intolerance of silence by some educators in Japan, Mulligan (2005: 33) asks, 'how many of us have observed the agonizing period of silence, the long pause, the language conversion process of translating what has been said into Japanese and then going through the same process when answering?'.

While the postgraduate student in the example above consulted his neighbours in a safety-seeking effort to ensure an accurate target language response, conversely another interviewee related how a safety behaviour she employed had been intended to ensure the inaccuracy of her responses. After having been privately tutored in English from an early age, this third-year education student had become far more proficient in the language than her classmates. She described how she felt that her good pronunciation made her stand out in class and her oral performances were negatively evaluated by peers. The student explained that as a consequence, 'I purposely tried to pronounce things badly so that it'd sound the same as everyone else'. This safety behaviour involved pretending to be disfluent by adopting *katakana* pronunciation (also known as vowel-marking - see Carroll, 2005) where vowels are added to word-final consonants (e.g. *good morning* is pronounced *goodo morning*u) and mixing up the letter *r* with the letter *l* – a common error for novice Japanese learners of English. She provided the following illustration:

> 'I want to have a <u>lice</u>!' Lice, you know? Lice! It's very- ((spoken while laughing)) I want to have lice or (..) I (.) will (.) go (.) to (.) *sho-pin-gu*. I (.) will (.) go (.) *sho-pin-gu* next, or something like that. I changed my accent, talking like my friend...I tried to- tried to cut my speaking time. I didn't want- I didn't want be laughed ((at)) by everyone. So when I- I talk in English only- ((it was)) only when I ((I was)) nominated by teacher so I- I wasn't active in the classroom.

Even though the socially anxious engage in safety behaviours in order to reduce anxiety, behaviours like this student described actually work to maintain a person's anxiety as they encourage self-monitoring and perpetuate biased predictions about how one will be perceived (Clark, 1999; Clark & Wells, 1995; McManus & Hirsch, 2007; Wells et al., 1995). Within language learning situations, safety seeking behaviours aimed at avoiding or minimising oral participation can make learners appear indifferent and unfriendly. Doing little for good interpersonal relationships and making cooperation between participants less likely, these strategies tend to make social interactions in the classroom less successful.

Somatic and cognitive symptoms

Somatic and cognitive symptoms make up the final component of the cognitive-behavioural model of Clark and Wells (1995). The socially anxious experience marked arousal in feared situations and consequently there is a range of symptoms associated with the condition. Sufferers tend to become concerned that others will notice their symptoms and therefore 'interpret them as signs of impending or actual failure to meet their desired standards of social performance' (Clark, 2001: 410). This leads to an increase in self-monitoring as individuals often become hypervigilant, searching for signs of anxiety which they believe are all too obvious to others. In this section I will briefly discuss some of the symptoms that learners described experiencing during their language classes.

One student, an English language major at a private university famous for its study abroad schemes, spoke of the tense atmosphere which dominated her intensive English class (15 hours of instruction per week) and described what she felt at the prospect of being called on to speak in the target language in front of her classmates:

> I can feel my heart- heart rate maybe going up or (..) I feel colder maybe (3.0) and I would feel inferior (.) I would feel I'm idiot (..) I wanna just run away, disappear ((laughs)).

The palpitations this learner experiences are a common physical symptom associated with social anxiety. In the extract she links her somatic symptoms to a negative self-image and a desire to seek safety by fleeing from the situation (an action she claimed never to have carried out, choosing instead to endure the situation in discomfort). Her description of feeling cold is somewhat odd as we could reasonably have expected the opposite; a feeling of being hot and sweaty. This is certainly what another interviewee described when she talked about the anxious feelings she experienced in her weekly English class:

> At first my hands become really sweaty, and then I kind of restlessly look back and forth between my dictionary and notebook and nervously look around to see if everybody else is following... it's kind of nerve-wracking and erm my brain's working hard and gets full.

Note how this student depicts not just the physical symptoms of her anxiety, but cognitive and behavioural components too. The account of her brain 'working hard' and getting 'full' suggests she has experienced a kind of cognitive overload brought about by the attention-draining activities of self-monitoring, scrutinising others' reactions and engaging in safety behaviours whilst at the same time trying to attend to the lesson content. It is no wonder this student described feeling 'absolutely flustered' in her language class and admitted to retreating into the safety that silence offered. A further interviewee, who spoke extensively about his feelings of embarrassment during lessons, recounted similar panicky experiences when he was called upon to speak English in front of his classmates:

> It's like my mind goes blank um (2) it goes into a panic. How can I say? I feel flustered like 'what can I do, what can I do?' comes one after another.

Mental blanks are recognised as a common cognitive symptom of social anxiety (Clark, 1999, 2001; Clark & Wells, 1995; McManus & Hirsch, 2007). They also represent a feared prediction for some learners, particularly when there is a requirement to perform some form of public speaking activity individually in the classroom (e.g. giving a presentation). Mental blanks, in common with other cognitive and somatic symptoms, tend to be exacerbated by safety behaviours.

Conclusion

There is a pronounced tendency for Japanese learners of English to avoid oral participation in their university language classrooms, and we should acknowledge that the reasons behind this phenomenon are numerous and complex. A learner's silence may emerge through any number of multiple, interconnected routes, and these routes are influenced by variables at individual, classroom, institutional and societal levels. From the testimony I have collected about their experiences of classroom-based language instruction, I believe one of the most salient conceptions of silence for these students is the silence of social anxiety – a silence born from inhibition, withdrawal, fear and distress. Based primarily on the work of Clark and Wells (1995) and adapted to summarise the main points of the arguments put forward in this chapter, I conclude by presenting a cognitive-behavioural model of an L2 learner's silence-inducing social anxiety (see Figure 13.1). The model illustrates how a skewed, negatively-biased self-concept, working in tandem with an overriding fear of negative evaluation, influences the cognitive processes and in-class behaviours of language learners who seek to minimise their oral participation and retreat into silence.

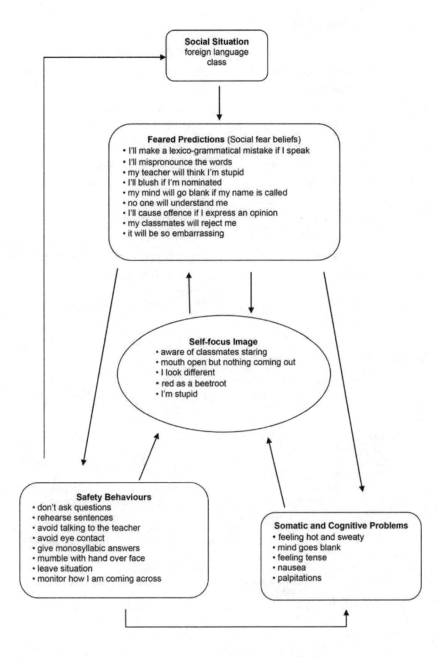

Figure 13.1 A cognitive-behavioural model of an L2 learner's silence-inducing social anxiety (Adapted from Clark & Wells, 1995; McManus & Hirsch, 2007)

Transcript convention

.	Falling 'final' intonation	That'll do just fine
,	Continuing 'list' intonation	We studied reading, writing, listening
?	Question intonation	Really?
↑	Shift into higher pitch	It was ↑ wonderful
!	Animated talk	Lice!
(.)	Pause of less than 0.5 second	I (.) will (.) go
(..)	Pause of about 0.5 second	But (..) it works anyway
(...)	Pause of about 1 second	I think (...) it takes time
(2)	Pause of about 2 seconds	It was (2) a Tuesday
-	Abrupt cut off	I- we were on time
(.hhh)	Inhalation	(·hhh) let me see
(( ))	Other details	You're terrible ((spoken while laughing))
....	Emphasis	Everybody was looking

(adapted from Richards, 2003)

References

Aida, Y. (1994) Examination of Horwitz, Horwitz, and Cope's constructs of foreign language anxiety: The case of students of Japanese. *The Modern Language Journal* 78 (2), 155–168.

American Psychiatric Association. (2000) *Diagnostic and Statistical Manual of Mental Disorders* (4th edn). Washington, DC: Author.

Barnlund, D.C. (1974) The public and the private self in Japan and the United States. In J.C. Condon and M. Saito (eds) *Intercultural Encounters with Japan: Communication - Contact and Conflict* (pp. 27–96). Tokyo: Simul Press.

Blackmore, M.A., Erwin, B.A., Heimberg, R.G., Magee, L., and Fresco, D.M. (2009) Social anxiety disorder and specific phobias. In M.G. Gelder, N.C. Andreasen, J.J. López-Ibor Jr. and J.R. Geddes (eds) *New Oxford Textbook of Psychiatry* (2nd edn, Vol. 1) (pp. 739–750). Oxford: Oxford University Press.

Breen, M.P. (1985) The social context for language learning – a neglected situation? *Studies in Second Language Acquisition* 7 (2), 135–158.

Carroll, D. (2005) Vowel-marking as an interactional resource in Japanese novice ESL conversation. In K. Richards and P. Seedhouse (eds) *Applying Conversation Analysis* (pp. 214–234). London: Palgrave Macmillan.

Clancy, P.M. (1990) Acquiring communicative style in Japanese. In R.C. Scarcella, E.S. Anderson and S.D. Krashen (eds) *Developing Communicative Competence in a Second language* (pp. 27–35). New York, NY: Newbury House.

Clark, D.M. (1999) Anxiety disorders: Why they persist and how to treat them. *Behavior Research and Therapy* 37 (Supplement 1), S5–S37.

Clark, D.M. (2001) A cognitive perspective on social phobia. In W.R. Crozier and L.E. Alden (eds) *International Handbook of Social Anxiety* (pp. 405–430). Chichester: Wiley.

Clark, D.M. and Wells, A. (1995) A cognitive model of social phobia. In R.G. Heimberg, M.R. Liebowitz, D.A. Hope and F.R. Schneier (eds) *Social Phobia: Diagnosis, Assessment and Treatment* (pp. 69–93). New York, NY: Guilford Press.

Dörnyei, Z. (2009) Individual differences: Interplay of learner characteristics and learning environment. *Language Learning, 59* (Issue Supplement s1), 230–248.

Essau, C.A., Sasagawa, S., Chen, J. and Sakano, Y. (2012) Taijin kyofusho and social phobia symptoms in young adults in England and in Japan. *Journal of Cross-Cultural Psychology* 43 (2), 219–232.

Granger, C.A. (2004) *Silence in Second Language Learning: A Psychoanalytic Reading.* Clevedon: Multilingual Matters.

Greer, D.L. (2000) "The eyes of *hito*": A Japanese cultural monitor of behavior in the communicative language classroom. *JALT Journal* 22 (1), 183–195.

Heinrichs, N., Rapee, R.M., Alden, L.A., Bögels, S., Hofmann, S.G., Ja Oh, K. and Sakano, Y. (2006) Cultural differences in perceived social norms and social anxiety. *Behaviour Research and Therapy* 44 (8), 1187–1197.

Hewitt, E. and Stephenson, J. (2012) Foreign language anxiety and oral exam performance: A replication of Phillips's MLJ study. *The Modern Language Journal* 96 (2), 170–189.

Hodson, K.J., McManus, F.V., Clark, D.M. and Doll, H. (2008) Can Clark and Wells' (1995) cognitive model of social phobia be applied to young people? *Behavioural and Cognitive Psychotherapy* 36 (Special Issue 4), 449–461.

Hofmann, S.G., Asnaani, A. and Hinton, D.E. (2010) Cultural aspects in social anxiety and social anxiety disorder. *Depression and Anxiety* 27 (12), 1117–1127.

Holliday, A. (1994) *Appropriate Methodology and Social Context.* Cambridge: Cambridge University Press.

Horwitz, E.K., Horwitz, M.B. and Cope, J. (1986) Foreign language classroom anxiety. *The Modern Language Journal* 70 (2), 125–132.

Ishii, S. and Bruneau, T. (1994) Silence and silences in cross-cultural perspective: Japan and the United States. In L.A. Samovar and R.E. Porter (eds) *Intercultural Communication: A Reader* (7th edn) (pp. 246–251). Belmont, CA: Thomson Wadsworth.

Kasahara, Y. (1986) Fear of eye-to-eye confrontation among neurotic patients in Japan. In T.S. Lebra and W.P. Lebra (eds) *Japanese Culture and Behavior: Selected Readings* (Revised edn, pp. 379–387). Honolulu: University of Hawaii Press.

Kawakami, N., Shimizu, H., Haratani, T., Iwata, N. and Kitamura, T. (2004) Lifetime and 6-month prevalence of DSM-III-R psychiatric disorders in an urban community in Japan. *Psychiatry Research* 121 (3), 293–301.

King, J. (2013a) *Silence in the Second Language Classroom.* Basingstoke: Palgrave Macmillan.

King, J. (2013b) Silence in the second language classrooms of Japanese universities. *Applied Linguistics* 34 (3), 325–343.

Kleinknecht, R.A., Dinnel, D.L. and Kleinknecht, E.E. (1997) Cultural factors in social anxiety: A comparison of social phobia symptoms and *taijin kyofusho. Journal of Anxiety Disorders* 11 (2), 157–177.

Korst, T.J. (1997) Answer, please answer! A perspective on Japanese university students' silent response to questions. *JALT Journal* 19 (2), 279–291.

Kring, A.M. and Johnson, S.L. (2012) *Abnormal Psychology* (12th edn) Hoboken, NJ: John Wiley and Sons.

Lane, C. (2008) *Shyness: How Normal Behaviour Became a Sickness.* New Haven, CT: Yale University Press.

Leary, M.R. (1995) *Self-presentation: Impression Management and Interpersonal Behavior.* Milwaukee, WI: Brown and Benchmark.

Lebra, T.S. (1976) *Japanese Patterns of Behavior*. Honolulu: University Press of Hawaii.

Lebra, T.S. (1987) The cultural significance of silence in Japanese communication. *Multilingua* 6 (4), 343–357.

Lebra, T.S. (1993) Culture, self, and communication in Japan and the United States. In W.B. Gudykunst (ed.) *Communication in Japan and the United States* (pp. 51–87). New York, NY: State University of New York Press.

Liu, M. and Jackson, J. (2008) An exploration of Chinese EFL learners' unwillingness to communicate and foreign language anxiety. *The Modern Language Journal* 92 (1), 71–86.

Long, M.H. (1996) The role of the linguistic environment in second language acquisition. In W.C. Ritchie and T.K. Bhatia (eds) *Handbook of Language Acquisition (Vol. 2: Second language acquisition)* (pp. 413–468). New York: Academic Press.

MacIntyre, P.D. and Gardner, R.C. (1994) The subtle effects of language anxiety on cognitive processing in the second language. *Language Learning* 44 (2), 283–305.

McManus, F. and Hirsch, C. (2007) Social phobia: Investigation. In S. Lindsay and G. Powell (eds) *The Handbook of Clinical Adult Psychology* (3rd edn) (pp. 206–226). Hove: Routledge.

McVeigh, B.J. (2002) *Japanese Higher Education as Myth*. New York, NY: M. E. Sharpe.

Mulligan, C. (2005) No English educational reforms will be effective unless Japanese English teachers can and will speak English in the classroom. *The Language Teacher* 29 (5), 33–35.

Purdon, C., Antony, M., Monteiro, S. and Swinson, R.P. (2001) Social anxiety in college students. *Anxiety Disorders* 15 (3), 203–215.

Ramsawh, H.J., Chavira, D.A. and Stein, M.B. (2010) Phenomenology of social anxiety disorder. In D.J. Stein, E. Hollander and B.O. Rothbaum (eds) *Textbook of Anxiety Disorders* (2nd edn) (pp. 437–452). Arlington, VA: American Psychiatric Publishing.

Rapee, R.M., Kim, J., Wang, J., Liu, X., Hofmann, S.G., Chen, J., Oh, K.J., Bögels, S.M., Arman, S., Heinrichs, N. and Alden, L.E. (2011) Perceived impact of socially anxious behaviors on individuals' lives in Western and East Asian countries. *Behavior Therapy* 42 (3), 485–492.

Richards, K. (2003) *Qualitative Inquiry in TESOL*. Basingstoke: Palgrave Macmillan.

Salkovskis, P.M. (1991) The importance of behaviour in the maintenance of anxiety and panic: A cognitive account. *Behavioural Psychotherapy* 19 (1), 6–19.

Schreier, S.-S., Heinrichs, N., Alden, L., Rapee, R.M., Hofmann, S.G., Chen, J., Oh, K.J. and Bögels, S.M. (2010) Social anxiety and social norms in individualistic and collectivistic countries. *Depression and Anxiety* 27 (12), 1128–1134.

Scott, S. (2006) The medicalisation of shyness: From social misfits to social fitness. *Sociology of Health & Illness* 28 (2), 133–153.

Stein, D. J. (2009) Social anxiety disorder in the West and in the East. *Annals of Clinical Psychology* 21 (2), 109–117.

Swain, M. (2005) The output hypothesis: Theory and research. In E. Hinkel (ed.) *Handbook of Research in Second Language Teaching and Learning* (pp. 471–483). Mahwah, New Jersey, NJ: Lawrence Erlbaum.

Tedeschi, J.T. (ed.) (1981) *Impression Management Theory and Social Psychological Research*. New York, NY: Academic Press.

Topham, P. and Russell, G. (2012) *Social anxiety in higher education. The Psychologist* 25 (4), 280–282.

Wakefield, J.C., Horwitz, A.V. and Schmitz, M.F. (2005) Are we overpathologizing the socially anxious? Social phobia from a harmful dysfunction perspective. *Canadian Journal of Psychiatry* 50 (6), 317–319.

Wells, A., Clark, D.M., Salkovskis, P., Ludoate, J., Hackmann, A. and Gelder, M. (1995) Social phobia: The role of in-situation safety behaviors in maintaining anxiety and negative beliefs. *Behavior Therapy* 26 (1), 153–161.

Woodrow, L. (2006) Anxiety and speaking as a second language. *RELC Journal* 37 (3), 308–328.

Young, D.J. (ed.) (1999) *Affect in Foreign Language and Second Language Learning: A Practical Guide to Creating a Low-anxiety Classroom Atmosphere.* Boston, MA: McGraw-Hill College.

14 Chinese University Students' Willingness to Communicate in the L2 Classroom: The Complex and Dynamic Interplay of Self-Concept, Future Self-Guides and the Sociocultural Context

Zhen Yue

Introduction

The central role of self-concept in shaping learners' engagement in learning activities is widely acknowledged. In Second Language Acquisition (SLA) research, self-related constructs have been recognised as playing a key role in contributing to successful language learning and use (e.g. Arnold & Brown, 1999; Cheng *et al.*, 1999; Dörnyei, 2005; Dörnyei & Ushioda, 2009; Mercer, 2011; Norton, 2000, 2001; Woodrow 2006; Yashima *et al.*, 2004). Furthermore, there is a growing awareness of the significance of learners' self-perceptions in contributing to one's willingness to communicate (WTC) in a foreign/second language (L2) (Cao & Philp, 2006; Kang, 2005; MacIntyre, 2007; MacIntyre *et al.*, 1998). However, although efforts to capture the role of the self across various contexts of WTC have been evident (e.g. MacIntyre & Legetto, 2011; MacIntyre *et al.*, 2011; Peng & Woodrow, 2010), few studies have focused on an in-depth exploration of learners' self-relevant constructs in actual L2 communication.

This study is part of a larger project investigating university English language learners' L2 WTC in a Chinese sociocultural context. The aim of the current chapter is to understand the way in which individual language learners perceive their sense of self and how this impacts on both their WTC and the actual communicative behaviour in the L2 classroom as they engage in specific communication activities. This chapter takes a closer look at one individual language learner and examines the complex self-related processes across various L2 communicative situations. The findings are discussed through the lens of a complex systems theory (Larsen-Freeman & Cameron, 2008), which is used in this study as an overarching framework to shed light on the interplay of self-concept, WTC and the sociocultural context.

Theoretical Background

L2 WTC

As self-concept is significant in L2 learning, it is therefore believed to play a key role in initiating L2 WTC and L2 use. The concept of WTC was traditionally considered from the psychological perspective as a personality trait (McCroskey & Baer, 1985), but has been reconceptualised in the SLA research to recognise both trait and state characteristics of WTC in the L2 context (MacIntyre et al., 1998). Accordingly, L2 WTC is defined as 'a readiness to enter into discourse at a particular time with a specific person or persons, using a L2' (MacIntyre et al., 1998: 547) and the resulting model of L2 WTC proposed by the same researchers integrates various linguistic, psychological and social variables as enduring and situational influences underlying L2 WTC and L2 use.

Particularly prominent among the empirical results from the growing research in this domain is the role of self-related constructs in shaping individuals' WTC in their L2. These include self-confidence, motivation, learners' beliefs, language anxiety, other-directed self and many others (MacIntyre et al., 1997, 1998, 2011; Peng & Woodrow, 2010; Wen & Clément, 2003). An interesting recent tendency in L2 WTC research is to view the construct through the lens of self-guides which usually concern a dynamic and forward-pointing process of how someone is moved from the current self-state towards future imaginative selves through self-regulated and motivated behaviour (Dörnyei & Ushioda, 2009). For example, MacIntyre (2007) has suggested that the initiation of L2 WTC concerns an individual's volitional process with both approach and avoidance tendencies, waxing and waning from moment to moment. Additionally, in a more recent study of MacIntyre and Legatto (2011) on the change of WTC, they also have identified that WTC as a dynamic system is self-organising into preferred states and repeller states. Following this argument, it may be productive to adopt self-concept as a broadly defined term and argue that L2 WTC is likely to be generated when individuals realise the discrepancy between their current L2 self-concept and L2 related future self-guides. Both constructs are reviewed next.

L2 self-concept

A person's self-concept concerns a set of beliefs or perceptions one holds about oneself (Mercer, 2011). Pajares and Schunk defined self-concept as 'a self-description judgment that includes an evaluation of competence and the feelings of self-worth associated with the judgment in question' in a specific domain (Pajeras & Schunk, 2005: 105). This self-related construct embraces both affective and cognitive dimensions and is defined broadly to capture sets of beliefs related to a specific domain and across a range of contexts. According to Mercer (2011), self-concept refers to the current self-state, and since it is closely tied to the specific situation, self-concept cannot be understood independently from its setting. In addition to the situatedness of self-concept, past research has also revealed its multi-faceted nature (Marsh et al., 2000a, 2001; Schunk, 2003; Yeung & Wong, 2004). It has been suggested that different domains of self-concept develop and change in different ways over time (Young & Mroczek, 2003). Around a person's core sense of self that is more stable across time and place, learners may also hold a working self-concept of the moment (Mercer, 2011). This dimension of the self-concept is most likely to fluctuate and be influenced by contextual factors and situational variables (Mercer, 2011). Therefore, an important emphasis is the consideration of context in understanding the variability of the self-concept and the ways in which self-concept may interact with and be influenced by other variables (Onorato & Turner, 2004). In line with this argument, this study focuses on the L2 self-concept defined as an individual's stable as well as situated self description of their current competence and evaluative perceptions as an English as a Foreign Language (EFL) learner and speaker in relation to specific communicative tasks in the L2 classroom at a Chinese university.

L2 possible selves

Future self-guides have been conceptualised in psychology as possible selves. These are taken to represent individuals' ideas of 'what they might become, what they would like to become, and what they are afraid of becoming' (Markus & Nurius, 1987: 157). Possible selves concern individuals' conceptualisation of their as-yet unrealised potential. In this sense, they function as future self-guides that shed light on how individuals are moved from the present towards the future and thus make an explicit link between the current self-system and self-guided behaviour (Dörnyei & Ushioda, 2009). In SLA research, two key aspects of possible selves have been identified: the Ideal L2 self and the Ought-to L2 self. The former refers to 'the L2 specific facet of one's ideal self' and the Ought-to L2 self concerns 'the attributes that one believes one ought to possess to meet expectations and to avoid possible negative outcomes' (Dörnyei & Ushioda, 2009: 29). In the L2 motivation domain, these two types of possible selves form two of the three main components of Dörnyei's (2005) L2 Motivational Self System along with the L2 learning experience. The L2 learning experience is associated with the direct impact of the individual's learning environment, which implicates the inseparable relationship between the self-related constructs and the social context.

Based on Higgins's (1987, 1996) self-discrepancy theory, possible selves as future self-guides could be powerful motivators for language learners to learn the L2 because of the desire to reduce the discrepancy between their current actual selves and the Ideal and Ought-to L2 selves (Dörnyei & Ushioda, 2009). In this vein, it is possible to argue that L2 WTC could be the outcome of one's self-discrepancy reduction process between the current self-state and future possible selves.

Emerging complex dynamics of self-related constructs

In recent years, following the trend to investigate self-concept in relation to specific domains, there has been a growing emphasis on the dynamic nature of self-concept (DeHart & Pelham, 2007; Harter, 2006; Young & Mroczek, 2003). Additionally, the movement from the current self-states to possible selves has been recognised as a dynamic and forward-pointing process. The complex interplay of learners' possible selves and L2 learning situations is evident in Asker's (2012) study, which highlights the multi-faceted and dynamic nature of students' images of future selves in motivating their L2 learning engagement across different microcontexts. Concerning learner's WTC in L2 learning, self-related constructs, namely self-concept and possible selves, are considered to play a significant role in understanding the individual's L2 WTC, and the discrepancy between the two self dimensions holds an explanatory power for understanding the individual's initiation of L2 WTC. The emerging evidence of the complex, dynamic and situated nature of both self-concept and possible selves indicates that any research aspiring to understand WTC will need to take these features into account.

The study

Although self-concept has traditionally been examined within the dominant experimental and quantitative paradigm, there have been important calls for more situated, holistic and qualitative investigations (de Saint Léger & Storch, 2009; Ellis, 2008; Morita, 2004; Mercer, 2011). Such methodological orientation, it has been argued, would allow more in-depth insights into the complex, unanticipated and dynamic development of self-related constructs in the foreign language learning context. Building on these arguments, the present study has adopted an ethnographic case study approach in order to explore ways in which the L2 language learner forms self-concepts in the EFL domain and how the interplay of learner's language-related self-concepts, future self-guides and the sociocultural context affects WTC and communicative behaviour in the L2 classroom.

The research context and the participant

The data were collected in a Chinese university setting. The university is one of the top 10 universities in mainland China and has been ranked highly for the quality of teaching and research across various fields (Academic Ranking of World Universities, 2012). English is taught as a foreign language and the university offers both general English classes (e.g. International communication) typically taught by Chinese teachers and foreign English classes (e.g. Speaking and Listening) taught by native speakers of English. English classes usually take place once a week with an allocation of three hours per week for the International communication class (referred to as Class A from now on) and two hours for the Listening and Speaking class (Class B). Students attend these classes in two different terms and are grouped based on their initial assessment results. Students with higher scores attend Class A, while those with lower scores are enrolled in Class B. Both types of classes normally consist of students from various majors except English-major students who usually have their own specialist language classes in their department.

The participant is one of the five participants who volunteered to take part in the larger study. Sarah (pseudonym) is a 25-year-old first-year postgraduate student majoring in microbiology. At the time of the study, she was assigned to Class B based on her prior English assessment results. She was studying with students from her own department and students of economy and finance. She started to learn English when she was 5 years old and developed an interest in learning English gradually thanks to her positive language learning experience. She indicated a preference to attend Class B, as, according to her, the learning atmosphere in that class was more relaxed, the foreign teacher was more encouraging and there was no pressure to produce correct answers in class discussions.

Data collection instruments

The data collection was carried out over a period of 14 weeks, which constitutes one academic semester at this university. Data came from the following three sources: (1) a life story interview, (2) classroom observation and (3) stimulated recall interviews. The life story interview was conducted with Sarah at the outset of the study to construct an initial in-depth portrait of her language learning experience and her sense of self-concept. In addition, 10 two-hour ethnographic classroom observations were carried out to capture Sarah's actual communication behaviour in her classes. The observations involved (1) detailed field notes of the overall classroom context, tasks and interactions and (2) audio recordings of Sarah's verbal interactions with the teacher and/or peers. Finally, stimulated recall interviews, conducted as soon as possible after each teaching session, examined Sarah's perceptions and evaluation of her communicative behaviour and probed further into Sarah's WTC, self-concepts and future self-guides in the context of Sarah's specific interactions. For a full summary of data sources concerning Sarah's WTC, please see Table 14.1.

Data analysis

The interviews were conducted in Chinese according to the participant's preference and also with an intention to maximise the accuracy of mutual comprehension between the researcher and the research participant. The field notes were summarised and reviewed after each observation session. The interview data were transcribed and prepared for further analysis. A Grounded Theory approach was adopted during the data analysis process (Charmaz, 2006) with the aim of generating findings embedded in the data without imposing any preconceived categories or theoretical frameworks on the data and to achieve a more holistic theoretical explanation of Sarah's WTC.

The data were coded line-by-line initially by identifying themes, such as 'parents' encouragement', 'anticipating praise from the teacher' and 'nervous when facing the teacher'. Having identified a number of recurrent thematic categories, I proceeded with a more analytical approach to coding (Richards, 2005, 2009). At this stage, earlier data across datasets and initial codes were reviewed and recoded critically, and further, often unexpected, concepts emerged. For example, as

Table 14.1 A summary of Sarah's data

Data sources	Sessions	Length
Life story interview	1	1 h 53 min
Ethnographic classroom observation	10	19 h 35 min
Stimulated recall interview	10	4 h 05 min

'anticipating praise from the teacher', 'parents' high value on English learning', 'pursuing high marks in schools' and 'emphasis on future success' all implicate the orientation of meeting expectations of teachers, parents, educational settings and also wider society, 'meeting expectations' was created as a more broader concept to integrate the original labels. This, in turn, led to a theoretical insight which revealed possible relationships between the Ought-to L2 self, L2 WTC and other variables, around which a conceptually sound and empirically grounded theory of Sarah's L2 WTC could be built (Charmaz, 2006). Annotations and memos were written during the coding and analysis process, which further facilitated theoretical thinking (Kubanyiova, 2012). Due to space limitations, the following discussion of findings will be based on Sarah's life story interview and two sessions of classroom observation since they capture recurrent themes which appeared across all datasets, which are representative of Sarah's overall dataset.

Results and Findings

Sarah's dynamic L2 self-concept

Findings of this study shed light on the dynamic interplay of the sociocultural context and Sarah's evaluative perception of her current L2 competence. Above all, Sarah's family background, particularly parental support, appears to have played a dominant role in shaping her L2 self-concept. Sarah grew up as the only child and her parents always placed a high value on the knowledge of English and, consequently, on Sarah's English language education. As a result, Sarah was enrolled in the so-called English interest class at the age of five, which marked the beginning of her English language learning. This kind of parental encouragement had run throughout her English studies in primary, middle and high schools. As a result, Sarah was well aware of the significance of English and, like her parents, seemed to highly value the outcomes of her English studies. Interestingly, Sarah never perceived studying English as a burden, possibly an outcome of parental influence, but she admitted that becoming proficient in English was 'not a piece of cake'. She believed that although she was 'not bad at English', she still needed to 'invest a great effort' in learning English, such as attending extracurricular classes.

These mixed feelings about her own competence become more obvious when different reference points are brought into her reflections. Comparing herself with her peers both in class and outside of the class, she perceived her current English competence as intermediate and comparable to others. However, she came up with a less favourable assessment of her competence when she reflected on it in relation to the years of 'great effort', hinting at her disappointment with the results. It seems, therefore, that Sarah's L2 self is heavily dependent on her reference points, which, in her case, come mainly from her perceptions of her parents' values and satisfaction with her progress, peers' proficiency and the amount of effort invested in her English studies.

The picture becomes even more complex when Sarah's L2 self-concept is examined against the backdrop of the wider sociocultural and educational context. For example, Sarah's school teachers' emphases on the value of high marks in English exams led Sarah to identify with the main purpose of learning English in middle and high schools, which she saw as 'passing exams' and 'pursuing high marks'. These seemed to be the main motivation for Sarah to invest effort in learning English outside the classroom in order to become 'more competitive'. However, as soon as the exam-orientation became less prominent at university, Sarah seemed to pay considerably less attention to her English studies, even though she claimed that she still perceived learning English as important. In this sense, it could be argued that Sarah's L2 self-concept follows a fluctuating trajectory with different external pressures and values exerting an influence on Sarah's perceptions of her self-concept with different impacts on her actual investment in studying English.

On the other hand, permeating Sarah's data is a unifying theme, attesting to the fairly stable dimension of her L2 self-concept. Throughout her reflections on English learning across different stages of her past, present and even hoped-for future experiences, Sarah refers to herself as 'aspiring', 'autonomous' and 'competent' in English language learning and also 'guilty' if she fails to achieve her desired outcomes. As a postgraduate student, she finds it impossible to pay complete attention to her English studies, but, at the same time, shifts her emphasis towards a more meaningful engagement with English that is relevant to her major at present, such as reading academic journal articles and familiarising herself with academic conventions for conducting and reporting research in English. Sarah believes that these have a close relationship with her future development, as she hopes to be an active member of the academic community in her chosen field, which also involves a high proficiency in English.

This section has shown that Sarah's self-concept appears to be linked to a variety of external forces and pressures, but there is, at the same time, an overarching theme which points to a more internalised reference point against which Sarah assesses her current L2 self-concept. This suggests an interesting interplay between Sarah's self-concept and her Ought-to L2 self as well as her Ideal L2 self. Because Sarah's Ought-to L2 self is particularly strong in her dataset, I will examine it in more detail along with her Ideal L2 self in the following section.

Sarah's Ought-to L2 self and Ideal L2 self

From Sarah's description about her review of her previous English language learning experience, current perception of her L2 studies and prospect for future development, her Ought-to L2 self appeared prominently as the dominant future self-guide during her L2 learning process. Meeting parents' and teachers' expectations acts as a dominant driving force in guiding Sarah's L2 learning. As a result of her parents' high value placed on her education, and particularly investment in studying English language, such as extracurricular classes, buying learning materials and encouraging her to study English on a daily basis, Sarah was aware of the significance of learning English, and realised the future vision that her parents desired for her, which leads Sarah to believe that she 'ought-to' learn English successfully. Otherwise, she would 'disappoint' her parents and feel 'guilty'. The role of parents' support is also identified as being prominent across other participants and existing literature investigating EFL in China (Chen et al., 2005; Hu, 2002). In addition, meeting teachers' expectations was also obvious during Sarah's L2 learning in middle and high schools where there was a focus on examination results. For example, Sarah perceived that 'If you want to have a good relation with teachers, you need to study well. Teachers like good students'. Additionally, she also felt 'embarrassed' when she failed the exam, as the teacher would call her name to pick up the exam papers in front of the class. It is seen that either meeting teachers' expectations or avoiding the negative outcomes associated with failing exams, or a combination of both could be the key impetus in guiding Sarah to move towards what she perceived she ought to become as an L2 learner.

Moreover, concerning Sarah's current L2 self-state and her L2 possible selves in the future, her Ought-to L2 self provides possibilities for a dynamic link between the two self dimensions. The main aspects referring to Sarah's Ought-to L2 self and Ideal L2 self are proficiency in English and professional advancement. One of the goal-directed behaviours in moving towards proficiency in English is attending the International English Language Testing System (IELTS) exam.

> I will take IELTS exam next year...friends and classmates around me all take the exams, and also my parents encourage me to try...it is a kind of way to test my English competence.

In this case, Sarah viewed the IELTS exam as a criterion to evaluate her English proficiency. Together with her parents' expectations and influences from her peers, Sarah started to visualise the discrepancy between her current L2 self and her Ought-to L2 self. Sarah's Ought-to L2 self functions as a driving force to motivate her to invest more effort in L2 learning in daily life, such as preparing for the exam, and speaking more in the L2 in the classroom in order to achieve a higher mark in the exam, and move closer to the possible self she generated.

Similarly, regarding professional advancement and future career development, Sarah's Ideal L2 self and Ought-to L2 self are mainly concerned with publishing new research in English and pursuing advanced studies abroad.

> I think I wasted too much time and my parents' money...I'm so guilty...My parents want me to be brilliant and successful in the future, just like other Chinese parents. That's why they invest so much on my education, particular English study.

In the Chinese sociocultural context, collectivism is the main constituent of Chinese culture. The success of someone is the pride of not only the individual but also the parents as well as the entire family. Chinese parents usually place great expectations on their children and hope that they can have a bright future. In this sense, the 'guilty' of as-yet unrealised desire from her parents can be interpreted as a predominant impetus for Sarah. The Ideal and Ought-to L2 selves can point the direction for Sarah to move towards her unrealised potential and relieve her feeling of guilt.

The complex interplay of the L2 self-concept on L2 WTC

The L2 self-concept as mentioned above is constructed according to one's living and learning experiences, and these also have an impact on the individual's L2 learning on a more general level. When focusing on the learner's actual L2 communication in the classroom, the situatedness of self-concept, especially the complexity of the working self-concept plays a key role in dynamically affecting the learner's L2 WTC. One aspect of the learner's L2 working self-concept concerns the insider orientation that refers to a sense of group belongingness and is closely related to collectivism in the Chinese culture (Wen & Clément, 2003), which has different impacts on the individual's L2 WTC in different communicative situations.

L2 communication excerpt 1 (19 March 2012):

(Students were reading the questions)
Sarah: Discuss the questions...(silence)...OK, the first question, I think they're a kind of rude, right?... a kind of rude, because as senior they can't do quickly about the new things. They make mistakes, but they soon ... they soon accepted them. As a junior, we can give advice, but can't criticise the senior people.
... (silence)...
Other student: Let's look at the second one.
(Students read the next question)

In this communicative situation, Sarah generated the discussion within her group by talking about the first question. At the beginning of the discussion, Sarah tended to keep silent like her other group members by prompting others to speak. However, after realising others' reluctance to speak, and her sense of belonging within the L2 group, Sarah decided to start talking.

> I'm a hero, because they didn't speak, so I need to say something. We can't get stuck there.

Rather than the initial willingness to engage in the discussion, Sarah's motivation was derived from her sense of being a hero that is the responsibility referring to one's Ought-to L2 self, in order to keep group cohesiveness which particularly emphasises successful completion of the task. Group cohesiveness in the Chinese setting stems from the insider orientation which concerns a Chinese cultural expectation that ingroup members should be treated with a high level of familiarity and obligation because they share a common sense of unity and interdependence (Wen & Clément, 2003). In this case, the insider orientation contributes to a supportive climate for Sarah to produce L2 communicative behaviour because of responsibility and a sense of 'we-ness' and 'belongingness' she felt as a member of the group.

On the other hand, on some occasions, the learner's sense of being an insider may work in a contradictory way. In an L2 communicative situation where students were talking about Western festivals, Sarah showed frequent code switching between her L1 and L2.

> I was talking to my partner in English, but I was not sure 'Treat or Trick' is for Halloween or Easter, so I asked my partner, but she didn't know, and asked me 'what' in Chinese. Then I said 'Easter egg' to her. It seems she also didn't understand, and she asked me 'what does it mean' in Chinese, so I changed to speak Chinese to her.

Although Sarah had the desire to communicate in English, she perceived it as inappropriate to insist on using her L2 when her interlocutor seemed to request that she use her mother tongue. In this sense, between the desire and willingness to communicate, the individual may undergo a complex process whereby social and affective factors interact with each other. Only when she feels effectively comfortable will she be ready to engage in her L2. However, in this situation, Sarah's working self-concept was interacting with the situated context, where she employed the insider orientation to protect her sense of belongingness and avoid the possible negative outcome of being considered as showing off to her group members. Therefore, in this specific situation, her insider oriented working self-concept may act as an obstructor in generating her L2 WTC.

The dynamic role of the ought-to L2 self in L2 WTC

As identified above, Sarah's Ought-to L2 self is mainly concerned with meeting parents' and teachers' expectations and avoiding failing exams in general. Among these three concerns, meeting her parents' expectations is the most dominant motivator. As for L2 communication in the classroom, the intention of meeting teachers' expectations displayed dynamic roles in guiding the learner's L2 WTC according to different L2 communicative situations.

In the same group discussion about Western festivals, Sarah showed a kind of communicative behaviour by reluctantly talking about a topic that she was uncertain about when the teacher was walking around her.

> I was a little bit nervous at that moment, as I was not quite sure the 'treat or trick'...but the teacher was there. I need to say something, so I just repeat the words...just make sure what I was speaking is correct because you were facing the teacher.

It is evident that Sarah's L2 WTC was dynamically affected by the anxiety of uncertainty when facing the teacher. Although Sarah kept talking, her communicative behaviour is more appropriate to be interpreted as pleasing her teacher with proper performance rather than her initial willingness to speak.

> Teacher means marks. I mean it's internalised and developed from previous learning experience. For example, in high school, when we had exams in class, teachers usually walked around you to see how you did in the exams, whether you did correctly. If you did it wrong, teachers would not be happy, so you would be very nervous at that moment. Day after day, if the teacher stands beside or near me, I felt nervous, so make sure your performance is good, your answer is correct.

Sarah's interpretation is important in explaining that the learner's Ought-to L2 self was constructed based on her previous learning experience, which to some extent was internalised and stable within the individual's sense of self across time and situations. Although Sarah perceived her preference to attend this class because of no pressure to produce correct answers in the class discussion, in this actual L2 communication, she still showed her anxiety because she was uncertain about the correct answer which is contrary to her internalised Ought-to L2 self. This Ought-to L2 self concerns the teacher's expectations, good L2 performance and examination orientation. The realisation of this discrepancy to some extent supports the production of some communicative behaviour in the L2 in this specific situation. However, on the other hand, it actually restrained the learner's initial L2 WTC.

Sarah's Ought-to L2 self functions in a different way in another situation. After the group discussion about festivals, the teacher asked for feedback about Halloween in front of the class. Sarah provided the answer directly by speaking it out, even without raising her hand in order to 'attract the teacher's attention' and 'leave a good impression to the teacher', 'I hoped the teacher can notice my answer and kept on talking with my words'.

In this situation, the Ought-to L2 self acted as an impetus in initiating Sarah's L2 WTC and producing L2 communicative behaviour. It is possible to argue that the learner's L2 WTC is capable of being changed and dynamically influenced by the Ought-to L2 self with an intention to meet the teacher's expectations. According to different situational variables internal and external to the individual, such as state self-confidence, anxiety, interpretation of situated context, discussion topics and teachers, the Ought-to L2 self dynamically interplays with these variables and guides the learner's L2 WTC in complex ways.

Working towards L2 possible selves

As shown above, during L2 communicative interactions, the learner undergoes a complex and forward-pointing process in generating L2 WTC. At the heart of this process is the dynamic interplay of the learner's L2 self-concept, future self-guide, the sociocultural context and its impact on purposive L2 behaviour. In some occasions, the interaction of these components may not effectively produce one's L2 WTC. However, the learner's WTC in the L2 most likely occurs when she realises the discrepancy between her current L2 self-state and future as-yet unrealised potential, and she is simultaneously ready or effectively comfortable at that moment to reduce the discrepancy and move towards her Ideal or Ought-to L2 selves.

Referring to the L2 communication excerpt I mentioned above, after students completed the discussion, the teacher asked them for feedback on it. When the teacher asked the first question that Sarah talked about in her group before, Sarah immediately responded to it.

I talked about the first question, so I had already organised my speech and was well prepared. It was a good opportunity to let the teacher know me. I hope I can leave a good impression to the teacher, so that maybe she can give me a higher mark in the finally examination, you know, the emotional mark.

In this communicative situation, Sarah perceived that the prior L2 communicative experience positively constructed her state communicative self-confidence, which ensured her readiness both psychologically and linguistically to engage in a L2 conversation at that moment. Simultaneously, meeting her teacher's expectations and the examination orientation, particularly 'the emotional mark' that concerns a subjective evaluation based on the teacher's impression of the student, supported Sarah to visualise her possible L2 self with a higher mark, and then realise the discrepancy between her current self and future self. Accordingly, Sarah was willing to provide a perfect answer in order to impress her teacher, by which she was moving towards the future self she perceived that she ought to become.

Similarly, in the same communicative situation, Sarah showed her motivation and willingness to generate the conversation by sharing her ideas.

> My uncle often talks about the Western festivals with me. He has lots of opportunities to go abroad. After listening I started to be interested on these, and also learned many things. It's good to tell people what I know, I mean share with others, as they may not know about these interesting things.

Sarah's previous living experience shows an impact on her L2 working self-concept. She perceived herself as being more knowledgeable than other group members regarding Western cultures, which leads her to feel comfortable with her current self. The vision of sharing with others and being a knowledgeable source of information could be an effective impetus employed as a future self-guide supporting Sarah to initiate her L2 WTC, and work towards her Ideal L2 self.

Discussion

Learner's L2 self-concept and L2 possible selves

The language learner constructed a unique picture about her sense of L2 self based on her own learning and life experience in a Chinese sociocultural context in which her self-concept is embedded. The components within the L2 self-concept are unique to the individual. Within this picture, there are various facets related to her sense of self, such as her parents' values, perceived L2 competence, obligation, feared L2 self and her L2 working self-concept showing dynamic interplays with variables within the L2 situation and sociocultural context, which provides evidence for the multidimensional, complex and dynamic nature of self-concept (Mercer, 2011). There is some extent of consistency and coherence between the learner's L2 self-concept and her L2 possible selves (i.e. her Ideal L2 self and her Ought-to L2 self), as the construction of one's possible selves cannot be separated from the current self. The learner's Ought-to L2 self is identified as sharing some common features (i.e. meeting parents' and teachers' expectations, being responsible for higher marks and future development, and avoiding failing exams) with other Chinese EFL learners' sense of future selves due to the particular Chinese sociocultural context by comparing it with other participants in the current study and also based on evidence from the contemporary SLA literature across investigations of Chinese learners' L2 motivation, L2 WTC and EFL teaching in China (Chen *et al.*, 2005; Hu, 2002; Matsukawa & Tachibana, 1996; Peng & Woodrow, 2010; Warden, 2000; Warden & Lin, 2000; Wen & Clément, 2003). The culturally valued and internalised motivation to meet societal, parental and educational expectations, and examination requirements is specific to Chinese Confucian culture, which then acts as a dominant force in shaping the individual's Ought-to L2 self and is manifested in dynamically impacting the learner's L2 WTC in L2 communication.

The complexity of L2 WTC

In L2 communicative situations, the learner's L2 self-concept and Ought-to L2 self interact dynamically with various contextual factors and situated elements such as group cohesiveness, feedback from interlocutors, teacher's support and perceived anxiety. These variables are the indicators of the development of a particular L2 phenomenon, which provides possibilities for the learner to reduce the discrepancy between the current L2 self and the possible L2 selves, and have as an outcome the initiation of the learner's L2 WTC and related L2 communicative behaviour. During this complex process, the learner's L2 WTC can be created and changed in unpredictable ways. In this sense, L2 WTC is complex and dynamic, which works at a system level, within which every component is interconnected and interacts with each other in directing the development of L2 WTC. As a part of the system, the learner's L2 self-concept and perceived L2 possible selves play a significant role in contributing to the development of one's L2 WTC system. It is suggested that the learner's L2 WTC is more likely to be initiated in the L2 communicative situation when the language learner can visualise specific L2 possible selves and realise that the discrepancy between the current self and future possible selves is possible to be reduced by following specific feasible L2 action plans.

Conclusion

The current chapter focusing on the EFL domain, particularly EFL speakers in a Chinese sociocultural context, presents a picture of how an individual L2 learner constructed her L2 self-concept and L2 possible selves, and how these self-related constructs act dynamically in complex ways affecting one's L2 WTC and communicative behaviour in specific L2 situations. A complex systems theory is considered particularly useful in thinking about and researching WTC and self-concept, which is effective in providing a more holistic perspective in understanding the issue. Additionally, the study also provides empirical implications of EFL teaching, particularly communicative language teaching (CLT) in China. It is suggested that although English is a global language and there is a particular emphasis on importing CLT into the L2 classroom in China, decisions about standards, pedagogy and assessments for these teaching programmes should consider learner's EFL self-concepts, especially those formed particularly within a Chinese sociocultural context in order to avoid potential conflicts and resistance to importing the pedagogy. For example, teachers can encourage collaborative learning by assigning different tasks to each individual in groups. At the same time, they should be aware of and sensitive to sociocultural influences and other factors related to the learners' L2 self when engaging them in discussions.

References

ARWU (2012) Academic Ranking of World Universities, See http://www. shanghairanking.cn/Country2012 (accessed March 2012).

Arnold, J. and Brown, H.D. (1999) A map of the terrain. In J. Arnold (ed.) *Affect in Language Learning* (pp. 1–27). Cambridge: Cambridge University Press.

Asker, A. (2012) Future self-guides and language learning engagement of English-major secondary school students in Libya: Understanding the interplay between possible selves and the L2 learning situation. Unpublished PhD thesis, University of Birmingham.

Cao, Y. and Philp, J. (2006) Interactional context and willingness to communicate: A comparison of behaviour in whole class, group and dyadic interaction. *System* 34 (4), 480–493.

Charmaz, K. (2006) *Constructing Grounded Theory*. London: Sage.

Cheng, Y.S., Horwitz, E. and Schallert, D.L. (1999) Language anxiety: Differentiating writing and speaking components. *Language Learning* 49 (3), 417–446.

Chen, J.F., Warden, C.A. and Chang, H.T. (2005) Motivators that do not motivate: The case of Chinese EFL learners and the influence of culture on motivation. *TESOL Quarterly* 39 (4), 609–633.

de Saint Léger, D. and Storch, N. (2009) Learners' perceptions and attitudes: Implications for willingness to communicate in an L2 classroom. *System* 37 (2), 269–285.

DeHart, T. and Pelham, B.W. (2007) Fluctuations in state implicit self-esteem in response to daily negative events. *Journal of Experimental Social Psychology* 43 (1), 157–165.

Dörnyei, Z. (2005) *The Psychology of the Language Learner*. Hillsdale, NJ: Lawrence Erlbaum Associates.

Dörnyei, Z. and Ushioda, E. (eds) (2009) *Motivation, Language Identity and the L2 Self*. Bristol: Multilingual Matters.

Ellis, R. (2008) Learner beliefs and language learning. *Asian EFL Journal* 10 (4), 7–25.

Harter, S. (2006) The self. In W. Damon and R.M. Lerner (eds) *Handbook of Child Psychology: Social, Emotional, and Personality Development* (Vol. 3) (pp. 505–570). Hoboken, N.J: John Wiley and Sons.

Higgins, E.T. (1987) Self-discrepancy: A theory relating self and affect. *Psychological Review* 94 (3), 319–340.

Higgins, E.T. (1996) The "self digest": Self-knowledge serving self-regulatory functions. *Journal of Personality and Social Psychology* 71 (6), 1062–1083.

Hu, G. (2002) Potential cultural resistance to pedagogical imports: The case of communicative language teaching in the PRC. *Language, Culture and Curriculum* 15 (1), 30–49.

Kang, S.-J. (2005) Dynamic emergence of situational willingness to communicate in a second language. *System* 33 (2), 277–292.

Kubanyiova, M. (2012) *Teacher Development in Action: Understanding Language Teachers' Conceptual Change*. Basingstoke, UK: Palgrave Macmillan.

Larsen-Freeman, D. and Cameron, L. (2008) *Complex Systems and Applied Linguistics*. Oxford: Oxford University Press.

MacIntyre, P.D. (2007) Willingness to communicate in the second language: Understanding the decision to speak as a volitional process. *The Modern Language Journal* 91 (4), 564–576.

MacIntyre, P.D., Noels, K.A. and Clément, R. (1997) Biases in self-rating of second language proficiency: The role of language anxiety. *Language Learning* 47 (2), 265–287.

MacIntyre, P.D., Clément, R., Dörnyei, Z. and Noels, K.A. (1998) Conceptualizing willingness to communicate in a L2: A situational model of L2 confidence and affiliation. *The Modern Language Journal* 82 (4), 545–562.

MacIntyre, P.D. and Legatto, J.J. (2011) A dynamic system approach to willingness to communicate: Developing an idiodynamic method to capture rapidly changing affect. *Applied Linguistics* 32 (2), 149–171.

MacIntyre, P.D., Burns, C. and Jessome, A. (2011) Ambivalence about communicating in a second language: A qualitative study of French immersion students' willingness to communicate. *The Modern Language Journal* 95 (1), 81–96.

Marsh, H.W., Hau, K.-T. and Kong, C.-K. (2000a) Late immersion and language instruction in Hong Kong high schools: Achievement growth in language and non-language subjects. *Harvard Educational Review* 70 (3), 302–346.

Marsh, H.W., Kong, C.K. and Hau, K.T. (2001) Extension of the internal/external frame of reference model of self-concept formation: Importance of native and non-native languages for Chinese students. *Journal of Educational Psychology* 93 (3), 543–553.

Matsukawa, R. and Tachibana, Y. (1996) Junior high school students' motivation towards English learning: A cross-national comparison between Japan and China. *ARELE: Annual Review of English Language Education in Japan* 7, 49–58.

McCroskey, J.C. and Baer, J.E. (1985) Willingness to communicate: The construct and its measurement. Paper presented at the annual conference of the Speech Communication Association, Denver.

Mercer, S. (2011) *Towards an Understanding of Language Learner Self-concept*. Dordrecht: Springer.

Morita, N. (2004) Negotiating participation and identity in second language academic communities. *TESOL Quarterly* 38 (4), 573–603.

Norton, B. (2000) *Identity and Language Learning: Gender, Ethnicity and Educational Change*. London: Longman.

Norton, B. (2001) Non-participation, imagined communities and the language classroom. In M. Breen (ed.) *Learner Contributions to Language Learning: New Directions in Research* (pp. 157–171). Harlow: Pearson Education.

Onorato, R.S. and Turner, J.C. (2004) Fluidity in the self-concept: The shift from the personal to social identity. *European Journal of Social Psychology* 34 (3), 257–278.

Pajares, F. and Schunk, D.H. (2005) Self-efficacy and self-concept beliefs. In H.W. Marsh, R.G. Craven and D.M. McInerney (eds) *International Advances in Self Research*, vol. 2. (pp. 95–121). Greenwich, Connecticut: Information Age Publishing.

Peng, J. and Woodrow, L. (2010) Willingness to communicate in English: A model in the Chinese EFL classroom. *Language Learning* 60 (4), 834–876.

Richards, L. (2005) *Handling Qualitative Data: A Practical Guide*. London: Sage.

Richards, L. (2009) *Handling Qualitative Data: A Practical Guide*. (2nd edn). London: Sage.

Schunk, D.H. (2003) Self-efficacy for reading and writing: Influence of modeling, goal setting, and self-evaluation. *Reading and Writing Quarterly* 19 (2), 159–172.

Warden, C.A. (2000) EFL business writing behaviour in differing feedback environments. *Language Learning* 50, 573–616.

Warden, C.A. and Lin, H.J. (2000) Existence of integrative motivation in an Asian EFL setting. *Foreign Language Annals* 33 (5), 535–547.

Wen, W.P. and Clément, R. (2003) A Chinese Conceptualisation of Willingness to Communicate in ESL. *Language, Culture and Curriculum* 16 (1), 18–38.

Woodrow, L.J. (2006) A model of adaptive language learning. *The Modern Language Journal* 90 (3), 297–319.

Yashima, T., Zenuk-Nishide, L. and Shimizu, K. (2004) The influence of attitudes and affect on willingness to communicate and second language communication. *Language Learning* 54 (1), 119–152.

Yeung, A.S. and Wong, E.K.P. (2004) Domain specificity of trilingual teachers' verbal self-concepts. *Journal of Educational Psychology* 96 (2), 360–368.

Young, J.F. and Mroczek, D.K. (2003) Predicting intraindividual self-concept trajectories during adolescence. *Journal of Adolescence* 26 (5), 586–600.

15 The Interaction of the L2 Motivational Self System with Socialisation and Identification Patterns and L2 Accent Attainment

Nihat Polat

Introduction

Second language acquisition (SLA) research has recently intensified the direction and effort in the study of a multidimensional self-concept, a learner's evaluative beliefs about herself/himself in affective and meta-cognitive competence. Thus far, affective variables such as motivation and metacognitive variables like beliefs and identity have been most commonly studied as constitutive elements of the internal structure of a second language (L2) learner's self-concept (Dörnyei & Ushioda, 2009; Mercer, 2011; Pajares & Schunk, 2005). The actual self is the perception of identity individuals have of themselves or the perception of identity people have according to what they think other people define them as. The ideal self is a depiction of a person's identity in an ideal state, also defined as attributes a person ideally wishes to possess, while the ought self involves perceived attributes that a person ought to possess (Higgins, 1987). Thus, a person's effort to become less like her/his actual self and more like her/his Ideal or Ought-to L2 self can be indicative of her/his form of motivation (Csizér & Kormos, 2009). Nevertheless, research on how a learner's L2 self (perceptions individuals have of their self as an L2 learner and user) and Ideal L2 self (attributes a person ideally wishes to possess as an L2 learner and user) concepts interact with identification and socialisation patterns in affecting success in L2 attainment is markedly limited. In light of self-discrepancy (Higgins, 1987), the L2 Motivational Self System (Dörnyei, 2005) and social identity and investment theories (Norton-Peirce, 1995), one could argue that it is of grave importance to identify compatibilities or congruencies between L2 learners' self-concepts and their identification patterns (Duff, 2002) of varying strengths as they relate to learning an L2. For example, do the identification patterns of learners with low versus high levels of L2 proficiency differ, and if so, do these differences significantly relate to different forms of L1 or L2 dominant socialisation patterns and success in L2 accent attainment?

Although SLA research has yet to fully unravel the complexities and intricacies of the internal structure of L2 learners' self-concepts, it is not too frivolous to argue that, whether momentary or long-lasting, or haphazard or consistent, L2 learners seem to have some forms of motivation and belief systems behind their situational or permanent or even self-conflicting investment efforts in their self-concepts. In view of a possible economic theory of L2 acquisition, investment (Norton-Peirce, 1995) in self-concept may involve complex comparisons and may as well be analogous to building and maintaining a financial portfolio; people sometimes buy stocks that they assume will always do well, they sometimes invest in companies that are in high demand at the time of purchase and they sometimes do both to diversify their portfolios. Sometimes these investments may seem contradictory to each other and sometimes people go against their financial advisors to have control over their investments, but it is hard to argue that their decision-making is governed by haphazard powers.

One dangerous thing to do here is to make causality assumptions about the decision-making processes involved in investment in L2 self-concepts. Nevertheless, it is possible that learners' perceptions of the importance of an L2, even on a global level, may affect whether or not they will invest in learning it successfully. If learners view the L2 as a valuable commodity, they may likely invest in it and have higher success in acquiring it than those who believe otherwise (Csizér & Kormos, 2009; Norton-Peirce, 1995). Undoubtedly, the prestige and dominance associated with the L2 (demand drives investment) may affect L2 learners' perceptions about the language, or conversely, having dominant social networks with an L2 community may lead to establishing such motivations and belief structures about the L2. L2 learners' decision-making in self-concept investments can also be affected by the L2 portfolio in which they are interested because societal factors can sometimes hinder social interaction (in this case, access to investment) between first language (L1) and L2 communities, diminishing an L2 learner's ability to envision themselves as a part of that community (Lamb, 2009; Schumann, 1978). Such situations underscore the significance of sociopsychological factors in L2 learners' self-concepts and reaffirm the volatility that social comparisons lend to understanding self-concepts in L2 learning (Mercer, 2011).

This study examines the complex system of self, Ideal L2 self and identification patterns in Kurdish-speaking communities in Turkey as they relate to success in the acquisition of a native-like Turkish accent in speaking Turkish. It addresses whether the perceptions of (1) self and Ideal L2 self predict degrees of accentedness in an L2, (2) self and Ideal L2 self predict dominance in L1 versus L2 networks, (3) L1 versus L2 communities predict dominance in L1 versus L2 networks and (4) L1 versus L2 communities predict degrees of accentedness in an L2. In addition to examining the interaction of multiple variables in a politically charged setting, this study's uniqueness comes from its focus on the acquisition of accent, a salient source of linguistic profiling (Baugh, 1999) and socio-cultural identification (Labov, 1972; Moyer, 2007). Below, firstly, I describe the historical context of Kurds as a minority group in Turkey. Secondly, I summarise previous research related to the variables under study. Thirdly, I explain the research methodology. Finally, I present the findings and interpret them in light of existing SLA theory and research.

Background: Kurds in Turkey

The Kurdish-speaking community lived under the Ottoman Empire, a loosely integrated group of entities that encompassed a wide variety of cultures and languages, stretching at various times from what is today Algeria to the Caspian Sea, and from Yemen to Hungary and Southern Poland. Under the Millet System, the right to practise one's own religion and speak one's own language was upheld (Kenanoglu, 2005). This case is generally referred to as tolerance rights in the literature (Hassanpour, 1992). In contrast to the Ottoman Empire, the Republic of Turkey took great interest in the regulation of languages other than Turkish. From the inception of the modern Turkish Republic in 1923, government policy sought to create a national identity under the guise that Turkey was populated by only one group of people with a single language, Turkish. The official language of Turkey is to this day Turkish only. To varying degrees over the past 80 years, it has been illegal to speak, write, publish, broadcast or essentially communicate in minority languages in government offices in the country (Hassanpour, 1992; Kendal, 1980; May, 2001; Skutnabb-Kangas & Bucak, 1995).

In 1961, Turkey adopted a new constitution in which some publications in Kurdish were allowed, but from the late 1960s until the early 1990s, there was an increased suppression of Kurdish culture/language as relations between the military-dictated governments and the political Kurdish activist movement worsened, after several military coups and a war declared by the Kurdish Workers' Party (PKK) (Koivunen, 2002), which resulted in the death of thousands of people. In the new constitution of 1982, the laws enacted in 1923 were reiterated, banning the use of Kurdish in the public realm (May, 2001) and establishing new programmes to improve literacy in Turkish (Hassanpour, 1992). In 1991, a new law permitted the use of Kurdish in contexts other than radio and television broadcasts, publications and education (Koivunen, 2002). However, once again anti-Kurdish laws were reintroduced by the late 1990s. There were criminal proceedings against those who promoted Kurdish language courses (May, 2001) because the Kurdish language was construed as a danger to the existence and independence of the state and the security of the community (May, 2001; Skutnabb-Kangas et al., 2009).

In recent years, the Turkish government, partially due to pressure from the European Union, has lifted the ban on speaking Kurdish in public, making radio broadcasts, publishing in Kurdish and having language education in Kurdish possible. Recently, private Kurdish language courses have been offered in many regions of Turkey. Although the situation is still restricted, with people not having a full and free range of possibilities such as bilingual education, the government has relaxed its earlier full prohibition against the public use of Kurdish. The current government has passed new regulations about Kurdish language rights, establishing a national TV station (TRT Şeş) that broadcasts in Kurdish, while also promising to improve the situation of minorities in a new constitution to be enacted soon.

Currently, Kurds live in almost all geographical regions in Turkey, with the majority residing in the east and southeast. According to the European Commission on Racism and Intolerance (ECRI, 2011), most areas where many Kurds live are among the poorest provinces and villages. They speak Kurdish, which belongs to the western Iranian branch of the Indo-European language family and is written in Arabic, Cyrillic and Roman scripts. Most Kurds who live in Turkey are bilingual (proficiency in Kurdish is limited to speaking and listening) in Turkish and Kurdish. While only few are simultaneous bilinguals and were exposed to both languages before schooling at around the age of 7, most were monolingual in Kurdish until they began formal education in Turkish (consecutive bilingualism). There are also Kurds who live in big cities and grew up as monolingual Turkish speakers or monolingual Kurdish speakers. They are mainly women and older individuals who live in rural areas and have not received the Turkish-only government schooling (Smits & Gündüz-Hoşgör, 2003). It is very hard to determine the actual Kurdish population in Turkey. Indeed, a rather substantial discrepancy has been observed between the numbers reported by the Turkish governmental and nongovernmental agencies as well as international organisations. According to the European Commission on Racism and Intolerance (ECRI, 2011), the Kurdish population in Turkey is estimated to be between 12 and 15 million.

L2 Socialisation and Investment

L2 learners act both as subjects and objects of socioculturally constituted structures, norms and relations that cannot be separated from their
motivations and behavioural patterns (Ushioda, 2009). They continuously
contribute to the shaping of their immediate and broader environments
(ecologies) while simultaneously being shaped by them. They move from
partially participating to fully participating in the act of learning (Lamb,
2009). More specifically, L2 learners constantly transform their identity
repertoires while participating in communities of practice because they
ultimately attempt to re-situate their identities according to the actions
of those deemed as experienced and important (Lamb, 2009; Polat &
Mahalingappa, 2010). That is why, in their situated learning theory, Lave
and Wenger (1991) emphasise social interaction to be an essential part of
knowledge expansion and comprehension, a notion shared by sociocon-
structivists who champion the primacy of the social over the individual
in any kind of learning. Indeed, every social ecology offers different affordances, and humans capitalise on each affordance in different ways (van
Lier, 2004), astutely comparing and measuring their extrinsic gains, losses,
competence, relatedness and control and autonomy (Deci & Ryan, 1987)
over the utilisation of each affordance.

The composition of an L2 learner's self-concept (Mercer, 2011) inevitably involves making comparisons and choices, because people are moved
to engage in a task in the presence of multiple possibilities and opportunities. Thus, self-concepts can be positive, negative, weak or strong, but
they are hard to predict and are relative to how well an individual attends
to available affordances in a setting. For instance, if a student who is
learning an L2 views the language as a principal necessity in her/his
world, she/he will find multiple reasons to socialise and socially identify
with the users of that language, which in turn may trigger the utilisation
of many other facilitating opportunities. Similarly, L2 learners who view
the target language as an investment in their identity (Dörnyei &
Ushioda, 2009; Norton-Peirce, 1995) may compare their identity to those
of others who speak the target language and make modifications accordingly (Mercer, 2011); the ideal modifications would undoubtedly be that
L2 learners make an effort to add the L2 identity to their repertoire of
identities. The sociolinguistic theory of accommodation (Giles & Coupland, 1991), which affirms that people exert an effort to adjust their communication behaviours to those of the target speech community in
exchange for possible gains is a good example of such trading acts of linguistic capital (Bourdieu, 1991). Hence, since it is hard to probabilistically
compute human behaviour, one can argue that the constitutive components of L2 learners' self-concepts are interactionally complex, situational,

ever-changing and even self-contradictory (Dörnyei & Ushioda, 2009; Higgins, 1987). This study aims to add to this line of research in untangling some of the complex interactions between certain constitutive elements of L2 self-concept and learners' patterns of L1 and L2 dominance.

Identification Patterns: Self and Ideal L2 Self

Although unclear and premature, early SLA research on motivation did include learners' social identification (Gardner & Lambert, 1972), a notion also underscored in the current research that learners who want to learn an L2 must have a genuine motivation to identify with members of that culture. Currently, identifying with a particular social community is perceived as a socioculturally constituted phenomenon rather than a natural inclination (integrative or intrinsic) (Ushioda & Dörnyei, 2009). Hence, one could argue that investment in an L2 self is a self-determined volitional act that is linked to numerous affective (e.g. motivation, identity) and metacognitive factors (e.g. beliefs) that interact in complex ways in different social settings. The relationships among L2 self, identity and motivation are therefore experiencing a paradigm shift and reconceptualisation with new support in L2 motivation research in different settings (Dörnyei, 2005; Taguchi et al., 2009; Ushioda & Dörnyei, 2009).

Dörnyei's (2005) L2 Motivational Self System re-conceptualises L2 motivational behaviour based upon the L2 self-concept because L2 motivation is somewhat related to a learner's ability to imagine herself/himself as a native speaker of that language (Dörnyei & Ushioda, 2009). In fact, Norton (2000) argues that people construct their identities based on their perceived association and affiliation with the L2 world. Dörnyei (2005) bases the L2 Motivational Self System on the self-discrepancy theory (Higgins, 1987), which categorises the self into three domains: actual, ideal and ought. The actual self is the perception of identity individuals have of themselves or the perception of identity people have according to what they think other people define them as. The ideal self is a depiction of a person's identity in an ideal state (Higgins, 1987), also defined as attributes a person ideally wishes to possess while the ought self involves perceived attributes that a person ought to possess (Dörnyei, 2005). Thus, a person's effort to become less like her/his actual self and more like her/his ideal or ought self can be indicative of her/his form of motivation (Csizér & Kormos, 2009).

Current research has generated some evidence and support for the L2 Motivational Self System as a promising theory that encompasses elements of identity and L2 learners' self-identification patterns (for more studies, see Dörnyei & Ushioda, 2009). According to this theory, motivation partially depends on L2 learners' self-concepts that cannot be separated from their patterns of identification and socialisation with L2 speakers (Dörnyei, 2009; Taguchi *et al.*, 2009; Ushioda & Dörnyei, 2009), which provide exposure opportunities for comprehensible input (Polat, 2011). For example, in a study where Csizér and Kormos (2009) examined the effects of the Ideal L2 self and the Ought-to L2 self on learners' motivated behaviour, they found that the Ideal L2 self partially predicted the motivation of the Hungarian learners of English at both secondary and higher education levels. These findings were corroborated in a large-scale study by Taguchi *et al.* (2009) in three different settings, including Japan, China and Iran. While this study does not explore motivation per se, it seeks to examine if a learner's perceptions about self and Ideal L2 self and her or his identification patterns contribute to her or his L2 self-concept that has also been linked to L2 motivation.

Method

Research questions

In this study, L2 self is used as an umbrella construct that entails numerous constitutive elements that are manifested in L2 learners' behaviours as coherent yet sometimes contradictory manifestations of their self-concept. The nature of inconsistencies in one's self can be emotional, cognitive, metacognitive or a combination of these traits (Higgins, 1987), and L2 learners have different belief systems, rationalisations and motivations to justify such language behaviours (Dörnyei & Ushioda, 2009). This study explores the L2 self (perceptions individuals have of their self as an L2 learner and user) together with the Ideal L2 self (attributes a person ideally wishes to possess as an L2 learner and user) in the context of the variables under study because both are constitutive elements of the L2 self-concept. In addition, theoretically one can assume that the ways in which L2 learners position their Ideal L2 selves cannot be separated from their perceptions about their L2 selves. This study examines the complex system of the L2 self and the Ideal L2 self, L2 dominance and socialisation and perceptions about the Kurdish and Turkish-speaking communities in Turkey as they relate to varying degrees of accentedness in speaking Turkish. Specifically it addresses the following questions:

(1) Do perceptions of one's self and Ideal L2 self predict degrees of accentedness in an L2?
(2) Do perceptions of one's self and Ideal L2 self predict dominance in L1 versus L2 networks?
(3) Do perceptions about L1 versus L2 communities predict dominance in L1 versus L2 networks?

(4) Do perceptions about L1 versus L2 communities predict degrees of accentedness in an L2?

Participants and setting

Eighty-eight students, whose ages ranged from 16 to 18 years, participated in this pilot study that was conducted prior to a subsequent multivariate study on L2 identity, social networks and motivation (Polat, 2007). Participants came from two public high schools in eastern Turkey. These schools were purposefully selected to be ethnically diverse to make sure that all kinds of social networks were available to them. The selection of the sample was based on the assumptions of the statistical procedures used in the study. There were more females ($n = 51$) than male participants who had undergone the mandatory monolingual schooling in Turkish without any instructional accommodations or support in their native language. Participants, who came from rather low socio-economic backgrounds, were ethnically Kurdish and had been born and lived in the research setting all of their lives. Only four participants had spent some time in another city with the amount of time ranging from one to seven weeks.

On the social network questionnaire, participants reported very little exposure to the Turkish language prior to their formal schooling (around 6 or 7 years) and had grown up speaking Kurdish in their household. Since the youngest participants in this study were 16 years old, all participants had a fairly good spoken and written command of standard Turkish at the high school level. In terms of issues of sampling bias and generalisability, it is important to note that although approximately 70% of Kurdish children living in urban areas receive middle-school education, only around 30–40% of them receive a high school education in eastern Turkey due to monetary constraints. Therefore, the sample in this study may represent a slightly higher socio-economic status level.

The setting is a fairly large historical city in eastern Turkey with a sizeable population. According to the socio-economic rankings of cities in Turkey, this setting had a medium-level socio-economic level with a Kurdish population of around 16% (*Yearbook of Turkish Statistics*, 2009). Given the study objectives, the data for this project could not have been collected in settings in which social interactions between the Turkish and Kurdish communities were either denied to people due to present ethnic conflicts or one culture had entirely assimilated into the other. The study setting was selected to ensure that it did not have a history of extremism in terms of the long-lasting ethnic clashes between Kurdish separatists and the Turkish Republic.

Data sources and analysis

Accent measurement data came from audio recorded speech tokens based on 10 selected phrases that were quintessential in the speech of Kurds while speaking Turkish. The 10 sounds included six consonants and four vowels (see Table 15.1). Three native speaker ethnic Turks, who were trained on accent rating procedures by the researcher, served as judges. All three judges were college educated (one man and two women) and had language education backgrounds. Such phrase-stimuli based accent measurement scales have been commonly used in the field as valid and reliable procedures (Derwing & Munro, 1997; Flege, 1984; Magen, 1998; Major, 1987). Participants' degrees of accentedness were represented by the number of targeted sounds that they pronounced correctly in each phrase based on a binary judgment of correct (native-like) or incorrect (non-native-like) pronunciation. Therefore, each participant could possibly receive a score between 0 and 10 as a representation of her or his native-like Turkish accent.

Socialisation and language community allegiance patterns were measured through a social network survey and a semantic differential technique. The social network questionnaire measured participants' exchange, interactive and passive networks to determine their L1 and L2 dominance. For each participant, two language dominance scores (Turkish and Kurdish) were established to be used in regression analyses. More specifically, a participant reported how dominant the uses of both Turkish and Kurdish

Table 15.1 Phonemic features used in the determination of the degree of accentedness of Kurdish learners while speaking Turkish

Linguistic Features	Kurdish Pronunciation	Turkish Pronunciation
diğer yerler	ʁ	J
bayağı farklıdır	İ	ɫ
bayağı farklıdır	Q	K
harbi yaşarız	X	H
otlarin yeşermesini	Ë	ε
Kadar hissederiz	Ħ	H
çiçeklerle süslenir	G	K
bembeyaz olur	ɨr	Ur
üfül kokar	U	Y
zamanlar vardır	W	V

were in their conversations with each network that they reported, using a scale of 1 (least dominant) to 5 (most dominant). Moreover, participants reported for each network the frequency, place, nature and reason for language use while also indicating degree of closeness with and socio-emotional or capital dependency on each network they reported. The data on self, Ideal L2 self and perceptions about the Kurdish and Turkish-speaking communities were collected via a semantic differential technique (Spolsky, 1969) that consisted of four sections (self, Ideal L2 self, the Kurdish-speaking community and the Turkish-speaking community) based on a list of 30 positive words/phrases that could be used to describe people (e.g. confident, considerate). Participants reported how well they believed each adjective described their self, Ideal L2 self, the Kurdish-speaking community and the Turkish-speaking community on a scale from 1 meaning the adjective does not at all describe these attributes to 5 meaning the adjective describes these attributes very well.

To determine if each of these four semantic differential instruments was measuring what it was assumed to measure, four exploratory factor analyses (EFA) were conducted using a principal axis factoring (PAF) extraction method with a promax rotation. All four tests met the criteria for factorability and sampling adequacy of the data (Mertler & Vannatta, 2010). The results revealed that each section (self, Ideal L2 self, Kurdish-speaking community and Turkish-speaking community) measured only one factor, with the first eigenvalues being approximately three times greater than the second for Self – First: 8.31, Second: 2.14; Ideal self – First: 9.42, Second: 2.28; Turkish-speaking community – First: 9.62, Second: 2.41 and Kurdish-speaking community – First: 9.80, Second: 2.70.

Data were analysed using a series of multiple regressions, using the accent scores, L1 and L2 dominance scores and participants' perception scores about their self, their Ideal L2 self, the Kurdish-speaking community and the Turkish-speaking community. A regression model was appropriate for data used in this study because it not only helped to determine how the self, the Ideal L2 self, perceptions about L1 and L2 communities and L1 and L2 dominance relate to each other but also measure how they predict varying degrees of accentedness, allowing for the interaction effect and possible multicollinearity calculations.

Results

The results suggest that the participants' degrees of accentedness, measured by the number of sounds pronounced correctly in phrasal tokens, varied from 1 to 10 (Table 15.2). To make the reporting and interpretation of results easier, participants' accentedness degrees were denoted by five levels. Those who pronounced between one and two sounds

Table 15.2 Distribution of participants by the number of words pronounced correctly

Accentedness levels	Number of words	Number of participants
Level 1	1	4 (4%)
	2	11 (13%)
Level 2	3	8 (9%)
	4	17 (19%)
Level 3	5	11 (13%)
	6	7 (8%)
Level 4	7	9 (10%)
	8	8 (9%)
Level 5	9	4 (5%)
	10	9 (10%)
Total		88 (100%)

correctly (Level 1) were identified as having a 'Very strong foreign accent' while participants in Level 5, who pronounced between nine and ten sounds correctly, were identified as having 'No foreign accent'. The results revealed that the whole group correctly pronounced around half of the sounds ($M = 5.3$, SD = 2.6) presented in the phrasal tokens. The findings also indicated that variation in degrees of accentedness was rather remarkable. Table 15.2 shows that almost 50% of the participants were in Levels 2 and 3, with Level 5 having the fewest number of participants. The rather high inter-rater reliability coefficients (.88 to .92) suggested that the judges were in agreement in their binary evaluation of accent levels.

A regression model was used to determine how the self, the Ideal L2 self, perceptions about L1 and L2 communities and L1 and L2 dominance measures interact with each other to predict varying degrees of accentedness. Table 15.3 shows the descriptive statistics for all variables entered into the regression model. The results suggested a significant association ($R^2 = .46$, $p < .001$) between the six predictors and the degree of accentedness in Turkish as the outcome variable. There was no significant correlation between perceptions about self and degrees of accentedness; however, participants who reported higher levels of positive perceptions about their Ideal L2 self (.21, $p < .05$) also obtained higher native-like accent scores. Two other variables that also seemed to positively

Table 15.3 Descriptive statistics of all the variables

	M	SD
Self	4.03	.464
Ideal L2 self	4.03	.512
Kurdish	3.38	.648
Turkish	3.42	.715
Turkish dominant	3.23	.555
Kurdish dominant	3.03	.534
Ratings	5.32	2.64

contribute to the degrees of accentedness included Turkish dominant networks (.59, $p < .001$) and perceptions about the Turkish-speaking community (.47, $p < .001$). In other words, participants whose socialisation patterns were more of Turkish-dominance and those who reported to hold higher levels of positive perceptions about the Turkish-speaking community seemed to have a less accented Turkish accent. Interestingly, a perception about the Kurdish-speaking community was not a significant predictor of a native-like accent.

To unravel how these variables interact with each other as manifestations of an L2 learner's self-concept, correlations among measures of the self, the Ideal L2 self, Turkish dominant and Kurdish dominant networks as well as perceptions about the Turkish and Kurdish-speaking communities were also examined. Table 15.4 shows that perceptions about L1 and L2 communities were not only correlated with each other but also related to dominance in the participants' language socialisation. In other words, the more positive their perceptions were about the Kurds, the less positive they were about the Turks (-.23, $p < .05$). Similarly, participants who reported higher levels of positive perceptions about the Kurds also had Kurdish dominant networks (.48, $p < .001$) while participants with Turkish dominant networks were those who held higher levels of positive perceptions about the Turks (.37, $p < .001$). Note that in cases where independent variables are correlated, also known as multicollinearity, it is hard to determine which variable is generating the effect on the dependent variable (accentedness).

Conclusions and Discussion

In sum, the findings revealed a remarkable amount of variation in the degrees of accentedness of the high school students in this study when

Table 15.4 Significant bivariate correlations among all variables

	Self	Ideal L2S	Kurdish	Turkish	DomT	DomK	Ratings
Self							
Ideal L2S							
Kurdish							
Turkish			-.229*				
DomT				.374**			
DomK			.479**				
Ratings		.211*		.467**	.587**		

Notes: *$p < .05$; **$p < .01$; Ideal L2S: Ideal L2 self; DomT: Turkish dominant; DomK: Kurdish dominant.

speaking in Turkish as measured by binary judgments based on 10 phrasal tokens. The results suggested that three of the six variables, namely the Ideal L2 self, Turkish dominant networks and perceptions about the Turkish-speaking community, were positive significant predictors of degrees of accentedness. The findings also indicated a few multicollinearity (when predictor variables correlate with each other in a regression model) cases among some predicting variables; specifically, participants who reported higher levels of positive perceptions about Kurds had more Kurdish dominant networks and lower levels of positive perceptions about Turks while participants with Turkish dominant networks were those who reported higher levels of positive perceptions about Turks.

Of the three variables that seemed to predict variation in degrees of accentedness, having L2-dominant (Turkish) networks was the strongest contributor followed by holding favourable perceptions about the L2 community (Turkish-speaking) and their Ideal L2 selves. In general, this finding corroborates previous research on the role of L2 dominance in L2 attainment, particularly comparable research on L2 socialisation patterns and dominance and the acquisition of L2 phonological features (Dowd et al., 1990; Lybeck, 2002; Polat, 2011). Similarly, this finding confirms the results of Flege et al. (2002), who reported that bilinguals with L2 dominant socialisation patterns attained higher levels of native-like accent.

The result that the Ideal L2 self significantly correlated with degrees of accentedness is also in line with previous research that the Ideal L2 self is a significant predictor of success in L2 attainment (Csizér & Kormos, 2009). Furthermore, in light of evidence reported in support of the L2

Motivational Self System (Dörnyei, 2005) in the Japanese, Chinese and Iranian settings by Taguchi *et al.* (2009), this finding also demonstrates that the Ideal L2 self is a significant contributor to L2 learners' motivated behaviour in the sociopolitically charged Turkish setting. This could be explained by the constitutive elements of other related variables (e.g. motivation, identity) that form the L2 self-concept. Indeed, from a self-discrepancy theory (Higgins, 1987) perspective, motivation is described by Dörnyei (2009: 18) as 'a desire to reduce the discrepancy between one's actual self and the projected behavioral standards of the ideal/ought selves'. We could then assume that these young Kurdish adolescents attained a less accented Turkish speech by attaching extrinsic values to building an L2 self (Csizér & Kormos, 2009; Lamb, 2009), socialising with the Turkish-speaking community, and investing more time and effort in gaining the linguistic capital (Norton, 2000) of the Turkish-speaking community.

Theoretically speaking, these findings can be situated within social SLA theories, particularly broad applications of Vygotskyian sociocultural views (Pavlenko & Lantolf, 2000) and L2 socialisation research (Duff, 2002; Watson-Gegeo, 2004). In addition, such results can be interpreted from the lenses of specific applications of the L2 Motivational Self System (Dörnyei, 2005) and social identity and investment theories (Norton-Peirce, 1995). In other words, in light of all of these theories one can argue that perceptions about L1 and L2 communities and self-concepts are constructed in social interactions, a two-way street that involves conscious acts of identity while indexing varying socialisation and acculturation patterns that roughly represent learners' social self-definitions as evaluated against what they consider stereotypical for their native speech communities as opposed to the L2 community (Polat, 2011; Woolard, 1991). Thus, how much time and effort learners invest in L2 identity building depends on not only how they situate their multiple selves in the L1 and L2 communities, but also how their selves are perceived by the members of L1 and L2 communities (Atkinson, 2002).

Finally, the results indicated some correlation amongst a few predictor variables (e.g. more positive perceptions about Kurds and more Kurdish dominant networks). In other words, higher levels of positive perception about Kurds imply lower levels of positive perceptions about Turks, or more dominant socialisation with Turks means less dominant socialisation with Kurds. We know that this cannot be true because above, in the same regression model, I found that a perception about the Turkish-speaking community was a significant predictor of a native-like accent whereas a perception about the Kurdish-speaking community was not. Similarly, while having Turkish dominant networks seemed to be a positive predictor of native-like accentedness, Kurdish dominant ones were not. Taken together these results suggest that these variables are different from each other, confirming the validity of current operationalisations of them in the field.

Implications

The results suggest that the Ideal L2 self, Turkish dominant networks and perceptions about the Turkish-speaking community significantly contributed to the acquisition of a more native-like Turkish accent by high school students of Kurdish ethnic backgrounds. We can deduce the following implications from these results. Firstly, in their instructional practices (e.g. curricula, and tasks and activities), L2 teachers should help their learners set the building of a positive L2 self-concept as the ultimate goal. In so doing, teachers can help L2 learners imagine their potential selves (Kubanyiova, 2009) performing various culturally appropriate speech acts and communicative tasks that are typical of native speakers. Secondly, such instructional practices require careful planning and delicate implementation because we know that accented speech is no longer considered a language deficiency as long as it is intelligible (Braine, 2010), and L2 learners construct debilitating affective filters when they perceive that their native linguistic and cultural identity (i.e. actual self) is being threatened. To do so, teachers need to re-evaluate and reform their pedagogical belief systems about their own roles by hopefully switching from L2 information transferors to L2 self-concept builders.

Thirdly, L2 education as a field needs restructuring: the curriculum, teacher preparation, instructional materials and tasks, and L2 assessment and evaluation systems should be centered around the notion of L2 self-building. Finally, given the finding that learners' perceptions about L1 and L2 communities correlate with their socialisation patterns and success in L2 attainment (Polat, 2009), a more in-depth analysis of L2 learner profiles may be critical. In other words, examining and understanding learners' pedagogical beliefs about and attitudes towards the L2 language, culture and community as well as their perceived identities and motivational patterns would help L2 educators offer better support systems to help learners build more productive L2 self-concepts.

References

Atkinson, D. (2002) Toward a sociocognitive approach to second language acquisition. *The Modern Language Journal* 86 (4), 525–545.

Baugh, J. (1999) *Out of the Mouths of Slaves*. Austin, TX: University of Texas Press.

Bourdieu, P. (1991) *Language and Symbolic Power*. Cambridge, MA: Harvard University Press.

Braine, G. (2010) *Nonnative Speaker English Teachers: Research, Pedagogy and Professional Growth*. New York, NY: Routledge.

Csizér, K. and Kormos, J. (2009) Learning experiences, selves and motivated learning behaviour: A comparative analysis of structural models for Hungarian secondary and university learners of English. In Z. Dörnyei and E. Ushioda (eds) *Motivation, Language Identity and the L2 Self* (pp. 98–119). Bristol: Multilingual Matters.

Deci, E.L. and Ryan, R.M. (1987) The support of autonomy and the control of behavior. *Journal of Personality and Social Psychology* 53 (6), 1024–1037.

Derwing, T. and Munro, M.J. (1997) Accent, intelligibility and comprehensibility: Evidence from four L1s. *Studies in Second Language Acquisition* 19 (1), 1–16.

Dowd, J., Zuengler, J. and Berkowitz, D. (1990) L2 social marking: Research issues. *Applied Linguistics* 11 (1), 16–29.

Dörnyei, Z. (2005) *The Psychology of the Language Learner.* Mahwah, NJ: Erlbaum.

Dörnyei, Z. (2009) The L2 motivational self system. In Z. Dörnyei and E. Ushioda (eds) *Motivation, Language Identity and the L2 Self* (pp. 9–42). Bristol: Multilingual Matters.

Dörnyei, Z. and Ushioda, E. (eds) (2009) *Motivation, Language Identity and the L2 Self.* Bristol: Multilingual Matters.

Dörnyei, Z. and Ushioda, E. (2009) Motivation, language identities and the L2 self: Future research directions. In Z. Dörnyei and E. Ushioda (eds) *Motivation, Language Identity and the L2 Self* (pp. 350–356). Bristol: Multilingual Matters.

Duff, P.A. (2002) The discursive co-construction of knowledge, identity, and difference: An ethnography of communication in the high school mainstream. *Applied Linguistics* 23 (3), 289–322.

ECRI (European Commission on Racism and Intolerance) (2011) ECRI Report on Turkey. Council of Europe. See http://www.coe.int/t/dghl/monitoring/ecri/Country-by-country/Turkey/TUR-CBC-IV-2011-005-ENG.pdf (accessed April 2013).

Flege, J.E. (1984) The detection of French accent by American listeners. *Journal of Acoustical Society of America* 76 (3), 692–707.

Flege, J.E., MacKay, I.R.A. and Piske, T. (2002) Assessing bilingual dominance. *Applied Psycholinguistics* 23 (4), 567–598.

Gardner, R.C. and Lambert, W.E. (1972) *Attitudes and Motivation in Second Language Learning.* Rowley, MA: Newbury House.

Giles, H. and Coupland, N. (1991) *Language: Contexts and Consequences.* Keynes: Open University Press.

Hassanpour, A. (1992) *Nationalism and Language in Kurdistan, 1918–1985.* San Francisco, CA: Mellen Research University Press.

Higgins, E.T. (1987) Self-discrepancy: A theory relating self and affect. *Psychological Review* 94 (3), 319–340.

Kenanoglu, M.M. (2005) *Osmanlı Millet Sistemi: Mit ve Gerçek [The Ottoman Millet System: Myth and Reality].* Istanbul: Klasik Yayinlari.

Kendal, N. (1980) The Kurds under the Ottoman Empire. In G. Chaliand (ed.) *People without a Country: The Kurds and Kurdistan* (pp. 67–83). London: Zed Books Ltd.

Koivunen, K. (2002) The Invisible War in North Kurdistan. Unpublished PhD Dissertation. University of Helsinki.

Kubanyiova, M. (2009) Possible selves in language teacher development. In Z. Dörnyei and E. Ushioda (eds) *Motivation, Language Identity and the L2 Self* (pp. 314–332). Bristol: Multilingual Matters.

Labov, W. (1972) *Sociolinguistic Patterns.* Philadelphia, PA: University of Pennsylvania Press.

Lamb, M. (2009) Situating the L2 self: Two Indonesian school learners of English. In Z. Dörnyei and E. Ushioda (eds) *Motivation, Language Identity and the L2 Self* (pp. 229–247). Bristol: Multilingual Matters.

Lave, J. and Wenger, E (1991) *Situated Learning: Legitimate Peripheral Participation.* Cambridge: Cambridge University Press.

Lybeck, K. (2002) Cultural identification and second language pronunciation of Americans in Norway. *The Modern Language Journal* 86 (2), 174–191.

Major, R.C. (1987) Phonological similarity, markedness, and rate of L2 acquisition. *Studies in Second Language Acquisition* 9 (1), 63–82.

Magen, H.S. (1998) The perception of foreign-accented speech. *Journal of Phonetics* 26 (4), 381–400.

May, S. (2001) *Language and Minority Rights: Ethnicity, Nationalism, and the Politics of Language*. New York: Longman.

Mercer, S. (2011) *Towards an Understanding of Language Learner Self-concept*. Dordrecht: Springer.

Mertler, C.A. and Vannatta, R.A. (2010) *Advanced and Multivariate Statistical Methods: Practical Application and Interpretation*. Los Angeles: Pyrczak.

Moyer, A. (2007) Do language attitudes determine accent? A study of bilinguals in the USA. *Journal of Multilingual and Multicultural Development* 28 (4), 502–518.

Norton-Peirce, B. (1995) Social identity, investment, and language learning. *TESOL Quarterly* 29 (1), 9–31.

Norton, B. (2000) *Identity and Language Learning: Gender, Ethnicity, and Educational Change*. London: Longman.

Pajares, F. and Schunk, D.H. (2005) Self-efficacy and self-concept beliefs. In H.W. Marsh, R.G. Craven and D.M. McInerney (eds) *International Advances in Self Research* (Vol. 2) (pp. 287–305). Greenwich, CT: Information Age.

Pavlenko, A. and Lantolf, J.P. (2000) Second Language Learning as Participation and the (Re)construction of Selves. In J.P. Lantolf (ed.) *Sociocultural Theory and Second Language Learning: Recent Advances* (pp. 154–177). Oxford: Oxford University Press.

Polat, N. (2007) Socio-psychological factors in the attainment of L2 native-like accent of Kurdish origin young people learning Turkish in Turkey. Unpublished PhD dissertation. The University of Texas at Austin.

Polat, N. (2009) Matches in beliefs between teachers and students, and success in L2 attainment: The Georgian example. *Foreign Language Annals* 42 (2), 229–249.

Polat, N. and Mahalingappa, L. (2010) Gender differences in identity and acculturation patterns and L2 accent attainment. *Journal of Language, Identity, and Education* 9 (1), 17–35.

Polat, N. (2011) Examining the nature and content of L2 socialization patterns: Attainment of a native-like Turkish accent by Kurds. *Critical Inquiry in Language Studies* 8, 261–288.

Schumann, J.H. (1978) The acculturation model for second language acquisition. In R.C. Gingras (ed.) *Second Language Acquisition and Foreign Language Teaching* (pp. 27–50). Arlington, VA: Center for Applied Linguistics.

Skutnabb-Kangas, T. and Bucak, S. (1995) Killing a mother tongue: How the Kurds are deprived of linguistic human rights. In T. Skutnabb-Kangas and R. Phillipson (eds) *Linguistic Human Rights: Overcoming Linguistic Discrimination* (pp. 347–370). Berlin: Mouton de Gruyter.

Skutnabb-Kangas, T., Phillipson, R., Mohanty, A. and Panda, M. (eds) (2009) *Social Justice Through Multilingual Education*. Bristol: Multilingual Matters.

Smits, J. and Gündüz-Hoşgör, A. (2003) Linguistic capital: Language as a socio-economic resource among Kurdish and Arabic women in Turkey. *Ethnic and Racial Studies* 26 (5), 829–853.

Spolsky, B. (1969) Attitudinal aspects of second language learning. *Language Learning* 19 (3–4), 272–283.

Taguchi, T., Magid, M. and Papi, M. (2009) The L2 motivational self system among Japanese, Chinese, and Iranian learners of English: A comparative study. In Z. Dörnyei and E. Ushioda (eds) *Motivation, Language Identity and the L2 Self* (pp. 66–97). Bristol: Multilingual Matters.

Ushioda, E. (2009) A person-in-context relational view of emergent motivation, self and identity. In Z. Dörnyei and E. Ushioda (eds) *Motivation, Language Identity and the L2 Self* (pp. 215–228). Bristol: Multilingual Matters.

Ushioda, E. and Dörnyei, Z. (2009) Motivation, language identities and the L2 self: A theoretical overview. In Z. Dörnyei and E. Ushioda (eds) *Motivation, Language Identity and the L2 Self* (pp. 4–8). Bristol: Multilingual Matters.

van Lier, L. (2004) *The Ecology and Semiotics of Language Learning: A Sociocultural Perspective*. Boston: Kluwer Academic.

Watson-Gegeo, K.A. (2004) Mind, language, and epistemology: Toward a language socialization paradigm for SLA. *The Modern Language Journal* 88 (3), 331–350.

Woolard, K.A. (1991) Linkages of language and ethnic identity: Changes in Barcelona, 1980-87. In J. Dow (ed.) *Language and Ethnicity: Focusschrift in Honor of Joshua Fishman* (Vol. 2) (pp. 61–81). Amsterdam/Philadelphia: John Benjamins.

Yearbook of Turkish Statistics [in Turkish] (2009) Ankara: Turkish Statistics Association (TUIK) Publications.

Part 3

Self-Concept and Language Teaching

16 The Effect of Motivational Strategies on Self-related Aspects of Student Motivation and Second Language Learning

Gabriella Mezei

Introduction

There is a growing interest in self-related concepts in second language (L2) teaching and learning since it has been found that self-related concepts such as the Ideal L2 self, self-efficacy or self-confidence affect second language acquisition (SLA) and language learning in many important ways. One such area of interest is the interface between the Ideal L2 self and student motivation as motivation has a fundamental role in contributing to language achievement (Dörnyei, 2005, 2009; Dörnyei & Ushioda, 2009). This line of research has started to generate interesting results for the role that the self and identity play in motivation, which has many far-reaching implications. For instance, several studies showed that the Ideal L2 self is a very good predictor of motivated language learning behaviour (e.g. Csizér & Kormos, 2009; Ryan, 2009; Taguchi *et al.*, 2009). The concept of integrativeness (Gardner, 1985) has been broadened and specified (Csizér & Dörnyei, 2005; Dörnyei & Csizér, 2002; Dörnyei *et al.*, 2006). Also visual style and imagination have been linked to motivation (Al-Shehri, 2009). Furthermore, self-concept is believed to have motivational properties (Marsh & Köller, 2003). In addition, other self-related concepts such as self-confidence, self-efficacy and metacognition also play an instrumental role in shaping language learning behaviour and have an effect on learning outcomes (Covington, 1992; Mercer, 2011). Most of the studies on these self-related concepts have mainly focused on language learners. However, in an instructed SLA setting, such as the classroom, the role of the teacher cannot be neglected. Motivational strategies are techniques that are at the disposal of the teacher to help students foster motivation and thus make them more successful in language learning. It is believed that motivational strategies directly contribute to motivated language learning behaviour (Guilloteaux & Dörnyei, 2008); nevertheless, this statement needs further evidence. The novelty of this paper is that it intends to go beyond the seemingly logical but maybe simplistic statement that the use of motivational strategies directly leads to motivated language learning behaviour, a proposition in line with the suggestion of Larsen-Freeman and Cameron (2008) that there might be a non-linear relationship between teaching and learning.

Theoretical Background

In Hungary, where the present study was carried out, most language learning takes place in the classroom, since the country is monolingual. The classroom can easily become a dull and uninspiring environment for L2 learners unless the teacher raises the students' interest and applies some forms of motivational techniques. The most obvious and straightforward techniques are motivational strategies, which 'refer to (a) instructional interventions applied by the teacher to elicit and stimulate student motivation and (b) self-regulating strategies that are used purposefully by individual students to manage the level of their own motivation' (Guilloteaux & Dörnyei, 2008: 57). This paper focuses on the first definition above, that is, the teacher-initiated aspect of motivational strategies. Motivational strategies have been identified as contributing to motivated language learning behaviour directly in various important ways although their systematic investigation started only some decades ago (Dörnyei, 1997, 1998).

Researchers who conducted longitudinal case studies among elementary school students between 1977 and 1995 (Nikolov, 1995, 1999, 2003, 2004) and among secondary school students for four years (Heitzmann, 2008) have come to the conclusion that various teacher-related forms of behaviour (that were not labelled as motivational strategies in these studies) directly foster motivated language learning behaviour. For elementary school students, the most important motivational tool was task-based motivation and the learning situation and context. In addition, the teacher had a dominant influence on their motivation. Praise and rewards also played a key role in motivating elementary students to learn English. On the other hand, secondary school students' motivation was intricately interwoven: at the onset, positive L2 experiences and instrumental motives proved to fuel their motivation, but later on short-term goals were set and were linked to their mastery motivation. This sense of achievement led to higher levels of intrinsic motivation, and thus the students found themselves in a self-strengthening cycle of motivated language learning behaviour. Both Dörnyei's (1994) three-level motivational conception and the process model of motivation of Dörnyei and Ottó (1998) were found to be applicable in a classroom setting. Mezei and Csizér (2005) found similar results in a case study of an experienced L2 teacher. It was found that motivational strategies and motivational teaching practices can indeed be linked to motivated language learning behaviour. The motivational strategies mostly concerned the first and third phases of the motivational teaching practice (Dörnyei, 2001): creating basic motivational conditions, and maintaining and protecting motivation (see also the four scales of the Motivational Strategies Questionnaire). Guilloteaux and Dörnyei (2008) designed an observational scheme, the Motivational Orientation of Language Teaching (MOLT), to follow and tally motivational strategies as they are happening. The authors identified a direct link between the use of motivational strategies and motivated language learning behaviour with the help of a correlational design, and highlighted that, in the long run, motivational teaching practice enhances course-related attitudes, which feeds back on the students' task-based attitudes. According to the authors, 37% of the variance in motivated language learning behaviour can be explained with the help of motivational strategies.

Apart from the teacher and the motivational strategies at her disposal, other equally important points that contribute to an elevated level of motivation and motivated language learning behaviour are the students themselves and some of the characteristics they possess. As such, their self-confidence, their image about themselves and language learning (i.e. their Ideal L2 self), their self-efficacy (i.e. the belief in one's own capacity to achieve results) (Bandura, 1986, 1994) and metacognition (i.e. a form of conscious monitoring and the knowledge of oneself) (Paris & Winograd, 2001), especially in the case of older learners (Csíkos, 2007), as was identified in the case of good language learners (Rubin, 1975; Stern, 1975), are of utmost importance when conceptualising L2 motivation. This raises the need to incorporate self-related concepts into models of motivation. Research on self-regulation (i.e. how the students manage their learning) (Boekaerts & Niemivirta, 2000), which includes studies on students, clinical patients and organisations (Boekaerts et al., 2000), has made an attempt to identify what students do to reach a goal or manage their learning. Nevertheless, the self is the basis of the self-regulatory system (Brownlee et al., 2000), and self-regulation results in enhanced efficiency and performance.

In education-related research, self-regulation can be defined as 'an active, constructive process whereby learners set goals for their learning and then attempt to monitor, regulate, and control their cognition, motivation, and behavior, guided and constrained by their goals and the contextual features in the environment' (Pintrich, 2000: 453). The emphasis is on the process, that is, monitoring, controlling and reflecting on one's self, but at the same time the vision of the individual is also called for (a special feature of one's Ideal L2 self, see e.g. Al-Shehri, 2009; Dörnyei, 2009; see also this volume chapters 18, 19 and 20), in that it is the reflection of what one can identify and visualise as a potential goal to achieve. Furthermore, according to Demetriou (2000: 245), self-regulation is the 'dynamic or active aspect of self-understanding'. It means that one's self-concept plays a crucial role in how he or she approaches learning, in this case; including various subprocesses (e.g. planning, monitoring or reflecting) and cognitive elements (e.g. self-efficacy or goal-setting). Therefore, students' personal responsibility in learning becomes essential as a basic precondition of self-regulation, and combined with autonomy, students become more intrinsically motivated if they develop through self-regulation (Noels et al., 1999). For this to happen, metacognition, being strategic, expectancy-value beliefs, goal-setting and self-efficacy are needed to complement the learning process (Paris & Winograd, 2001). In short, self-regulation research has shown how self-related elements in learning can contribute to learning from an active-constructive aspect. In other words, the self-concept feeds on the learning process and students can make use of their own resources, not only by managing their learning but by applying their vision (Ideal L2 self), their beliefs (self-efficacy), their self-confidence and even their metacognition.

Dörnyei (2005, 2009), drawing on previous work on possible, ideal and ought selves (Higgins, 1987, 1996; Markus & Nurius, 1986), has incorporated self-related concepts into his L2 Motivational Self System, rooted in research on self and identity. This theory discusses motivation in terms of the Ideal L2 self, the Ought-to L2 self and the language learning experience. Future-oriented self types (in the form of goals), imagery (visual style), strategies and a promotion-prevention focus (to approach or avoid a goal or task) come into play, in that the wish to reduce the gap between one's current self and future self fuels people's motivation to learn a language. What is important from the point of view of the present study is how to identify the points where teacher intervention (i.e. motivating students to learn by motivational strategies) is possible in order to affect students' self-concept through their motivation. The third element of the theory is the language learning experience, including an individual's language learning history, the setting and context where the actual language learning takes place, the teacher and peers. The L2 Motivational Self System theory, being the most up-to-date in current L2 motivation research, serves as an excellent basis for investigating the effects of self-concept on language learning from a motivational point of view.

In sum, the theoretical framework for the present study includes three aspects of motivation and self-concept research: (1) motivational teaching practices (Dörnyei, 2001), operationalised as motivational strategies to measure teacher intervention; (2) the motivation of students, operationalised with the help of the L2 Motivational Self System, and including motivated language learning behaviour as an outcome of language learning (and as a dependent variable), and (3) self-related concepts operationalised as self-regulation (Stockdale, 2003), including self-efficacy and control, in order to measure the students' attempts to manage their motivation, cognition and behaviour.

Method

Participants

In this research, two groups of students were investigated, one from Budapest, the capital of Hungary, and one from a town of county status. The two learner groups can be considered different in two aspects: the size of Budapest is approximately 40 times bigger, and, being the capital, it attracts a great deal more tourists (*Demographic Yearbook*, 2004). The students of these schools are monolingual. The social background of the students can be considered similar since the schools they attended are secondary grammar schools. In Hungary, the secondary school system consists of three types of schools among which grammar schools are thought to be of higher quality than the other two types of schools. The schools that the participants attended are considered average according to rank orders of secondary schools in Hungary using various indicators (Neuwirth & Horn, 2007). However, upon observation and discussions with the teachers, it turned out that the teachers in those schools place a strong emphasis on language teaching and learning. One teacher from each school was selected by using purposive sampling (Dörnyei, 2007) and all of their students, except for the ones in their final year, filled in the questionnaires. The students in their final year were eliminated from the sample because they were busy preparing for their school-leaving examination. Altogether 92 students (31 males and 58 females) responded and three students failed to provide data on their gender. The mean age of the students was 15 years, most of them being in their 9th year of studies (and 1st year of secondary level studies). The study concentrates on English as a foreign language, which is the most frequently taught L2 in Hungary (Halász & Lannert, 2006), although all students in this type of secondary school learn a second foreign language as well, and some students also reported learning three foreign languages. The students were in six groups (two groups of the teacher in Budapest and four groups of the other teacher), were streamed according to the level of proficiency and were pre-intermediate, intermediate or advanced levels. At the time of data collection, nine of the students had already acquired a state-recognised intermediate level language certificate and eight of them were preparing to take one. In addition, seven students had already acquired a C1 level (according to the Common European Framework of Reference, Council of Europe, 2001) language certificate. The teachers were rather different from each other in terms of experience since the teacher in Budapest had over 25 years of experience and was a mentor teacher, while the other teacher had 10 years of teaching experience and was a teacher of history as well.

Instruments

This paper reports the quantitative part of a mixed methods study. The quantitative data include three questionnaires, each concentrating on a different area of interest. Each area has been measured by questionnaire items using five-point rating scales. The questionnaires were adapted or designed and validated for the purpose of this study as the brief summary that follows describes.

Motivation questionnaire (adapted from Kormos & Csizér, 2008):

(1) *Ideal L2 self* (five items): the students' views of themselves as successful L2 speakers. Example: Speaking English would help me with my future career (Cronbach $\alpha = .84$).

(2) *Ought-to L2 self* (five items): students' views of language-related issues and attributes they think they should possess. Example: To become an intelligent person, I need to speak English (Cronbach $\alpha = .72$).

(3) *Instrumental orientation* (four items): pragmatic aspects of being able to speak a language well, such as a higher salary. Example: Nowadays, those who speak English have better jobs (Cronbach $\alpha = .72$).

(4) *International orientation* (six items): students' views about English as an international language. Example: English is one of the most important languages in the world (Cronbach $\alpha = .76$).

(5) *Self-confidence* (five items): students' conviction as to how easily and how successfully they can learn English. Example: I am sure that I can learn a foreign language well (Cronbach $\alpha = .94$).

(6) *Motivated language learning behaviour* (five items): students' efforts and persistence in learning English. Example: It is very important to me to learn English (Cronbach $\alpha = .84$).

Self-regulation questionnaire (based on Stockdale's Learning Experience Scale, 2003):

(1) *Initiative* (four items): students' effort to do work after finishing it in school or their desire to find materials outside of school without the help of the teacher. Example: I frequently do extra work in a course just because I am interested (Cronbach $\alpha = .76$).

(2) *Control* (four items): organising learning to become more successful and more motivated. Example: I always effectively take responsibility for my own learning (Cronbach $\alpha = .61$).

(3) *Self-efficacy* (four items): belief in one's capacity to produce effects. Example: I am certain about my capacity to take primary responsibility for my learning (Cronbach $\alpha = .75$).

(4) *Motivation* (four items): motivation to take part in lessons, enjoy the lessons and complete course requirements. Example: I complete most of the activities because I WANT to, not because I HAVE to (Cronbach $\alpha = .75$).

Motivational strategies questionnaire (based on Dörnyei, 2001):

(1) *Creating the basic motivational conditions* (four items): the preconditions that are necessary to further motivational attempts. Example: The atmosphere in the English lessons is pleasant (Cronbach $\alpha = .66$).

(2) *Generating initial motivation* (six items): ways of encouraging learners to identify with the goals of the classroom, enhancing values and attitudes and increasing expectancy of success. Example: We formulated and accepted explicit class goals (Cronbach $\alpha = .80$).

(3) *Maintaining and protecting motivation* (seven items): preventing students from abandoning goals, getting bored of activities and being distracted. Example: The teacher uses goal-setting methods in the classroom (Cronbach $\alpha = .82$).

(4) *Encouraging positive retrospective self-evaluation* (five items): appraisals and reactions to successes and failures. Example: The teacher promotes effort attributions in the students (Cronbach $\alpha = .73$).

The study involved interviews to further probe teachers and students about the motivational teaching practice. Firstly, the teacher interview was designed and validated (Mezei, 2006). Then the student interview was modelled on the teacher interview so that a comparison between them would be more straightforward. The interviews centred on the following issues:

- Background questions: subject matter the teachers teach, teaching experience, information about the school.
- General questions about teaching.
- Motivational strategies: Dörnyei's (2001) motivational strategies – whether they are used, how, examples where relevant.
- Self-regulation and autonomy: whether the teacher spends time developing the students' autonomy, and if so, how; the role of personal experience in this.
- Rounding off: what it means to motivate the students to learn, or to be motivated, and what the motivational strategies are.

Procedure

The questionnaires were piloted and went through reliability analysis with the help of principal component analysis. The Motivation questionnaire was designed and validated by Kormos and Csizér (2008) and was used in the same format due to the similarity of the samples (i.e. Hungarian secondary schools of average quality). The Self-regulation questionnaire was built upon the one that Stockdale (2003) designed. Translation, appropriate adaptation and validation for the Hungarian sample were carried out in order to make it appropriate and usable for the given population. The Motivational strategies questionnaire was designed on the basis of Dörnyei's (2001) motivational teaching practice and the four phases it comprises. Items were drawn up, piloted and validated using principal component analysis. Unreliable items were removed, while other items were reworded and tested again. Scales with a reliability coefficient higher than .60 were kept.

Apart from testing the reliability of the scales, the following procedures were computed using SPSS 13.0 (Coakes *et al.*, 2006). Regression analysis showed which scales played the most important role in predicting motivated language learning behaviour. Furthermore, after identifying the variables that best predict the dependent variable, the model was broken down to identify the variables that best predict the independent variables. Thus, a chain of regressions was established in order to build up the final model, which shows all the independent variables that play a role in predicting motivated language learning behaviour, and also the strength of these links. This procedure has allowed for identifying a potential path of motivating students to learn. In addition, correlations helped to identify a link between the motivational strategies of the teachers and the motivated language learning behaviour of the students. In order to compare the strength of the correlations, the Fisher r-to-z transformation was used.

The interviews were recorded with the consent of the participants. The length of the interviews with the teachers varied between 45 and 70 minutes, while the interviews with the students lasted between 15 and 25 minutes on average. The interview data were subjected to qualitative content analysis.

Results

Table 16.1 contains information about the basic statistics of the scales used in this study. It can be seen that all the scales have a satisfactory reliability (above. 61), that the means vary between 2.92 (Initiative) and 4.38 (Ideal L2 self), with all the scales having a relatively low standard deviation.

Firstly, a regression model was built in order to predict motivated language learning behaviour as the dependent variable, using all the other variables as independent variables (Table 16.2). The aim was to establish

Table 16.1 Descriptive statistics of the scales

Scales	Mean	St. dev.	Cr. Alpha
Creating the basic motivational condition	4.23	.52	.66
Generating initial motivation	3.63	.66	.80
Maintaining and protecting motivation	3.48	.67	.82
Encouraging positive retrospective self-evaluation	3.60	.63	.73
Initiative	2.92	.78	.76
Control	3.79	.67	.61
Self-efficacy	3.80	.72	.75
Motivation	3.66	.67	.75
Ideal L2 self	4.38	.64	.84
Ought-to L2 self	3.91	.68	.72
Instrumental orientation	4.13	.65	.72
International orientation	4.31	.53	.76
Self-confidence	3.62	.83	.94
Motivated language learning behaviour	3.93	.69	.84

Table 16.2 Results of the regression analysis with motivated language learning behaviour as the criterion measure

Scale	B	SE B	β
Ideal L2 self[a]	.52	.07	.48**
Motivation[b]	.26	.07	.26**
Control[b]	.24	.06	.23**
Instrumental orientation[a]	.15	.07	.14*
R^2		.72	

Notes: *$p < .05$; **$p < .01$; [a]Motivation questionnaire; [b]Self-regulation questionnaire.

which variables play the most important role in motivating students to learn, and, somewhat surprisingly, it turned out that motivational strategies do not form part of the variables that do so. Instead, two scales of the Motivation questionnaire and two scales of the Self-regulation questionnaire best predict motivated language learning behaviour. The fact that the Ideal L2 self is the best predictor is in line with other studies (Csizér & Kormos, 2009; Dörnyei & Csizér, 2002; Dörnyei et al., 2006; Kormos & Csizér, 2008; Ryan, 2009; Taguchi et al., 2009) and also strengthens the validity of Dörnyei's (2005, 2009) L2 Motivational Self System.

The scales of each questionnaire were investigated separately as well in order to identify which variables have potentially a key role in predicting motivated language learning behaviour. Table 16.3 shows the model which used the scales of the Motivation questionnaire as independent variables. It can be seen that two scales play an important role. Apart from the Ideal L2 self, which has the strongest predicting power of all the variables, another self-related concept seems crucial, and that is self-confidence. The appearance of two self-related concepts is not surprising considering the fact that a sense of self plays a crucial role in individual development (Mercer, 2011; Zentner & Renaud, 2007) and the role of personal theories students hold does have far-reaching effects on their beliefs, goals and ultimately on their motivation (Dweck, 1999). The combination of these two variables indicates that in this sample of students the vision of being a successful language learner and the belief of being able to become one are combined to form the basis of motivated language learners. In terms of the L2 Motivational Self System, it means that a strong vision and conviction can reduce the gap between the students' present self and ideal self so that they become more motivated to learn English.

Table 16.3 Results of the regression analysis (Motivation questionnaire) with motivated language learning behaviour as the criterion measure

Scale	B	SE B	β
Ideal L2 self	.70	.08	.65**
Self-confidence	.18	.06	.22**
R^2		.59	

Note: **$p < .01$

Table 16.4 Results of the regression analysis (Self-regulation questionnaire) with motivated language learning behaviour as the criterion measure

Scale	B	SE B	β
Motivation	.57	.09	.55**
Control	.19	.09	.18*
R^2		.46	

Notes: *$p < .05$; **$p < .01$

It was also crucial to probe to what extent the scales of the Self-regulation questionnaire contribute to motivated language learning behaviour because it was hypothesised that students' autonomy-related characteristics have an impact on their motivation. When only the Self-regulation questionnaire was examined (Table 16.4), Motivation to participate in classes/activities and Control over the learning environment turned out to be powerful enough to be part of the model. This suggests that students who are motivated to actively take part in the lessons, enjoy the lessons and complete requirements display higher levels of motivated language learning behaviour. In addition, the presence of the variable Control suggests that students who organise learning in order to become more successful will eventually achieve this goal. Thus, students who want to participate, enjoy lessons and can organise the environment to serve these points will be more motivated to learn the language. Initiative (that is, the students' effort to do work in addition to requirements) and self-efficacy beliefs (beliefs in one's capacity to produce effects) do not play a role. The lack of impact of the latter variable is somewhat surprising, considering the effect attributions and beliefs have on behaviour and

Table 16.5 Results of the regression analysis (Motivational strategies questionnaire) with motivated language learning behaviour as the criterion measure

Scale	B	SE B	β
Generating initial motivation	.37	.13	.36**
Creating the basic motivational conditions	.35	.16	.26*
R^2		.34	

Notes: *$p < .05$; **$p < .01$

motivation (Bandura, 1986, 1994; Markus & Nurius, 1986; Skaalvik & Bong, 2003).

Examining the Motivational strategies questionnaire on its own (Table 16.5) has revealed that the first two phases of the motivational teaching practice play a role in motivated language learning behaviour. The teachers seem to be better at generating and creating basic motivational conditions than maintaining and protecting motivation or fuelling positive self-evaluation. This could be due to the following reasons. For instance, the initial phases usually correspond to the early stages of the academic year when the teachers (and the students) have more energy and enthusiasm to motivate (and be motivated). It is also possible that an overly strong beginning in motivating the students can make later stages comparatively low when a routine sets in. This issue definitely deserves further research.

The fact that the effects of the motivational teaching practice and that of self-confidence disappear when all the variables are entered into the model points to the fact that either a false causal relationship is suggested by the results in Tables 16.2–16.4 or a correlation is partialled out by entering further variables. This led to the investigation of how correlations between the individual variables and the dependent variable (motivated language learning behaviour) work. Formerly, a link between the use of motivational strategies and motivated language learning behaviour was identified with the help of correlations (Guilloteaux & Dörnyei, 2008) and case studies (Mezei & Csizér, 2005). However, a closer look at the variables with the help of regression has revealed that the direct link hypothesised earlier might need reconceptualising. Therefore, the links between the four phases of the motivational teaching practice and motivated language learning behaviour were investigated in the case of the two teachers individually and also in the case of the whole sample. Table 16.6 shows that in each case there is a moderate or relatively strong correlation, all correlations being significant at the .01 level. The strength

Table 16.6 Correlations among the phases of the motivational teaching practice and motivated language learning behaviour

Motivational teaching practice	Teacher 1 (n = 29)	Teacher 2 (n = 63)	Whole sample (N = 92)
CBMC	.66**	.42**	.54**
GIM	.53**	.52**	.58**
MPM	.62**	.33**	.54**
EPRS	.59**	.33**	.47**

Notes: **p < .01; CBMC = creating the basic motivational conditions; GIM = generating initial motivation; MPM = maintaining and protecting motivation; EPRS = encouraging positive retrospective self-evaluation.

of the correlations was compared using the Fisher r-to-z transformation and none of the comparisons proved significant in either of the phases.

These figures can be considered typical and meaningful within this field (Dörnyei, 2007; Guilloteaux & Dörnyei, 2008). In addition, Guilloteaux and Dörnyei (2008) found a correlation of .61 between the teacher's motivational teaching practice and the learners' motivated language learning behaviour, explaining 37% of the variance in motivated language learning behaviour (although the methodology was slightly different, this percentage covered all the four phases as opposed to the present study

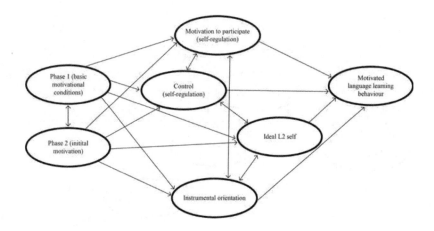

Figure 16.1 The initial model

where only the first two phases are responsible for 34% of the variance, see Table 16.5). Furthermore, entering other areas of interest into the model can contribute to a higher explanatory power of motivated language learning behaviour, with the motivational strategies having a limited or rather different role.

Considering the above, it was found that studying these motivational strategies (i.e. the motivational teaching practice) and self-related concepts (i.e. Ideal L2 self and self-regulation) individually was not satisfactory on its own and a closer look at the variables is needed in order to disentangle how motivational strategies and self-related concepts come into play when motivating students to learn. The initial model, presented in Figure 16.1, was drawn up to be tested. After running further regressions in order to establish the predicting power of the remaining variables, the final model, shown below in Figure 16.2, was drawn up.

Discussion

The final model (Figure 16.2) shows how motivational strategies can indirectly contribute to motivated language learning behaviour mediated by the Ideal L2 self, two scales of self-regulation and instrumental orientation. The most important conclusion is that motivational teaching practice does not shape motivated language learning behaviour directly, but only through self-regulation and the Ideal L2 self. The motivational strategies do not affect instrumental orientation. However, phase 1, which

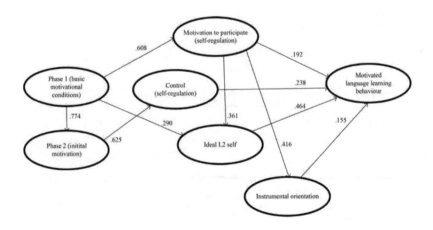

Figure 16.2 The final model

involves generating basic motivational conditions, does have a weak effect on the Ideal L2 self. Motivational teaching practices can have a relatively strong effect on students' motivation to participate in class with the help of basic motivational conditions and a relatively strong effect on control via the initial motivational techniques. The model also shows that the Ideal L2 self is the strongest contributor to motivated language learning behaviour and that self-regulation has an impact in the form of motivation to participate (and enjoy classes) and control.

The emergence of the four variables that are the direct predictors of motivated language learning behaviour suggests that this latter variable is more closely related to factors that are internal to the students, that is, how motivated and how self-directed they are as individuals, as opposed to how the teachers attempt to motivate them to learn. However, motivational teaching practices, in the form of motivational strategies, indirectly influence motivated language learning behaviour, and ultimately language learning. The presence of this indirect effect surfaced because correlations can hide important links between variables, and, as the regression model showed, motivational strategies do not participate in predicting it. In this sample, the same power of correlations was found as in the case of the Guilloteaux and Dörnyei (2008) study, but the model is refined. Upon a closer look at the data, it emerged that the younger teacher placed a far greater emphasis on student autonomy, and in comparing the two subsamples of the two teachers, it turned out that the younger teacher's students were more motivated and displayed a higher level of motivated language learning behaviour. This finding, combined with the fact that the more experienced teacher's students' correlations were higher (Table 16.6), led to the conclusion that there is something more to the link between the effect of motivational strategies and motivated language learning behaviour than was previously thought. This and the regression model led to the drawing up of the final model in Figure 16.2.

There may exist a link between the use of motivational strategies and motivated language learning behaviour, but there are other variables that more powerfully predict it, such as the Ideal L2 self. This finding is consistent with the results of other studies that have identified the Ideal L2 self as one of the key predictors of motivated language learning behaviour (Csizér & Kormos, 2009; Dörnyei & Csizér, 2002; Dörnyei et al., 2006; Kormos & Csizér, 2008; Ryan, 2009; Taguchi et al., 2009). Although self-efficacy, self-confidence and metacognition did not emerge as predicting motivated language learning behaviour either because they were not significant in the final regression model (self-efficacy and self-confidence) or because no scale was set up to measure it (metacognition), the qualitative data suggest that all three concepts are important when it comes to language learning and teaching. The following is a brief selection of quotes from the interviews illustrating this point:

- Self-efficacy and self-confidence:
  'It's enough for me if the teacher tells me what the test is going to cover [...] it's perfectly enough for me [to get prepared]' (student interview)
- Or the lack of the above:
  'sometimes I'm really disappointed at my English knowledge' (student interview)
- Metacognition, especially making the students realise the importance of the English language, stressing that making mistakes is part of the language learning process, making students accept the fact that there are different needs and minimising the negative effects of a task:

'In my opinion it's important that making a mistake is not a negative thing. I try to make them understand that making a mistake is part of the learning process, [...] and that I'm not angry with them at all [...] and if others laugh at someone, I tell them it wasn't nice'. (teacher interview)

'I say this in class. You are different. You want different things. This time we do this. Next time another thing'. (teacher interview)

'I often tell them, when I know that something isn't going to be too exciting, that this is a very important issue or [...] I tell them that I love this or that thing'. (teacher interview)

Further research needs to add to our understanding about the role of the above variables. It must also be reiterated here that self-efficacy beliefs do not form part of the regression model. Self-efficacy is a learner characteristic component in the Self-regulation questionnaire (Stockdale, 2003), which means that it is the students' belief in their capacity. The quotes above point to the idea that self-efficacy has not reached its full potential in students. Sometimes they focus on what they do not know instead of how they could develop. This can take extreme forms, to the extent of having debilitating effects on the student: 'They imposed everything on us. I didn't feel they'd help. [They] weren't interested in what I do or how I go about things'. Also, it has been pointed out that the Hungarian educational system does not favour student initiatives (Mezei, 2012), which might be the reason why initiative is also missing from the regression model.

Based on the above, motivational strategies should aim for the self-regulation of students for two main reasons. Firstly, the students' self-concept is the basis of achievement (Covington, 1992). Secondly, providing the students with control and autonomy over their learning process is an effective way of motivating them.

Consequently, self-regulation mediates the effect of the motivational teaching practices in general and of motivational strategies in particular. Creating basic motivational conditions and generating initial motivation affect the students' motivation to participate and their organisation of learning, respectively. Motivated language learning is affected by these first two phases of motivational teaching practices. Furthermore, they contribute to two aspects of motivation: the Ideal L2 self and instrumental orientation. Thus, the model has revealed that although motivational strategies are closely associated with motivated language learning behaviour, there are variables that mediate this link. Further research needs to identify how best these self-related aspects can be supported by language teachers in order to maximise their contribution to language learning motivation, motivated language learning behaviour and ultimately language learning.

Conclusion

The initial presupposition that motivational strategies contribute to motivated language learning behaviour and thus shape language learning has been strengthened. This paper has put forward the idea that the teachers' effort to motivate their students to learn with the help of motivational strategies is justifiable inasmuch as it targets two aspects of student motivation, namely, the Ideal L2 self and instrumental orientation, and two aspects of student self-regulation, namely, motivation to participate and control, indicating that an intricate relationship between various motivational and self-related variables is at play when it comes to motivated language learning behaviour, an indispensable aspect of language learning (Dörnyei, 2005, 2009; Dörnyei & Ushioda, 2009).

Some limitations of the study need to be mentioned. Firstly, the small number of participants makes it difficult to generalise the findings. At the same time, it allowed for interviews with several of the participants, including teachers and students. Although the results of the qualitative methods were not the main focus of this paper, the interviews greatly contributed to drawing up the model presented and to running the set of regressions that served as the basis of the final model. In addition, the interviews provided more ideas as to how to further this research project. An additional problem arose with the difficulty of conceptualising self-regulation in a form that is digestible for teachers and students. The literature on self-regulation and autonomy holds that these are two different concepts (e.g. Benson, 2001; Hiemstra, 2004; Little, 1990, 2007). For the purposes of this study, however, it was not possible to treat them as such notions.

The pedagogical implications include the need to reconceptualise how teachers motivate their students to learn. The most important finding is that various aspects of the students' self-concept and their self-regulation should be targeted in the hope of higher levels of achievement. Shouldering the responsibility of motivating students to learn has somewhat shifted from the teacher to the student, and, from this point of view, the teacher's role has changed as well, in that a more dynamic aspect of learning is the target of an intervention. In the future, more dynamic methods need to address these issues.

References

Al-Shehri, A.S. (2009) Motivation and vision: The relation between the Ideal L2 self, imagination and visual style. In Z. Dörnyei and E. Ushioda (eds) *Motivation, Language Identity and the L2 Self* (pp. 164–171). Bristol: Multilingual Matters.

Bandura, A. (1986) *Social Foundations of Thought and Action: A Social Cognitive Theory.* Englewood Cliffs, NJ: Prentice-Hall.

Bandura, A. (1994) Self-efficacy. In V.S. Ramachaudran (ed.) *Encyclopedia of Human Behavior* (Vol. 4, pp. 71–81). New York, NY: Academic Press.

Benson, P. (2001) *Teaching and Researching Autonomy in Language Learning.* Harlow: Longman.

Boekaerts, M. and Niemivirta, M. (2000) Self-regulated learning. Finding a balance between learning goals and ego-protective goals. In M. Boekaerts, P.R. Pintrich and M. Zeidner (eds) *Handbook of Self-regulation* (pp. 417–450). San Diego, CA: Elsevier Academic Press.

Boekaerts, M., Pintrich, P.R. and Zeidner, M. (eds) (2000) *Handbook of Self-regulation.* San Diego, CA: Elsevier Academic Press.

Brownlee, S., Leventhal, H. and Leventhal, E.A. (2000) Regulation, self-regulation, and construction of the self in the maintenance of physical health. In M. Boekaerts, P.R. Pintrich and M. Zeidner (eds) *Handbook of Self-regulation* (pp. 369–416). San Diego, CA: Elsevier Academic Press.

Coakes, S.J., Steed, L. and Dzidic, P. (2006) *SPSS version 13.0 for Windows: Analysis without Anguish.* Milton: John Wiley & Sons.

Council of Europe (2001) *Common European Framework of Reference of Languages: Learning, Teaching and Assessment.* Cambridge: Cambridge University Press.

Covington, M.V. (1992) *Making the Grade. A Self-worth Perspective on Motivation and School-Reform.* Cambridge: Cambridge University Press.

Csíkos, C.S. (2007) *Metakogníció. A Tudásra Vonatkozó Tudás Pedagógiája [Metacognition. The Pedagogy of Metaknowledge].* Budapest: Műszaki Kiadó.

Csizér, K. and Dörnyei, Z. (2005) The internal structure of language learning motivation and its relationship with language choice and learning effort. *The Modern Language Journal* 89 (1), 19–36.

Csizér, K. and Kormos, J. (2009) Learning experiences, selves and motivated learning behaviour: A comparative analysis of structural models for Hungarian secondary and university learners of English. In Z. Dörnyei and E. Ushioda (eds) *Motivation, Language Identity and the L2 Self* (pp. 98–119). Bristol: Multilingual Matters.

Demetriou, A. (2000) Organization and development of self-understanding and self-regulation. Toward a general theory. In M. Boekaerts, P.R. Pintrich and M. Zeidner (eds) *Handbook of Self-Regulation* (pp. 209–251). San Diego, CA: Elsevier Academic Press.

Demographic Yearbook (2004) Budapest: Central Statistical Office.

Dörnyei, Z. (1994) Motivation and motivating in the foreign language classroom. *The Modern Language Journal* 78(3), 273–284.

Dörnyei, Z. (1997) What can researchers offer teachers? The case of motivation. *Novelty* 4 (4), 6–19.

Dörnyei, Z. (1998) Motivation in second and foreign language learning. *Language Teaching* 31 (3), 117–135.

Dörnyei, Z. (2001) *Motivational Strategies in the Language Classroom*. Cambridge: Cambridge University Press.

Dörnyei, Z. (2005) *The Psychology of the Language Learner: Individual Differences in Second Language Acquisition*. Mahwah, NJ: Lawrence Erlbaum.

Dörnyei, Z. (2007) *Research Methods in Applied Linguistics. Quantitative, Qualitative and Mixed Methodologies*. Oxford: Oxford University Press.

Dörnyei, Z. (2009) The L2 motivational self system. In Z. Dörnyei and E. Ushioda (eds) *Motivation, Language Identity and the L2 Self* (pp. 9–42). Bristol: Multilingual Matters.

Dörnyei, Z. and Csizér, K. (2002) Some dynamics of language attitudes and motivation: Results of a longitudinal nationwide survey. *Applied Linguistics* 23 (4), 421–462.

Dörnyei, Z., Csizér, K. and Németh, N. (2006) *Motivation, Language Attitudes and Globalisation: A Hungarian Perspective*. Clevedon: Multilingual Matters.

Dörnyei, Z. and Ottó, I. (1998) Motivation in action: A process model of L2 motivation. *Working Papers in Applied Linguistics* (Vol. 4, pp. 43–69). London: Thames Valley University.

Dörnyei, Z. and Ushioda, E. (eds) (2009) *Motivation, Language Identity and the L2 Self*. Bristol: Multilingual Matters.

Dweck, C.S. (1999) *Self-Theories: Their Role in Motivation, Personality, and Development*. Philadelphia, PA: Psychology Press.

Gardner, R.C. (1985) *Social Psychology and Second Language Learning: The Role of Attitudes and Motivation*. London: Edward Arnold.

Guilloteaux, M.J. and Dörnyei, Z. (2008) Motivating language learners: A classroom-oriented investigation of the effects of motivational strategies on student motivation. *TESOL Quarterly* 42 (1), 55–77.

Halász, G. and Lannert, J. (2006) *Report on the Hungarian State Education 2006*. Budapest: OKI.

Heitzmann, J. (2008) The ups and downs of motivation: A longitudinal study of a group of secondary-school learners of English. PhD thesis. Budapest: Eötvös Loránd University.

Hiemstra, R. (2004) Self-directed learning lexicon. *International Journal of Self-Directed Learning* 1 (2), 1–6.

Higgins, E.T. (1987) Self-discrepancy: A theory relating self and affect. *Psychological Review* 94 (3), 319–340.

Higgins, E.T. (1996) The 'self-digest': Self-knowledge serving self-regulatory functions. *Journal of Personality and Social Psychology* 71 (6), 1062–1083.

Kormos, J. and Csizér, K. (2008) Age-related differences in the motivation of learning English as a foreign language: Attitudes, selves, and motivated learning behavior. *Language Learning* 58 (2), 327–355.

Larsen-Freeman, D. and Cameron, L. (2008) *Complex Systems and Applied Linguistics*. Oxford: Oxford University Press.

Little, D. (1990) Autonomy in language learning. In I. Gathercole (ed.) *Autonomy in Language Learning* (pp. 7–15). London: CILT.

Little, D. (2007) Language learner autonomy: Some fundamental considerations revisited. *Innovation in Language Learning and Teaching* 1 (1), 14–29.

Markus, H. and Nurius, P. (1986) Possible selves. *American Psychologist* 41 (9), 954–969.

Marsh, H.W. and Köller, O. (2003) Bringing together two theoretical models of relations between academic self-concept and achievement. In H.W. Marsh, R.G. Craven and D.M. McInerney (eds) *International Advances in Self Research* (pp. 17–47). Greenwich, CT: Information Age Publishing.

Mercer, S. (2011) *Towards an Understanding of Language Learner Self-concept.* Dordrecht: Springer.

Mezei, G. (2006) Egy interjúkérdéssor validálása: A motivációs tanítási gyakorlat vizsgálata [Validating an interview guide: Investigating the motivational teaching practice]. *Iskolakultúra* 16 (10), 128–132.

Mezei, G. (2012) The motivational teaching practice of teachers and the self-regulatory system of students in the English language classroom. PhD thesis. Budapest: Eötvös Loránd University.

Mezei, G. and Csizér, K. (2005) Második nyelvi motivációs stratégiák használata az osztályteremben [L2 motivational strategies in the classroom]. *Iskolakultúra* 15 (12), 30–42.

Neuwirth, G. and Horn, D. (2007) *A Középiskola Néhány Mutatója 2006 [Some Indices of Secondary Schools 2006].* Budapest: Oktatáskutató és Fejlesztő Intézet.

Nikolov, M. (1995) Általános iskolás gyerekek motivációja az angol mint idegen nyelv tanulására [Elementary school pupils' motivation to learn English as a foreign language]. *Modern Nyelvoktatás* 1 (1), 7–20.

Nikolov, M. (1999) 'Why do you learn English?' 'Because the teacher is short.' A study of Hungarian children's foreign language learning motivation. *Language Teaching Research* 3 (1), 33–56.

Nikolov, M. (2003) Angolul és németül tanuló diákok nyelvtanulási attitűdje és motivációja [The attitudes and motivation of students of English and German]. *Iskolakultúra* 13 (8), 61–73.

Nikolov, M. (2004) Az életkor szerepe a nyelvtanulásban [The role of age in language learning]. *Modern Nyelvoktatás* 10 (1), 3–26.

Noels, K.A., Clément, R. and Pelletier, L.G. (1999) Perceptions of teachers' communicative style and students' intrinsic and extrinsic motivation. *The Modern Language Journal* 83 (1), 23–34.

Paris, S.G. and Winograd, P. (2001) The role of self-regulated learning in contextual teaching: Principles and practices for teacher preparation. See http://www.ciera.org/library/archive/2001-04/0104prwn.pdf (accessed November 2012).

Pintrich, P.R. (2000) The role of goal orientation in self-regulated learning. In M. Boekaerts, P.R. Pintrich and M. Zeidner (eds) *Handbook of Self-regulation* (pp. 451–502). San Diego, CA: Elsevier Academic Press.

Rubin, J. (1975) What the "good language learner" can teach us. *TESOL Quarterly* 9 (1), 41–51.

Ryan, S. (2009) Self and identity in L2 motivation in Japan: The Ideal L2 self and Japanese learners of English. In Z. Dörnyei and E. Ushioda (eds) *Motivation, Language Identity and the L2 Self* (pp. 120–143). Bristol: Multilingual Matters.

Skaalvik, E.M. and Bong, M. (2003) Self-concept and self-efficacy revisited. In H.W. Marsh, R.G. Craven and D.M. McInerney (eds) *International Advances in Self Research* (pp. 67–89). Greenwich, CT: Information Age Publishing.

Stern, H.H. (1975) What can we learn from the good language learner? *The Canadian Modern Language Review* 31 (4), 304–318.

Stockdale, S. (2003) Development of an instrument to measure self-directedness. PhD thesis. Knoxville, TN: University of Tennessee.

Taguchi, T., Magid, M. and Papi, M. (2009) The L2 motivational self system among Japanese, Chinese, and Iranian learners of English: A comparative study. In Z. Dörnyei and E. Ushioda (eds) *Motivation, Language Identity and the L2 Self* (pp. 66–97). Bristol: Multilingual Matters.

Zentner, M. and Renaud, O. (2007) Origins of adolescents' ideal self: An intergenerational perspective. *Journal of Personality and Social Psychology* 92 (3), 557–574.

17 ELT Motivation from a Complex Dynamic Systems Theory Perspective: A Longitudinal Case Study of L2 Teacher Motivation in Beijing

Yuzo Kimura

Introduction

In the research field of second language acquisition (SLA), second language (L2) motivation is described as a subset of individual differences along with, among others, aptitude, language styles and learning strategies. In the 1990s, the study of L2 motivation recorded an unprecedented number of article publications (Dörnyei & Skehan, 2003), and this eventually led to multiple diverse methodological pathways. The proliferation of L2 motivation studies was a welcome phenomenon for L2 motivation researchers because since then, L2 motivation studies have become a fertile ground for ongoing developments. For one thing, quantitative approaches to investigating L2 motivation have reached a sophisticated stage by employing higher standards of statistical procedures (see for example, Csizér & Dörnyei, 2005; Taguchi et al., 2009). These studies show the possibility of a multifaceted causal structure to L2 motivation from a macro perspective. On the other hand, more attention has started to be paid to L2 motivation on an individual basis through qualitative and longitudinal research paradigms. This trend of L2 motivation research 'has merged into a rapidly emerging broader strand within SLA, the study of complex dynamic systems' (Dörnyei & Ushioda, 2011: xii).

In this chapter, I will address L2 teaching and learning motivation in the context of L2 classrooms in Beijing from a Complex Dynamic

Systems Theory (CDST) perspective. Firstly, I will provide an overview of the history of L2 motivation studies and then discuss the theoretical rationale of CDST. Secondly, I will briefly summarise teacher beliefs and teacher motivation research before describing the current study.

L2 Motivation: Past and Present

According to Dörnyei (2005), the history of L2 motivation research can be described in three distinct periods: the social psychological period between 1959–1990, the cognitive-situated period during the 1990s and the process-oriented period in more recent years. The social psychological approach, introduced by Lambert, Gardner and their associates, described L2 motivation with a view to correlating it with macro factors such as ethno-linguistic communities (see Gardner & Lambert, 1972). This approach yields averaged or aggregated traits for those who belong to a certain group and thus tells us little about L2 motivation among individuals. In contrast to this broad view of L2 motivation, the cognitive-situated period of L2 motivation pays more attention to the situated contexts in which learning takes place, including teachers and learner groups (Dörnyei, 2005). As Ushioda points out, the traits of L2 motivation studies in these two periods can be described in such a manner that, firstly, L2 motivation is investigated using a distinction between the inner mental world of individuals and the environment which surrounds them, and secondly, the primary research goal is to uncover 'rule-governed psychological laws that explain how context affects motivation' (Ushioda, 2009: 217). Recently, within the process-oriented period, L2 motivation has been considered distinctive, neither a static nor a cause–effect attribute but a dynamic and complex system that displays continuous fluctuation. When viewed from such a perspective, L2 motivation may be investigated longitudinally, focusing more on individuals in ongoing teaching and learning situations. Such a contextually embedded model of L2 motivation can hardly be approached in traditional linear models using cross-sectional analysis, but is more appropriately addressed through investigating individuals' processes of L2 motivation using grounded theory, which makes such research qualitative in nature.

As such, the process-oriented period of L2 motivation research has witnessed a small but steady increase in qualitative approaches to investigating L2 motivation (Nikolov, 2001; Syed, 2001; Ushioda, 2003; Williams et al., 2001). These studies have common core features and the following set of criteria seems to be an appropriate summary: (a) a limited number of participants, (b) the application of semi-structured interviews and (c) interpretations of transcribed narrative text in a grounded theory manner.

In the current era, described as the socio-dynamic period by Dörnyei and Ushioda (2011), L2 motivation studies have evolved into further stages of exploration. The L2 Motivational Self System is a new theory of L2 motivation that was created by Dörnyei (for a comprehensive summary, see Dörnyei, 2009) during this most recent period of L2 motivation research. Originally derived from Markus and Nurius (1987) and created from the need to re-interpret Gardner's concept of 'integrativeness' (Gardner, 2001: 5), the L2 Motivation Self System captures one's 'desire to reduce the discrepancy between one's actual and ideal or ought-to selves' (Dörnyei, 2005: 101). The desire to reduce the gap between one's current L2 self and one's Ideal L2 self theorised by the L2 Motivation Self System can wisely express one's continuous future state of motivation, and thus, it is ideally suited to a longitudinal qualitative view as a framework for interpreting participants' language identity and L2 motivation. During the socio-dynamic period, L2 motivation research has been merging with other alternative approaches in SLA (Atkinson, 2011). Since the paper of Firth and Wagner (1997) was written, there has been a crucial theoretical and methodological debate in SLA between cognitivism and positivism (Larsen-Freeman, 2007; Zuengler & Miller, 2006). This conflict led to recent renewed calls for viewing SLA more broadly, including the socially situated dimension of the language acquisition process. These calls further differ according to the extent to which the social context is considered to play a role, either a full role such as in Sociocultural Theory or with the social and psychological aspects forming a unity such as in the Sociocognitive Approach or CDST (Larsen-Freeman, 2010). In L2 motivation research, already small but promising results have emerged (Kim, 2009, 2011; Lamb, 2009). This trend of merging different branches of SLA motivation research seems not only promising but also timely as 'the move towards more socially grounded, dynamic and complex interacting systems in the analysis of L2 motivation is also in keeping with wider contemporary trends within the field of applied linguistics that has highlighted emergenist and dynamic systems approaches to understanding SLA' (Dörnyei & Ushioda, 2011: 72).

CDST and L2 motivation studies

L2 motivation research seems to have reached a turning point where it has met with a theory which sustains the analysis of more socially grounded, dynamic and complex phenomena, such as CDST. A complex system in CDST consists of heterogeneous agents, and interaction among them often brings unpredictable and non-linear results. It is interconnected with a specific context, and at the same time, it is open to allow energy from other systems. A complex system in seeming equilibrium also changes continually both on its own and as a result of this influx of energy from other systems. It is, however, highly adaptable to change from other systems, but once the change is adapted to, the system itself may change entirely (Larsen-Freeman & Cameron, 2008). As such, change is an essential tenet of CDST and it is due to this trait that the system can draw non-linear trajectories. However, in the course of system development, it may also experience stable and predictable phases when the system is ruled by strong forces called attractors which drive it to those stable phases (Dörnyei, 2012).

In this vein, the L2 classroom in a formal school context is a good example of, and thus can be defined as a complex system: It consists of heterogeneous agents (e.g. teachers, students, curriculum, etc.), and while teachers may put in almost the same effort towards teaching individual students every year, the results often do not reflect the effort they have invested. L2 classes in schools are often susceptible to external influence from other factors such as school policy, parental pressure and, more broadly, the national curriculum. Teachers usually change (or are at least expected to change) their instruction at every necessary occasion in order to fine-tune and maximise their efforts.

Applications of CDST in SLA are emerging, and rewarding results have just started to accumulate, primarily in the area of L2 emergence and development (for a recent example, see Verspoor *et al.*, 2011). L2 motivation studies in light of CDST are currently on the research agenda (for self-concept and beliefs in DST perspective, see Mercer, 2011), but several potential lines of inquiry are available. For example, Dörnyei (2012) proposes three research strategies to investigate complex dynamic systems: (1) a focus on identifying strong attractor-governed phenomena, (2) a focus on identifying typical attractor conglomerates and (3) a focus on identifying and analysing typical dynamic outcome patterns or the signature dynamics of systems.

Teacher beliefs and teacher motivation

In SLA, language teaching and learning beliefs are also individual differences along with motivation. Because of their mutual closeness, beliefs are sometimes treated almost interchangeably with motivation. This is perhaps because of the vagueness of belief traits which are expressed in different terms by scholars with different research agendas (Barcelos, 2006a). However, I believe that it is crucial to clear up the distinction between beliefs and motivation before conducting interpretive studies. In this regard, Pajares (1992) is insightful. As he says:

> The construct of educational beliefs is itself broad and encompassing. For purposes of research, it is diffuse and ungainly, too difficult to operationalise, too context free. Therefore, as with more general beliefs, *educational beliefs about* are required beliefs about confidence to affect students' performance (teacher efficacy), about the nature of

knowledge (epistemological beliefs), about causes of teachers' or students' performance (attributions, locus of control, motivation, writing apprehension, math anxiety), about perceptions of self and feelings of self-worth (self-concept, self-esteem), about confidence to perform specific tasks (self-efficacy). There are also educational beliefs about specific subjects or disciplines (reading instruction, the nature of reading, whole language). (Pajares, 1992: 316)

This suggests that from what participants say during interviews or in journal logs, for example, the researcher can carefully select the portion that relates to the participants' understanding of teaching and learning motivation. Due to the overlap of the constructs, researchers should take into account that what participants describe as their language teaching and learning beliefs may underpin their language teaching and learning motivation.

In addition to the issue of belief/motivation clarification, one of the important issues of L2 motivation still to be fully investigated is L2 teacher motivation. And yet, the literature on L2 teacher motivation in the field of applied linguistics remains limited in comparison with that in the field of educational psychology (Dörnyei & Ushioda, 2011). One promising study, however, was conducted by Kubanyiova (2012), which explores an L2 teacher's conceptual change by proposing Language Teacher Conceptual Change (LTCC), an integrated model to gauge the impact of teacher education. LTCC is unique in that it encompasses Possible Language Teacher Selves: (a) the Ideal Language Teacher Self, (b) the Ought-to Language Teacher Self and (c) the Feared Language Teacher Self, all based on Dörnyei's (2005) L2 Motivational Self System. Through ethnographic classroom observations and interview data from eight in-service teacher participants, Kubanyiova attempts to explain the mixed impact and curious pattern of teacher development in a language teacher training course. The study is compelling in that on the one hand, it demonstrates how individual complexities of L2 teacher motivation may be influenced by contextual conditions and demands from the lens of the Possible Language Teacher Self, and on the other, it addresses the link between teacher cognition, L2 teacher motivation and teacher development. It must be pointed out, however, that no research has attempted so far to investigate L2 teacher motivation from a CDST standpoint.

Thus, amid the current turning point for L2 motivation research where teacher motivation investigations in light of other SLA disciplines are still scarce, exploring L2 teachers' teaching motivation from a CDST viewpoint will cast a pioneering light on the field of L2 motivation. The present study illustrates such a case with the intention of further enriching and expanding the conversation of L2 teaching motivation and L2 learning motivation more generally.

The Study

This study aims to investigate L2 teachers' motivation with a focus on two English teachers and their learners in the settings of two different middle schools in Beijing, China. The investigation uses the framework of CDST by paying particular attention to the changes in L2 teachers' motivation from both micro and macro perspectives, wherein salient attractors which appear to govern the system of middle school L2 teaching in Beijing are explored. Based on the attractor explorations, I will try to identify the salient system components and then analyse signature dynamics, or typical dynamic outcomes, of L2 teaching motivation in Beijing. To this end, I address the following research questions:

(1) How can changes in L2 teaching motivation be described from a shorter/micro and longer/macro perspective?
(2) In what way can micro/macro changes in L2 teaching motivation be described by attractors in the different L2 teaching systems in Beijing?
(3) What are the signature dynamics in the middle school L2 teaching system in Beijing?

Although not necessarily a full-fledged ethnography, this study is ethnographic in nature as it employs careful observations of teachers and students within their school community over an extended period of time. In this regard, an ethnographic case study seems most appropriate to address the research questions for three reasons. Firstly, ethnography tries to uncover participants' emic views, or their views of reality. Secondly, ethnography looks at phenomena from a holistic view, taking into account both the behaviour of subjects and the context in which they are embedded (Nunan, 1992). This is especially crucial to investigate contextually embedded L2 motivation from a CDST stance because a complex system itself is interconnected with a specific context. Finally, an ethnographic case study requires a certain length of time to conduct. A longitudinal, case-study and time-series approach 'enables connections to be made across levels and timescales' (Larsen-Freeman & Cameron, 2008: 245), which in turn enables us to uncover changes in L2 teachers' motivation.

Settings, participants and data collection

Fieldwork was conducted at two different middle schools, both located in a district of Beijing. The main participants were two English teachers, Mary, a junior middle school English teacher, and Sarah, a senior middle school[1] English teacher (both pseudonyms). The primary data consist of their videotaped classroom practices at two different phases at different intervals. Data were collected in March 2007 and September 2009 at a junior middle school and in March 2005 and March 2007 at a senior middle school, respectively. During the 2007 fieldwork, before each classroom practice was conducted at the two sites, I attended each of their in-school pre-teaching discussions[2]. I also visited the district's teachers training college several times to interview some supervisors about the system and the functions of the school, and attended lectures as well as an open class for in-service English teachers in that district. An open class is a lesson conducted by an experienced teacher with his/her students that other teachers may observe in order to learn how to apply a variety of teaching strategies effectively when teaching their own students. I also had the opportunity to observe Mr Wang's (pseudonym) lessons. Mr Wang was one of Sarah's colleagues as well as her mentor with a teaching career that spanned 35 years. These secondary data and voices from the participants' colleagues (six colleagues of Mary and two colleagues of Sarah) were used in my interpretation of the participants' L2 teacher motivation.

The final and main data consisted of semi-structured interviews with the two teachers and seven students, conducted two to seven months after the initial teaching practices; in October 2007 and in March 2010 for the junior middle school, and in May 2005 and in October 2007 for the senior middle school. After watching segments of video clips from the primary data as stimulated recalls, these two teachers were asked a series of questions. The seven students who joined the interviews were: Mandy and Sam as 2007 junior middle school 1st year students; Sherry, Lucy and Fiona as 2009 junior middle school 2nd year students; and Susan and Nancy as 2005 senior middle school students (all pseudonyms). Table 17.1 summarises the contexts, participants and data collection phases.

Data analysis and interpretation

To conduct deep theory-building explorations, this qualitative research employs constructivist grounded theory. Constructivist grounded theory differs from the way ethnographers employ grounded theory from an objectivist standpoint. While objectivist grounded theory pays no attention to how data are generated between the researcher and participants, constructivist grounded theory draws on an interpretive tradition whereby data and analysis are co-constructed through interaction (Charmaz, 2006). From this view, interview narratives were interpreted by paying careful attention to the interview context. Also, triangulation was set for both methods and data to ensure credibility and trustworthiness (e.g. Barcelos, 2006b). The former indicates the employment of different sources of data collection: observations with field notes, stimulated

Table 17.1 Summary of the research contexts

March 2005	March 2007	September 2009

. Sarah
  SMS English teacher
  8 years of experience
. Susan and Nancy
  SMS 1st year students
. Mr Wang
	⇨ . Sarah
	. Sarah's two colleagues	

	. Mary
	  JMS English teacher
	  1.5 years of experience
	. Mandy and Sam
	  JMS 1st year students
	. Mary's six colleagues
		⇨ . Mary
		. Sherry, Lucy and Fiona
		  JMS 2nd year students

Note: JMS and SMS stand for junior and senior middle school, respectively.

recalls and semi-structured interviews. The latter refers to collecting data from different kinds of participants: teachers, learners, colleagues and out-of-school supervisors.

Following Miles and Huberman (1994), codes were created progressively. Firstly, descriptive coding of transcribed interview narratives was processed by an L2 research expert in addition to me, and any discrepancy was discussed to reach a final agreement. These coded narratives were further explored by revising initial descriptive codes and creating more inferential ones for higher level of analysis, to 'relate to one another in coherent, study-important ways' (Miles & Huberman, 1994: 62). This was done using NVivo 10 [Computer software] (2012) until coding categories were '"saturated" when gathering fresh data no longer sparks new theoretical insights' (Charmaz, 2006: 113).

Findings

Micro/macro change of L2 teaching motivation

Timescales are one of the crucial factors in conducting CDST studies. As van Geert (2008) suggests, the short-time dynamics movement will affect the long-term dynamics in small but interesting ways, whereas some traits of the long-term dynamics can suggest the nature of underlying short-term dynamics. In this regard, micro/short-term and macro/long-term L2 teaching motivation of Mary and Sarah reveals the interesting dynamism of L2 teaching motivation.

When I observed Mary's class in March 2007, she was among the newest and youngest of seven English teachers at her junior middle school. She had graduated from a local university majoring in English literature and had only 1.5 years of teaching experience. Young as she was, she had a heavy burden as a homeroom teacher, or a 'head teacher' in the Chinese context of an experimental class[3]. The following quote illustrates the extrinsic reasons for her job settlement:

> I'm an English major and most of my classmates in my university became an interpreter or some translation works. Very few of us become teachers. At my last year of my university, I took the test of postgraduate of English literature and I failed. So at last, I had to work. (INT, Mary, 10/17/2007)[4]

My observation was timed to take advantage of her open class. When Mary presented her teaching procedures at her in-school pre-teaching discussion three days before her open class, she explained her rough teaching idea for Unit 1 in book 2 of *Go for It!*, 'Where's your pen pal from?'[5]. As the second lesson of this unit, she said that she would use a real map to describe people, languages and cities in the world. The ultimate goal of this lesson was for students to be able to write a real letter to look for real pen pals. Supporting this goal was her strong teaching belief which seems to be the foundation of her L2 teaching motivation, to use English in a real context:

> I think it's [writing a real letter to their pen pal] a real use of our language. I think in my personal opinion. (PTD, Mary, 3/1/2007)

Based on this belief, she constructed her own way of task arrangement and task association. Although she was young, she seemed to be motivated to arrange textbook tasks towards this goal:

> I will not just teach the book, like I say to them, 'Open your books and turn to page 3, let's look at 3B'. I will do something more. Sometimes I choose other things to add in this unit. (INT, Mary, 10/18/2007)

This motivation for arranging and associating tasks was still present two years later in 2009 when she taught Unit 2 of book 1 of *Go for It!*, 'What's the matter?', for the 8th grade students. In this lesson about health issues, her growth was evident in terms of task selection and task arrangement. She chose several tasks in the textbook to arrange and link them, so that students were able to proceed through their health-related learning from shorter, simpler and fixed language structures (e.g. words and phrases for body parts) to longer, creative and more complex structures (e.g. pair work and role play). As she said:

> I think this one [the order of selecting and linking tasks] is interesting. I think trying to relate the tasks is very interesting. (INT, Mary, 3/19/2009)

In contrast to this strong task-association motivation, Mary was young and received many comments and constructive criticism from her colleagues. Two prominent suggestions from her colleagues were a good source for the micro aspect of her L2 teaching motivation, because both of them somehow changed or influenced Mary's teaching practice during her open class. The first suggestion was related to the need to use either realia or digital materials. Initially, she planned to use a real map to introduce her lesson, but eventually, her colleagues were sceptical about the use of the map, partly because the position of each nation was unclear on it and partly because her students lacked geographical knowledge. Instead, they suggested using a PowerPoint (PPT) slide with national flags and pictures of celebrities who were familiar to all the students. In doing so, students could easily catch the theme of the lesson. She accepted this suggestion because she thought that it was important to employ materials that would be interesting for her students (PTD, Mary, 3/1/2007). Therefore, in her open class she decided to use PPT slides with 14 national flags and pictures of famous people from around the world on them. The following quote demonstrates her belief in the importance of capturing her students' interest when teaching them:

> We have used many different things in our class to interest students. I think the interest is very important for students to learn English now. Instead of world map, I used PPT. But last year I used the map. Some of the lessons they can't use real things. So if they use the PPT, usually use PPT. (INT, Mary, 10/18/2007)

Thus, for Mary, the use of realia or digital materials depends on the extent to which they can promote her students' interest. It is interesting to note that two of Mary's students in 2007 expressed very different attitudes towards her lesson. While Mandy said that the PPT slides attracted her very much, Sam denied his interest in this style of practice, and preferred other tasks such as the teacher introducing a nation of interest to the students (INT, ST, 10/18/2007).

The second suggestion is with regard to the balance between the time allocated for a task and to what extent Mary should give feedback to her students. This is a difficult issue for a novice teacher such as Mary and she needed assistance from her colleagues. Before she raised this issue, at the earlier stage of the discussion with her colleagues, she was heavily criticised for the uneven distribution of time allotment in dealing with Unit 1. Then, the discussion topic turned to the formation of groups and the time allotment for each group to present their results. Here, Mary mentioned the following dilemma: How could she encourage students to present voluntarily with an atmosphere of poor engagement in her experimental class? Having heard lengthy suggestions from other experienced teachers, she finally said that she would do her best to say something to as many of the 30 students as possible. At this stage of the interview, she also mentioned the important role that a single male colleague with six years of teaching experience played in her decision by describing that she had borrowed many teaching ideas and PPT slides from him during her early days of teaching (PTD, Mary, 3/1/2007).

A post-observational task distribution analysis prepared by myself revealed, however, that her 2007 practice was still heavily uneven with 40% allotted to the introduction followed by 33% to pair work and another 27% to small segments such as the warm-up (6%), two other tasks (12%) and a summary (9%). My overall impression of her practice was that her classroom was predominantly 'teacher-led' (FN, 3/5/2007). The following quote from the 2007 interview further illustrates her difficulty as a homeroom teacher of the class. Her motivation to solve this problem is obvious, but she is struggling to resolve the issue:

> Some students can answer the questions. But they won't hand up. So I don't know their own thoughts, but it's problem in my class. I must have my own way to deal with them, or it will be worse and worse. (INT, Mary, 10/18/2007)

The post-observational task distribution analysis for her 2009 practice showed a significant difference with equal distributions of the lesson allotted to the introduction (13%), pair work (21%), listening comprehension (17%), role play (18%) and oral practice (16%), followed by another 15% allotted to two other small tasks. Mary said that she spoke more in 2007 and she asked students to speak more in 2009. She analysed her own growth by explaining that she took less time to prepare for class, dealt with more things in class and communicated with students more casually. She also felt capable of eliciting responses from many students and offering feedback (INT, Mary, 3/19/ 2010). As her three 2009 students, Sherry, Lucy and Fiona agreed, Mary's class required a moderate level of attentiveness, which they said was appropriate for maintaining their L2 learning motivation (INT, ST, 3/19/2010).

However, the most remarkable change in Mary's long-term motivation is her desire to pursue a postgraduate course of English language education. As she said:

> I didn't learn teaching at my university, but now, I will go to the Capital Normal University postgraduate course to learn the English teaching. I passed the exam at last. Sometimes I found teaching very interesting. (INT, Mary, 3/19/2010)

In response to my question of what motivated her most in terms of teaching English, she replied that it was her responsibility as a homeroom teacher to care for her students. She said that this was extremely challenging, but it made her grow remarkably (INT, Mary, 3/19/2010).

In contrast to Mary, when I conducted my first observation of Sarah in 2005, she already had eight years of teaching experience after graduating from a normal university majoring in English. The observation was conducted during her usual morning class, a single experimental class in her school with the top 50 students. The class was reading a 506-word expository English passage from the textbook, *Senior English for China* entitled 'The Birth of a Festival', about the origin of the Kwanzaa festival among African Americans. The class mainly consisted of fast reading (6 min), a quick glance at a whole passage (3 min), paragraph reading (26 min, i.e. reading aloud by one student, in-depth understanding of a paragraph, multiple choice questions and describing main ideas), true or false questions as a summary (1 min) and a retelling task (10 min). The lesson proceeded entirely by using PPT slides which were all prepared by Sarah.

Sarah had a strong belief in her love of her students, which in turn enhanced her L2 teaching motivation. As she said:

> Before I love English, I love my students first. Every time I come into a classroom, I know that our students want to learn something from me. So, that made me learn more. (INT, Sarah, 5/30/2005)

Her ultimate goal of teaching English was also for her students' sake, so that they would be able to communicate with foreigners in English at home or abroad in the future. In order to achieve this goal, she tried to make her classroom as comfortable as possible to maximise rapport with her students and let them speak more in their first and second year. Also, to promote students' smooth understanding of English passages, she arranged tasks from general (i.e. 'fast reading' and 'a quick glance at a whole passage') to specific (i.e. 'paragraph reading' with 'in-depth understanding' in particular). However, Sarah had another important motivation in designing her 2005 practice, which was to have her students prepare for the National College Entrance Examination (NCEE). For example, 'fast reading' was located at an earlier stage of her practice not only to have her students pick up general and important points, but also for them to acquire the speed necessary to answer all the NCEE questions within 120 minutes (INT, Sarah, 5/30/2005). The L2 learning motivation of Sarah's 2005 students, Susan and Nancy, seemed to be a perfect fit with Sarah's beliefs and motivation for the following reasons. Firstly, they were extremely fond of Sarah. Secondly, they both understood the importance of English as one of the main subjects in the NCEE. Thirdly, beyond this exam-related extrinsic motive to learn English, they both had clear intrinsic long-term future goals such as studying abroad or getting an English-related job (INT, ST, 5/28/2005).

Sarah's dual L2 teaching motivation would further accelerate its shift from a communication mode to a more exam-oriented mode when she taught 3rd year students:

> ...but in the third year, all of them [making dialogues, retelling a text] are unnecessary. In the third year, we do a lot of reading and multiple choices. That is the most important. (INT, Sarah, 5/30/2005)

In her 2007 practice with 3rd year students when she prepared for reading an 824-word expository passage entitled 'the Language of Honey-Bees' from Book 3 of *Senior English for China*, it was not surprising that the topic of her pre-teaching discussion primarily concerned NCEE related issues and not a single suggestion was made about her teaching procedure by her two colleagues. There were two factors that had an important impact on Sarah's long-term L2 teaching motivation. The first factor was a change in the level of the students that Sarah taught in 2005 and 2007. In 2005, the single experimental class accommodated the top 50 students, but in 2007 when they became 3rd year students, these gifted students were sorted into two different experimental classes. Sarah was only able to continue teaching 10 of these students in one of the experimental classes along with 40 new students, who although gifted, were not the top students in that school. Faced with such a significant demographic change, Sarah had to adjust the level of difficulty of the class activities accordingly (INT, Sarah, 10/19/2007). Since the overall level of the class in 2007 was much lower than the class that Sarah had taught in 2005, she was extremely motivated to use teaching approaches and materials that would be suitable for the students in her class. Indeed, in spite of their younger age, her 2005 students were actively able to express the main ideas of each paragraph they read on their own (SR, 5/3/2005), whereas most of her 2007 students were not able to do so. Therefore, in 2007 Sarah needed to add main idea descriptions as multiple choice questions on her PPT slides to scaffold the students' learning. (SR, 3/9/2007). To Sarah, this demographic change might have meant an entire system change between these two classes.

The second factor involves the powerful influence of Mr Wang on Sarah's motivation to use handouts comprised of both lead-in and reading activities. The handout with lead-in activities consisted of 18 gap-filling quizzes about idioms with animal names while the handout that contained reading for the students to complete was a written version of all of Sarah's PPT slides including key words and phrases. The purpose of the lead-in handout was to help students to be interested in English, while the purpose of the reading handout was to save time (INT, Sarah, 10/19/2007). When I observed Mr Wang's practice in 2005, he used very similar handouts to Sarah's, and as Sarah eventually revealed, the idea behind her handouts originally came from Mr Wang:

> When I prepare each unit, I try to make a long paragraph or some very difficult grammar easier. That is what I learned from Mr Wang. Mr Wang is my master. He had taught me a lot in a real teaching. (INT, Sarah, 5/30/2005)

Two teachers' trajectories of L2 teaching motivation: attractor-governed pathways

The primary attractors for Mary are her motivation for the arrangement and association of tasks and her motivation to use English in a real context. These attractors seem very powerful as she notes these interests and beliefs over the course of the observation period, yet questions remain regarding where these motivations originated.

In 2001, the Ministry of Education of China implemented a new national curriculum of English, *The English Curriculum Standard: Experimental version* (Ministry of Education, 2001). This new curriculum placed great importance on the learning process and advocated the use of various teaching methods, so that learners could discover grammar rules and develop effective learning strategies themselves (Tian & Qin, 2010). The district where Mary's school is located selected a new textbook, *Go for It!*, which implemented a strict Task Based Language Teaching (TBLT) syllabus. I believe this new concept of teaching was undoubtedly a big challenge for a new teacher like Mary, but I assume the challenge was seen as worthy by the young and curious novice teacher and eventually she may have found arranging and associating tasks interesting. In so doing, her motivation to teach and use English in a real communicative context may have been nurtured. Hence, this attractor can be named the *L2 teaching macro policy attractor*.

The second important attractor for Mary is her responsibility as a homeroom teacher. From the interpretation of her narratives, she coped with many difficulties with her students; however, she fulfilled her responsibility of getting them on the right track and having them attain a satisfactory achievement. Hence, this attractor can be described as the *teacher responsibility for student achievement attractor*. It is very interesting that as a novice teacher, her L2 teaching motivation was attracted not by ELT per se, but by her responsibility as a homeroom teacher. This shows evidence that a teacher–learner rapport can lead to enhanced L2 teaching motivation.

The last attractor, the *desire for professional development attractor*, finally led her to make her long-term dream come true. This long-term attractor should be particularly important for underpinning the professional career of someone like Mary who seems to have had no choice because of extrinsic reasons for immediate job placement after attaining initial qualifications.

In contrast, Sarah's attractors are simple and yet powerful, because her fundamental belief that makes up her attractors for L2 teaching seems to come from her strong love of students. It is reasonable to say, therefore, that her dual attractors, one which concerns her students and the other, her desire to construct English classes for the sake of her students' NCEE, coexist harmoniously in her classroom. Hence, they can be described as the *learner consciousness attractor* and the *NCEE attractor*, respectively. I believe that the coexistence of these dual attractors is only possible because she attained a stable teacher–learner rapport, which verifies the need for a positive student–teacher relationship (Murphey & Carpenter, 2008).

Thus, these two English teachers have different trajectories influenced by different attractors that govern their L2 teaching systems. However, there seems to be another strong common attractor between the two, a *dissemination attractor*. This governs L2 teaching motivation in terms of their lesson preparation having been assisted through the dissemination of other teachers' good practices to them. For example, both Mary and Sarah received intensive support from their teacher training college including free access to digital materials, open class observation and NCEE mock test results on a regular and frequent basis. Mary could visit the school every Tuesday afternoon to attend a lecture (INT, Mary, 10/18/2007) or Thursday morning for an open class observation taught by other key teachers in the district (FN, 3/17/2005). Also included in this attractor is a pre-teaching in-school discussion where more practical ideas can be disseminated from other colleagues in the same school (INT, Sarah, 10/19/2007) or individual mentors, or particular colleagues such as Mr Wang for Sarah and a male colleague for Mary.

The signature dynamics of L2 teaching motivation in Beijing

By now it is clear that in the L2 teaching environment in Beijing, systems that these L2 teachers belonged to were governed by different attractors and yet they also belonged to a common system. What is interesting is the role that this common system can play on each L2 teacher in individual and incidental ways. For example, in the case of Mr Wang, who had already retired by the time that I visited Sarah at her school in 2007, the essence of his teaching philosophy continued to be disseminated through her practice which she self-regulated without his assistance. This may have been realised through a number of incidental factors such as a suitable age gap between them, often found in a father–daughter relationship, or a prerequisite that Mr Wang was an expert of practical English classroom instruction and famous in Beijing. As for Mary, however, it is uncertain to what extent she will be able to realise such a mentor–mentee relationship between her male colleague and herself. If a good relationship is established, this system will have a tremendous role to play in Mary's teaching practice because unlike secondary school English teachers in the public school system in Japan and South Korea who usually move to different schools at set intervals, she can stay at her school for an extended period of time and enjoy the benefit of an apprenticeship from a supportive mentor and colleague based at the same school.

Summary and Future Implications

Given the increasing interest in CDST and its application to L2 motivation studies, I would like to address in this final section where CDST differs from two other theories as applied to L2 motivation research. Firstly, Kubanyiova (2012) devised the Possible Language Teacher Self in LTCC by conceptualising teachers' cognitive, affective and emotional changes in the context of teacher development and teacher education. The gap-filling desire of possible selves can capture teachers' motivational changes very well in the context of pre-service or in-service teacher training. However, it does not necessarily do so in contexts such as the current study where changes in L2 teaching motivation need to be addressed based on everyday classroom practice. This is perhaps because unlike teachers in a pre-service or in-service context in which they have relatively more time to reflect on their own teaching and therefore to evaluate their future prospects, those in actual everyday teaching contexts have seldom, if ever, the chance to express their gap-filling desire regarding a future self by reflecting on their everyday classroom practice. CDST, in contrast, can accommodate such a context broadly and flexibly since a classroom can be defined as a complex and dynamic system to be investigated in all its complexity.

Secondly, current neo-Vygotskian SLA researchers see social interaction, mediation in particular, as a crucial element to human actions (Lantolf & Thorne, 2006). Taken from this view of L2 motivation research, ESL learners' motivational changes, for example, can be conceptualised as a mediated phenomenon in Activity Theory among Subject, Instruments, Rules, Community, Division of Labor and Object (Kim, 2011). Although CDST shares with the Vygotskian paradigm the view that higher mental functions emerge through social interaction, it places its locus of interest 'neither in the brain/body nor social interaction, but in their intersection' (Larsen-Freeman, 2011: 66). In this vein, L2 motivation studies applying CDST can see L2 motivation from a much broader and flexible perspective and thus are able to conceptualise motivation within systems as well as across them. This difference between the two theoretical models may result in fundamental differences in interpreting the changes in L2 motivation even when considering similar data from similar participants.

However, this broadness and flexibility may bring with it the risk of applying CDST in an unsystematic manner. Careful and consistent attention should be paid to elaborate on the role that theory plays in L2 motivation studies. To do so, it is also crucial, particularly at the dawn of a new conceptual approach, to accumulate a variety of research projects using CDST as a theoretical underpinning to create reliable templates for L2 motivation studies over time.

Notes

This study was financially supported by a research grant from the Japanese Government (Japan Society for the Promotion of Science Grant-in-Aid for Scientific Research (C) 16520337, 18520428, 21520569) and an earlier version was presented at AILA 2011 in Beijing. I would like to express my sincere gratitude to the participants, school authorities and educational leaders who offered me the chance to conduct my extended fieldwork in Beijing. I would also like to thank Zoltán Dörnyei for his encouraging discussion, Luxin Yang and Theron Muller for their constructive comments on an earlier draft of this chapter.

(1) Junior middle school and senior middle school in China are equivalent to junior high school and senior high school in Japan and the US, and middle school and high school in South Korea.

(2) In Beijing, middle school English teachers usually gather to have a weekly in-school pre-teaching discussion, discuss ideas for teaching and share their materials before they conduct English lessons.

(3) In Beijing, gifted middle school students are often placed into a special class which is called an experimental class. The lessons that teachers conduct in the experimental class are more challenging than those conducted in regular classes in order to meet the needs of the gifted students.

(4) References to data follow these systems of conventions: INT – interview; SR – stimulated recall (teaching practice segments shown in the interview); PTD – pre-teaching discussion; FN – field notes. Each reference contains the person with whom I conducted the interview and the date of the data collection. Therefore, (INT, ST, 5/30/2005) represents the narrative data from the interview with students dated May 30th 2005.

(5) The series Go for It! is an English textbook for junior middle school students published by People's Educational Press created by the Curriculum Material Institute of China in collaboration with Thompson Learning of US. It is a typical TBLT syllabus textbook prepared for the experimental version of the new national curriculum that was implemented in 2001 in Beijing.

References

Atkinson, D. (ed.) (2011) *Alternative Approaches to Second Language Acquisition*. Abingdon: Routledge.

Barcelos, A.M.F. (2006a) Researching beliefs about SLA: A critical review. In P. Kalaja and A.M.F. Barcelos (eds) *Beliefs about SLA: New Research Approaches* (pp. 7–33). New York, NY: Springer.

Barcelos, A.M.F. (2006b) Teachers' and students' beliefs within a Dewean framework: Conflict and influence. In P. Kalaja and A.M.F. Barcelos (eds) *Beliefs about SLA: New Research Approaches* (pp. 171–199). New York, NY: Springer.

Charmaz, K. (2006) *Constructing Grounded Theory: A Practical Guide Through Qualitative Analysis*. London: Sage Publication Limited.

Csizér, K. and Dörnyei, Z. (2005) The internal structure of language learning motivation and its relationship with language choice and learning effort. *The Modern Language Journal* 89 (1), 19–36.

Dörnyei, Z. (2005) *The Psychology of the Language Learner: Individual Differences in Second Language Acquisition*. Mahwah, NJ: Lawrence Erlbaum.

Dörnyei, Z. (2009) The L2 Motivational Self System. In Z. Dörnyei and E. Ushioda (eds) *Motivation, Language Identity and the L2 Self* (pp. 9–42). Bristol: Multilingual Matters.

Dörnyei, Z. (2012) Researching complex dynamic systems: 'Retrodictive qualitative modelling' in the language classroom. *Language Teaching*. Advance online publication. doi:10.1017/S0261444811000516.

Dörnyei, Z. and Skehan, P. (2003) Individual differences in second language learning. In C.J. Doughty and M.H. Long (eds) *The Handbook of Second Language Acquisition* (pp. 589–630). Malden, MA: Blackwell Publishing.

Dörnyei, Z. and Ushioda, E. (2011) *Teaching and Researching Motivation* (2nd edn). Harlow: Pearson Education Limited.

Firth, A. and Wagner, J. (1997) On discourse, communication, and (some) fundamental concepts in SLA research. *The Modern Language Journal* 81 (3), 285–300.

Gardner, R.C. (2001) Integrative motivation and second language acquisition. In Z. Dörnyei and R. Schmidt (eds) *Motivation and Second Language Acquisition* (pp. 1–19). Honolulu, HI: University of Hawaii Press.

Gardner, R.C. and Lambert, W.E. (1972) *Attitudes and Motivation in Second Language Learning*. Rowley, MA: Newbury House.

Kim, T.-Y. (2009) The sociocultural interface between Ideal Self and Ought-to Self: A case study of two Korean students' ESL motivation. In Z. Dörnyei and E. Ushioda (eds) *Motivation, Language Identity and the L2 Self* (pp. 274–294). Bristol: Multilingual Matters.

Kim, T.-Y. (2011) Sociocultural dynamics of ESL learning (de)motivation: An activity theory analysis of two adult Korean immigrants. *The Canadian Modern Language Review* 67 (1), 91–122.

Kubanyiova, M. (2012) *Teacher Development in Action: Understanding Language Teachers' Conceptual Change*. Basingstoke: Palgrave Macmillan.

Lamb, M. (2009) Situating the L2 self: Two Indonesian school learners of English. In Z. Dörnyei and E. Ushioda (eds) *Motivation, Language Identity and the L2 Self* (pp. 229–247). Bristol: Multilingual Matters.

Lantolf, J.P. and Thorne, S.L. (2006) *Sociocultural Theory and the Genesis of Second Language Development*. Oxford: Oxford University Press.

Larsen-Freeman, D. (2007) Reflecting on the cognitive-social debate in second language acquisition. *The Modern Language Journal* 91 (Focus Issue), 773–787.

Larsen-Freeman, D. (2010) The dynamic co-adaptation of cognitive and social views: A complex theory perspective. In R. Batstone (ed.) *Sociocognitive Perspectives on Language Use and Language Learning* (pp. 40–53). Oxford: Oxford University Press.

Larsen-Freeman, D. (2011) A complexity theory approach to second language development/acquisition. In D. Atkinson (ed.) *Alternative Approaches to Second Language Acquisition* (pp. 48–72). Abingdon: Routledge.

Larsen-Freeman, D. and Cameron, L. (2008) *Complex Systems and Applied Linguistics*. Oxford: Oxford University Press.

Markus, H. and Nurius, P. (1987) Possible selves: The interface between motivation and the self-concept. In K. Yardley and T. Honess (eds) *Self and Identity: Psychosocial Perspectives* (pp. 157–172). Chichester: John Wiley & Sons Ltd.

Mercer, S. (2011) Language leaner self-concept: Complexity, continuity and change. *System* 39 (3), 335–346.

Miles, M.B. and Huberman, A.M. (1994) *Qualitative Data Analysis: An Expanded Sourcebook. Second Edition*. Thousand Oaks, CA: SAGE Publications.

Ministry of Education (2001) *Yingyu Kecheng Biaozhun: Shiyangao* [English Curriculum Standard: Experimental Version]. Beijing: Beijing Normal University Press.

Murphey, T. and Carpenter, C. (2008) The seeds of agency in language learning histories. In P. Kalaja, V. Menezes and A.M.F. Barcelos (eds) *Narratives of Learning and Teaching EFL* (pp. 17–34). New York, NY: Palgrave Macmillan.

Nikolov, M. (2001) A study of unsuccessful language learners. In Z. Dörnyei and R. Schmidt (eds) *Motivation and Second Language Acquisition* (pp. 149–169). Honolulu, HI: University of Hawaii Press.

Nunan, D. (1992) *Research Methods in Language Learning*. Cambridge: Cambridge University Press.

NVivo 10 [Computer software] (2012) Doncaster: QSR International Pty Limited.

Pajares, M.F. (1992) Teachers' beliefs and educational research: Cleaning up a messy construct. *Review of Educational Research* 62 (3), 307–332.

Syed, Z. (2001) Notions of self in foreign language learning: A qualitative analysis. In Z. Dörnyei and R. Schmidt (eds) *Motivation and Second Language Acquisition* (pp. 127–148). Honolulu, HI: University of Hawaii Press.

Taguchi, T., Magid, M. and Papi, M. (2009) The L2 motivational self system among Japanese, Chinese, and Iranian learners of English: A comparative study. In Z. Dörnyei and E. Ushioda (eds) *Motivation, Language Identity and the L2 Self* (pp. 66–97). Bristol: Multilingual Matters.

Tian, J. and Qin, J. (eds) (2010) *Zhongxue Yingyu Jiaoxuelun [The Theory of Middle School English Language Teaching]*. Beijng: Beijing Normal University Press.

Ushioda, E. (2003) Motivation as a socially mediated process. In D. Little, J. Ridley and E. Ushioda (eds) *Learner Autonomy in the Foreign Language Classroom: Teacher, Learner, Curriculum, Assessment* (pp. 90–102). Dublin: Authentik Language Learning Resources.

Ushioda, E. (2009) A person-in-context relational view of emergent motivation, self and identity. In Z. Dörnyei and E. Ushioda (eds) *Motivation, Language Identity and the L2 Self* (pp. 215–228). Bristol: Multilingual Matters.

van Geert, P. (2008) The dynamic systems approach in the study of L1 and L2 acquisition: An introduction. *The Modern Language Journal* 92 (2), 179–199.

Verspoor, M.H., de Bot, K. and Lowie, W. (eds) (2011) *A Dynamic Approach to Second Language Development: Methods and Techniques*. Amsterdam: John Benjamins Publishing Company.

Williams, M., Burden, R.L. and Al-Baharna, S. (2001) Making sense of success and failure: The role of the individual in motivation theory. In Z. Dörnyei and

R. Schmidt (eds) *Motivation and Second Language Acquisition* (pp. 171–184). Honolulu, HI: University of Hawaii Press.

Zuengler, J. and Miller, E.R. (2006) Cognitive and sociocultural perspectives: Two parallel SLA worlds? *TESOL Quarterly* 40 (1), 35–58.

Part 4
Intervention Studies

18 A Motivational Programme for Learners of English: An Application of the L2 Motivational Self System

Michael Magid

Introduction

Language teachers all over the world are faced with the challenge of motivating their students to learn. In response to this challenge, there have been some publications on motivational strategies in the language classroom during the past 20 years (e.g. Chang, 2010; Cheng & Dörnyei, 2007; Dörnyei & Csizér, 1998; Guilloteaux & Dörnyei, 2008; Oxford & Shearin, 1994), with Zoltán Dörnyei's (2001) book offering the most comprehensive summary of second language (L2) motivational strategies to date. My L2 motivational programme that I will describe in this chapter is novel in the sense that it contains new motivational strategies to motivate English language learners based on the recent theoretical approach to L2 motivation, Dörnyei's L2 Motivational Self System (see Dörnyei & Ushioda, 2009, 2011, and especially Dörnyei, 2009a), including the use of scripted imagery.

Imagery is defined as 'an internal representation of a perception of the external world in the absence of that external experience' (Hall et al., 1990: 28). Hall et al. (1990) define scripted imagery as a situation in which a script on a variety of themes, especially as a stimulus for an imagined journey, is read to an individual or group, who is usually relaxed with their eyes closed. Scripted imagery has been used in schools as a part of social and health education development (e.g. Hall & Hall, 1988; Hall et al., 1990; Hornby et al., 2003). Imagery is employed in subjects such as drama and art to generate creativity and imagination. Imagery activities have also been developed especially for L2 learners (e.g. Arnold et al., 2007; Hadfield & Dörnyei, 2013). In this chapter, I will describe my motivational programme in which imagery was incorporated as a key component to motivate learners of English from China to devote more time and effort to learning English by enhancing their vision of their Ideal L2 self. This chapter has five main objectives: (1) to describe the main components of my intervention programme, (2) to offer evidence that my programme increased the strength of my participants' vision of their Ideal L2 selves, (3) to demonstrate that my programme effectively motivated my participants to learn English, made them more confident in their English, improved their attitudes towards learning English and offered numerous other benefits, (4) to examine the relationships between my participants' motivation, confidence, their vision of their Ideal L2 self and their goals for learning English and (5) to share recommendations with language practitioners who may be interested in designing L2 motivational programmes following a similar approach.

The L2 Motivational Self System

The L2 Motivational Self System has been widely tested and validated in a number of different countries such as Hungary, Saudi Arabia, China, Japan and Iran (Al-Shehri, 2009; Csizér & Kormos, 2009; Ryan, 2009; Taguchi et al., 2009). It is based on the theory of possible selves (Higgins, 1987; Markus & Nurius, 1986). In their seminal paper about possible selves, Markus and Nurius (1986: 954) identified three main types of possible selves when they wrote that, 'possible selves are the ideal selves that we would very much like to become. They are also the selves we could become, and the selves we are afraid of becoming'. The three kinds of possible selves they referred to were ideal selves, expected selves and feared selves. Markus and Nurius (1986: 954) provided examples of ideal selves including 'the successful self, the creative self, the rich self, the thin self, or the loved and admired self' and the feared selves being 'the alone self, the depressed self, the incompetent self, the alcoholic self, the unemployed self, or the bag lady self'. However, they did not elaborate on the meaning of the selves that we could become. According to Dörnyei (2009a), these selves refer to our expected selves; the selves that we are likely to become. Among the other possible selves that Markus and Nurius (1986: 958) mentioned in their paper were the ought selves which they defined as 'an image of self held by another'.

Possible selves, especially the ideal selves and ought selves, are often called future self-guides since they have the capacity to regulate behaviour. Higgins and his associates (e.g. Higgins, 1987, 1998; Higgins et al., 1985; Higgins et al., 1994) have conducted a great deal of research which demonstrated that learners' ideal selves act as academic self-guides. It is noteworthy that Higgins's work on selves precedes that of Markus and

Nurius and that the two key components of Higgins's theory of possible selves (e.g. Higgins, 1987; Higgins *et al.*, 1985) are the ideal self and the ought self, which he defined more precisely than Markus and Nurius. According to Higgins (1987: 320), the ideal self refers to the 'representation of the attributes that someone would ideally like to possess (i.e. a representation of hopes, aspirations, or wishes)' and the ought self is defined as the 'representation of the attributes that someone believes you should or ought to possess (i.e., a representation of someone's sense of your duty, obligations, or responsibilities)'.

The Ideal L2 self is a central component of the construct of L2 motivation within Dörnyei's L2 Motivational Self System which consists of three dimensions: the Ideal L2 self, the Ought-to L2 self and the L2 learning experience. The Ideal L2 self as defined by Dörnyei (2009a: 29) is 'the L2-specific facet of one's ideal self'. According to Dörnyei (2009a: 29), the Ought-to L2 self is defined as 'the attributes that one believes one ought to possess (i.e. various duties, obligations, or responsibilities) in order to avoid possible negative outcomes'. The L2 learning experience refers to 'situation-specific motives related to the immediate learning environment and experience' (Dörnyei, 2009a: 29).

Since our possible selves are perceptions we hold of ourselves in the future, they include images and in this way are related to vision. Marilyn King, a former Olympic athlete said that it is not will-power and determination that enables Olympic athletes to work so hard. 'It's the vision. It's the power of an image that inspires great passion and excitement – so much so that you have enormous energy to do what you want' (Murphey, 2006: 95).

It has been found that nine conditions are required in order for future self-guides to exert their full motivational capacity. Firstly, the L2 learner should have a desired future self-image. Ruvolo and Markus (1992) found that there are differences in how easily people can generate a positive possible self. Therefore, it is not expected that everyone will possess a developed ideal or ought self-guide.

Secondly, the future self should be sufficiently different from the current self. The L2 learner should be aware of a gap between his/her current and future selves in order to feel that an increased effort in learning the L2 is necessary.

Thirdly, the future self-image should be elaborate and vivid. Markus and Ruvolo (1989: 228) remarked that the more specific and vivid one's positive possible selves are, 'the more one's current state can be made similar to the desired state'. They concluded that the more elaborated the possible self is in terms of imaginal representations, the more motivationally effective it will be.

The fourth condition is that the future self-guides should be plausible. Ruvolo and Markus (1992) affirmed that possible selves must be perceived as being plausible in order to have their full impact on motivation. Therefore, in terms of motivational strategies employing imagery, it is important that the imagery be presented in a realistic manner.

The fifth condition is that the future self-image is not perceived as comfortably certain. The L2 learner must believe that the future self-image will not automatically occur without a significant increase in effort. Oyserman and James (2009) point out that effort will not be exerted if the attainment of the future self is too likely or too unlikely, which takes into account the condition about plausibility as well.

The sixth condition is that there should be harmony between the ideal and ought selves. According to Dörnyei (2009a: 20), effective possible selves 'should feel congruent with important social identities' because a clash between the future self-guides could have a negative impact on motivation. For example, one's ideal self could be to excel in one's studies, but one's ought self, especially for adolescents, may contain views from peers that being popular does not involve academic achievement. Oyserman et al. (2006) discovered that among school children, negative group images of academic achievement are often highly accessible and conflict with academic self-guides. The researchers suggested that the most effective strategy to increase the motivation towards academic achievement is to augment the perceived congruence between the academic possible selves and social identity.

The seventh condition that is required for the future self-guides to exert their full motivational capacity is for them to be activated. Sherrill and Hoyle (2006) affirm that possible selves need to be activated in order to become a part of the working self-concept, so that they can have an impact on behaviour.

The eighth condition is that procedural strategies to achieve language learning goals are in place. Oyserman et al. (2006) state that future self-guides will only be effective if they contain plausible and specific action plans that are automatically cued by images. Therefore, according to Dörnyei (2009a: 21) 'effective future self-guides need to come as part of a "package", consisting of an imagery component and a repertoire of appropriate plans, scripts and self-regulatory strategies'.

The ninth condition is that the desired self is offset by the feared self. Oyserman and Markus (1990) proposed that a hoped for possible self will have maximal motivational effectiveness when it is offset or balanced by a countervailing feared self in the same domain. They argued that this kind of balance would create an optimal motivational situation because there would be both a goal to achieve and a goal to avoid.

The motivational programme that I designed and that I will describe in the following section was the first one that applied the L2 Motivational Self System with the purpose of developing an ideal language self by generating a language learning vision and through imagery enhancement. It was an application of the L2 Motivational Self System since I motivated learners of English by enhancing their vision of their Ideal L2 self and designed the programme in such a way as to meet the nine conditions that I mentioned above.

Design

The main objectives of my programme were to motivate my participants to put more time and effort into learning English (1) by enhancing their vision of their Ideal L2 self; (2) helping them to develop clear and specific goals and action plans in order to attain their Ideal L2 self; (3) helping them to create action plans to achieve their goals and (4) offsetting their Ideal L2 self with their Feared L2 self. I also examined the temporal development of L2 motivation as well as the future self-guides.

My programme included some components that were based on Oyserman's (2003, see also Oyserman et al., 2002) nine-week possible selves intervention programme, called the School-to-Jobs Programme, involving 62 African American secondary school students in which she developed an after-school programme to enhance the students' abilities to imagine themselves as successful adults and connect these future images to current school involvement. The School-to-Jobs Programme had the three following main objectives: (1) to help youth develop proximal and distal goals as well as strategies to achieve these goals, (2) to increase the youth's concern about school and create a sense of academic efficacy and (3) to develop positive communication skills and active listening. The activities in the intervention that I will be describing below were created in order to improve the students' academic self as a short term goal and connect that self to their ideal adult future selves.

In one of the first sessions, in order to enhance the students' vision of their ideal selves, they were asked to choose at least 10 photographs out of 200 that were provided portraying successful African American adults that they would like to become in four life domains: work, family, community and lifestyle. They were instructed to state the age that they think they will be when they will achieve these ideal selves and explain each of their choices to the rest of the class. The photos depicted positive and plausible future self-guides, which was an important aspect of the intervention. In addition, the photos portrayed successful African Americans in order to ensure harmony between the ideal self and the ought self.

In a follow-up session, students were given four sheets to fill out which each contained one of the four domains mentioned above. They were asked to write down as many goals as they could for each domain as well as the name of a positive and a negative role model in each domain. The positive role model served to activate their vision of their ideal self and the negative role model activated their vision of their feared self, in this way creating a balance between them.

In the next session, students were instructed to draw a timeline to depict their future. They had to include their future goals, forks in the road when one or more options were available, obstacles they thought they might encounter and strategies to overcome these obstacles. The students were again encouraged to consider the domains of work, family, community and lifestyle. Thinking about obstacles and ways to overcome them taught the students to think about their future in a realistic manner.

In one of the following sessions, students were asked to write down specific action plans to achieve the goals they had noted on their timeline in each of the four domains. They were instructed to write down which actions they would take to achieve their goals and when they intended to perform these actions. Two of the sessions focused on the students' possible selves. In the first of these sessions, the students had to list their ideal and feared next year selves as well as the strategies they would adopt to attain their ideal selves and avoid their feared selves. In the second session, they were instructed to list their ideal and feared adult selves as well as the strategies they would employ to achieve their ideal selves and avoid their feared selves. Following sessions included discussions about university entrance requirements and careers, so that students could develop realistic strategies to achieve their goals.

The main findings were that the intervention helped the students to develop more balanced possible selves, gain strategies to attain these possible selves and link the possible selves to the effort that they put into their studies. It increased their concern about school and also helped them to develop positive communication skills as well as active listening. In the section on the structure of my programme, I will indicate which parts of my programme were based on Oyserman's programme.

My intervention programme and follow-up interviews lasted a total of four months. The programme consisted of a series of four two-hour workshops. During the first hour of each workshop, I taught my participants ways to improve their English skills, make new friends in Britain, prepare for job interviews and write a CV. I chose these topics because most of my participants indicated on a preliminary questionnaire that they would like to learn more about them in order to adapt better to living in Britain. In the second hour of each workshop, I used motivational strategies that I will describe in the section on the structure of my programme in order to enhance my participants' vision of their Ideal L2 self and motivate them to devote more time and effort to learning English. Due to space limitations, I will focus on the motivational part of my programme in the rest of this chapter. Readers interested in the details of the programme may refer to my thesis and an article that I wrote with my colleague (Magid, 2011; Magid & Chan, 2012).

Participants

The intervention programme involved 31 participants (14 males and 17 females) who were international students from cities all over mainland China taking a wide variety of courses at a British university. They ranged in age from 20 to 40 years with a mean age of 24 years. There were 17 participants doing a bachelor's degree, 12 doing a master's degree and 2 working on a PhD. Their English language proficiency ranged from intermediate to advanced levels.

Instruments

The intervention programme employed two questionnaires. The first questionnaire was administered before the programme was designed and consisted of questions about the learners' background information as well as questions about the kinds of topics that they would be interested in studying during the workshops. The second questionnaire was administered at the very beginning of the first workshop immediately after the participants signed the consent form and at the end of the final workshop. This questionnaire was composed of five items drawn from Taguchi et al. (2009) which measure the strength of the vision of the Ideal L2 self. Two interviews were conducted with each participant after the end of the workshops. The two interview schedules consisted of 20 questions in the first interview and 30 in the second one. The first three questions of the first interview measured changes in the participants' motivation towards learning English, their goals for learning English, their goals for the future, their Ideal L2 self and their confidence in their English. The remaining questions served the purpose of gaining feedback from the participants about the programme and evaluating the effect that the different activities from the programme had on them.

The first question of the second interview again addressed changes in the participants' motivation towards learning English, their goals for learning English, their goals for the future, their Ideal L2 self, and their confidence in their English. Most of the remaining questions focused on vision, imagination, imagery and goals. For example, there were questions to assess how the participants' vision of their Ideal L2 self and their goals for learning English had changed as a result of the programme and the impact that their vision of their Ideal L2 self had on their motivation towards learning English. I asked about the effect that the scripted imagery used in the programme had on the participants' emotions, confidence level and motivation towards learning English. The last few questions were about the participants' reasons for learning English and how the amount of time and effort that the participants devoted to studying English had changed as a result of the programme. Having a qualitative aspect to my research in the form of interviews enabled me to gain a deeper understanding of the changes in my participants' motivation towards studying English.

The structure of the programme

I will briefly describe the main components of the workshops by presenting the structure of the programme which was divided into four units. In the first unit, I asked my participants to write about their goals for their future jobs, relationships and lifestyle as well as their Ideal L2 self in each of those domains in order to help them create a vision of their Ideal L2 self. Each of the participants was instructed to write down as many goals as they could think of for each of the domains. They were also asked to write down the names of positive and negative role models for each domain. This task was based on one of Oyserman's (2003) activities that was used in the School-to-Jobs Programme in order to help the participants define their goals in different areas of their life.

In the first unit, I also asked the participants to listen to two scripted imagery situations about themselves using English effectively in the future in order to strengthen their vision of their Ideal L2 self by making it more elaborate and vivid. In every unit, I asked the participants to imagine situations that I wrote based on interviews I conducted with participants in a previous study (Magid, 2009) about the changes in their Ideal L2 self and motivation over time. These scripted imagery situations were used to enhance my participants' vision of their Ideal L2 self and their Feared L2 self. Please refer to Appendix A for an example of a positive situation and Appendix B for an example of a negative situation in the domain of career that I used during my programme.

In the second unit, after reading a positive situation to my participants about their Ideal L2 self, I asked them to draw a timeline and indicate in which year they expect to achieve their goals for their Ideal L2 self, career, relationships and lifestyle by noting down everything they hope will happen. They were also asked to indicate forks in the road to illustrate the various options they may have even if they don't achieve their primary goals in order to make their vision of their Ideal L2 self plausible.

In the third unit, I read a positive and a negative situation to the participants to offset their Ideal L2 self with their Feared L2 self. I then instructed the participants to develop action plans in order to achieve their major objectives for their Ideal L2 self. Then, they had to decide on a date when they would start working on their objectives as well as when and how they would review their progress.

In the fourth unit, I read a positive and a negative situation to the participants. Then, I asked them to write about their Feared L2 self by describing the kind of person they were afraid of becoming if their English would not improve. They were also asked to write down ways in which they could avoid becoming that kind of person. The purpose of this activity was again to offset the Ideal L2 self with the Feared L2 self and to make their vision of their Feared L2 self more clear and specific. The timeline, action plans and Feared L2 self activities resembled Oyserman's (2003) activities that I described in the Design section of the chapter. However, her activities did not deal with possible L2 selves.

Throughout the workshops, I continued to activate my participants' vision of their Ideal L2 self with excerpts from the film *Dead Poets' Society* (Haft *et al.*, 1989), poetry and music. For example, I shared the poem, 'The Road Not Taken' by Frost (1916) and the song, 'Father and Son' by Stevens (1975) with the participants in order to encourage them to try to make their dreams come true and follow their heart. I believe that even if people have a clear vision of their Ideal L2 self, they need to have the courage to attain it, especially if it clashes with their Ought-to L2 self. I also activated their vision of their Ideal L2 self during the time that the workshops were delivered and after they ended by asking them to listen to recordings at home on a daily basis of the situations that they had listened to in class and that they had written themselves.

Procedure

The data were collected in England in 2008 and 2009. My participants had no difficulty in answering the interview questions or understanding the activities from the programme because they were all advanced learners of English. I measured the strength of my participants' vision of their Ideal L2 self at the very beginning of the programme and at the end to examine the impact that the intervention programme had on their vision of their Ideal L2 self. I also conducted two semi-structured interviews with each participant. The first interview was given six weeks after the programme had ended and the second interview was given six weeks after the first interview. Both interviews lasted about one hour. Although there were fewer questions in the first interview, I spent more time during that interview reviewing the participants' work on the four activities (i.e. the goals activity, time-line, action plans and Feared L2 self activity) that I had asked them to do during the workshops.

Data analysis

The data that I collected were both quantitative and qualitative. The quantitative data consisted of my participants' ratings of the strength of their vision of their Ideal L2 self on the pre-workshop and post-workshop questionnaires. In order to analyse the quantitative data, I conducted a paired-samples t-test on the data from both questionnaires to assess whether or not the changes in the strength of my participants' vision of their Ideal L2 self were statistically significant.

The qualitative data consisted of my participants' responses to the two post-workshop interviews as well as responses from a retrospective interview containing their explanations of their ratings on the question-naires which measured the strength of their vision of their Ideal L2 self. The interviews were transcribed, resulting in a corpus of more than 200,000 words. The interviews were coded into the following four broad categories: (1) An Evaluation of the Programme, (2) The Vision, (3) The Activities and (4) Recommendations for Future Programmes. The emerg-ing themes that were related to the evaluation of the programme were the general benefits of the programme for the participants, the effect of the programme on their motivation towards learning English, the effect of the programme on confidence and the relationship between motiva-tion and confidence. The emerging themes pertaining to the vision were the relationship between vision and motivation, the relationship between vision and confidence, support for the nine conditions which enhance the motivational impact of the future self-guides, as well as the effect of the positive and negative situations on vision, goals, imagination and emotions. The emerging themes within the activities category were the effect of the activities on vision, goals, imagination and emotions. The emerging themes that corresponded to recommendations for future programmes were recommendations for the structure of future pro-grammes as well as the possible situations and activities that may be used when designing future programmes. A further in-depth analysis and categorisation was then carried out to investigate the interaction within and between the major themes by using NVivo version 8.0 (see Magid, 2011 for further details on the statistical analyses and research methodology).

Results

Firstly, I would like to mention that there was a significant increase in the strength of my participants' Ideal L2 self as a result of my programme. A paired-samples t-test was conducted on the data from the pre-workshop and post-workshop questionnaires to evaluate the impact of the intervention programme on the strength of my participants' Ideal L2 self. There was a statistically significant increase in their Ideal L2 self from Time 1 before the programme began (M = 5.30, SD = .82) to Time 2 which was after the programme ended (M = 5.46, SD = .53), $t(30)$ = –4.40, p < .0005 (two-tailed).

The mean increase in the strength of the Ideal L2 self was .43 with a 95% confidence interval ranging from –.63 to –.23. The eta squared statistic (.39) indicated a large effect size which demonstrates that my programme substantially strengthened my participants' Ideal L2 self. This result proves that it is possible to enhance L2 learners' vision of their Ideal L2 self through visualisation training.

The main findings from the interview data revealed interesting relationships between my participants' motivation, confidence, their vision of their Ideal L2 self and their goals for learning English. I will illustrate each of my main findings with key extracts which I have selected from the interview data. All of the participants felt more motivated to learn English and more confident in their English after they finished the programme. Their increased confidence enabled them to imagine themselves more clearly using English in their future. More than 80% of the participants reported that feeling more confident in their English made them feel more motivated to learn English. More than half of the participants reported that feeling more motivated to learn English made them feel more confident in their English.

More than 80% of the participants put more time and effort into learning English after taking part in the programme. During the post-workshop interviews, I asked them if they exerted more of an effort towards learning English and devoted more time to learning English because of my programme. I have summarised their responses in Table 18.1. Please note that the amount of time they put into learning English does not include the time they spend on their coursework. It refers specifically to time spent on learning English outside of their classes. Table 18.1 illustrates that 28 out of 31 participants exerted more effort towards learning English and 25 participants devoted more time to learning English as a result of my programme. All names are pseudonyms to ensure anonymity.

In the following interview extract, Amy told me that not only did she become more motivated to learn English because of my programme, but that her motivation is more constant:

> My motivation would sometimes disappear before I took your classes, but after taking them, it exists more often. It persists more. (Amy)

Most of the participants found that both the positive and negative situations motivated them to learn English. As Evan explains below, imagining the positive and negative situations helped him to realise the importance of English and motivated him to study English hard.

> The most impressive thing in your classes is that you told me to imagine the positive and negative situations. I never took those measures before. They made me realise more directly the importance of English. I enjoyed imagining those situations and they motivated me to study English harder! (Evan)

As Justin explains in the following interview extract, he felt more motivated to learn English when he realised that the difference between the two types of situations depends on how hard he will study English as well as his course in the next few years:

> When I realised that the difference between these two situations depends on my actions in the following two years, I decided to focus

Table 18.1 Effort and time devoted to learning English after the programme

Participants	Effort after programme	Time after programme (hours per week)
Charlie, Emma, Sophie	Same	Same
James, Ken, Carol	More	Same
Jason, Kurt	More	2 hours more
Jane, Marina	More	3 hours more
Amy, Bill, Crystal, Justin, Karen, Linda	More	3.5 hours more
Nancy, Ray	More	5 hours more
Betty, Evan, Jessie, Joy, Maria, Paul Robin, Susie, Tammy	More	7 hours more
Brian	More	9 hours more
Annabella, Kevin, Leo	More	14 hours more

most of my time on studying English and my course. I never spend any time playing computer games anymore. (Justin)

It was found that the situations had a long-term impact on the motivation of some of my participants towards learning English. For example, Paul told me that the situations he listened to during my workshops still motivate him.

I was changed by the class and I imagine situations without thinking. Though it has been a long time since I took your classes, the situations you read to me still motivate me to learn English. (Paul)

The positive and negative situations also had a long-term effect on Ken's motivation towards learning English as he describes below.

The recordings affected me not only for a short term; not only during the session. I always think about them, so they are in my mind. The situations affect me by motivating me to study English harder and warning me not to be so lazy; not to do bad things to ruin my career and my future. (Ken)

Kevin told me that what he remembers the most about my workshops are the positive and negative situations that I described to him when he said, 'They have stayed in my mind forever'. The situations were more motivating when they were plausible and matched the participants' goals. Nearly 80% of the participants reported that the emotions caused by the positive and negative situations motivated them to learn English. The positive situations gave most of the participants confidence in their English. The negative situations gave them pressure to learn English. Both confidence and pressure motivated the participants to learn English. As is illustrated by the following interview extract, there was a long-term impact from the positive situations on Robin's confidence in his English:

Listening to the positive situations gave me confidence in my English which I now feel all the time! (Robin)

When I asked Evan which of the two situations motivated him most to study English hard, he replied in the following way:

I think that both of them played an equally important role. I need both of them to create a balance! Imagining the positive situations makes me feel excited to study English. When I feel very satisfied with my English, I need some pressure from negative situations to motivate me to study English. (Evan)

Sophie also said that both of the situations motivated her to study English hard.

> The positive ones gave me confidence in my English and helped me set my goals for learning English. The negative ones reminded me that if I don't study English hard, I won't succeed. (Sophie)

Many of my participants also mentioned that they gained confidence in their English because my programme helped them to develop clear goals for learning English and in other aspects of their life. Linda told me that my classes helped her to learn how to set up her goals for learning English and for her future. When her goals for learning English became more clear, she became more confident in her English, which suggests a relationship between the clarity of goals and confidence.

Most of my participants believe that motivation and confidence mutually affect each other. Amy explained the relationship between motivation and confidence quite well in the following interview extract:

> If I feel confident, I will think that I can improve my English by studying hard, so my confidence pushes me to study English hard. When I feel motivated to learn English, I will study English hard and my English will improve which will make me feel more confident in my English. (Amy)

It is interesting to note that confidence gives Nancy motivation towards learning English because it makes her feel that the positive situations I described in the workshops are possible for her to achieve. This supports the plausibility condition that I described in the section on the conditions that enhance the motivational impact of the future self-guides.

> I feel confident in my English when I imagine the positive situations. The confidence makes me feel that one day those situations might come true and that motivates me. (Nancy)

Crystal's confidence in her English makes her feel more motivated to learn English because her confidence helps her to make her goals for learning English and her vision of her Ideal L2 self more clear as she explains below.

> When I feel more confident in my English, it makes me feel more motivated to learn English because I can see the goal I can achieve. Then the ideal vision is not so far away. (Crystal)

The extract above supports the condition that the future self-image should be elaborate and vivid in order to exert a maximum impact on the motivation towards L2 learning. Having examined the benefits of my intervention programme, the effect of the programme on motivation and confidence and the relationship between motivation and confidence, I will focus on the visionary aspect of my programme in the following section.

The relationship between vision and motivation

My participants' vision of their Ideal L2 self and their Feared L2 self motivated them to study English hard via the powerful emotions that they elicited. For many participants, their vision made them feel energetic and excited, which provided them with the energy to study English hard. In the following extract, Susie explains how her vision of her Ideal L2 self motivates her to learn English:

It can make me feel very energetic and I want to study English hard to achieve this vision. The motivation comes from a deep part of my mind and my heart! (Susie)

Evan's vision of his Ideal L2 self motivates him to learn English because it makes him feel excited and gives him a desire to achieve his vision as is illustrated in the following extract:

When I think about my vision, I feel excited and I have a strong desire to make it come true. The feeling of excitement motivates me to learn English. I realised that I need to put more time and effort into learning English to achieve my vision. That's the way that my vision encourages me! (Evan)

My participants reported that their vision of their Ideal L2 self motivates them to learn English by giving them goals to achieve, which illustrates the close relationship between vision and goals.

Without goals, I don't have motivation. My vision of my Ideal L2 self gives me goals for learning English. Those goals motivate me to learn English. (Sophie)

On the topic of goals, it is noteworthy that the clearer one's vision of one's goals is for learning English, the more motivating they are as Charlie revealed during his interview.

I feel more motivated to study English hard because my goals are becoming clearer and I can see my goals, so I have a direction to work towards, which makes me want to study English harder. (Charlie)

The programme made my participants' vision of their Ideal L2 self and their goals for learning English more clear and specific, which motivated them to learn English. Having goals for learning English gave some participants more confidence in their English and pressure to learn English. It was found that for some participants, their confidence in their English and their vision of their Ideal L2 self had a mutual effect on each other. For example, Brian's confidence in his English helped him to clearly imagine himself using English well in the future. At the same time, his clear vision of himself speaking English fluently in the future gave him more confidence in his English.

For other participants, their vision of their Ideal L2 self gave them more confidence in their English. James provided the following explanation of the impact of the vision of one's Ideal L2 self on one's confidence level:

> Imagining the Ideal L2 self really helps to build confidence in English. If you guide people to think a lot about what kind of ideal future they could have, they will discover their own advantages and then become more and more confident. I think that discovering your advantages and thinking about your ideal situation are both extremely beneficial in building confidence. (James)

Tammy's vision of her Ideal L2 self gave her confidence in her English because it was plausible since it contained realistic goals as she explains below.

> My vision of my Ideal L2 self depends on what I think I can achieve. If I think I can achieve my goals, then I have the confidence that I can do that! (Tammy)

The extract above suggests that the more realistic language learners' goals are, the more confident they will feel that they can achieve them. It is reminiscent of one of the conditions for the motivational capacity of the future self-guides that I described, namely that the future self-guides should be plausible.

More than half of the participants reported that their imagination improved as a result of the programme. In other words, they use their imagination now more often than they did before they took my workshops and are able to imagine situations related to learning English, how they will use English in their future and their future in general. My participants told me that their imagination improved because they had many opportunities to practise using it during my workshops when I asked them to imagine the situations that I described above as well as their own positive and negative situations related to using English in their future. This suggests that imagination can be enhanced with practice.

Some participants mentioned various benefits of using their imagination such as enabling them to become more creative and prepare for the future. More than 80% of the participants can imagine situations, especially those involving English, in more detail than they could before the programme. The following extract from Kurt's second interview represents the thoughts of many of my participants.

> My imagination of how I can use English in the future became better and more detailed because I had the chance to practise using my imagination in your classes. Now, I can imagine things on more levels and in a more detailed way than before I took your classes. I have very strong images in my mind sometimes! (Kurt)

More than half of the participants now use their imagination to motivate themselves to learn English. Although I never explicitly told my participants during the workshops that they can imagine their Ideal L2 self and their Feared L2 self in order to motivate themselves to learn English, I was astonished that many of them automatically started to use this motivational strategy without being asked to do so. Evan told me that imagining positive and negative situations of himself using English helps him a great deal to learn English, especially when he feels tired of studying.

> Sometimes when I am lazy and I don't want to study English, I think about a situation in which one day I will be able to speak English fluently like a native speaker. I will think how exciting life will be if I can learn English well. I use my imagination as a method to encourage myself to learn English. (Evan)

These findings lead me to conclude that it is possible to motivate language learners by enhancing their vision of their Ideal L2 self.

Additional benefits of the programme

Although the main objectives of my programme were to motivate my participants to study English by enhancing their vision of their Ideal L2 self and by making their goals for learning English more clear and specific, there were many other positive outcomes from the programme that I will describe in this section. Firstly, my participants reported that their speaking and listening improved and that their vocabulary expanded as a result of my programme. Besides improving their English, the participants acquired many new methods to develop their speaking, listening, reading and vocabulary. More than 80% of the participants are using these new methods to learn English.

The workshops helped my participants to become more aware of the importance of English for their future. Linda said that my programme helped her to understand the importance of English and made her goals for learning English more clear.

> Once I realised that English was important and my goals for learning English became more clear, I realised that I should grab the chance to speak English more and set up my goals for the future. (Linda)

My programme also helped to improve my participants' attitudes towards learning English, which made them want to devote more time and effort to learning English. Nancy told me that the workshops made her attitudes towards learning English more positive. She said that her attitudes towards learning English were quite negative before she took my classes. Now, she really wants to study English hard and is very eager to speak English fluently. The findings demonstrated the power of emotions on the motivation towards language learning, which supports Dörnyei's (2009b) proposal of a dynamic tripartite framework composed of three interacting systems – motivational, emotional and cognitive – that could be used to understand the individual differences of language learners.

Conclusion

One of the main findings with regard to my intervention programme was that there was a significant increase in the strength of my participants' Ideal L2 self as a result of my programme. This finding showed that it is possible to enhance L2 learners' vision of their Ideal L2 self through visualisation training and that strengthening of the vision can be done in a relatively short amount of time. The enhancement of language learners' vision of their Ideal L2 self through the use of imagery is an effective motivational strategy that may be employed by language teachers, writers of language textbooks and language learners themselves.

My programme made most of my participants more motivated to learn English and all of them more confident in their English for the following reasons. Firstly, my programme enhanced their vision of their Ideal L2 self. Secondly, their vision of their Ideal L2 self and their goals for learning English became more clear and specific due to my programme. Furthermore, since my programme helped my participants to develop clear goals, they became more confident in their English.

With regard to the relationship between motivation and confidence, I found that motivation and confidence mutually affect each other. The findings demonstrated the key role that confidence in the target language plays in the language learning process. It motivates language learners to continue improving their target language and helps to make their vision of their Ideal L2 self more clear, which was also found to be motivating.

My findings supported the conditions that are required in order for the future self-guides to exert their full motivational capacity, namely that the future self-image should be elaborate and vivid, the future self-guides should be regularly activated and plausible. They should contain specific action plans that are automatically cued by images and the hoped for possible self should be balanced by a feared self in the same domain. It was found that language learners are motivated to learn their target language when they have clear and specific language learning goals.

Besides increasing my participants' motivation towards learning English and their confidence in their English, there were other benefits of the programme that I would like to mention. Most of my participants' imagination improved as a result of my programme. This finding demonstrates that it is possible to improve one's imagination through visualisation training. My participants' speaking and listening improved and their vocabulary expanded. They learned new ways to improve their English, how to write a CV, covering letter and prepare for job interviews. In addition, my participants became more aware of the importance of English and their attitudes towards learning English became more positive. My programme can be easily implemented by language teachers and offers a wide variety of benefits to language learners ranging from increasing their motivation and their confidence in learning languages to improving their L2 proficiency and their attitudes towards learning languages. The programme does not need to be long in order to be effective and all of the activities in the programme are done in the target language, which allows learners to improve their L2 proficiency while at the same time becoming more motivated and confident. I strongly believe that there is a great potential to develop many more of these types of programmes based on Dörnyei's (2009a) L2 Motivation Self System that will be suitable for language learners of all ages, levels of proficiency and target languages.

The main limitation of my intervention programme was that there were not enough visualisation training activities to enable the participants to practise using their imagination before they were exposed to the scripted imagery situations. This was due to the fact that the programme only contained four workshops. Therefore, I suggest that future programmes for university students should consist of six workshops instead of four. The first two workshops could focus on activities to stimulate and train the participants' imagination such as the ones that may be found in Arnold *et al.* (2007), which is a fascinating teachers' resource book on using imagery to teach English.

Although in my programme I was able to compare the strength of my participants' vision of their Ideal L2 self before and after the programme, another method to assess the effect of the programme on the participants could be to have a control group that would only be given the part of the workshops not dealing with the enhancement of the future self-guides through visualisation and an experimental group that would receive the full treatment. It would be important to ensure that the strength of the vision of the Ideal L2 self of the members of both groups is similar before they begin to participate in the programme. In addition, I would suggest that the groups be matched in terms of their L2 motivation, confidence in their L2 and their attitudes towards learning the L2. Then, it would be possible to evaluate the impact of the programme on all of these factors as well.

I think that if the programme would be designed for primary or secondary school students, it could be even longer since these students tend to have more free time than university students, but of course this depends on the country where they live. Such a programme could be eight weeks long and the first four weeks could be devoted to visualisation training activities. I have already developed a motivational programme (Magid, 2014) for year 5 primary school students in Singapore and found that eight weeks was sufficient to motivate the children, make them feel more confident in their English and improve their attitudes towards learning English. I would like to see programmes designed for learners of languages besides English as well as for working professionals. My dream is to collaborate with linguists, L2 teachers and L2 students all over the world in order to create programmes that will make the process of learning languages more motivating and enjoyable. I hope that I will be able to collaborate with others by using one of my second languages: Chinese, French or Russian. In that sense, I will achieve my vision of my Ideal L2 self!

References

Al-Shehri, A.S. (2009) Motivation and vision: The relation between the ideal L2 self, imagination and visual style. In Z. Dörnyei and E. Ushioda (eds) *Motivation, Language Identity and the L2 Self* (pp. 164–171). Bristol: Multilingual Matters.

Arnold, J., Puchta, H. and Rinvolucri, M. (2007) *Imagine that! Mental Imagery in the EFL Classroom*. Cambridge: Cambridge University Press.

Chang, L.Y-H (2010) Group processes and EFL learners' motivation: A study of group dynamics in EFL classrooms. *TESOL Quarterly* 44 (1), 129–154.

Cheng, H.-F. and Dörnyei, Z. (2007) The use of motivational strategies in language instruction: The case of EFL teaching in Taiwan. *Innovation in Language Learning and Teaching* 1 (1), 153–174.

Csizér, K., and Kormos, J. (2009) Learning experiences, selves and motivated learning behaviour: A comparative analysis of structural models for Hungarian secondary and university learners of English. In Z. Dörnyei and E. Ushioda (eds) *Motivation, Language Identity and the L2 Self* (pp. 98–119). Bristol: Multilingual Matters.

Dörnyei, Z. (2001) *Motivational Strategies in the Language Classroom*. Cambridge: Cambridge University Press.

Dörnyei, Z. (2009a) The L2 motivational self system. In Z. Dörnyei and E. Ushioda (eds) *Motivation, Language Identity and the L2 Self* (pp. 9–42). Bristol: Multilingual Matters.

Dörnyei, Z. (2009b) *The Psychology of Second Language Acquisition*. Oxford: Oxford University Press.

Dörnyei, Z. and Csizér, K. (1998) Ten commandments for motivating language learners: Results of an empirical study. *Language Teaching Research* 2 (3), 203–229.

Dörnyei, Z. and Ushioda, E. (2009) *Motivation, Language Identity and the L2 Self*. Bristol: Multilingual Matters.

Dörnyei, Z. and Ushioda, E. (2011) *Teaching and Researching Motivation* (2nd edn). Harlow: Pearson Education.

Frost, R. (1916) *Mountain Interval*. New York: Holt & Company.

Guilloteaux, M.J. and Dörnyei, Z. (2008) Motivating language learners: A classroom-oriented investigation of the effects of motivational strategies on student motivation. *TESOL Quarterly* 42 (1), 55–77.

Hadfield, J. and Dörnyei, Z. (2013) *Motivating Learning*. Harlow: Longman.

Haft, S., Thomas, T. and Witt. P.J. (Producers), Weir, P. (Director). (1989) *Dead Poets Society [Motion picture]*. United States: Touchstone Pictures.

Hall, E. and Hall, C. (1988) *Human Relations in Education*. London: Routledge.

Hall, E., Hall, C. and Leech, A. (1990) *Scripted Fantasy in the Classroom*. London: Routledge.

Higgins, E.T. (1987) Self-discrepancy: A theory relating self and affect. *Psychological Review* 94 (3), 319–340.

Higgins, E.T. (1998) Promotion and prevention: Regulatory focus as a motivational principle. *Advances in Experimental Social Psychology* 30, 1–46.

Higgins, E.T., Klein, R. and Strauman, T. (1985) Self-concept discrepancy theory: A psychological model for distinguishing among different aspects of depression and anxiety. *Social Cognition* 3 (1), 51–76.

Higgins, E.T., Roney, C.J.R., Crowe, E. and Hymes, C. (1994) Ideal versus ought predilections for approach and avoidance: Distinct self-regulatory systems. *Journal of Personality and Social Psychology* 66 (2), 276–286.

Hornby, G., Hall, C. and Hall, E. (2003) *Counselling Pupils in Schools: Skills and Strategies*. London: Routledge.

Magid, M. (2009) The L2 motivational self system from a Chinese perspective: A mixed methods study. *Journal of Applied Linguistics* 6 (1), 69–90.

Magid, M. (2011) A validation and application of the L2 motivational self system among Chinese learners of English. PhD Thesis, University of Nottingham.

Magid, M. (2014) An application of the L2 Motivational Self System to motivate elementary school English learners in Singapore. *Journal of Education and Training Studies* 2 (1), 228–237.

Magid, M. and Chan, L. (2012) Motivating English learners by helping them to visualise their ideal L2 self: Lessons from two motivational programmes. *Innovation in Language Learning and Teaching* 6 (2), 113–125.

Markus, H. and Nurius, P. (1986) Possible selves. *American Psychologist* 41 (9), 954–969.

Markus, H.R. and Ruvolo, A. (1989) Possible selves: Personalized representations of goals. In L. A. Pervin (ed.) *Goal Concepts in Personality and Social Psychology* (pp. 211–241). Hillsdale, NJ: Lawrence Erlbaum.

Murphey, T. (2006) *Language Hungry: An Introduction to Language Learning Fun and Self-esteem*. London: Helbling Languages.

Oxford, R.L. and Shearin, J. (1994) Language learning motivation: Expanding the theoretical framework. *The Modern Language Journal* 78 (1), 12–28.

Oyserman, D. (2003) *School-to-jobs Facilitators Manual.* University of Michigan: Ann Arbor.

Oyserman, D., Bybee, D. and Terry, K. (2006) Possible selves and academic outcomes: How and when possible selves impel action. *Journal of Personality and Social Psychology* 91 (1), 188–204.

Oyserman, D. and James, L. (2009) Possible selves: From content to process. In K. Markman, W.M.P. Klein and J.A. Suhr (eds) *The Handbook of Imagination and Mental Stimulation* (pp. 373-394). New York: Psychology Press.

Oyserman, D. and Markus, H.R. (1990) Possible selves and delinquency. *Journal of Personality and Social Psychology* 59 (1), 112–125.

Oyserman, D., Terry, K. and Bybee, D. (2002) A possible selves intervention to enhance school involvement. *Journal of Adolescence* 25 (3), 313–326.

Ruvolo, A.P. and Markus, H.R. (1992) Possible selves and performance: The power of self-relevant imagery. *Social Cognition* 10 (1), 95–124.

Ryan, S. (2009) Self and identity in L2 motivation in Japan: The ideal L2 self and Japanese learners of English. In Z. Dörnyei and E. Ushioda (eds) *Motivation, Language Identity and the L2 Self* (pp. 120–143). Bristol: Multilingual Matters.

Sherrill, M.R. and Hoyle, R.H. (2006) Future orientation in the self-system: Possible selves, self-regulation, and behaviour. *Journal of Personality* 74 (6), 1673–1696.

Stevens, C. (1975) *Father and Son. On Cat Stevens Greatest Hits [CD]*. Santa Monica, CA: A & M Records.

Taguchi, T., Magid, M. and Papi, M. (2009) The L2 motivational self system among Japanese, Chinese, and Iranian learners of English: A comparative study. In Z. Dörnyei and E. Ushioda (eds) *Motivation, Language Identity and the L2 Self* (pp. 66–97). Bristol: Multilingual Matters.

Appendix A

Positive scripted imagery situation

The perfect job

Close your eyes. I would like you to imagine yourself five years from now as being very successful in your work thanks to your knowledge of English. One of the reasons why you have an important position, a high salary and a rewarding, interesting job is because of your excellent English. You were able to develop a wide professional network with international colleagues all over the world and work in an English environment where you need to use English all the time to communicate with your colleagues. You have a large office, a big comfortable house, take expensive vacations and are able to provide everything that your family needs.

You are able to take good care of your parents and this makes you feel very happy and proud. They have given you so much during their life and now you are able to pay them back. You have attained all of their expectations and even exceeded them. You always make a good impression on the people you meet at work and in your community because of your ability to speak English so fluently and all of your other skills. Your parents are very proud of you and talk about your success in front of their friends. In fact, they don't need to work anymore because they live such a comfortable life thanks to you. You have given them a lot of honour and have raised your whole family to a higher position in society. You also have a high position in society because of your knowledge and success and are part of a high social class.

Since you are one of the best English speakers in the company, you are very powerful and make many important decisions every day. You supervise your colleagues and tell them what they should do to improve their work. Everyone respects and admires you. Your plan in the next five years is to start your own business. You already have started to negotiate with possible business partners, many of whom are English-speaking people. You are excited about your bright future and are sure that all of your dreams will come true. Stay with this feeling of excitement as you open your eyes and come back to this room.

Appendix B

Negative scripted imagery situation

A boring job

Close your eyes. I would like you to imagine yourself five years from now doing a job that you really don't like. You were not able to get your dream job because your English wasn't good enough and now you have a boring job in China with a low salary. You work really long hours and often have to work on the weekend. You speak Chinese at work most of the time and are forgetting your English as well as much of the knowledge you gained at university. You feel like you have disappointed your parents. They spent so much money on your studies in England, but they feel like it was not worth it. You hoped that you would be able to pay them back for everything they gave you, but you cannot.

It's difficult for you to support yourself on your salary and you are not able to support your family. Your parents still need to keep working hard, even though they are not so young anymore. You need to live with your parents because you can't make enough money to buy your own place. You feel like you are a burden on your parents, which makes you feel ashamed. Your boss orders you around all day, but you must follow his orders since you are in a low position. You feel like you have no freedom to decide anything in your life. You wish you would have tried harder to improve your English while you were at university and gain more skills so you could find a better job, but now it is too late. Stay with this feeling for a moment before you open your eyes and come back to this room.

19 Effects of an Imagery Training Strategy on Chinese University Students' Possible Second Language Selves and Learning Experiences

Letty Chan

Introduction

The use of mental imagery is ubiquitous in human experience, from reminiscing about the past to anticipating the future. When we consciously engage in visualisation, it can improve our recall (e.g. de la Iglesia *et al.*, 2005), enhance interview performance (e.g. Knudstrup *et al.*, 2003), ease psychological distress (e.g. Hackmann *et al.*, 2011) and develop creativity (e.g. Finke, 1990). In relation to language learning, the use of imagery can improve listening comprehension (e.g. Center *et al.*, 1999), vocabulary learning (e.g. Cohen, 1987; Shen, 2010; Stevick, 1986) and writing (e.g. Jampole *et al.*, 1994). These studies highlight the various ways in which imagery can assist learners to acquire a second language (L2).

Indeed, imagery plays an important role in human emotion, cognition and behaviour, and a line of enquiry in psychology has been conducted to explore its impact. In comparing the effects of imagery and verbal processing, studies reveal that imagery can greatly influence people's affect. For example, given various negative and neutral scenarios, participants become significantly more anxious if they imagine fearful scenarios as compared to when they listen to the same scenarios and think about their meaning (Holmes & Mathews, 2005). A similar experiment, using positive scenarios, shows that participants' positive affect increases significantly in the imagery context (Holmes *et al.*, 2006).

Imagery not only influences human emotion but also cognition. When images are conjured up, goal-specific information becomes accessible in our cognitive system and, in turn, provides an impetus for action (Conway *et al.*, 2004) and increases people's motivation to achieve target goals (Anderson, 1983). Mental simulations also have various cognitive functions, such as increasing the perceived probability of an event occurring (Anderson *et al.*, 1980) and checking the viability of plans (Taylor & Schneider, 1989).

Finally, imagery's powerful effects on behaviour have also been supported in various studies. For example, Martin and Hall (1995) demonstrated the effect of imagery on beginner golfers' motivation to practise a golf putting task. The main findings were that the imagery group visualising positive performance spent the longest period of time practising golf putting of their own accord. Another study conducted by Knäuper *et al.* (2009) found that mental imagery can enhance motivation. That is, participants who were asked to employ mental imagery of the task were significantly more likely to complete the task than those who did not use imagery (see Dörnyei & Kubanyiova, 2014).

Possible Selves

Mental imagery has a close connection with another construct in psychology known as Possible Selves, which consists of cognitive components representing individuals' ideas of 'what they might become, what they would like to become, and what they are afraid of becoming' (Markus & Nurius, 1986: 964). Similar to imagery, possible selves relate to cognitions and emotions. They are manifested as goals, aspirations, motives, fears and threats, and can symbolise a variety of positive future self-constructs contextualised in different settings, such as the agile self in sport, the successful self at work or the confident self at a party. Alternatively, possible selves can also include feared selves, such as the unpopular self, the lonely self or the unemployed self. According to the seminal paper written by American psychologists Markus and Nurius (1986) who introduced the concept, possible selves contain the following key characteristics: (a) they are intricately intertwined with one's present and past selves; (b) they are highly personalised and socialised, defined by individual contexts as well as social comparisons; and (c) they are more unstable and sensitive to changes in the environment, especially when compared to one's present or past selves that are anchored in one's experiences and memories. Possible selves also vary in the amount of cognitive and affective elaborations, in that there is a graded continuum as to how intricate and detailed a possible self can become.

Possible selves can powerfully exert motivation as the constructs are said to have 'incentives for future behaviours' (Markus & Nurius, 1986: 954). Possible selves not only provide a context for people to evaluate and interpret the current selves but they also possess self-regulatory effects if linked with specific roadmaps and behavioural strategies, and are therefore known as 'self-regulatory possible selves' (Hoyle & Sherrill, 2006: 1677). The motivational effects can be exercised when a possible self is recruited and activated in the working self-concept. Likewise, a future self-guide which is not activated in one's working self-concept does not have an impact on one's current self and subsequent behaviours (Markus & Nurius, 1986).

The L2 Motivational Self System

The theory of possible selves has influenced research in L2 motivation with the inception of a motivation theory known as the L2 Motivational Self System developed by Dörnyei (2005, 2009). The proposed framework includes three major components: (a) the ideal L2 self, which is the L2-related facet of one's ideal self; (b) the ought-to L2 self, which relates to the L2-specific traits that a person believes he or she ought to possess; and (c) the L2 learning experience, which is motivation related to the immediate learning environment and experience (e.g. the positive rapport built in the classroom and learners' dynamics). Studies conducted over the past few years have converged in confirming the validity of Dörnyei's framework, supporting the ideal L2 self as a substantive predictor and determiner of motivated L2 behaviour (e.g. Csizér & Kormos, 2009; Csizér & Lukács, 2010; Kormos et al., 2011; Papi, 2010; Taguchi et al., 2009). Interestingly, recent studies have confirmed that learners' ideal L2 selves are positively associated with both visual and auditory components of imagery (Dörnyei & Chan, 2013; Kim, 2009; Kim & Kim, 2011), and the ideal L2 selves are not only positively correlated with learners' intended effort but their actual grades (Dörnyei & Chan, 2013). These results suggest that imagery plays a key role in the development of future self-guides, and that learners with a vivid L2 self-image, in which imagery is an integral component, are more likely to be motivated and to take actions in language learning.

Apart from the ideal L2 selves, the feared L2 selves are also important future self-guides in counterbalancing and offsetting students' ideal selves. In the original theory of Markus and Nurius (1986: 954), the feared selves are 'selves we are afraid of becoming'. They could be the 'alone self, the depressed self, the incompetent self, the alcoholic self, the unemployed self, or the bag lady self'. Examples of the L2-specific feared selves could be someone who finds it difficult to comprehend an L2 or a person who has great difficulty in expressing him/herself in speaking and writing. Although the feared L2 self is not one of the constructs in the L2 motivational self system, the entity could be vital in that it 'regulates behaviour by guiding the individual away from something' (Dörnyei, 2009: 13) and it induces maximal motivational capacity of an ideal self (Oyserman & Markus, 1990).

The Use of Imagery and Possible Selves in Learning

From a practical point of view, language educators are most interested in how they can use imagery and possible selves in the L2 classroom. As Ruvolo and Markus (1992) suggest, one's possible selves can generate feelings of efficacy, competence, control and optimism, which would then provide an impact on behaviour. However, it is unlikely that learners' ideal selves could be constructed and developed from scratch. It would be more realistic to raise learners' awareness about their past achievements, their own strengths and weaknesses when envisioning future aspirations (Dörnyei, 2009).

Such endeavours have been made by researchers who conducted possible selves programmes to enhance student motivation in the academic arena. For example, Hock et al. (2006) have guided students to contemplate their hopes, expectations and fears for the future in a programme in which students were prompted to reflect on their future roles and create a Possible Selves Tree, a drawing that represents one's hoped-for and expected selves. It was found that the use of possible selves resulted in higher academic performance, higher retention rates and higher graduation rates for university student-athletes than for those in the control group. A number of other studies have also explored the effects of possible selves interventions on students' general academic achievements (e.g. Oyserman et al., 2006; Oyserman et al., 2002; Sheldon & Lyubomirsky, 2006), and the results have shown that such enhancement programmes could enhance learners' future identities and their motivation in learning.

In recent years, L2-specific intervention programmes have been conducted with the aim of enhancing learners' future identities and L2 motivation (Fukada et al., 2010; Magid, 2011; Sampson, 2012). Evidence suggests that helping students to develop and strengthen their ideal L2 self may have a positive impact on their L2 motivation. Despite the initial interest, however, relatively few studies have used both imagery and possible selves in a compulsory, credit-bearing university language course or have examined the specific changes in participants' L2-specific future identities within the context of an intervention. The purpose of this paper is to investigate the impact of an imagery intervention on the students' ideal and feared L2 selves, and to explore the students' responses to the intervention in the context of autonomous L2 learning.

Research Aims

This study aims to explore the impact of an imagery training strategy (which incorporates the use of visualisation exercises, the creation of an Ideal Selves Tree and language counselling) on university students' possible L2 selves and their learning experiences. The main research questions are as follows:

(1) How do students' possible L2 selves – that is, their ideal L2 self and feared L2 self – change as a result of the imagery training strategy?
(2) How do students respond to the three intervention components utilised in the study, namely: visualisation exercises, the creation of an Ideal Selves Tree and language counselling?

Methods

Participants

Eighty second-year Chinese university science students (50 males and 30 females) participated in the study in a mid-sized, English-medium university in Hong Kong. These students were advanced English learners with language proficiencies ranging from high intermediate to advanced level. They ranged in age from 20 to 23 years with a mean age of 21 years.

Possible selves intervention

This study was conducted as part of a 12-week compulsory university English course in spring 2010[1], which aimed to develop autonomous language learners through a self-access language learning (SALL) component. As students had to learn English independently in the course, the goals were to help students create a vision of their ideal L2 self and to chart their progress throughout the course.

At the beginning of the course, students were introduced to the concept of the ideal self and how visualising their successful future selves could enhance their motivation in learning. Students were then asked to draw an Ideal Selves Tree[2] with stems envisioning (a) the ideal L2 learners they would like to become in the future, (b) their ideal future selves as a worker and the use of English in their future workplace and (c) their ideal

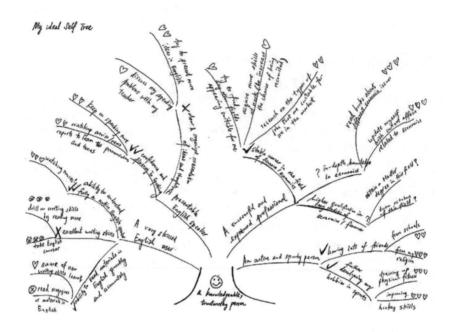

Figure 19.1 Sample of a student's ideal selves tree

selves in personal arenas. Students were also asked to draw smaller branches growing from the stems to indicate their action plans. Figure 19.1 shows a tree that was drawn by a student.

In addition, four visualisation exercises were conducted in class, which took place in the last ten minutes of class when the lights were dimmed and students were asked to close their eyes when imagining situations in which they felt confident using English. In the first practice task, students were familiarised with this technique by looking at two pictures on the screen and recalling the images in their mind. In the remaining three sessions, learners were asked to visualise a scenario where they felt confident in their use of English. The teacher did not use a particular script, but prompted students by using a few guidelines (see Table 19.1). Learners were encouraged to talk about their experience in as much detail as possible afterwards.

Finally, there were two 20-minute language counselling sessions incorporated in the intervention in which it was arranged for students to meet the teacher researcher in pairs. The aim was to help students envision who they could be as an English user, raise their awareness of their learning attitudes and set concrete learning goals.

Table 19.1 Imagery script

I would like you to close your eyes. This is a time for you to relax and to think about some positive experience that can happen in your life. This is a time to nurture yourself and to build a positive experience in your mind. I would like you take a deep breath and exhale slowly.

I would like you to come to this place where you will have a positive experience using English. This can be anything you want it to be. You could be giving an English presentation confidently in a classroom. You could be chatting with a friend in English fluently. You could be writing an essay in English. You are feeling very confident and this is a happy moment. Enjoy this moment. Try to look around you. What can you see? Try to take a close look at everything around you, the people and the surroundings. Take a close look at the people and their response. Try to listen to what they are saying to you. They are very happy with you. Try to enjoy this positive feeling in you. I will now give you some time to enjoy this moment. Try to see, hear and feel this moment.

I will now count to three. When I do so, you will be back to the present and you can open your eyes. One, two, three.

Data collection

Pre-course and post-course questionnaires that measured the strength of the participants' vision of their possible L2 selves were administered during Week 1 and Week 12 of the course. The items were taken from an established motivation inventory in Ryan (2009), and questions concerning students' evaluations of the intervention were included in the second survey.

Qualitative data were collected during three phases in the second week, the tenth week and two months after the course had finished. Table 19.2 summarises the details of each phase of the qualitative data collection.

Interview questions drawn from Ryan (2009) were used to investigate students' ideal and feared L2 selves at Time 1 and Time 2. Students' views of the intervention components were explored at Time 3. Data collection at Time 1 and Time 2 was conducted in English whereas the interviews at Time 3 were conducted in either Cantonese (the participants' first language) or in English.

Table 19.2 Information on the three phases of the qualitative data collection

	Time of data collection	No. of informants
Time 1	2nd week of the course	23 (13 males & 10 females)
Time 2	10th week of the course	15 (8 males & 7 females)
Time 3	2 months after the course	14 (8 males & 6 females)

Ethical procedures

To protect the students' rights in this research study especially because it was related to a credit-bearing course, strong measures were implemented to ensure appropriate ethical conduct. This was mainly to avoid a conflict of interests as the teacher researcher also had the role of evaluating participants' work which would eventually lead to a final grade for the course. In this case, although the teacher researcher taught the classes, the recruitment of participants and the administration of data collection in the first and second phases were undertaken by a separate data collector[3]. The recruitment for the final interview was carried out via the post-course survey and students who indicated an interest were contacted after the course had finished. Pseudonyms were also employed in the report.

Data analysis

Data from the pre-course and post-course questionnaires were processed by SPSS version 18.0 using parametric paired-samples t-tests to explore whether there were statistical differences in students' ideal and feared L2 selves. Content analyses of the nearly 71,000-word corpus of interview data were carried out using NVivo 8.0. The researcher first read through the transcriptions identifying the emerging themes and then the text was coded into categories, such as the ideal L2 selves, the feared L2 selves, visualisation and an evaluation of the intervention.

Results

Quantitative analyses of students' ideal and feared L2 selves

Internal consistency reliability

Table 19.3 shows the Cronbach's alpha reliability coefficients for the two multi-item scales: Ideal L2 self and Feared L2 self. The reliability coefficients for both scales are above or close to the recommended .70 threshold, which suggests that there is a display of homogeneity among the items of the two composite factors.

Quantitative changes of students' ideal and feared L2 selves

Paired-samples t-tests were conducted to evaluate the impact of the intervention on students' ideal and feared L2 selves (see Table 19.4). The results showed that students' ideal L2 self increased but their feared L2 self did not change significantly as a result of the imagery intervention.

Table 19.3 Cronbach's alpha coefficient for the multi-item scales

Variables	Cronbach's alpha	Questionnaire items
Ideal L2 self	.73	- I have a role model to look up to as an ideal English user. - I imagine/visualise myself being someone who can communicate with others fluently in English. - I imagine/visualise myself being someone who is a good English writer. - I imagine/visualise myself reading English texts effectively.
Feared L2 self	.64	- I am scared that my English standard will decline. - Because I have experienced some embarrassing situations when I have used English, I feel more motivated to improve the language. - The fear of losing my knowledge of English motivates me to keep on studying the language. - I worry about the consequences of not becoming the English user I would like to be.

Table 19.4 Comparing the quantitative temporal changes in learners' future self-guides: Paired-samples t-tests

	M	SD	D	T	Effect size[1]
Pre ideal L2 selves	3.86	.82	79	-2.65*	0.08
Post ideal L2 selves	4.16	.76			
Pre feared L2 selves	4.32	.79	79	-.01	0.00
Post feared L2 selves	4.17	.70			

Notes: *$p < 0.01$. [1]Eta squared.

The change to the various facets of possible L2 selves

To measure the change to students' possible L2 selves in the intervention, three coding categories[4] were employed, namely: (a) emergent (i.e. selves which were not present at Time 1 but present at Time 2), (b) fading (i.e. selves which were present at Time 1 but not at Time 2) and (c) stable (i.e. selves which were present both at Time 1 and Time 2). The qualitative data were categorised by domains (e.g. listening versus speaking self) as well as by the nuance differences in contexts (e.g. academic

Table 19.5 Frequencies in the direction of change in various facets of possible L2 selves

Emergent L2 selves	Fading L2 selves	Stable L2 selves
Ideal speaking self (7/14)	Feared speaking self (3/14)	Ideal speaking self (6/14)
Ideal writing self (3/14)	Ideal listening self (5/14)	Feared speaking self (4/14)
Feared speaking self (3/14)	Feared writing self (1/14)	Feared reading self (1/14)
Feared writing self (2/14)	Feared reading self (1/14)	General feared L2 self (2/14)
General feared L2 self (1/14)		

Note: $N = 14$.

versus work) shown in informants' responses. Table 19.5 presents an overview of the development of informants' possible L2 selves.

The qualitative data revealed five facets of possible L2 selves which were categorised as the 'emergent possible selves' and the most notable emerging self was the ideal speaking self with half of the participants having an emergent change in this facet. This could be because the course had a heavy speaking component and students were also encouraged to envisage the ideal speaking self both in the creation of the Ideal Selves Tree and in the visualisation exercises. A positive change in the emergent ideal speaking self could be seen particularly in four of these students whose ideal future self-guides became more specific towards the end of the intervention. For example, Jade who did not have an idea of her ideal L2 self at Time 1 gradually developed a concrete, established ideal L2 self at Time 2:

> I guess it would still be the imagery I did in class. In my imagination, I was doing a presentation introducing something to an audience. I was just talking or explaining. It motivated me because this could be a job I would like to do in the future. This is what I expect myself to be. And to achieve that, I would try my best to learn English... hard. (Time 2, focus group 1)

Similarly, the ideal L2 self of three other students became more specific and their future self-guides changed from having general attributes (e.g. someone who speaks fluently) to acquiring a specific role model. In John's own words:

I have a vision which is job- or career-related. I have a role model who is one of my seniors. His English and accent is not so good, but he can speak fluently during an interview or can communicate with other foreign exchange students. (Time 2, focus group 4)

In the category of the 'fading possible L2 selves', apart from witnessing a diminishing ideal listening self, the feared selves related to speaking, writing and reading were also weakening towards the end of the course. This was seen in Betty who mentioned that she was scared of having daily conversations in English at Time 1, but this fear diminished at Time 2.

Yes, in fact, I know that I cannot speak as well as a foreigner, but I just imagine that I can speak like him. For the fear, I just want to try my best. So I really am not afraid. There's no fear. (Time 2, focus group 4)

Finally, four facets of possible L2 selves remained stable, namely: the ideal speaking self, the feared speaking self, the feared reading self and the general feared L2 self[5] with more informants demonstrating stability in the speaking L2 self.

Participants' evaluation of the intervention components

Visualisation

Approximately two-thirds of the students found the in-class visualisation exercises useful, with 68.8% rating the usefulness of visualisation as 4 or above. For the survey item 'The in-class visualisation practice was useful', descriptive data show a mean score of 3.98 out of 6 (SD = 1.09; $n = 80$) in students' evaluations.

Many informants found the in-class visualisations a pleasant and relaxing experience, especially for those who understood the rationale behind them and for those who were already practising the use of visualisation. This was true for Adam who appreciated the use of imagery:

For me, I think visualisation has its potential because it is a kind of self-motivation exercise. I read a book years ago about this technique and in the past I visualised quite often. (Time 3, focus group 1)

This was the same for Jade who suggested that visualisation motivated her to learn English:

Interviewer: Do you think the visualisation exercises helped you with the SALL component?
Jade: Yes, it did help because I gained more confidence to chat with other foreigners or students from other countries.

Interviewer: Did it help you to try to create more opportunities to talk to others?

Jade: Yeah. Yeah.

Interviewer: It did?

Jade: Yeah. I did grab the chance to talk to the students from other countries or the exchange students. (Time 3, interview 3)

Although some students found the visualisation exercises motivating, it appeared that the positive impact was sustained only for a short period of time and the motivation gradually declined after the initial boost, which was commented on by Phil:

I have an image in my mind. After that day, I have more motivation. That only lasted for a few days. After those few days, I returned to normal. It gave me confidence because if I dream that I am a successful guy, I have more confidence. As I said before, it gave me a goal. (Time 3, focus group 2)

The effectiveness of visualisation also depended on the students' ability to visualise. Learners in this study found it relatively easy to visualise in general and tended to find it effortless to reconstruct actual scenarios that had occurred, as mentioned by Jackson:

I think… it's easy because I have encountered such a scenario before. I just recall it from my memory. (Time 3, interview 4)

However, there was a minority of students who found it difficult to visualise, especially influenced by the time of the day in which the visualisation was conducted. In Sam's words:

As my class is in the late afternoon, doing visualisation is very difficult. We are very tired and our brain is in a traffic jam. (Time 3, focus group 2)

Ideal selves tree

The Ideal Selves Tree seemed to be moderately effective in motivating students in SALL, and the descriptive data showed a mean score of 3.71 out of the six-point Likert scale for the survey item 'The Ideal Selves Tree helped me to be more motivated in SALL' (SD = 1.12; n = 80). 60.3% of the students rated four or above in the Likert scale for this item.

Among the 14 informants, 7 of them found the task helpful in shaping their goals as the schematic representation in the Ideal Selves Tree helped them to envision their future and it also acted as a reminder, which was the case for James:

> I seldom set goals for myself. I do have a final goal, but I don't come up with some short-term goals. As I imagine those situations, I have some motivation to work harder and to improve my English. It keeps reminding me of what I have to do when I come across the Ideal Selves Tree on my desk. I remember what I have drawn. (Time 3, interview 5)

Filling the SALL record was a compulsory task for students which would be submitted at the end of the course, but Zac suggested that there were additional benefits of using the Ideal Selves Tree:

> [The Ideal Selves Tree] helps me to think about the whole thing more systematically. There are some lines connecting ideas, which is similar to a mind-map. With the SALL record, it's perhaps just words on separate pages. It's more difficult for me to see the connections. (Time 3, focus group 2)

Language counselling sessions

Many students found the language counselling motivating, with 81.3% of students rating it 4 or above on the Likert scale. The mean score obtained for the item 'The two language counselling sessions motivated me to do SALL' is 4.22 out of a six-point Likert scale (SD = 1.03; n = 80).

From the qualitative data, eight students found the counselling sessions helpful. The two language counselling sessions served various purposes for these students. While some learners felt the pressure to present their learning goals and to report their progress in these sessions, others saw it as an opportunity to build rapport with the teacher, a chance for both the students and the teacher to become more familiar with one another. The sessions were also opportunities for learners to be challenged, to reflect upon their independent L2 learning and to refine their goals, which was the case for Dana:

> I think it was quite good. When you saw the tree, you asked me some challenging questions. When I went back home, I thought about that point and agreed that the goals didn't really match what I had in mind. (Time 3, focus group 2)

Discussion

The intervention strategy can be considered moderately successful as its impact was strong in many ways but less pronounced in others. It was successful in significantly enhancing the strength of the participants' ideal L2 self, which meant that the students had a stronger and more positive future L2-related identity towards the end of the intervention. This suggested that the participants could better visualise themselves as someone who could communicate with others fluently in English, someone who would be a good English writer and who could read English texts effectively as shown in the questionnaire items. The ideal L2 selves of some students also became more specific and were extended to different contexts (e.g. at a work-related context) as indicated by the qualitative data.

Encouraging comments were received for all three core intervention components. The participants found it constructive to present their learning goals and to report their progress in independent learning during the language counselling sessions. The instructor was seen as a mentor, helping students evaluate their own progress, reflect upon their learning and refine their goals. Any misconceptions regarding learners' perceptions of visualisation were also clarified. More importantly, it was encouragement and support given to the students as well as the rapport built that was valued by the informants. The findings echo Voller's (1997) assertion that teachers can be seen as facilitators, counsellors and resources in an autonomy-centred classroom.

Regarding the Ideal Selves Tree, the task created the time and space for students to reflect upon their intended actions for goal achievement. It helped students to construct and record who they would like to be in the future, and it also acted as a reminder for them. It was particularly helpful for learners who were serious about setting realistic goals.

As for the in-class visualisation exercises, the strength and effectiveness of imagery was influenced by various factors, namely the imagery generating abilities, the number of visualisation exercises used, the time of day of the class and whether learners understood and identified with the benefits of the technique. Drawing from the students' experience in using imagery in this study and from other research findings, issues pertaining to the practicality of using mental imagery in the classrooms will be further delineated in the next section.

The intervention was also successful in developing and maintaining the students' L2 speaking self, which was the most stable and emerging construct with 10 out of 14 informants mentioning a feared and ideal speaking self at Time 1 and Time 2, respectively. In fact, it was the most significant self construct with all 14 informants mentioning it at some point in time. When students envisioned their L2 speaking self, they were searching for role models. Many students used native English speakers, foreigners or locals who sound like foreigners as benchmarks; and evaluated who they would like to become accordingly. The emergence of a prominent L2 speaking self may have developed among the students because they were encouraged to imagine various speaking-related scenarios in the visualisation exercises, including giving oral presentations and chatting with native speakers, which could have encouraged a more prominent L2 speaking self. It could also be due to the nature of the course, which aimed to develop students' oral proficiency by providing oral discussions in most lessons.

Although the intervention was successful in the aforementioned areas, the results revealed less of an impact on alleviating the strength of the students' feared L2 self. The fear-related future self-guides remained relatively strong (i.e. in the range of four on a six-point Likert scale) in the post-course survey. This could be because the intervention focused on enhancing the students' ideal L2 self without aiming to specifically alleviate the feared L2 self. The period in which the intervention was conducted (i.e. at the end of their second year) could also play a role since the pressure of preparing for examinations, end-of-term assignments, summer internship applications and interviews, as mentioned by some participants, could have evoked or maintained the feared L2 self. Although the feared L2 self can offset the ideal L2 self (Dörnyei & Ushioda, 2011), the ramifications of having an intensified feared L2 self could lead to an increase in L2 anxiety and debilitate students' L2 learning (Papi, 2010). The presence of fear or anxiety in L2 learning has been noted in Chinese students (e.g. Tsui, 1996; Zhang & Head, 2010), which could be related to the generally low levels of self-esteem found in Hong Kong Chinese children (as compared to Chinese and Caucasian children who live in Britain), resulting from the pressurising educational environment and cultural values in Chinese society (Chan, 2000).

Lessons from the intervention

Lesson 1: Students' readiness to visualise in class

From the feedback received, most participants welcomed the opportunity to visualise in class, even those with relatively poor imagery generating ability, but some students displayed scepticism about the use of imagery as a motivational strategy in language learning. It is therefore important for students to understand both the benefits and the process of imagery use. In addition, teachers can explain to students some theoretical materials and scientific evidence that support imagery use (Sargent, 1996). Simple guided imagery exercises can also be tried out in the introductory sessions.

Lesson 2: Environment

To achieve the best results, it is vital to provide a safe, comfortable and quiet environment for the participants (Glouberman, 1989). Various factors such as temperature, noise level and the time of the day will affect imagery. Participants could be asked to sit in a comfortable way, for example with their legs uncrossed and arms unfolded. They could also remove their glasses and have their eyes closed.

Lesson 3: Contents of visualisation

Since some informants commented on the differences between realising the ideal L2 self in the near future (e.g. someone who is learning autonomously on a daily basis) as compared to attaining the ideal L2 self in the distant future (e.g. joining an exchange programme), practitioners may consider informing participants of the effects of the different psychological temporal dimensions in imagery production.

Research has found that a goal may exert more motivational impact if it is considered to be more 'psychologically imminent rather than remote' (Perunovic & Wilson, 2009: 356). Seeing proximal future success can also instigate a confidence boost in the current self. Therefore, conducting mental simulations with one's proximal future self may have a more positive influence on students' motivation and choice of decision.

Participants can consider using their autobiographical memory as a basis for their visualisation by reconstructing their past experiences and creating new ones. This was the experience of some participants who modified the unsuccessful experience with slight modifications into a successful one. Even visualising unhappy moments and evoking some strong emotions could act as a reminder of a person's feared L2 self, which can then offset his or her ideal L2 self (Dörnyei & Ushioda, 2011).

Lesson 4: Frequency of visualisations

A few informants mentioned the short-lived duration of the motivational effects of visualisations, which coincides with a research finding that suggests that the effects of imagination on personal intention persist at least over a 3-day period (Anderson, 1983). In order to prolong the motivational effects and keep the vision alive, participants can be encouraged to use visualisation by producing personalised imagery scripts and recordings to be used outside of their class. These can be used on a regular basis, preferably within a 3-day timeframe.

Lesson 5: Language counselling sessions

As suggested by some students, an individual visualisation exercise can be conducted in the language counselling sessions to help students to further create, clarify and develop their ideal L2 selves.

Lesson 6: Ideal selves tree

Regarding the Ideal Selves Tree, the success of the task depended on the students' view of the possibility and feasibility of achieving the goals they set for themselves. This is in line with Markus and Nurius (1986), who suggest that the ideal selves should be possible. In order for students to find the task useful, it is vital for them to be specific as to what they could achieve within a particular timeframe. It is also important for the diagram to be put in a prominent place in order to remind them of their goals.

Conclusion

All in all, the present study has provided interesting insights into the way an imagery strategy exerted a positive impact on students' possible L2 selves and learning experiences. The intervention significantly increased the learners' ideal L2 self although the feared L2 self remained relatively stable. The results also revealed that different facets of possible L2 selves showed stability and changes in the intervention. Most of all, the study demonstrates how imagery, when used appropriately, has the potential to be an effective tool in motivating L2 learners and a powerful reminder of future goals.

Acknowledgements

The author would like to express her deepest gratitude to Professor Zoltán Dörnyei and the editors of this volume for their invaluable comments on earlier drafts. She would also like to thank Dr David Gardner for his continuous help and support throughout the study. A special thanks goes to all of the participants who provided valuable insights into the use of imagery strategy in L2 learning.

Notes

(1) Some of the results in this study have been presented in a paper published by Magid and Chan (2012).
(2) The activity was adapted from the Possible Selves Intervention conducted by Hock *et al.* (2006).
(3) The data collector has obtained a doctorate degree and is experienced in English teaching as well as L2 research.
(4) The categories were adapted from the study conducted by Frazier *et al.* (2000).
(5) 'General feared L2 self' entails a general fear of becoming a poor English user in the future.

References

Anderson, C.A. (1983) Imagination and expectation: The effect of imagining behavioral scripts on personal intentions. *Journal of Personality and Social Psychology* 45 (2), 293–305.

Anderson, C.A., Lepper, M.R. and Ross, L. (1980) Perseverance of social theories: The role of explanation in the persistence of discredited information. *Journal of Personality and Social Psychology* 39 (6), 1037–1049.

Center, Y., Freeman, L. Robertson, G. and Outhred, L. (1999) The effect of visual imagery training on the reading and listening comprehension of low listening comprehenders in Year 2. *Journal of Research in Reading* 22 (3), 241–256.

Chan, Y.M. (2000) Self-esteem: A cross-cultural comparison of British-Chinese, white British and Hong Kong Chinese children. *Educational Psychology* 20 (1), 59–74.

Cohen, A. (1987) The use of verbal and imagery mnemonics in second-language vocabulary learning. *Studies in Second Language Acquisition* 9 (1), 43–61.

Conway, M.A. Meares, K. and Standart, S. (2004) Images and goals. *Memory* 12 (4), 525–531.

Csizér, K. and Kormos, J. (2009) Learning experiences, selves and motivated learning behavior: A comparative analysis of structural models for Hungarian secondary and university learners of English. In Z. Dörnyei and E. Ushioda (eds) *Motivation, Language Identity and the L2 Self* (pp. 98–119). Bristol: Multilingual Matters.

Csizér, K. and Lukács, G. (2010) The comparative analysis of motivation, attitudes and selves: The case of English and German in Hungary. *System* 38 (1), 1–13.

de la Iglesia, C. Buceta, J. and Campos, A. (2005) Prose learning in children and adults with Down syndrome: The use of visual and mental image strategies to improve recall. *Journal of Intellectual and Developmental Disability* 30 (3), 199–206.

Dörnyei, Z. (2005) *The Psychology of the Language Learner: Individual Differences in Second Language Acquisition*. Mahwah, NH: Lawrence Erlbaum.

Dörnyei, Z. (2009) The L2 motivational self system. In Z. Dörnyei and E. Ushioda (eds) *Motivation, Language Identity and the L2 Self*. Bristol: Multilingual Matters.

Dörnyei, Z. and Chan, L. (2013) Motivation and vision: An analysis of future L2 self images, sensory styles, and imagery capacity across two target languages. *Language Learning* 63 (3), 437–462.

Dörnyei, Z. and Kubanyiova, M. (2014) *Motivating Students, Motivating Teachers: Building Vision in the Language Classroom*. Cambridge: Cambridge University Press.

Dörnyei, Z. and Ushioda, E. (2011) *Teaching and Researching Motivation* (2nd edn). Harlow: Longman.

Finke, R. (1990) *Creative Imagery: Discoveries and Inventions in Visualization*. Hillsdale, NJ: Lawrence Erlbaum.

Frazier, L.D., Hooker, K., Johnson, P.M., Kaus, C.R. (2000) Continuity and change in possible selves in later life: A 5-year longitudinal study. *Basic and Applied Social Psychology* 22 (3), 237–243.

Fukada, Y. Fukuda, T. Falout, J. and Murphey, T. (2010) Increasing motivation with possible selves. In A. Stewart (ed.) *JALT 2010 Conference Proceedings*. Tokyo: JALT.

Glouberman, D. (1989) *Life Choices and Life Changes Through Imagework: The Art of Developing Personal Vision*. London: The Aquarian Press.

Hackmann, A., Bennett-Levy, J. and Holmes, E.A. (2011) *Oxford Guide to Imagery in Cognitive Therapy*. New York, NY: Oxford University Press.

Hock, M.F., Deshler, D.D. and Schumaker, J.B. (2006) Enhancing student motivation through the pursuit of possible selves. In C. Dunkel and J. Kerpelman (eds) *Possible Selves: Theory Research and Applications* (205–221). New York, NY: Nova Science.

Holmes, E.A. and Mathews, A. (2005) Mental imagery and emotion: A special relationship? Emotion. *Emotion* 5 (4), 485–497.

Holmes, E.A. Mathews, A. Dalgleish, T. and Mackintosh, B. (2006) Positive interpretation training: Effects of mental imagery versus verbal training on positive mood. *Behavior Therapy* 37 (3), 237–247.

Hoyle, R.H. and Sherrill, M.R. (2006) Future orientation in the self-system: Possible selves, self-regulation, and behavior. *Journal of Personality* 74 (6), 1673–1696.

Jampole, E.S., Mathews, F.N. and Konopak, B.C. (1994) Academically gifted students' use of imagery for creative writing. *The Journal of Creative Behavior* 28 (1), 1–15.

Kim, T.-Y. (2009) Korean elementary school students' perceptual learning style, ideal L2 self, and motivated behavior. *Korean Journal of English Language and Linguistics* 9 (3), 261–286.

Kim, Y.-K. and Kim, T.-Y. (2011) The effect of Korean secondary school students' perceptual learning styles and ideal L2 self on motivated L2 behavior and English proficiency. *Korean Journal of English Language and Linguistics* 11 (1), 21–42.

Knudstrup, M., Segrest, S.L. and Hurley, A.E. (2003) The use of mental imagery in the simulated employment interview situation. *Journal of Managerial Psychology* 18 (6), 573–591.

Knäuper, B., Roseman, M., Johnson, P.J. and Krantz, L.H. (2009) Using mental imagery to enhance the effectiveness of implementation intentions. *Current Psychology* 28 (3), 181–186.

Kormos, J., Kiddle, T. and Csizér, K. (2011) Systems of goals, attitudes, and self-related beliefs in second-language-learning motivation. *Applied Linguistics* 32 (5), 495–516.

Magid, M. (2011) A validation and application of the L2 motivational self system among Chinese learners of English. Unpublished PhD Thesis. University of Nottingham.

Magid, M. and Chan, L. (2012) Motivating English learners by helping them visualise their ideal L2 self: Lessons from two motivational programmes. *Innovation in Language Learning and Teaching* 6 (2), 113–125.

Markus, H. and Nurius, P. (1986) Possible selves. *American Psychologist* 41 (9), 954–969.

Martin, K. and Hall, C. (1995) Using mental imagery to enhance intrinsic motivation. *Journal of Sport and Exercise Psychology* 17 (1), 54–69.

Oyserman, D., Bybee, D. and Terry, K. (2006) Possible selves and academic outcomes: How and when possible selves impel action. *Journal of Personality and Social Psychology* 91 (1), 188–204.

Oyserman, D., Terry, K. and Bybee, D. (2002) A possible selves intervention to enhance school involvement. *Journal of Adolescence* 25 (3), 313–326.

Oyserman, D. and Markus, H. R. (1990) Possible selves and delinquency. *Journal of Personality and Social Psychology* 59 (1), 112–125.

Papi, M. (2010) The L2 motivational self system, L2 anxiety, and motivated behavior: A structural equation modelling approach. *System* 38 (3), 467–479.

Perunovic, W.Q.E. and Wilson, A. E. (2009) Subjective proximity of future selves: Implications for current identity, future appraisal, and goal pursuit motivation. In K.D. Markman, W.M.P. Klein and J.A. Suhr (eds) *Handbook of Imagination and Mental Simulation* (pp. 347–358). New York, NY: Psychology Press.

Ruvolo, A.P. and Markus, H. (1992) Possible selves and performance: The power of self-relevant imagery. *Social Cognition* 10 (1), 95–124.

Ryan, S. (2009) Self and identity in L2 motivation in Japan: The ideal L2 self and Japanese learners of English In Z. Dörnyei and E. Ushioda (eds) *Motivation, Language Identity and the L2 Self* (pp. 120–143). Bristol: Multilingual Matters.

Sampson, R. (2012) The language-learning self, self-enhancement activities, and self perceptual change. *Language Teaching Research* 16 (3), 317–335.

Sargent, G. (1996) Developing a mental skills training program 3. *Sports Coach* 8, 26–27.

Sheldon, K.M. and Lyubomirsky, S. (2006) How to increase and sustain positive emotion: The effects of expressing gratitude and visualising best possible selves. *Journal of Positive Psychology* 1 (2), 73–82.

Shen, H.H. (2010) Imagery and verbal coding approaches in Chinese vocabulary instruction. *Language Teaching Research* 14 (4), 485–500.

Stevick, E.W. (1986) *Images and Options in the Language Classroom*. Cambridge: Cambridge University Press.

Taguchi, T., Magid, M. and Papi, M. (2009) The L2 motivational self system among Japanese, Chinese, and Iranian learners of English: A comparative study. In Z. Dörnyei and E. Ushioda (eds) *Motivation, Language Identity and the L2 Self* (pp. 66–97). Bristol: Multilingual Matters.

Taylor, S.E. and Schneider, S.K. (1989) Coping and the simulation of events. *Social Cognition* 7 (2), 174–194.

Tsui, A.B.M. (1996) Reticence and anxiety in second language learning. In K. Bailey and D. Nunan (eds) *Voices from the Language Classroom* (pp. 145–167). New York, NY: Cambridge University Press.

Voller, P. (1997) Does the teacher have a role in autonomous learning? In P. Benson and P. Voller (eds) *Autonomy and Independence in Language Learning* (pp. 98–113). London: Longman.

Zhang, X. and Head, K. (2010) Dealing with learner reticence in the speaking class. *ELT Journal* 64 (1), 1–9.

20 Applications and Implications of the L2 Motivational Self System in a Catalan EFL Context

Jessica Mackay

Introduction

The field of second language (L2) motivation research is undergoing a fascinating period of change and expansion. As Dörnyei and Ushioda point out in the introduction to the second edition of *Teaching and Researching Motivation*, 'Since the publication of the first edition [in 2001] the research landscape of language learning motivation has changed almost beyond recognition' (2011: xi). Dörnyei himself is at the forefront of the change in the direction of L2 motivation research with his 2005 proposal of a new theory, the L2 Motivational Self System.

The origin of the L2 Motivational Self System lies in the results of extensive, longitudinal research in Hungary (Csizér & Dörnyei, 2005a, 2005b; Dörnyei & Csizér, 2002). Dörnyei concluded that there was a need to reconceptualise the construct of integrativeness (Gardner & Lambert, 1959) that would be both compatible with the changing global profile of English and would incorporate research theories from motivational psychology. To do this, he drew upon the idea of possible selves and future self-guides (Higgins *et al.*, 1985; Markus & Nurius, 1986). Possible selves theory suggests that motivated human behaviour is guided by the visions we have of our future selves, including both positive selves (e.g. ideal self), negative selves (e.g. feared self) or the vision that others have for us (ought self). Working together in optimum conditions these future self-guides can create the initial need and desire to maintain effort to achieve a goal. The L2 Motivational Self System consists of three components: (1) The Ideal L2 self, which is the vision of our future L2-speaking self, incorporating both integrative and internalised instrumental motives; (2) The Ought-to L2 self, which includes the qualities one feels one should possess to meet external expectations and avoid undesirable consequences, including less internalised instrumental motives; and (3) the L2 learning experience, which refers to situated, executive motives concerned with the immediate learning environment and experience (Dörnyei & Ushioda, 2009).

There is increasing quantitative, empirical evidence to support the validity of the theory (Al Shehri, 2009; Csizér & Kormos, 2009; Taguchi *et al.*, 2009). However, to date, few mixed-methods or qualitative studies have been completed (Lamb, 2009; Magid & Chan, 2012; Ryan, 2009). These studies provided compelling insights into the practical potential of the L2 Motivational Self System. The present study seeks to explore the construct in a different educational context, Spain, and by using a control group for the purpose of comparison.

It is clearly a very exciting time to be both a researcher and a teacher working in this field and, unsurprisingly, this theory of language learning motivation has struck a chord with many language teaching practitioners, especially those working in the context of English as a Foreign Language (EFL). The notion of the Ideal L2 self offers a possible explanation for some of the apparent ambiguities in the EFL classroom. The motivation of highly engaged and enthusiastic learners cannot necessarily be explained by the construct of integrativeness, whose underlying principle, the wish to identify oneself with the community of the language being learnt, is losing relevance in a globalised context or is simply 'untenable for second-language learners in world Englishes contexts' (Coetzee Van-Roy, 2006: 447). Furthermore, possible selves theories work on the visceral level of imagination and emotions, human factors ever present in a classroom situation which we ignore at our peril. As Dörnyei states 'it goes beyond logical, intellectual arguments when justifying the validity of the various future-oriented self types' (2005: 15). Last but not least, this reinterpretation offers the enticing prospect of possible classroom application, using techniques such as positive visualisation which have been used successfully in clinical, educational and sport psychology. According to Dörnyei, there is a 'considerable body of literature on the conscious use of imagery to good effect in varied disciplines' (Dörnyei & Ushioda, 2009: 35). He goes on to suggest a number of conditions which need to be fulfilled in order to 'devise creative ideal-self-generating activities' (Dörnyei & Ushioda, 2009). The nine conditions he specifies (Dörnyei & Ushioda, 2011: 83-84) can be summarised as follows:

(1) The learner must have or create a desired self-image.
(2) This image is sufficiently different from the current self.
(3) The image is strengthened with elaborate and vivid detail.
(4) The image is substantiated; it is plausible and realistic in the individual's circumstances.

(5) The desired self-image is not comfortably certain; the learner perceives the need to exert effort.

(6) The image is acceptable in the learner's environment and does not contradict the expectations of significant others.

(7) The image is regularly activated and maintained over time.

(8) The image can be operationalised by appropriate procedural strategies.

(9) The image is counterbalanced by awareness of the Feared L2 self; the potential negative consequences of failure to attain the desired future L2 self.

A teachers' resource book (Hadfield & Dörnyei, 2013) has since been published, which rises to the challenge of translating these theories into practice. In this collaboration, the authors distinguish between the initial genesis of the vision (creating, strengthening, substantiating and counterbalancing) and the processes needed to maintain motivation over time (operationalising and keeping the vision alive). They also suggest a further step, unifying the vision (Hadfield & Dörnyei, 2013: 8), which integrates the Ideal, Ought-to and Feared L2 self visions. Material from this collaboration was piloted as part of this research, following the sequencing suggested by the authors. Further material was specifically designed to reflect the Catalan EFL context. The result was a motivational programme aimed at developing the learners' Ideal L2 self. Data pertaining to the learners' self-concept and language learning motivation were collected and subsequently analysed. The objective of this chapter is therefore to discuss the implications and applications of the L2 Motivational Self System as a potential motivational tool in a Catalan EFL classroom context.

Motivation in the Catalan EFL Context

In the Catalan education system, English is introduced as a compulsory subject in state schools at Grade 1, which means that by the time they reach university, most Catalan students will have already studied English for 12 years, often supplemented by classes in private language schools. In a survey of students of English aged 15 years conducted by the Catalan Government's Department of Education (Departament d'Educació. Informes d'Avaluació 12, 2006: 115), learners' attitudes towards studying English were found to be generally positive. The previous survey into learners on pre-university courses conducted between 2000 and 2004 also showed a generally positive attitude, although slightly less than that of learners two years behind in the system.

The data in the Catalan surveys coincide with evidence from other contexts. Learner motivation appears to decrease over the length of a student's school career (Tachibana et al., 1996). Furthermore, initial enthusiasm for languages among child learners often suffers a downturn before it is replaced with more realistic goals (Nikolov, 1999). Catalan university students are fully aware of the importance of English as a global language. However, they can also bring with them a set of expectations about how a language should be taught and learnt derived from their previous learning experience and occasionally a certain disillusionment about a perceived lack of progress up to that point (Mackay, 2009).

Contact with the target language

Part of the impetus behind the development of Dörnyei's L2 Motivational Self System (2005) was the need to explain the construct of integrativeness (Gardner & Lambert, 1959) in EFL contexts where the population had little contact with the target language (TL) community. It cannot be denied that there is access to English and potential interaction with native speakers (NSs) in the Catalan context. According to the UK Institute for Public Policy Research, more than one million British passport holders currently reside in Spain, and the Spanish National Institute for Statistics claims that Barcelona is the most popular destination for foreign visitors (INE, 2012).

Nevertheless, most learners in this study appear to have little contact with NSs at a community level other than the occasional encounter with tourists. In the interview data, 12 of the 22 participants had infrequent contact with NSs of English. However, in all but two of these cases, the NSs were residents of other countries. This is in keeping with the results of an extensive study conducted on school-age learners of English in Catalonia (Muñoz & Tragant, 2001; Tragant & Muñoz, 2000) which showed 'no explicit references to communicating with NSs but with speakers from "other countries" around the world' (Tragant, 2006: 249). In the case of university learners, English also seems to represent a tool for global communication rather than entry to the local TL community.

Method

Context

This study took place in the language school of a large Catalan university. The school is fee-paying and offers general foreign language (FL) courses in 18 different languages. Classes are taught in various university departments in different locations across Barcelona. These courses do not form part of the students' degree courses and are taken on an optional basis. The English department is the largest section within the school, accounting for 2,766 (76.45%) of the 3,618 students enrolled in the 2010–2011 academic year, with a mean age of 25.6 years. The majority of learners (68.2%) in the English department are full-time university students, while the remainder (31.7%) are members of the wider university community; teaching and administrative staff or graduates employed elsewhere. The majority of EFL students in the school are women (65.9%).

Participants

The participants in this study were learners enrolled in four intact groups (two intervention groups and two control groups) at the upper-intermediate level, equivalent to the Council of Europe common European framework of reference for languages (CEFR) level B2:1. This particular level was chosen as there seems to be a motivational hiatus post Cambridge First Certificate in English, equivalent to CEFR B2:2. Many students in this context aim to pass this internationally-recognised official exam and then choose to discontinue their studies. Furthermore, this particular level is the largest level in the school, which facilitated the administrative problems of organising two similar groups at the same level for two different teachers.

Table 20.1 summarises some of the general characteristics of the groups. Inevitably, given the context of a working language school, there was some variation in the times and locations of the groups. The teachers who took part in the study are both female British native speaker EFL teachers who are permanent members of staff. Teacher 1 (the researcher), who has worked at the school since 1995, has more than 20 years of teaching experience and holds the Royal Society of Arts (RSA) Diploma in Teaching English as a Foreign Language to Adults (TEFLA) and an MA

Table 20.1 General group characteristics

Group	Gender	Mean age (years)	Teacher	Occupation
A. N = 22 (Intervention)	M 20% F 80%	28.9	1	Student 73.3% Working 26.7%
B. N = 23 (Control)	M 26.3% F 73.3%	24.3	1	Student 84.2% Working 15.8%
C. N = 25 (Intervention)	M 53.3% F 46.7%	21.4	2	Student 86.3% Working 13.7%
D. N = 28 (Control)	M 10.5% F 89.5%	26.1	2	Student 52.6% Working 47.4%

in Applied Linguistics. Teacher 2 also has 20 years of teaching experience, is qualified to RSA Diploma TEFLA level and has worked at the school for more than 10 years.

Due to the structure of courses at the school, a number of students change groups at the end of the winter term when their university time-tables change. The high mortality rate prompted the decision to combine the four groups into two 'macro' groups comprising those students who had responded to the questionnaires both at T1 and T2: 'Treatment' ($N = 25$) and 'Control' ($N = 36$) for the purposes of analysis.

The intervention programme

In this chapter, the practical applications of the L2 Motivational Self System will be discussed using data drawn from a larger study (Mackay, forthcoming). This study sought to analyse the effects of a specifically designed Ideal L2 self intervention on learners' motivation, self-concept and motivated behaviour. In this chapter, I will limit my discussion to the aspects of motivation and self-concept which were pertinent to the L2 Motivational Self System. The 12-week intervention was conducted with two intact groups taught by two different teachers, who also taught a control group at the same level. The intervention activities, which took approximately one hour of the groups' four weekly contact hours, were designed specifically to develop the learners' Ideal L2 self and were cate-gorised into three areas:

- Preparation and visualisation training (approximately 3 hours of class time).
- Ideal, Ought-to and Feared L2 self visualisations (approximately 4 hours of class time).
- Practical strategies (approximately 5 hours of class time).

The visualisation training stage familiarised the learners with the technique of positive visualisation (PV) by using readings on the benefits of visualisation in sport psychology and also introduced and practised short activities employing mental imagery drawn from published material (Arnold et al., 2007). The next stage involved the introduction and visual-isation of possible future L2 selves. The first visualisation session aimed to introduce participants to the technique of PV in combination with breathing and relaxation exercises. As this was an introductory session, the theme of the general ideal future self was chosen. The learners viewed a PowerPoint presentation of aspects of their future selves (i.e. health, family, studies, home and career) and were asked to visualise their ideal future self and then compare with their partners in small group work.

Once the learners were comfortable with the techniques, the three subsequent visualisations took place over the three following weeks. These visualisations each focused specifically on an aspect of the learners' future L2 selves (Ideal L2 self, Ought-to L2 self and Feared L2 self). For these visualisations, learners were also shown a PowerPoint slideshow of images related to the possible future selves pertinent to that particular session and were then given different reading texts based on the wishes, needs or worries of four fictional learners of English, Greek or Maori (Hadfield & Dörnyei, 2013). The following example is one of the texts used in relation to the Ideal L2 self visualisation.

The students summarised the content of their text to each other and then compared these accounts to their own experiences and feelings. The groups were given the opportunity to discuss to what extent they identified with the learners in the texts. The students then closed their eyes

---

Jill's Future Ideal Greek Self

My imagined Future Self is on holiday in Greece. We have rented a car (managing all the paperwork in Greek) and are driving through a town in Greece and I can read all the street signs easily and fluently without spelling out the letters. We stop and park the car. I read the instructions on the meter and know how much to put in. I only have a note but I am able to ask someone for change for the meter.

Next, we have to find the museum. The map is not clear so I ask a passerby for directions. Not only can she understand me – but I understand everything she says! We reach the museum and I buy a guidebook in Greek. I can read fluently and understand everything it tells me about the objects in the museum and their history.

After the museum, we go for lunch in a little *taverna*. I can read the menu and order in Greek. When the meal comes, it is exactly what I thought I was ordering too! It's hot in the afternoon so we go back to the villa for a rest and then down to the beach. I read the newspaper on the beach.

On the way back I do the shopping for supper and can ask for what I want, identify the labels on the packets, understand how much it comes to and chat a little to the shopkeeper about where we come from and what I'm cooking for supper. In the evening, the landlady invites us in for a drink and I can chat to her easily and fluently. We talk about families, different customs in Greece and England and politics. I even make a joke!

(Hadfield & Dörnyei, 2013: 19)

and listened to a series of instructions and questions read from a script by the teacher, encouraging them to build a vivid mental image of this particular aspect of their future self. The learners subsequently described and compared their visualisations in small groups. They were asked to produce a written version as homework, giving them an opportunity to further develop and enhance their mental images. The final stage of the intervention focused on strategies which could lead to the realisation of students' visions. These activities included, for example, an analysis of the language course and programme syllabus, to select and prioritise the aspects of language which would be pertinent to the learners' personal needs. Furthermore, the learners elaborated a timeline to describe their language learning objectives. This activity was introduced by the teacher's own example of her learning goals (in Catalan) over a short-term period (by the end of the language course) and a long-term period (each year for the following five years). The teacher's timeline was projected onto the screen and the group was encouraged to offer opinions and suggestions. As homework, the individual learners produced personalised timelines. A selection of these timelines was shown to the group, to discuss the achievability of the learners' objectives. Individual feedback was provided by the teacher and the learners re-wrote the timelines to incorporate any necessary changes to make the goals more plausible. To illustrate this, an example is shown in Table 20.2 of the initial timeline produced by Óscar, a 32-year old university lecturer.

This study aimed to analyse the pedagogical implications of materials designed to develop the learners' Ideal L2 self. Both qualitative and quantitative methods were used to collect and analyse data. Given time and space considerations, the present analysis focuses on the data specifically

Table 20.2 Example of student timeline

2010	2011	2012	2013	2014	2015	2020 +
Restart to learn English. I try to improve my will power (2010–2011).	I would like to travel and stay in California for 3 months for work and improve my English.	I hope to buy finally a village house near the Pyrenees. There are English speaking people in the village I can to practise.	I will do an especial course for academic writing.	I will finish my research contract and have a new contract as Senior Lecturer.	I hope to write alone my first article in English for an specialised and scientific journal.	I can write and speak English without having to think. I travel to do lectures abroad. The people understand me without problems.

related to changes in the learners' self-concept in order to evaluate the effect of classroom activities of this type on language learner motivation.

Instruments

Quantitative data

The collection of quantitative data followed the methods developed by Dörnyei and his colleagues for their large-scale surveys in Hungary (Csizér & Dörnyei, 2005a, 2005b; Dörnyei & Csizér, 2002), which were subsequently used in further studies in the field (Csizér & Kormos, 2009; Ryan, 2009). In order to elicit data relevant to possible changes in learners' self-concept, an established and validated instrument was used: The Motivation Questionnaire (MQ) (Ryan, 2009, based on Dörnyei & Csizér, 2002). After piloting and adapting the wording to the Catalan context (Japanese → Catalan), the instrument was used verbatim. The final version of the instrument consisted of 82 six-point Likert scale items, spread over 15 scales. These scales reflect diverse aspects of learner motivation, including the pragmatic benefits of learning English (e.g. Instrumentality and International contact), the advantages and disadvantages of English as a global tool for communication (International empathy, Travel and Fear of assimilation), attitudes (e.g. Attitudes to the L2 community, Attitudes to learning English and Intended learning effort), future self-guides, in particular the Ought-to L2 self and the Ideal L2 self, affective aspects (L2 self-confidence, Willingness to communicate (WTC) and English anxiety) and intrinsic motivation (Cultural interest and Interest in foreign languages). The full list of scales is presented below together with a sample item.

(1) Cultural interest (five items)

    e.g. *Do you like Hollywood films?*

(2) Attitudes to L2 community (eight items)

    e.g. *Do you like the people of the United States?*

(3) Instrumentality (seven items)

    e.g. *Studying English will help me to get a good job.*

(4) International contact (four items).

    e.g. *I would like to be able to use English to communicate with people from other countries.*

(5) Interest in foreign languages (five items)

    e.g. *I would like to learn a lot of foreign languages.*

(6) International empathy (three items)

    e.g. *Studying English is important to me because I would like to become close to other English speakers.*

(7) Fear of assimilation (four items)

e.g. *As internationalisation advances there is a danger of losing the Cata-lan/Spanish culture.*

(8) Travel orientation (four items)

e.g. *Studying English will be useful when I travel overseas.*

(9) English anxiety (six items)

e.g. *If I met an English speaker, I would feel nervous.*

(10) Attitudes to learning English (six items)

e.g. *Learning English is really great.*

(11) Ought-to L2 self (five items)

e.g. *Few people around me think that it is such a good thing to learn foreign languages.*

(12) Ideal L2 self (six items)

e.g. *I often imagine myself as someone who is able to speak English.*

(13) L2 self-confidence (four items)

e.g. *Learning a foreign language is a difficult task for me.*

(14) WTC in English (eight items)

e.g. *How likely would you be to initiate communication in English in the following situations? (i) Talking in a small group of strangers.*

(15) Intended learning effort (seven items)

e.g. *I am the kind of person who makes great efforts to learn English.*

The quantitative data collection was timed to coincide with the beginning (November 2010) and the end (March 2011) of the intervention programme. The questionnaire was administered to all four groups (Intervention and Control) by the group teacher during class time. The students were given approximately 20 minutes to complete the question-naire and the teacher was available throughout to clarify doubts and answer questions.

The 15 scales on the questionnaire were submitted to reliability tests using SPSS version 18.0. All those scales that were found to have reached a Cronbach's Alpha level of less than 0.70 were considered not to be reli-able. After the tests of reliability, only seven scales were found to be reli-able and the others, including the scale used by Ryan (2009) as a criterion measure (scale 15, Intended learning effort), were therefore eliminated from the analysis. This may be due to the small sample compared to pre-vious studies. A Factor Analysis (FA) was performed on all 82 items of the original questionnaire in order to further explore the data. The FA also suggested seven scales, in keeping with the original results, but after

Table 20.3 Comparison of scales extracted from the FA with original scales on the MQ

FA scale x 5	Alpha	Equivalent to MQ scale	Alpha
Scale 1	.837	International contact	.706
Scale 2	.858	WTC	.867
Scale 3	.811	Attitudes to learning English	.844
Scale 4	.502	Ideal L2 self	.770
Scale 5	.765	English anxiety	.744

excluding items that loaded on more than one scale and those that had a value of less than 0.4, only five clear scales emerged. After an item-by-item comparison, these scales were found to correspond to five of the scales in the original MQ, shown in Table 20.3.

The scales extracted from the FA were then subjected to tests of reliability and only those with an alpha value >0.7 were found to be reliable. Consequently, scale 4, the Ideal L2 self scale, was not found to be reliable according to this analysis. In conclusion, the four scales found to be reliable after both rounds of tests were the following:

- International contact
- WTC
- Attitudes to learning English
- English anxiety

Following this further analysis, these remaining four scales may be interpreted as representative of this educational context and as such could be used as the starting point for analysis of the qualitative data.

Qualitative data

Semi-structured interviews were conducted with participants from each of the four intact groups involved in the study. Learners from each group were chosen 'for having diverse motivational profiles on the basis of their survey responses and teacher comments' (Lamb, 2009: 232). The characteristics of those learners are summarised in Table 20.4.

In total, 22 individual participants were interviewed. Fifteen students were interviewed only at T2. Seven participants from the treatment group A (teacher 1) were interviewed at T1 pre-intervention but two later changed groups so five of the seven were also interviewed post-intervention. This gives a final tally of 27 interviews. The average length of the interviews was 38 min 10 s. In total, more than 17 hours of

Table 20.4 Participants in the semi-structured interviews

	Mean age (years)	Gender		Occupation	
Intervention (N = 12)	32	Male 2 Female 10	(17%) (83%)	Student 5 Working 7	(42%) (58%)
Control (N = 10)	24	Male 5 Female 5	(50%) (50%)	Student 6 Working 4	(60%) (40%)

interview data were recorded, which were then transcribed by the researcher providing a corpus of 140,664 words.

The interview questions were designed to elicit further data on the scales used in the MQ. These included questions in the following areas:

- Language learning history/experiences of learning English.
- General orientations: Attitudes, Travel, Instrumentality.
- Hopes and expectations: Language learning objectives, visions of Ideal, Ought-to and Feared L2 self.
- WTC; self-confidence when using the TL.
- International posture/contact.

The analysis in this chapter focuses on data obtained from the semi-structured interviews and in particular, those observations which relate directly to the three tenets of Dörnyei's L2 Motivational Self System: the Ideal L2 self, the Ought-to L2 self and the L2 learning experience. The initial analysis was based on the interview questions and the findings of the quantitative data but also followed grounded theory (Maykut & Morehouse, 1994) as relevant patterns emerged from the data during analysis.

After the quantitative data analysis, four scales on the MQ were found to be particularly salient for the EFL learners in a Catalan university context (International contact, WTC, Attitudes to learning English and English anxiety). These areas were used as a starting point for coding the interview data and were subsequently divided into categories and themes, following the method suggested in Heigham and Croker (2009: 55) An example is given below:

Area: Attitudes to learning English.

Category: Experience of learning English in the current language course.

Theme: L1 use in class

Example: (S5, T1, 33:00) 'If you ask me to speak (in English) with another person who is Spanish or Catalan, it is unnatural'.

A coding scheme was devised by the researcher which identified 52 themes within the interview data, giving examples of each. This scheme was then used by a second teacher to categorise a sample of interview data. The two raters coincided on 92% of the categories.

Results

Quantitative data

The aim of this research was to ascertain the potential effects of an Ideal L2 self intervention. Therefore, the objective of the quantitative data analysis was to observe any development in the learners' self-concept by contrasting data collected at T1 and T2. As the data obtained from the MQ did not satisfy the assumptions of parametric statistics, the data were analysed using non-parametric tests. A Wilcoxon signed ranks test was used to compare the mean scores of the two macro-groups (Treatment and Control) between T1 and T2. The results are summarised in Tables 20.5a and 20.5b.

Only two significant results can be observed. Both of these results were to be found in scales that had been extracted and found to be reliable after the FA. Within the Treatment group the results indicate that

Table 20.5a Results of Wilcoxon signed ranks test: Contrast T1 & T2 by macro-group (Treatment)

Group	Scale	First data collection (T1) (n = 38)		Second data collection (T2) (n = 30)		Sig (T1 → T2) (n = 25)
		Mean	SD	Mean	SD	
Treatment	Instrumentality	5.28	0.68	5.22	0.53	0.705
(Groups A	International contact	5.12	0.73	4.89	0.98	0.242
& C)	Travel orientation	5.21	0.80	5.19	0.81	0.684
	English anxiety	3.12	0.92	3.24	0.85	0.977
	Attitudes to learning English	4.25	0.77	4.40	0.82	0.977
	Ideal L2 self	5.03	0.80	5.07	0.75	0.353
	WTC	3.44	1.18	4.05	1.03	0.030*

Table 20.5b Results of Wilcoxon signed ranks test: Contrast T1 & T2 by macro-group (Control)

Group	Scale	First data collection (T1) (n = 43)		Second data collection (T2) (n = 41)		Sig (T1 → T2) (n = 36)
		Mean	SD	Mean	SD	
Control	Instrumentality	5.51	0.47	5.27	0.71	0.065
(Groups B	International contact	5.38	0.55	5.04	0.81	0.019*
& D)	Travel orientation	5.56	0.47	5.41	0.65	0.176
	English anxiety	3.22	0.92	3.35	0.91	0.622
	Attitudes to learning English	4.67	0.97	4.53	0.80	0.560
	Ideal L2 self	5.34	0.57	5.18	0.69	0.484
	WTC	3.72	1.06	3.86	1.05	0.561

there was a statistically significant increase in WTC ($p = 0.030$), while the increase in this scale for the Control group was not significant. In contrast, the results from the Control group indicate a significant decrease in the scale relating to International contact ($p = 0.019$). The Treatment group also showed a decrease in motivation in this scale, but the change was not significant.

Qualitative data

The purpose of the qualitative data analysis was to shed light on any issues which may influence student self-concept and motivation in this particular context and to further observe the effects of the intervention programme.

L2 learning experience

As one of the fundamental tenets of Dörnyei's L2 Motivational Self System, this area was of particular interest in the present study and indeed proved to be a rich source of data. During the interviews, the participants were asked to respond to the two following questions about their English learning experiences:

Can you describe your experience of learning English at school?
Can you describe your experience of learning English in your current
   English course?

20 of the 22 interviewees had studied English between 6 and 12 years as a compulsory subject at school. Table 20.6 summarises the responses to the first question, regarding English at school.

The majority of learners (60%) had negative experiences of English at school. The most common reason given (9/12 responses) was that the subject became repetitive and dry at secondary level. For example an 18-year-old Law student observes: 'At first it was really funny but after you were learning grammar and things like that, all the time the same things, so it's boring' (Carmen, T1). She was not alone in stating the lack of native speaker teachers (8/12 responses), the general low level of English proficiency and English teaching in Spain (9/12 responses) as factors contributing to this negative experience: 'I hated that my teachers were Spanish. Everybody says that we are very good at grammar but very bad at accent' (Carmen, T1).

The second question pertains to the learners' current experience in the university language school. While it is true that 14 of the 22 participants were being interviewed by their own teacher (the researcher) which may have influenced their responses to this question, it is also pertinent that the responses extended to more general experiences in the school as 17 of the 22 participants had taken at least one previous course in the same

Table 20.6 Responses concerning experiences of learning English at school

Categories	N		
Negative experiences at school	10	Negative experiences	
		Repetitive	9
		NNSTs*	8
		No speaking	7
		Discipline problems	3
Positive experiences at school	0		
Both positive and negative	2		
No response	8		
Total	20		27

Note: *Non-native-speaker teachers.

Table 20.7 Responses concerning experiences of learning English in the present language course

Categories	Intervention (N = 10)	Control (N = 10)
English course		
Used only English in class	8	5
Perceives progress	6	9
Experienced a 'turning point'	7	7
(Lack of) maturity of classmates	2	2
Positive classroom dynamics	6	0
Negative classroom dynamics	1	3
Total	30	26
Outside class		
Contact with English	9	9
Type of contact		
Films	9	8
TV	8	7
Books	3	1
Internet	5	4
Total	25	20

institution. These responses are taken from the 20 (10 treatment, 10 control) participants interviewed at T2, post-intervention. This allowed time for those participants who were new to the school to form a clear opinion of their experiences. A summary of the responses is shown in Table 20.7.

The first observation that can be made here is that there is still a tendency to use the first language (L1) in the classroom, even at tertiary level, with the consequent effects on group dynamics. The students in the intervention groups were more likely to use only English in class but even in these groups there was some discomfort about L1 use. This observation was made by a 28-year-old optician in intervention group A: 'I like to feel OK in class, not feel like "el raro del turno" (the odd one out). If you try to speak in English a lot of people call you an "empollona" (swot)'. (Rachel, T1).

A general observation was that the more mature the student, the more likely they were to use English in class. The oldest participant in the interviews, a 62-year-old retired literary editor commented: 'I am a little astonished to see people who use Catalan or Spanish. I don't understand them because our willingness is the only way (to learn)'. (John, T2). It may not be a coincidence that the younger students have recently emerged from a school system that does not promote speaking skills. It is also possible that they are not yet aware, as the more mature students are, of the potential benefits of TL use in a classroom context. This comment from an 18-year-old in the intervention group sounds almost resentful about being obliged to speak English:

> If people don't correct me when I go abroad, then why should people in class correct me when they have the same level as me? I will make the same mistakes if I speak to them in English or not. (Carmen, T2)

The interview data do not indicate any difference between the intervention and control groups in terms of students who actively seek contact with English outside of class. However, the intervention group mentions a wider variety of sources of contact, which seems to support the findings of the quantitative data, as this group did not experience a significant reduction in the scale relating to International contact. Nevertheless, very few learners (2/20 responses) mentioned regular contact with NSs at a local level, which is surprising given the very real presence of an English-speaking community, especially in Barcelona.

Ought-to L2 self

In the online feedback given by students specifically on the intervention activities at the end of the course, the activity which received the most positive comments was 'The Mom Song' (Hadfield & Dörnyei, 2013: 77), an activity designed to promote awareness of the pressures that learners experience. Even so, among the reasons given for learning English, there were very few responses that could be directly related to the concept of the Ought-to L2 self. This in itself seems to corroborate the findings of the quantitative data analysis, which found that the Ought-to L2 self scale was not reliable in this particular context. Only 2 of the 22 participants (1 intervention, 1 control, both T2) mentioned external pressures from family, peers or society. However, the two learners who did mention these pressures felt them very strongly:

> (I don't want to) disappoint my family or my friends, or myself. But I have motivation and I would like to continue studying for, of course, my family, my mother. They (my parents) repeat every day, every day, you must study, you must study, you must study. So that is my fear...to disappoint my family. (Mark, Control, T2)

In some cases, the external pressures to learn English were interpreted as a demotivating factor. For example, one participant said '(English) is an obligation and people don't like obligations' (Carmen, Intervention, T2). One possible explanation for the lack of data on the Ought-to L2 self is that the intervention itself, in developing the Ideal L2 self-image, has caused the learners to de-emphasise the Ought-to L2 self, as in this example from a 24-year-old graduate student: '(The intervention) is useful to stop and think. What do you want? Are you studying English only because somebody told you that you have to study English or do you want to learn English?' (Natalie, T2).

Ideal L2 self

In order to obtain data pertaining to the participants' vision of their Ideal L2 self, interviewees were asked to imagine themselves in 5 years' time speaking English and describe the situation. The responses were first categorised according to whether or not the learners had a clear vision. Vague or noncommittal answers such as 'I think my English will be better' were not considered as perceptions of the Ideal L2 self. Those responses that included a clear and detailed description of the vision were further categorised as to the type of situation described: personal, e.g. 'I imagine myself maybe talking with some English friends in English, in a group of friends, in a bar. (It's) more social life than work because I don't think that I will use English in my ideal job'. (Natalie, T2) or pragmatic, e.g. 'I am studying English for business so I am visualising an interview or a business conference. I can understand what people say and I can speak.' (Rose, T2), or including elements of both. The responses are summarised in Table 20.8.

According to Higgins's self-discrepancy theory (1987), a learner first needs to perceive the difference between their desired self and their actual

Table 20.8 Responses relating to learner's Ideal L2 self vision at T2

Categories		Intervention (N = 10)	Control (N = 10)
Able to articulate Ideal L2 self vision		9	6
Ideal L2 self vision:	Personal	5	0
	Pragmatic	3	5
	Both	1	1

self in order to develop a relevant self-guide. The students who had taken part in the Ideal L2 self intervention, with its focus on positive visualisation, were more likely to have a clear vision of what they wish to do with English in the future, summarised by this participant: '(The intervention) makes you think about what you want to do in the next few years' (Helen, T2). The intervention programme proved successful in helping many of the students to develop their Ideal L2 self:

> I think that the visualisations and these things were good because I saw myself doing things that I had never thought of, so the activity made me think of it and think that maybe in three, four years I could talk as well as other people around me and English will not be a problem. (Oona, T2)

For some, however, the discrepancy may be perceived as too wide to be motivating, as is the case of this student in the intervention group: 'It's a curious thing because when I imagine in my head, I speak English and I can say a lot of things, but when I want to explain it in real words I'm choked and I'm not so fluent' (Rose, T2).

It is interesting to note that those learners from the intervention group who were interviewed at both T1 and T2 had developed their visions to include both personal and pragmatic elements. For example, Carmen, an 18-year-old Law student, only mentioned the pragmatic future benefits of knowing English at T1 'I'm in a work conference. I'm giving the conference so I have to know a lot of English, perfect English'. This continued to be important to her at T2: 'I give a presentation and the people understand me. At the end I can answer their questions without problems', but she also introduced aspects related to her personal life: 'I see myself with my host family. We are talking and laughing and I can understand everything'. In general, the intervention group was more likely to visualise scenarios grounded in social situations, often revolving around food and drinks. For example, 'I am with friends, maybe drinking a beer and then walking on the beach' (Rachel, T2). This suggests that the vision of the Ideal L2 self for the learners in the intervention group has become more personalised and intimate. When listing the prerequisites for successful future self-guides, Dörnyei and Ushioda (2009: 34) state that in order to be effective, the learner's desired self-image should have 'a sufficient degree of elaborateness and vividness'. The more personal visions of the intervention students include more nuances and details than those that are work-related, as in this example from a 19-year-old Economics student:

> It was a sunny Sunday lunch and I was pregnant. I was next to Jeong Rim, my cousin's wife and we were talking about my future baby

which is a funny situation because she is going to have a baby soon. In the visualisation she was giving me some advice about the pregnancy and I was feeling really proud of myself for understanding all the things she was telling me. (Oona, T2)

Furthermore, it seems that the intervention may have been useful to help learners develop strategies in order to attain their desired self-image. Those activities which focused on 'operationalising the vision' (Dörnyei & Ushioda, 2009: 37), such as creating a time line for language learning goals, were particularly effective for certain learners. This is illustrated by these comments from participants in the two intervention groups: 'Thanks to the activities, my goals are more specific now than the first time (we did an interview)' (Rachel, T2).

They (the intervention activities) prepare for you for the next months, not only the first months. It's your English. In this exercise you have to think about your English, not the English of the class or the school, or of level 4, no, no! Your English. (Helen, T2)

A further observation was that all the visions elaborated by the control group used, or attempted to use, future tenses, whereas a number of the intervention group (3/9 responses) used present or even past tenses when describing the Ideal L2 self, as in these two examples, first from a 24-year-old architecture student: 'I always imagine myself in a pub, meeting some people. It would be great' (Anna, T2) and secondly from a 62-year-old retired book editor: 'I imagine I was in California, where my son is working as a doctor. Now he is living here, but he went to California for a year and he liked this country very much' (John, T2). This temporal aspect cannot be explained by proficiency alone as all of those interviewed were at the same level within the academic system. It may be evidence instead of the intervention group's greater ability to anchor their vision in the here and now rather than in some distantly perceived future.

Discussion

The results of the quantitative analysis above demonstrate that both control and intervention groups increased in the scale related to WTC, but this increase was only significant in the case of the intervention group, possibly related to the positive group dynamics described by the participants in the interview data. Conversely, both groups demonstrated a downward tendency in the scale related to International contact, but only the control group suffered a significant decrease. Therefore, the intervention conducted in this study initially appears to have been successful in combatting the effects of demotivation over time as well as maintaining and even increasing L2 learning motivation in the treatment group. However, Ushioda (1996) warns against the temptation to measure motivational loss or gain in isolation, but rather to explore the motivational process as a complex, dynamic system using more sensitive qualitative techniques.

One issue arising in particular from the qualitative data in the present study was the role that age and/or maturity may play in the participants' ability to develop a vivid Ideal L2 self-image. In their Hungarian research, Kormos and Csizér (2008) found that university students had the strongest Ideal L2 self-image of the three age groups measured (secondary, university and adult) in line with the study by Carlson (1965), which states that students of university age have a relatively stable, but flexible self-image. Given these conditions, university students should be at the optimal age to take full advantage of an intervention of this type. However, in the sample of participants in the semi-structured interviews, this was not the case. The mean age of the intervention group interviewees was higher (Intervention 32, Control 24) and there was a higher proportion of participants who were working (intervention 58%, control 40%). The more mature students in the intervention group indicated in their responses that they were more open to experimenting with new techniques in the classroom, and indeed were able to produce more detailed and nuanced descriptions of their Ideal, Ought-to and Feared L2 selves. One possible implication may be that a certain level of emotional maturity is necessary in order to derive the maximum benefit from these classroom techniques.

Another observation that emerged from the qualitative data was the participants' general dissatisfaction with their previous language learning experience. In this respect, this study differs from Ushioda's findings in her longitudinal study with learners of French at university in Ireland (2001). In her study it was more common for the learners to cite a positive learning experience to explain their L2 learning motivation than to focus on future goals. In this study, the opposite seems to be true as the majority (12/20 responses) reported negative experiences at school and an even larger number (15/20 responses) were able to articulate a future vision of themselves as a successful L2 user, indicating that they had developed a clear Ideal L2 self. The negative experience at school for many of the participants certainly accounts for the lack of motivational intensity that many demonstrate when embarking on their EFL courses. It also seems that the L2 learning experience has set in place a system of beliefs about each individual's lack of progress. This can be related in turn to Attribution Theory for as Dörnyei summarises (Dörnyei & Ushioda, 2011: 15) 'different types of causal attributions affect behaviour differently'. In this context, lack of success or progress is commonly attributed to educational factors such as NNSTs or undemanding curricula. Perhaps the most relevant and positive outcome of the intervention was to set in motion a change in perspective regarding the causes and possible routes to progress among the learners who took part.

Conclusion

Research conducted with intact groups in real classrooms is inevitably subject to a number of limitations. In this case, the quantitative data analysis was limited by the relatively small number of learners involved. Furthermore, the timing of the intervention, spread over the first and second university term, interrupted by the Christmas break, resulted in a high mortality rate which affected both the quantitative and qualitative analysis. Based on this experience, one clear recommendation would be to compress the intervention into a shorter period, within a single academic term, in order to avoid the loss of participants over time.

The data suggest that an Ideal L2 self intervention can have a positive effect on the learner. The initial findings in the quantitative data suggested that the intervention group had improved or maintained certain aspects of motivation when compared to the control group. The qualitative data confirm that the intervention was generally well-received by the participants and may have helped some learners to develop a clearer mental image of their future English-speaking self. However, the differences between the intervention and control groups are quite subtle. Participants in both groups were able to describe a future Ideal L2 self. The image of a successful L2-speaking career self was common to both groups and may reflect the aspirations of Catalan university students in general. Nevertheless, those in the intervention group produced more detailed descriptions, more often related to aspects of their personal lives. These personalised details may help to satisfy the condition of strengthening the vision, which is one of the prerequisites outlined by Dörnyei and Ushioda (2009) as necessary for an Ideal L2 self vision to be an effective motivator.

However, it is not entirely evident whether any improvement in motivational factors was due specifically to the development of an Ideal L2 self or simply to the novelty of the approach in this particular educational context. Further research in both English as a Second Language (ESL) and EFL contexts with varying age groups in different educational settings is necessary in order to fully explore the effectiveness of these classroom techniques. Furthermore, future research may include more longitudinal studies in order to measure to what extent the intervention has an effect on learners' long-term motivation.

References

Al-Shehri, A.S. (2009) Motivation and vision: The relation between the ideal L2 self, imagination and visual style. In Z. Dörnyei and E. Ushioda (eds) *Motivation, Language Identity and the L2 Self* (pp. 164–171). Bristol: Multilingual Matters.

Arnold, J., Puchta, H. and Rinvolucri, M. (2007) *Imagine That! Mental Imagery in the EFL Classroom*. London: Helbling Languages.

Barcelona Tourism Board. Statistics compiled by the Spanish National Institute for Statistics (INE) See http://www.barcelonaturisme.cat/statistics (accessed November 2012).

Carlson, R. (1965) Stability and change in the adolescent's self-image. *Child Development* 36, 659–666.

Coetzee-Van Rooy, S. (2006) Integrativeness: Untenable for world Englishes speakers? *World Englishes* 25 (3/4), 437–450.

Csizér, K. and Dörnyei, Z. (2005a) The internal structure of language learning motivation: Results of structural equation modelling. *The Modern Language Journal* 89 (1), 19–36.

Csizér, K. and Dörnyei, Z. (2005b) Language learners' motivational profiles and their motivated learning behavior. *Language Learning* 55 (4), 613–659.

Csizér, K. and Kormos, J. (2009) Learning experiences, selves and motivated learning behavior: A comparative analysis of structural models for Hungarian secondary and university learners of English. In Z. Dörnyei and E. Ushioda (eds) *Motivation, Language Identity and the L2 Self* (pp. 98–119). Bristol: Multilingual Matters.

Dörnyei, Z. (2005) *The Psychology of the Language Learner. Individual Differences in Second Language Acquisition*. Mahwah, NJ: Lawrence Erlbaum.

Dörnyei, Z. and Ushioda, E (eds) (2009) *Motivation, Language Identity and the L2 Self.* Multilingual Matters.

Dörnyei, Z. and Ushioda, E. (2011) *Teaching and Researching Motivation* (2nd edn). Harlow: Longman.

Dörnyei, Z. and Csizér, K. (2002) Some dynamics of language attitudes and motivation: Results of a longitudinal nationwide survey. *Applied Linguistics* 23, 421–462.

Gardner, R.C. and Lambert, W.E. (1959) Motivational variables in second language acquisition. *Canadian Journal of Psychology* 13, 266–272.

Hadfield, J. and Dörnyei, Z. (2013) *Research and Resources in Language Teaching: Motivating Learning*, London, UK: Pearson.

Heigham, J. and Croker, R. (eds) (2009) *Qualitative Research in Applied Linguistics,* Basingstoke, Hampshire: Palgrave Macmillan.

Higgins, E.T., Klein, R. and Strauman, T. (1985) Self-concept discrepancy theory: A psychological model for distinguishing among different aspects of depression and anxiety. *Social Cognition* 3 (1), 51–76.

Higgins, E.T. (1987) Self-discrepancy: A theory relating self and affect. *Psychological Review* 94, 319–340.

Institute for Public Policy Research. Source of statistics for UK citizens resident in Spain. See http://www.ippr.org (accessed November 2010).

Kormos, J. and Csizér, K. (2008) Age-related differences in the motivation of learning English as a foreign language: Attitudes, selves and motivated learning behaviour. *Language Learning* 58 (2), 327–355.

Lamb, M. (2009) Situating the L2 self: Two Indonesian school learners of English. In Z. Dörnyei and E. Ushioda (eds) *Motivation, Language Identity and the L2 Self* (pp. 229–247). Bristol: Multilingual Matters.

Mackay, J. (forthcoming) An Ideal L2 self intervention: Implications for self-concept, motivation and engagement with the target language. Forthcoming PhD thesis, University of Barcelona.

Mackay, J. (2009) Attitudes towards Target Language cultures among EFL learners at a Catalan university. Relationship between attitudes, motivation and rate of learning. Unpublished MA dissertation, University of Barcelona.

Magid, M. and Chan, L. (2012) Motivating English learners by helping them visualise their Ideal L2 Self: Lessons from two motivational programmes. *Innovation in Language Learning and Teaching* 6 (2), 113–125.

Markus, H. and Nurius, P. (1986) Possible selves. *American Psychologist* 41 (9), 954–969.

Maykut, P. and Morehouse, R. (1994) *Beginning Qualitative Research*. London: The Falmer Press.

Muñoz, C. and Tragant, E. (2001) Motivation and attitudes towards L2: Some effects of age and instruction. In S. Forster-Cohen and A. Nizegorodcew (eds) *EUROSLA Yearbook* Vol. 1 (pp. 211–224). Amsterdam: John Benjamins Publishing Company.

Nikolov, M. (1999) 'Why do you learn English?' 'Because the teacher is short,' A study of Hungarian children's foreign language learning motivation. *Language Teaching Research* 3 (1), 35–56.

Ryan, S. (2009) Ambivalence and commitment, liberation and challenge: Investigating the attitudes of young Japanese people towards the learning of English. *Journal of Multilingual and Multicultural Development* 30 (5), 405–420.

SPSS Inc. Released 2009. PASW Statistics for Windows, Version 18.0. Chicago: SPSS Inc.

Tachibana, Y., Matsuwaka, R. and Zhong, Q.X. (1996) Attitudes and motivation for learning English: A cross-national comparison of Japanese and English high school students. *Psychological Reports* 79 (2), 691–700.

Taguchi, T., Magid, M. and Papi, M. (2009) The L2 motivational self system among Japanese, Chinese, and Iranian learners of English: A comparative study. In Z. Dörnyei and E. Ushioda (eds) *Motivation, Language Identity and the L2 Self* (pp. 66–97). Bristol: Multilingual Matters.

Tragant, E. and Muñoz, C. (2000) La motivación y su relación con la edad en un contexto escolar de aprendizaje de una lengua extranjera [Motivation and its relationship with age in a foreign language learning school context]. In C. Muñoz (ed.) *Segundas Lenguas. Adquisición en el Aula [Second Languages: Acquisition in the Classroom]* (pp. 81–105). Barcelona: Ariel.

Tragant, E. (2006) Language learning motivation and age. In C. Muñoz (ed.) *Age and the Rate of Foreign Language Learning* (pp. 237–268). Clevedon: Multilingual Matters.

Ushioda, E. (1996) Developing a dynamic concept of L2 motivation. In T. Hickey and J. Williams (eds) *Language Education and Society in a Changing World* (pp. 239–245). Dublin/Clevedon: IRAAL/Multilingual Matters.

Ushioda, E. (2001) Language learning at university: Exploring the role of motivational thinking. In Z. Dörnyei and R. Schmidt (eds) *Motivation and Second Language Acquisition* (pp. 91–124). Honolulu, HI: University of Hawaii Press.

Part 5

Future Research Directions

21 The Self-Concept and Language Learning: Future Research Directions

Michael Magid and Kata Csizér

Introduction

The chapters in this volume illustrate that the relationship between self-concept and language learning may be examined by applying a variety of research designs and addressing a wide range of questions. The studies which are both theoretical and practical in nature have deepened our understanding of the impact of self-concept on language learning by investigating language learners of different age groups, proficiency levels, studying in foreign and second language settings within public and private educational systems from extremely diverse cultural backgrounds. The research that was conducted in these studies demonstrates the impact of culture on self-concept, language learning and teaching in North America, Eastern and Western Europe, Asia and Australia. In this volume, self-concept has encompassed the following dimensions: possible selves, autonomy, self-regulation, identity, self-image, self-efficacy, self-confidence, social anxiety and willingness to communicate. It has been examined through the following theories: Dörnyei's (2009) L2 Motivational Self System, Gardner's (1985) Socio-Educational Model, the Self-Determination Theory of Deci and Ryan (1985), the Complex Dynamic Systems Theory (Van Geert, 1994) and Network Theory (Barabási, 2003). Given the breadth of theoretical paradigms and research designs as well as the complex, dynamic and multi-faceted nature of self-concept (see Mercer, Chapter 4), there are many exciting avenues of research that remain to be explored within the area of self-concept and language learning. In this concluding chapter, we would like to recommend future research directions based on the following topics that were discussed in the chapters in this volume: (1) Theoretical paradigms, (2) Self-Regulation, (3) Identity, (4) The language learning experience and (5) L2 motivational programmes.

Theoretical Paradigms

It is clear from the chapters in this volume that it is possible to investigate the impact of self-concept on both language learning and teaching through the lens of a range of theories such as the L2 Motivational Self System, the Self-Determination Theory, the Complex Dynamic Systems Theory and Network Theory since they take into account the dynamic, complex, emergent and multi-faceted nature of self-concept. From the review of empirical studies conducted in Chapter 3 which incorporate the L2 Motivational Self System and the Self-Determination Theory, it is evident that it would be helpful to have more research done within these theoretical paradigms in Western countries in order to have a clearer idea about the effect that culture has on the relationship between self-concept and language learning. As the authors of Chapter 3 suggested, there should be more longitudinal studies to incorporate the dynamic nature of self-concept and L2 motivation as well as the temporal aspect of the L2 Motivational Self System and the Self-Determination Theory.

Mercer's study (see Chapter 4) demonstrates how Network Theory can be used to examine the self-concept as a network of relationships. We look forward to more studies that apply Network Theory since it enables the self to be dynamic as the network and the relationships within it change and represents how the self is continually emerging. Researchers should consider the conclusion by Forgas and Williams (2003: 2) that 'a proper understanding of the self can only be achieved by considering the interaction of the individual, relational, and collective aspects of the self as a dynamic self-system'. To our knowledge, Kimura's study (see Chapter 17) was the first one to investigate L2 teacher motivation from a Complex Dynamic Systems Theory perspective. Since this approach effectively took into account individual differences as well as the dynamic nature of self-concept and motivation, we recommend adopting this approach in more studies on self-concept and language learning/teaching in the future.

Self-Regulation

As Csizér and Kormos point out (see Chapter 5), self-regulation, learner autonomy and motivation interact with each other dynamically and these concepts are often seen to overlap. Therefore, it is important to continue to explore the relationships between these concepts and find methods to establish a clearer distinction between them. In Chapter 6, Kim and Kim mention that it is still not clear if motivation causes self-regulated learning (SRL) or vice versa. This is a question that could be addressed in future studies. Another important research question related to self-regulation that was raised by Irie and Brewster (see Chapter 10) concerns investigating how the Ideal L2 self and the imagined community influence self-regulation.

Identity

The study conducted by Stracke, Jones and Bramley (see Chapter 9) was one of the few studies we have encountered involving participants with a bicultural identity. It would be valuable to conduct more research on the effect of a bicultural and a multicultural identity on self-concept, language learning and L2 motivation. Miyahara (see Chapter 12) raises important questions on identity by asking how, why and in what contexts language learners construct their identities. We recommend that researchers continue to explore the sources of language learners' identities as these could depend on the cultural background, educational setting, motivation and numerous other factors. Polat (see Chapter 15) mentions that studies on how a language learner's L2 self and Ideal L2 self interact with identification patterns are limited and warrant future research.

The Language Learning Experience

Since the language learning experience includes experiences both inside and outside of the classroom, it is important to focus on how teachers, classmates, significant others and members of the target language community communicate with language learners and how this communication affects their self-concept and language learning. Therefore, we agree with the authors' suggestion in Chapter 8 that there is a need to investigate how teachers, classmates, family members and others communicate with language learners in order to either facilitate or undermine their language learning and the development of their self-concept. As Miyahara suggests (see Chapter 12), it would also be interesting to explore through future research what kind of language learning environments are conducive to the formation and development of ideal selves. There could be a variety of conducive environments depending on the cultural background of the learners and the country in which they study. The role of culture would therefore be an important factor to consider when investigating the effect of the language learning experience on self-concept and language learning. In the study conducted by Iwaniec (see Chapter 11), since it was found that the self-concept is socially constructed, this highlights the importance of continuing to examine how the language learning experience influences one's self-concept. Miyahara points out (see Chapter 12) that how an individual sees himself/herself emotionally has an effect on his/her ability to respond to the environment. Positive emotions can enable language learners to respond flexibly to their environment, whereas negative emotions such as social anxiety may have the opposite effect. Therefore, it is important to consider the impact of emotions on the language learning experience. Scherer (2000: 70) affirms that emotions need to be seen within the framework of a 'dynamic time course of constantly changing affective tuning of organisms as based on continuous evaluative monitoring of their environment' and should be examined within a dynamic systems paradigm along with motivation and cognition.

L2 Motivational Programmes

The motivational programmes that were described in this volume all incorporated the use of imagery to enhance the participants' vision of their Ideal L2 self. When considering the relationship between vision and motivation, it is important to take into account the powerful impact that imagery has on our emotions as well as the relationship between emotions, motivation and cognition. Arnold (1999) argues that images can empower learning because they are related to creativity and to our emotions. Designers of future motivational programmes could consider new ways to enhance their participants' vision of their Ideal L2 self by making it more elaborate and vivid.

As Dörnyei suggests in chapter 2, in terms of applying his L2 Motivational Self System in future motivational programmes, they could be designed for learners of languages besides English and learners of other subject areas as well as a wider range of age groups. In Chapter 6, Kim and Kim mention that when training language learners to use SRL skills, the learners should be encouraged to discover which skills are most effective for them and the specific tasks they need to do in order to help them improve their English. Mezei (see Chapter 16) advocates that motivational strategies should aim for self-regulation because it will give students autonomy and control over their learning. Lyons writes in Chapter 7 that an important component to learners achieving a goal is having the ability to monitor and assess their progress towards it. As Lyons states, achieving their goals will most likely lead to more motivated behaviour and autonomy among language learners. Given the motivation and autonomy that may be obtained through self-regulation and self-monitoring, we recommend including training on SRL skills and on how to monitor one's progress towards goals in future L2 motivational programmes. We hope that our recommendations for future research in the area of self-concept and language learning will encourage both academics and teacher practitioners to continue unravelling the many mysteries that remain in this area. We are heartened by the excellent research that has been completed and await new discoveries with great anticipation!

References

Arnold, J. (1999) Visualization: Language learning with the mind's eye. In J. Arnold (ed.) *Affect in Language Learning* (pp. 260–278). Cambridge: Cambridge University Press.

Barabási, A.-L. (2003) *Linked*. New York, NY: Plume Books.

Deci, E.L. and Ryan, R.M. (1985). *Intrinsic Motivation and Self-determination in Human Behavior*. New York, NY: Plenum.

Dörnyei, Z. (2009) The L2 motivational self system. In Z. Dörnyei and E. Ushioda (eds) *Motivation, Language Identity and the L2 Self* (pp. 9–42). Bristol: Multilingual Matters.

Forgas, J.P. and Williams, K.D. (2003) The social self: Introduction and overview. In J.P. Forgas and K.D. Williams (eds) *The Social Self: Cognitive, Interpersonal, and Intergroup Perspectives* (pp. 1–18). Hove: Psychology Press.

Gardner, R.C. (1985) *Social Psychology and Second Language Learning: The Role of Attitudes and Motivation*. London: Edward Arnold.

Scherer, K.R. (2000) Emotions as episodes of subsystem synchronization driven by nonlinear appraisal processes. In M.D. Lewis and I. Granic (eds) *Emotion, Development, and Self-organization: Dynamic Systems Approaches to Emotional Development* (pp. 70–99). Cambridge: Cambridge University Press.

Van Geert, P. (1994) *Dynamic Systems of Development: Change between Complexity and Chaos*. New York, NY: Harvester Wheatsheaf.